JACK

JACK

The Biography of Jack Bruce

Steven Myatt

Aureus Publishing Limited

REVIEW COPY

NOT FOR RESALE

PLEASE SEND ANY REVIEWS TO:

Aureus Publishing Limited
Castle Court, Castle-upon-Alun, St. Bride's Major,
Vale of Glamorgan, CF32 0TN. Tel/Fax: (01656) 880033
sales@aureus.co.uk   www.aureus.co.uk

Aureus

Also by Steven Myatt and published by Aureus:

'Coghlan & Quo'

First Published 2005

This publication is printed on paper derived from sustainable forests. The cover is made from recycled material.

ISBN 10: 1 899750 36 3
ISBN 13: 978-1-899750-36-8

Printed in Great Britain.

A catalogue record for this book is available from the British Library.

Aureus Publishing Limited
Castle Court
Castle-upon-Alun
St. Bride's Major
Vale of Glamorgan
CF32 0TN

Tel: (01656) 880033 Fax: (01656) 880033
Int. tel: +44 1656 880033 Int. fax: +44 1656 880033

E-mail: sales@aureus.co.uk
Web site: www.aureus.co.uk

Acknowledgements

Particular thanks are due to:

Pete Brown

Charlie Bruce

Janet Bruce

Malcolm Bruce

Bob Brunning

Clem Clempson

Maurizio Comandini

Hugh Davies

Simon Emmerson

Peter Frampton

Mo Foster

Bruce Gary

Arthur Guinness

David Hadley

Jon Hiseman

Steve Hunter

Gary Husband

Mitchell Kane

Dennis Lawrenson

Ronnie Leahy

Lulu

Mark Marriott

Len Moskowitz

MPHM

Tony Hymas

Barbara & Lindley Nelson

Simon Phillips

Suzi Quatro

Grant Scales

Margrit Seyffer

Harry Shapiro

Chris Spedding

Klaus Voorman

Chris Welch

Bernie Worrell

Preface

Anyone who insists on compartmentalising Jack Bruce as a Sixties rock star is woefully misinformed. More accurately, they are perhaps under-informed. There are entries on him in all the usual rock reference books, but they are the thinnest sketches – a few facts and nothing more. In early 2004, when I first started scratching my head about his life and music, I was very surprised to find that no-one had written his biography. Spurred on by that discovery, and blithely thinking that I could rectify the deficiency, I started my preliminary research and only became more amazed that no such book existed.

Jack isn't a rock star in the accepted sense and never has been. It's an easy label to apply, and it seems to work well enough until you start scratching at the edges. Then you find it comes off rather easily. You see the Ferraris and the big house in the country and conclude that all that, plus Olympian drug excess, adds up to the job description which emerged out of nowhere through the second half of the Twentieth century and became the focus of envy for all lesser mortals; rock star. Jack had all that, but his background and the inter-connecting influences which made him the musician he is completely contradict that stereotype.

To a very large degree, pop and rock musicians who became famous during the Sixties and Seventies emerged from one of two backgrounds; they were inspired by straightforward rock 'n roll – Elvis and The Shadows are the influences most often quoted by British musicians of a certain age – or by the blues. Sometimes it was a mixture of the two, but if you're an analytic pedant and have a big black marker pen and a very large sheet of paper, it is a fairly easy exercise to draw two columns and put dozens of names on one side or the other.

The number of mainstream rock and pop stars who came up through the British jazz scene is tiny. To some degree it's a generational thing – for anyone who was a teenager in the mid-Sixties jazz was largely an irrelevance – but it also has a lot to do with the insularity and exclusivity of the form. Rock 'n roll and the blues have always been relaxed bed-fellows; fusing jazz with rock has always been vastly harder. To then market and promote the form to listeners who have no grounding in that music is even more difficult still.

Jack was completely immersed in jazz until some point around 1964. At that point he was astute enough to see that among the more cerebral musical forms it was the blues rather than jazz that was flexible enough to merge into the new music which was threatening to sweep everything else away. That's very much to his credit; a lot of people closed their ears and retreated into the safety of what they knew. Jack, courageous as ever, was one of those who, though an uncompromising purist for years, opened his ears and his mind to the new music and then immersed himself in those forms.

Coming out of the jazz scene made everything different. It meant that he was used to the notion of the individual virtuoso who played with a band but wasn't completely subsumed in it. It meant that he was accustomed to the fluidity within jazz line-ups, and the freedom that gave. And as one of the cocky young Turks trying to show the trad jazzers that modern jazz was the music of the future, he channelled his own natural rebelliousness into creative and constructive forms. He was constantly fighting the music – fighting against it, fighting with it, fighting for it. He wasn't fighting the Establishment or 'the system.' He didn't feel a need to piss up garage walls or smash his equipment on stage. Anyway, he needed all that energy for the music.

There are very few musicians whose records and CDs have sold in the tens of millions who are as musically well educated as Jack, or who have worked in and understood so many styles. Few composers of rock songs have come to their colleagues with much more than a few words on an envelope or a few notes in their heads – let alone a fully arranged and annotated score. Fewer still could muse, in their sixties, that perhaps they should move away from the music they have created and performed for more than forty years and, instead, might embark on a new career as a classical composer. Not without being laughed at mercilessly, that is.

Ninety-nine percent of everyone reading this will have, at the very least, a passing knowledge of Jack's music. Many will know every note by heart. Very few people know the man though; his upbringing, his influences and the personal details of his life in recent years. That's what the book is about. I haven't tried to talk to every musician Jack has ever played with, just as there isn't a list of every gig he ever played and what the temperature in the room was before and after the show.

Also, this isn't a book about Cream. That band made up just two and a half years of Jack's career (which is creeping towards fifty years in length). Cream is very important, of course, and it was hard to stop those times dominating the story. A balance had to be struck and one can only hope it was the right one.

In conclusion, it has to be said – and this is a point which is fundamental to how this book may be regarded – this is not a truly comprehensive biography of Jack Bruce. It is as comprehensive as you will ever read, but it is far from complete. Despite an initial agreement to tell the full story, when it came to talking about certain periods of his life, the drawbridge was pulled up with a resounding thud. The conversation stopped and nothing on this earth would ever have got it started again.

These weren't the parts of his life which one might expect him to be sensitive about; he spoke with devastating openness and honesty about some of the most difficult times in his life – especially in relation to the hardships of his childhood and his years as a heroin user – but in this book you will find almost nothing about his private life over the past few years. You will also read next to nothing about his 2003 liver transplant and his illness both before and after it. It's not, as one might expect, an attempt to whitewash history for reasons of vanity. His explanation is that it's nobody else's damned business, which is a suggestion which just leaves his biographer reeling and uncharacteristically speechless.

Faced with the door being slammed in his face, what is a biographer to do? This was never going to be a Kitty Kelley or Albert Goldman style of biography. No one was setting out to be destructive or unfairly critical; it was to be a celebration of a remarkable life, and an examination of the talent that has given such great pleasure and delight to so many. The life stories of musicians – or prime ministers or sculptors or scientists - should be as broadly-based as possible: The reader cannot understand or appreciate how outstanding people have managed their achievements without knowledge of their background and an appreciation of both what formed them, and what they are really like as human beings. One needs to understand the dynamics within a life, be it Mozart or Chuck Berry, to really appreciate how they came to write their music, and how their particular story fits within the far bigger picture.

It would have been dishonourable to have run round behind Jack and told his tale despite his wishes. It would not have been hard, but it wasn't ever really an option. For one thing, the story would have to have been told by his enemies – of whom there is no short supply – because it would not have been honest to hoodwink his friends. That means that the facts would inevitably have skewed, and the chances of this story treading a straight line would be slim. So what you have here is as much as can be written without duplicity. It isn't the whole story, but as I say, it's most certainly as good as you will ever see.

Steven Myatt
August 2005

Chapter 1

This was the concert that was never going to happen. Never. Cream – the very first super-group of the rock generation – had fallen apart in 1968 after less than two and a half years of frantic recording and touring. There was huge distrust between the three members of the band, and Jack Bruce and Ginger Baker – who had been at each other's throats quite literally in the past – were never again going to be in the same room, let alone share a stage. The mood was of anger, disappointment and undiluted hatred. Feelings had mellowed to some degree over the years, but even so, the three musicians were more likely to walk on the moon than ever play together as a band.

No matter how many music-lovers might want so much to see it, these three men were never going to run through their back catalogue. Separate hotels, separate limousines, separate dressing rooms wouldn't be enough. They would have had to have been in separate cities.

The relationship between them was actually quite complex; the perception was that Jack and Eric were wary of each other, just as Ginger made Eric very uncomfortable at best. Ginger resented Eric while Jack resented Eric, and Jack and Ginger utterly loathed each other. There was some truth in all that, but the feelings were less intense, or at least, they wavered, and the reality was far more subtle.

On the other hand, all three had matured as they had got older, and had moved away from each other, both as personalities and in terms of their musical fulfilment. They had revisited the forms that had most inspired them forty years ago; Eric had been able to exercise his passion for the blues, Jack had produced a long line of creative and individual albums, and Ginger had immersed himself in world rhythms (and polo ponies). In becoming more independent, musically, they moved three different ways round the same sphere and perhaps a reunion was inevitable rather than impossible. Now they could revisit their old music without revisiting their old selves.

The passage of time was another factor. The now-traditional rock 'n roll curses of

Fingers a blur as Jack delights thousands of music lovers;
Royal Albert Hall, May 2 2005 (Len Moskowitz)

drink and drugs had exacted a price on their contemporaries; the majority of other musicians they had played with in the Sixties were dead. It was astonishing that these three men, given the extent of their individual indulgences, should still be alive and able to play.

And, they had all passed the terrible, unforgiving landmark of sixty. Ginger was sixty-five, Jack was a few days away from his sixty-second birthday, and Eric had seen his sixtieth just a few weeks before. Time was not on their side. They weren't young any more, they weren't middle-aged any more, they were not far off being old men; when they were first Cream they would have thought anyone of that age to be truly ancient.

There are many rock 'n roll stars who haven't aged well. There have been some band reunions which simply shouldn't have happened. Jack, Eric and Ginger had one great psychological advantage though; they didn't identify with Elvis, overweight, drug-addled, dying constipated on the toilet, but with their jazz and blues heroes. These were men for who to be elderly meant to be venerable; the majority improved with age, played to larger and more sophisticated audiences, and never stopped recruiting new fans. Critics might suggest cruelly – but often accurately – that it was time for certain Sixties rock stars to retire and spend more time with their money, but no-one said that of the great jazz and blues men. Rock 'n roll is the music of the young – and those who are happy to temporarily suspend the ageing process, and can get away with it with dignity – but jazz and blues are ageless and timeless. Teenagers might mock a pop record that is forty years old, but a Robert Johnson track that's thirty years older than that is something else entirely. Nobody suggests that it's time for B B King to trade in his guitar, move to Florida and start playing bridge.

At nine minutes past eight on Monday May 2, Jack Bruce, Ginger Baker and Eric Clapton walked on stage at The Royal Albert Hall, and without any introduction – what introduction could there have been? – launched into I'm So Glad. One expensive box, curiously, was unoccupied, but otherwise there wasn't an empty seat in the house – except that at that moment every last member of the audience was on their feet, roaring with utter delight.

Behind them on a panel which stretched right across the stage was a delightfully old-fashioned light show; computer-generated now, but exactly replicating the coloured oil-in-glass slide projections of the Sixties. It was a nice touch. Otherwise, the stage was empty except for their amps and speakers (which, to the horror of the purists, weren't Marshalls). And the volume was never what it would have been four decades ago; nowhere near an eleven, seven at the most.

Eric, recently a father again, looked relaxed, slim and fit. Jack was slightly hunched, and of the three, the most obviously nervous. Ginger was all smiles and grins, and looked the most delighted to be there.

They hadn't been tempted to re-visit the paisley print shirts, satin trousers and velvet jackets of the Sixties, which was wise. Eric looked as if he was thinking of doing a little gardening, in a pale blue shirt and blue jeans. Ginger was wearing a black Cream T-shirt. Jack was in blue jeans and a red Liberty-print shirt over a black T-shirt. They could have been three middle-aged men heading down to the pub – until they picked up their instruments and started to play.

It was a magnificent gig – the first of four they played at The Royal Albert Hall during that week. By the third or fourth song all three were relaxed and comfortable. They had known from the rehearsals that it was going to work, but now they were completely certain of it. The audience didn't roar over the music as they might once have done, but were on their feet after every number. Eric in his role of showman extended the pause in the middle of Badge, to the crowd's delight, and then compounded their ecstasy but coming back – in his own good time – with a blistering take on that classic riff. Ginger got to sing Pressed Rat And Warthog – or rather speak it, as Jack and Eric thundered along beneath him. Ginger also showed that the extended drum solo is not dead by crashing through Toad just as elegantly, dextrously and pow-erfully as he might ever have done. The solo was well constructed, not too long, and including new and more modern licks. It was something that no one expected, and the audience was awed. His playing was as perfect as ever, and served as a stern warning to anyone who had either forgotten his unparalleled skills or had dared to think that they had faded over the years. For the audience it was a great treat, and for Ginger it must have been very satisfying indeed.

Crossroads was slower and more thoughtful than their immortal live version on 'Wheels Of Fire.' White Room was simply stunning; an immaculately mature perform-ance of a timeless, exquisite song.

There were a number of personal triumphs for Jack; opportunities to remind the world that he is a peerless musician, and he didn't let them slip away. He sang and playing harmonica on Rollin' And Tumblin', and put as much soul and muscle into the song as he did in the Sixties. At one point he dropped his harmonica, but caught it before it hit the floor and carried on without missing a beat. The next day The Daily Telegraph described his performance of Rollin' And Tumblin' as 'sensational, an express train of a song, hurtling along with purpose, power and unstoppable momen-tum.' Given the verve and vivacity with which he rocketed through the song, no one would ever have thought that the man was still recovering from a liver transplant. His only concession to his health was the occasional, brief use of a high stool.

We're Going Wrong was even more notable, especially as it's his own song. Ginger's drumming was so full-throated you could touch the rhythms and hold them, while Eric's guitar work was haunting and so light it defied gravity. Jack's bass playing was everything the audience expected, and more, but it was his vocals that made the hairs stand up on the back of the neck. As the song raged beneath, the lyrics soared away almost out of sight. Above all else, the song just sounded so modern; it could have been written and recorded in 2005 – and would still be stopping people in their tracks.

Jack and Eric were obviously actually listening to each other; there were grins flash-ing across the stage as they traded notes and phrases. Thirty-seven years ago they were often so preoccupied by what they were playing that they were oblivious to what else was being played. In 2005 there was a new maturity, and a sense of one-ness.

There were two small surprises; they played a soulful Stormy Monday, but didn't play I Feel Free – though admittedly that is a difficult song for a trio to play live. Also, at the point where they waved their goodbyes and left the stage, they hadn't played Sunshine Of Your Love. It was obviously being kept for the encore. Sure enough, they returned within a few minutes and Jack's immortal bass riff thundered through the hall. It would have been worth being there for that alone. The encore was just that one

'Seems to be going alright so far'; Ginger, Eric and Jack, first night of the Reunion concerts in London.
(LM)

song and then they were gone. They had played for an hour and fifty-five minutes, and if you had paid face value for a middling seat that would have worked out at slightly more than a pound a minute. A bargain.

'Everything to do with the concerts, from the rehearsals to the concerts themselves, was a joy from beginning to end', Jack says. 'There wasn't a single second that I could say anything negative about. It was wonderful. From the very first tune we played, it was like we hadn't played since the week before.

'We all ended up saying that it was a better band than it was in the old days; musically better. We just loved it.'

Jack had always been uncertain as to whether a reunion was ever going to happen. Interviewed in 2001 he almost contradicted himself, 'I think it may happen as a one-off kind of a thing. Maybe we can do something for some very good cause or something. It's kind of unlikely, but I guess it's possible. Certainly, Eric and myself are both playing. I don't know what Ginger's doing. He's living in South Africa, doing something. The other possibility might be, if we all were at loose ends sometimes, maybe we could see if we could do a record that was actually valid. Obviously, that would be a great challenge and a lot of fun to do.' In an earlier interview he had been more frank;

'It would be fabulous to do Cream again. I'd like to show everyone what the fuss was all about',

Jack, Eric and Ginger rehearsed five days a week for three weeks ('Though we took a couple of days off because we were getting over-rehearsed') through April at the sound stage in west London where the old Hammer horror films were shot. One can make of that connection what one will, but Jack's opinion is that Eric chose that location because he likes the canteen there, and in particular their steak and kidney pies.

They took it slowly, starting at about eleven each morning and went through until lunch – usually that steak and kidney pie followed by spotted dick and custard – and then playing until about four. Most of the afternoon was taken up with running through the set, as near to non-stop as they could.

Jack admits to having been very nervous about even going into the building when he first arrived. He waited outside for a while and he finally took a deep breath and went through the door only because it was raining so hard. As chance would have it, the first person he saw was Ginger, who was standing in the middle of the room. There has never been any secret of the fact that the two men have had more than their fair share of differences of opinion over the past forty years or so; differences of opinion which have descended into fury, recrimination and violence. 'I felt a bit awkward but he was very pleasant. There was no vibe whatsoever,' Jack said later.

They were there to do a job, and that was fine. They didn't socialise, didn't go down the pub together after each day's rehearsals – but that was neither expected nor required. They simply got on with the job; professional musicians acting professionally and doing what they were good at.

Jack was worried about his own ability, but only so far as his recent ill-health might have affected his performance. They had originally discussed doing two one-hour sets with an intermission, but soon decided that running straight through the set would work better. It was going to be a long run for a man who puts a lot of physical effort into his playing, and who had undergone very substantial surgery eighteen months previously. It was, he says, with perhaps a little understatement 'a bit daunting.' On the other hand, he had no doubts about his – or their – ability to still make great music together and deliver what their audience were hoping so much to hear.

'It was actually beneficial. When you get into the music it's like meditation. Physically you might get tired by mentally and spiritually you're completely refreshed and rejuvenated. It's the most wonderful thing.'

When it came to eight o'clock on that Monday night in early May though, it was a very different matter. Jack makes no bones about the fact that he was simply terrified; 'I was shitting myself.' All three were very nervous. There was no obvious reason why they should have been, and the fact will amaze just about everyone who was in that

Jack started the Reunion concerts playing the Gibson EB1 but switched to his fretless Warwick after a few songs (LM)

audience. With just a couple of steps to get before they were actually on stage, Eric dropped back and hissed to Jack, 'You go first!' Jack tried to but his legs simply wouldn't work for him. The saying is that they turn to jelly at a moment like that, and he says that's a good description. The hesitation only lasted for a second or two, until Jack – feeling that he was walking in slow motion – took the last steps from the twilight onto the brightly-lit stage.

'I was extremely nervous the first night, and pretty nervous every other night. Once we started playing though it wasn't too bad. It took me quite a while on the first night to get over the nerves and get into it.' It was about ten or fifteen minutes before all three settled down and the nervousness evaporated, but then they were flying. Jack shrewdly, mischievously, points out that though members of the audience might think that the band have really found the music after a couple of songs, it's often in fact the sound engineers who have had a chance to get the mix right.

It was a different matter two hours later when they finally left the stage; 'We were all feeling thrilled – mind you, Eric and I were thrilled when were sat at the side of the stage listening to Ginger's drum solo.'

The band greatly appreciated the audience – everyone in the hall entered almost consciously into a self-perpetuating circle; the band greatly appreciated the audience greatly appreciating them, and so it went on. There was a feeling that they couldn't let all these people down, but at the same time they were very much aware, Jack says, of being loved. He compares it to when he was playing with Ringo Starr's band in the Eighties; 'People loved The Beatles more than they loved any other band, and so there was this great wash of love towards Ringo. It was a very similar feeling. We were all in the right place at the right time.' He's correct in that; to stand on Kensington Gore at ten thirty on the Monday night was to be in a river of joy as hundreds of delighted, satiated people were making their way home - almost floating by.

The gigs were wonderful opportunities for spotting the famous. During the week the audience included Sir Paul McCartney, Ringo Starr, Roger Daltry, Jimmy Page, Bill Wyman, Roger Waters, Ray Cooper, Steve Winwood, Gary Moore, Brian May, Mick Taylor, Kris Kristofferson, Alice Cooper, Bryan Adams, Andy Fairweather Low, Glen Frey, Tom Hanks, Val Kilmer, Tim Burton, Helena Bonham Carter, Sean Penn, Jeremy Irons, Cilla Black, Chris Tarrant, Gary Kemp, Bill Oddie – and what other band reunion, anywhere on earth, would you found a guest list quite like that?

The concert was reviewed by all the quality papers the following morning; it was big news for the music press, obviously, but when The Times, The Daily Telegraph, The Guardian and The Independent all sit up and pay attention, it has to be something very special. And the following weekend most of the broadsheet Sundays reviewed the concerts as well.

David Cheal, writing in The Telegraph, said, 'Many reunions are tawdry, half-baked affairs. But this one was different, special ... In years to come I'll be able to say with pride: Cream, Albert Hall, 2005, I was there.'

The Times' reviewer wrote, 'You can't turn back the clock, and in truth, they didn't try ... it was a tremendous thrill to see the three of them together after all these years.'

Andy Gill from The Independent suggested that this time around they were perhaps even better than they had been in the Sixties, pointing out that the huge and diverse experience which each has amassed since then has added to their abilities. At one point Eric apologised to the audience for the band being 'cut off in its prime', and Jack countered with 'This is our prime!' Andy Gill finished his review by saying, 'He may be right, too.'

Writing in The Guardian, Alexis Petridis saw things very differently. Perhaps he was the wrong reviewer to send to the gig, perhaps he had his notions all ready mapped out before he arrived. He was appreciative of the band members' abilities, and praised several songs, but he seemed to think that there ought to be a 'best by' cut-off date for music lovers. He was snide about bald pates and 'nostalgia for a lost era', as if it was a sin to revisit great music from times gone by, and as if anyone over forty has no right to be stirred and enthused by exhilarating music.

He also said that young people were 'conspicuous by their absence', so he can't have met Rachel from Guildford, who was there to celebrate her nineteenth birthday. Or Simeon, sat behind her, who had told his father when asked how he wanted to celebrate his eighteenth birthday, that all he could possibly want was to be at the first night of the Cream reunion. So dad, to his eternal credit, brought him all the way from New York so that he could celebrate his coming of age as he wished. Asked why, Simeon said, 'Because it's Cream ...' as if the questioner were insane. What was truly surprising, even looking at the fans queuing to get in – as some did for hours before the gig started, was how many younger fans there were.

Tickets for the reunion concerts went on sale at 9am GMT on Monday January 24. They were only available over the phone or the internet. All the tickets for all four nights were sold within hours. That afternoon Johnny Walker, opening his BBC Radio 2 drive-time show, said, 'If you want to buy tickets for the Cream reunion ... you're too late. They've all gone.'

To the great distress of fans of the band who hadn't been able to get tickets, they began appearing at huge prices almost immediately. It seemed that touts had got hold of a large number, and also knew how much they could get for them. By the end of the day they were being auctioned on the eBay internet site, and it was obvious that fans who had missed out on the 24th were going to have to pay hundreds of pounds if they wanted to see the band. It wasn't difficult to pay £1,000 for a pair of tickets. In early April Radio 2 disc jockey Richard Allinson reported that one person had paid £2,850 for a single ticket.

Fan web sites bristled with disappointment and fury; it seemed unbelievably cruel that having waited thirty–seven years for this concert the sheer joy of it all would be denied to anyone who couldn't afford to put that sort of sum on their credit card. The price of the tickets, starting at £75 – but most being £125 (plus, for many, the cost of travel to and from London, and accommodation too) - was high enough; having to pay so much more than the real price was heartbreaking. There was talk of some fans cancelling their family holidays for the year so that they could have one evening of utter musical bliss.

The phrase 'the opportunity of a lifetime' is a cliché much loved by dodgy sales-men, but for Cream fans, the reunion concerts were nothing less than that. The organ-isers of the Glastonbury Festival had recently announced impressive plans to issue every visitor with a photo-ID ticket: All you had to do was send off a passport photo of yourself. Very many fans wanted to know why that hadn't also been the case for the Cream reunion. After all these years, weren't the fans worth it? Cream's promoters, 3A, issued a statement saying, 'It is our belief that we have made all possible efforts to make tickets available to the public but at the same time to make it as difficult as pos-sible for touts to get hold of tickets.' They added that they believed that the majority of tickets on sale at exploitative prices 'had been purchased not by touts, but by mem-bers of the public with a view to using one pair of tickets and selling the other pair on.' On May 2, fifteen minutes before the show started, prices had dropped, and touts out-side The Royal Albert Hall were asking between £250 and £350 for a single ticket.

Hugh Davies had broken the news of the reunion in The Daily Telegraph in mid-November 2004. Even a dozen years ago the worthy Telegraph would have sneered at rock music. Times have changed though, and their readership is getting older – and is made up of exactly the sort of people who would be prepared to put a few hundred pounds onto the gold card in return for a ticket to Cream's reunion.

There had been a hint of a rumour mentioned in The Daily Mail's 'Whispers' col-umn (in which the comedian Vic Reeves was amazed to find Jack asking for his auto-graph, to which he replied, 'No, this is all wrong. I'm a huge fan of yours. Can I have your autograph?'). Hugh decided to chase it up, unlikely though it seemed. He got his best clue that there was something going on when he dropped into The Royal Albert Hall and asked their marketing department about what they had booked in for the next few months. The instant clamming up, the nervous licking of a dry mouth and the wiping of sweating palms when he said the word Cream meant it was true. Even-tually he phoned Jack's wife, Margrit, and in an unguarded moment she admitted that the concerts were going to take place.

Hugh's piece ran to half a page, in colour, prominently sited on a right-hand page in the middle of the paper. He also quoted John Mayall, praising the band and perhaps going overboard in his praise of Eric, but adding snidely, 'It's probably Eric on one of his nostalgia trips, as Jack and Ginger are not exactly headline names of this generation.' He also said that he thought that any reunion might be in aid of charity.

The rock journalist Chris Welsh, who has written the definitive book on the band, was also completely taken by surprise. He hadn't heard it was going to happen. He didn't imagine that it would ever – could ever – happen. 'I am amazed they are getting back together again', he said. 'They were a juggernaut, streets ahead of anyone else.'

Writing in The Daily Express in early January, Mark Reynolds majored on the perceived animosity between the three men. He described Ginger and Jack as being 'in relative obscurity', which would have been surprising news to the very many people who have both seen Jack in concert and bought his CDs in recent years. Both The Telegraph and the Express's pieces were illustrated with a photo taken at the induction into the Rock 'N Roll Hall Of Fame, though they used different archive shots of Cream in the Sixties.

When The Daily Express revisited the subject after the shows, their new angle was to suggest that Ginger had actually tried to pull out at one stage, and had e-mailed Eric saying that he had got cold feet. The story was that Eric had then talked him round, and the paper quoted him as saying, 'I'm glad now that I've done it, because playing with Eric and Jack is a joy. It has been far better than I could have imagined in every way.'

Hugh Davies came back to the story again at the end of March – another half page spread – and mentioned the large sums that fans had to pay for black market tickets. He also quoted extensively from the first of the two interviews Eric recorded with Johnny Walker. Both celebrated their sixtieth birthday on March 30 and a special two-part interview of Eric, by Johnny, was broadcast.

Adrian Schweitzer was lucky; he got through on the phone and managed to buy tickets at face value. For him the cost was going to come in terms of a transatlantic airfare and hotel accommodation in London. The fact that he had to travel to the concert from his home in Garden Bay, fifty miles southwest of Vancouver in Canada wasn't a problem. He was going to be there.

He has been a fan of the band almost from the beginning, but has always been, in particular, a big fan of Jack's work; 'I think he is the greatest musician of our generation, and he has never been properly recognised. There has only ever been one musician for me that can transport me to other places. I find his new stuff to be superior to anything that is out there. He is a great singer, multi instrumentalist, composer and powerful bass player, and I have always thought of Cream as Jack Bruce's band - although popular opinion seems to be that it was Eric Clapton's band.

'I have always enjoyed Eric's playing but I believe he is hardly on the same level as

Jack, and I think he probably knows it. I think these concerts will cement Jack's credentials and bring him the recognition he so richly deserves.'

Mandy Wenzel is a German national living in Holland, who has a direct connection as she used to be the Bruce family's au pair. She is a fan from a younger generation, and was beside herself with delight when she managed to buy tickets for the last night of The Royal Albert Hall run; 'I did not know of Cream or Jack Bruce until around ten years ago. I went to England after leaving school, to be an au pair for a year. I landed in the Bruce household.

'I love his work. I love him even though he is a grumpy old Scot. I wanted to see him with Ginger because I knew it would be just awesome. I needed to be at The Royal Albert Hall so that I could catch up on an area that was been denied to me because of my age.'

Nicholas and Jill Gioello flew in from Sedona in Arizona for the reunion gig; 'I read something in November or December '04 in Mojo magazine about the rumoured reunion. I felt so excited, like I was a teenager again. I showed Jill and said 'Hey, if this happens let's get tickets and go make a whole week of it.' I'm not a rich man; by day I'm a city planner and my wife works at a local hotel, so this trip was always going to be a big thing for us

'I got up at 1am in preparation for the sale of tickets, which started at 2am our time', he says. 'I had my cell phone ready with a headset and mic and the phone number for The Royal Albert Hall set in the speed-dial. I logged on to the bookings website and waited. At 2am I started dialling the cell phone with my left hand, and with the mouse in my right hand I tried to navigate the web site.

'An hour and a half later and with no luck, I just about gave up. I actually had a few tears roll down my cheek, I was so disappointed, and I had not felt that kind of emotion in years. Then I started thinking 'What am I doing, quitting?' So I kept trying, and ten minutes later I had two tickets in the balcony!

'Around 1971, aged fifteen, I became interested in the guitar and I told anyone that would listen that I was going to be a guitar player. An older guy took me aside one day and said, 'If you really want to learn how to play the guitar, you gotta' get some Cream albums, man - Eric Clapton, Jack Bruce and Ginger Baker - that's the real music.' I bought 'Heavy Cream' - a two record set with all the essential songs on it – and oh, how many nights I spent with headphones on, so my parents wouldn't complain, listening over and over to those two records.

'Sure I loved Eric's stinging guitar solos, but Jack's vocals were also astonishing to me. The way he held a note or sang falsetto at the perfect time in a song was like nothing I'd ever heard before, so pure and clean and full of emotion. I also fell in love with Passing The Time and As You Said.

'I learned guitar tone and phrasing from Eric, and I learned vocal control and vocal dynamics, and bass counter melodies from Jack. I think I got turned on to poetry from them too. The music that Jack, Eric and Ginger created turned my head around at that crucial time in my early life. The chance to see Jack, Eric and Ginger play together again is something very special; it's the chance to go back to where my life's musical journey first began. '

Davy Rennie also managed to get tickets fore himself and his wife, and that meant they would be flying in from Glasgow. Jack's childhood home at Bishopbriggs is only a few minutes away from Davy and Angela Rennie's house. He has followed Jack's career, as he says, just about all his life; 'Just watch Jack's playing, the speed of his wrist and his fingers! In a three-piece band there's no hiding place. Jack is a genius, and a Caledonian genius at that!'

There was something fundamentally different about the band that played The Royal Albert Hall on May 2 2005. The same band, when it last played there on November 26 1968, was made up of three fiercely independent and ferociously competitive musicians. They worked as free spirits within the format of the trio, constantly battling against each other, trying to blow the others off the stage, determined to exert their individual supremacy: Like three lone wolves going for the throats of other males. There was no compromise; there was never any possibility of retreat, let alone giving ground. That was the secret of their success, but it was also an element in their demise.

In 2005 they worked as a team. They were all on the same side. Perhaps they had to be, because the possibility of the reunion gigs not working was unthinkable. More likely though, they had simply aged; not in the sense of having lost the will to do battle, but in that they simply didn't need to draw blood any more. Each still has his own demons, formed in childhood and reinforced by experience; his own personal history from which there is no real escape. However, as both human beings and musicians they had grown more comfortable with themselves and more self-confident. In 1968 each was utterly self-assured; none was genuinely, honestly self-confident. There was still something to be proved, and for them there always will be, but it was probably a very good think that the reunion didn't take place twenty or so years ago. Now they had matured.

They didn't all go out on the town together after the gig and double-check each other's addresses for their Christmas card lists. On stage at least they were no longer fighting each other; they were fighting, as one, to offer their audience the best possible musical experience. It made all the difference.

'Thank you for waiting', Eric had said to the audience at one point. We had waited, often thinking the wait was in vain, but it had been worth the wait.

Chapter 2

Jack was born in Lanarkshire on May 14 1943 in a modest house; 67 Beaufort Gardens in Bishopbriggs, which is a suburb about three miles to the north of Glasgow city centre, on the road to Kirkintilloch and the north-east. In the Seventies the area was 'moved' for administrative purposes and it is now included in East Dunbartonshire. In early times it had been a coal-mining town, with several large mines employing thousands of men from the town. If anyone describes Scotland in terms of the Highlands, snow-capped mountains, tumbling trout rivers and broad sea lochs then they're not thinking of Bishopbriggs.

He was born John Symon Asher Bruce, but was called Jack by his family from a very early age, and the nickname stuck. He keeps his full name on his passport and driving license, which allows him some anonymity when he wants it; particularly when travelling or booking into hotels.

Number 67 was a modest and undistinguished semi-detached house – a semi in the sense that it was at the end of a terrace. It was one of a large number of homes built in the Twenties and Thirties as an overdue move to create 'homes fit for heroes' as had been promised at the end of the First World War. It was actually owned by his parents, Charlie and Betty Bruce, which was a real achievement as previously they had spent all of their lives in rented homes. Jack remembers it as being particularly small, and it's likely that his parents could afford that house in particular because it was some way out of the city. Together with the adjoining houses it has long since been swept away and replaced with rather grander properties. Charlie and Betty were of a similar age, both were born in 1909.

Charlie had many different jobs throughout his working life, but when Jack was born he was selling insurance. That immediately summons up a certain image - of a neat and perhaps fastidious man in a white shirt and smart suit, with a full fountain pen and an ever-ready sheaf of printed forms. That wasn't Charlie Bruce though. He wasn't a white-collar worker by background or inclination. He was a short, lively, bright-eyed man who loved a good party. He was also a dapper man, always smart and proud of his appearance. He always left the house looking his best – and rarely without a hat.

The Bruce household was full of life, and at times was an exciting place to be. Charlie was an enthusiastic drummer and piano player, and at any party he would be sat at the piano stool, with the ash on his cigarette getting longer, as he thundered at the keys. He played for others rather than for himself; he played songs for folk to sing to, for them to dance to. His style was pure Fats Waller, Jack says, though 'His left hand was a little bit suspect.' He played fast and furious – and to the delight of his friends and family.

There wasn't a piano in the house until Jack's elder brother, also named Charlie, was encouraged to play as a teenager. He was a gifted pianist but music wasn't to become his life. He remembers Jack being born – in a bedroom upstairs. He recalls too, not long after, having to push the pram on endless walks.

When they were younger Charlie and Betty had been great ballroom dancers, and a weekend didn't go by when they didn't change into their very best clothes, shine up their shoes, slick down their hair, and go dancing at one of the city's large and stylish ballrooms. They first met at a dance, they conducted their courtship at dances and they danced as a handsome, newly married couple.

One of the most famous venues was The Barrowlands Ballroom on Gallowgate, just east of the city centre and north of the Clyde. It could accommodate 1,700, and with its glittering, sparkling décor it would have been an oasis of style and glamour. Appropriately it later became one of the city's best-loved rock venues.

Jack's mother doted on her younger son and he was her favourite. She had been very ill at the time of his birth and Jack had been taken from her and was brought up for the first few months of his life by one of her sisters. He wouldn't have been breast-fed, and though he would have been fussed over and cared for, he didn't receive the unreserved love that his mother would have given him.

Betty was a woman who knew what she wanted and was always very determined that she was going to get it. She clung to Jack, and nothing would ever be too good for him.

Betty's family were a rung or two higher up the social ladder, though they would still have considered themselves working class. Their home was in Springburn, and her father – originally from the eastern corner of the Highlands – was a coach painter for the railways. Prior to that her side of the family had come down from Easter Ross in the far north of Scotland, north of Inverness.

Her husband's parents had been very poor and he was brought up in unenviable circumstances. They lived in Bridgeton, not far from the infamous Gorbals, and while conditions wouldn't have been as bad as they were in the Gorbals itself, they would not have been very much noticeably better to an outsider. Things were undoubtedly tough; children were fortunate if they had good shoes to wear to school, and their diet would have been meagre at best.

His father had been an electrician before the First World War, which was a very high status occupation for a working man. Had all gone well, he might, given time, have managed to really improve his family's circumstances. However he suffered badly when he was gassed in his trench during the battle of Ypres, and as well as losing the sight of one eye, his general health was badly affected. The immediate effect was that he and his family were going to spend the rest of their lives in the poorer parts of the city.

Charlie had been a very bright child and had passed his examinations to go to the Scottish equivalent of the English grammar school, but that was quite beyond his par-

Jack's father Charlie Snr;
a left-wing political activist all his life. (Charlie Bruce)

ents' means. Instead he went out to work as soon as possible, to contribute to the household finances. This was far from unusual, not only was a contribution to the house coffers welcome; education was free, but until the end of the Second World War school books and other equipment had to be paid for.

He was a dedicated and uncompromising Marxist all his life, and was waiting for – and arguing for – the workers to rise up against the bosses and take control of the wealth of all nations. There was a strong and very well established Communist culture on Clydeside, and Charlie was far from alone in his views. It was a matter of personal pride that he had resisted the leader of The British Legion Of Fascists, Oswald Mosley, in his attempts to speak in Glasgow in the early Thirties. Mosley did have considerable support in the city and had been speaking at rallies there since 1931, and at one time he was nominated as the Rector of Glasgow University. The Fascists were allied to a number of other groups in Glasgow including the sectarian Scottish Protestant League and some of the city's criminal gangs – and at the other end of the social scale, The Earl of Erroll – Lord High Constable of Scotland – and a number of very prominent MPs, including Lord William Scott, Sir Adrian Bailie and Captain Archibald Ramsey.

For Charlie and his comrades – and their close allies in the Jewish community - the Fascists were a demonic presence, and while their ideological enemies were the employers and the wealthy, the Fascists represented, just as immediately, everything that they saw as utterly wrong. It was an almost religious, messianic crusade.

Terrifying violence between the two groups marked many of these events. The Communists were determined to deny Mosley an audience though, and they chopped down telegraph poles to form a barricade to physically stop him entering the city. Charlie was there, at the barricades, ready to be counted.

Charlie Jnr describes his father as a dogmatic man, never pragmatic in any way. His politics suited his style; neither had any truck with compromise. 'He always saw things in terms of black and white', Charlie says.

He was also a very fierce disciplinarian. To a degree that was the culture of the times, and as Charlie says of his father, 'He was never slow to hit you. Sometimes very severely. If he thought about it he'd strop you with a belt, but if it was spontaneous he would just punch us.'

He was exactly the opposite of today's enlightened 'new man.' Charlie says that he never saw him so much as wash a cup, and on one occasion when Betty was away for some reason their father was so adrift in the kitchen that he was reduced to trying to fry a meat and potato pie.

He saw all military conflict as 'class wars' – attempts by the ruling classes to both control the working classes and use them as disposable pawns in their power games - and would have refused to be a combatant on the grounds that he had no argument with the working man of any other land. These are views which, today, Jack has a lot of sympathy with – though he does see that it is much easier to make that case in relation to the First World War rather than the Second; 'There was an argument for the Second World War being necessary, but in essence all wars are unnecessary.'

Charlie worked as a fireman during World War Two, which meant that he didn't have to register as a conscientious objector, though Jack is certain that is what he would have done.

Being a fireman during the war wasn't a soft option. German bombers repeatedly targeted Glasgow. They wanted to inflict maximum damage on the docks and their warehouses, and of course the shipyards. Clydebank suffered more concentrated bombing that almost any other area in Britain. As well as being one of Britain's largest shipping-building areas, the Clyde was the main artery leading to the Atlantic and on to the USA.

The firemen would be dealing with fires in Victorian warehouses and huge warren-like workshops almost every night. It was dangerous, unpredictable, and often confused and confusing work. If a weakened, falling wall didn't kill you then a late-firing incendiary bomb might well – or even a delayed action anti-personnel mine, dropped specifically to kill, maim and cripple the morale of the emergency services.

The bombing had begun in March 1941, two years before Jack was born, and continued almost unabated. In that first attack over a thousand bombs were dropped and more than five hundred people were killed. 12,000 homes on Clydebank were damaged and 4,000 were completely destroyed.

For the Luftwaffe pilots it was a very long haul to targets on the west coast of Scotland, and by the time they were over their targets they would be both low on fuel and physically and mentally exhausted and terrified. They would have been sought out by searchlights and would have to fly through blazing curtains of anti-aircraft fire. Many bomber pilots turned away just a short distance from their intended targets and released their bomb load as soon as they could (lightening the plane considerably and allowing it to fly higher and faster immediately). Fireman and bomb disposal technicians had to broaden their operating range and attend to incidents in the city's suburbs and even out in the countryside. One night Jack's brother's school was flattened by a fleeing bomber dumping its ordnance – much to the delight of the younger Charlie Bruce; 'One of the main buildings took a direct hit and there was incendiary damage too, but we didn't get as much of a holiday as we'd hoped.'

Clydeside continued to be of critical importance to the war effort. In the months before Jack was born hundreds of thousands of American and Canadian troops disembarked there on their way to mainland Europe. In July 1943 The Queen Mary docked safely having crossed the Atlantic with 16,683 men on board – by far the largest number of people ever carried on a single sea crossing. This was the tortured city into which

Jack was born; by then the worst of the bombing was over and the emphasis was on offensive action rather than defensive. For the first two years of his life his native city was utterly involved in the 'total war.' It dominated just every aspect of daily life and was the biggest topic of conversation. It was an activity which occupied everyone around them, but Jack's parents remained implacably opposed to it.

The Communist ethic meant that no trace of religion was to be found in the Bruce home, and again Jack still shares his parents' views; 'All religion is a source of great evil in the world. It's just another way of keeping people's nose to the grindstone. It promises pie in the sky when you die! The theory is that you shouldn't worry if you've got nothing now, when you're dead you'll go to the Perfumed Garden.' Nonetheless, and confusingly, at one time Charlie was a leader at a local Sunday School.

Jack's earliest memory is, surprisingly, a pastoral one. He can vividly remember being with a childhood friend - he would probably have been less than two years old, with the end of the war still a year or so away. His companion was Doreen Battersby, the daughter of neighbours, who would have been much the same age. They were, he says, simply enjoying the new sensation of being able to walk. He recalls seeing everything from this new eye level, and being able to smell the flowers.

His brother says that both of them had a lot of freedom. There was no television

Jack, on right, with his elder brother Charlie – smart as ever. (CB)

of course, so they simply spent a lot of time outside in the streets and on neighbouring waste ground, playing with their friends and making up games. Similarly, they weren't driven to school, or even escorted there, so there were plenty of opportunities for diversions and adventures.

When he was older Jack would walk out of the city as often as he could, taking himself into the countryside – onto the hills if he could. When he got a bicycle he could get much further, and together with friends he would cycle a long way out of Glasgow's suburbs in search of an open landscape. Distance didn't matter. He would go as far as he could in just a day if need be, but come the holidays he and his friends could explore much further, staying at youth hostels and cycling many miles at a time, regardless of the weather.

'I never liked the city as a kid', he says, 'Whenever I had an opportunity to get out of Glasgow I did. I'd get on my bike I'd go up round Loch Lomond and round The Trossachs. It was just the beauty of the glens, the lochs, the rivers and the mountains. That's what I liked.' This is the landscape that he has returned to often – going north and north-west out of the Glaswegian conurbation; up into the Highland and Islands.

'If you went back and found my forebears' roots, I'm sure they were all from the Highlands and from the Border country.' He adds that as a child he always wanted to be in the country rather than in the city, and he never missed an opportunity to swap an urban environment for a rural one. If he couldn't get as far away he would find a substitute closer to home, such as the reservoirs which provided the city with its water supply, where he could fish – or just sit and think – or all three.

The family wasn't poor compared to the real poverty which existed in the worst parts of the city. The Bruce family was best described as solidly working class, but very respectable working class at that – with a lot of (what could be thought of as) lower middle class values; a strong work ethic, pride in one's appearance and, certainly so far as Betty was concerned, an ambition for them to better themselves.

When Jack was four years old the family emigrated to Canada. The Bruces were just one of many families who left Britain in search of a new home and a better quality of life – and, especially, better prospects for their children. Britain was only slowly recovering its spirits and its economy. Rationing was still in force for a broad range of goods – including, most critically, food. The heavily bombed cities were slowly being rebuilt. Hundreds of thousands of demobilised servicemen were trying to find jobs and re-start their interrupted careers. A Labour government had come to power as hostilities ended, with a radical manifesto of social change, but the pace was inevitably slow and the path uncertain. The Commonwealth countries were very popular with emigrants, and along with Australia, English-speaking Canada welcomed a whole wave of settlers from what was still regarded as 'the mother country.'

The driving force behind the move was Betty. She was the dominant partner in the marriage. That was – as in many working class families – of necessity. Charlie worked so hard, and such long hours, that when he was at home he was exhausted. Many men in his position, who to the outside world seemed to rule their domestic roost, where in fact happy to have their wives make the decisions and simply get on with things. As Jack recalls, 'My father made all the important decisions, such as who was going to win the war, and my mother made all the other decisions - which was everything else.'

For years Charlie was a fitter in a factory, and as well as working a long shift every working day, he would work an extra half shift on Tuesdays and Thursdays, and Saturday mornings and the occasional Sunday. And when he wasn't working he was as likely to be involved in political activities as be sat at home. This meant that his wife and two sons didn't see a lot of him. Like many children in working class families, Jack wasn't close to his father. It was as much social mores as the fact that working men laboured just about every hour they could. If you were lucky you might go to a football match with your dad on a Saturday afternoon, or if you were older, go for a pint with him. In the main though men socialised – when they did – with their work mates, and children played in the streets with their school friends.

The job that Jack remembers most fondly was when his father was a delivery driver for a chocolate company. He took the confectionery in bulk from the wholesaler's distribution centre to the various corner shops. He drove a small three-wheeled van, and occasionally Jack was allowed to go along for the ride. The chocolate didn't come ready-wrapped in convenient, pocket-sized bars, but was in large, heavy blocks. At each shop Charlie would cut a piece from the larger block, as required, and the lad was allowed to scrabble round and scoop up the shavings and crumbs and eat them. Understandably Jack remembers those days with very great affection.

The cost of the passage to Canada, and of housing once there, was considerable, and the money can only have come from making savings. Charlie's salary was the only income and was always fairly modest; the emigration must have taken a lot of thought and planning. It was Betty though who disciplined the household expenses and set aside the money they would need. She was the impetus behind the adventure, and at every stage the driving force. Betty always aspired to a better quality of life and more attractive surroundings for her family. She was undoubtedly a strong personality and a dominant force. Jack goes a little further though and describes his mother as 'pushy.' And others who knew her have put it more strongly still.

It's not hard to understand Charlie and Betty's thinking. Post-War Glasgow was an impoverished, dark city. Fifty or a hundred years earlier it had been a dynamic and ambitious city. Its Georgian and Victorian entrepreneurs had been clever, hard working and unerringly good at what they did.

The city is over a thousand years old, with its cathedral dating from 1136 and its university from 1451, but it really started to grow as a result of The Act of Union which legally joined England and Scotland in 1707. The previously shallow Clyde was dredged to allow larger, sea-going ships to enter more easily, and it became crucial to the tobacco trade. When the American Civil War threatened that activity, cotton and sugar were imported from the West Indies instead, and the iron founding and ship building industries started in earnest.

A huge amount of wealth was created in Glasgow over several generations, and the great men of the city were proud of their roots. As they did in many other parts of the country, they subscribed to impressive public works. These grandees supported art and education in particular; the Academy of Music and Drama was endowed in 1847, and the School of Art in 1845. These centres of culture were housed in magnificent build-ings and the city came to have a proud architectural identity very much its own.

By the end of the Second World War the momentum which had been created by both its mercantile middle class and its hard-labouring working class in the city had stalled. Like the great cities of Northern England, Glasgow had seen political power centralised in London. It was ignored politically, was left without investment, and its basic infrastructure was allowed to crumble. The city had some of the worst slum hous-ing in Britain, and it was only slowly being discussed, let alone tackled.

Glasgow was also eclipsed by Edinburgh, which saw itself as the hub of the law, medicine, culture and education north of the border. The good people of the Scottish capital looked down on the Glaswegians, and they in turn actively resented being patronised by the Edinburgians – who they saw as twee, prim and effete. Many Glaswe-gians, then and now, thought that their city had a better claim to the title of capital of Scotland than their smaller neighbour to the east. As Glaswegians used to say, 'Edin-burgh is the capital but Glasgow has the capital'; contrary to perception south of the border, the great trading city was always wealthier than its historic rival.

The Bruce family sailed to New York on the SS Franconia, which made the Atlantic crossing from Liverpool or Glasgow. Owned by the famous Cunard White Star line, it was a sizeable boat, with six passenger decks. The accommodation wasn't designed for maximum comfort but for maximum profit, and there would have been a couple of thousand people making each passage.

It was winter, and Jack has vivid memories of seeing icebergs as they crossed the North Atlantic. Both he and his brother were terribly seasick during the violent storms which assaulted the ship. One night Jack saw the first 'coloured person' he had ever met; a stewardess, who he remembers as kindly, jolly and 'very black.' She brought the sickly boy a large plate of sandwiches. He was hugely impressed both by her kindness and because all the crusts had been carefully cut off the bread.

1948: Jack, aged five,
started school in Weston in Canada. (CB)

There was a ballroom on the boat, and four year-old Jack took to conducting the dance band that played for the passengers. He adored this performance and he was given a chair to stand on, so he could be better seen by audience and musicians alike. It could be said, just, that his musical career started there, in the middle of the North Atlantic in the winter of 1947.

They disembarked in New York and had a wander round a city, which wasn't only much bigger than Glasgow, but also had the tallest buildings they had ever seen – the streets were almost like ravines cut into the ground. The people there were speaking the same language, to a greater or lesser degree, but everything else was very new and different. From there they took a train journey up into Canada, which took the best part of twenty-four hours.

The family settled in Hardington, which was a suburb of Weston, not far from Toronto. They enjoyed a significantly higher standard of life almost immediately. They lived in a good-sized bungalow, with a verandah and their own back garden – with,

Jack on a family picnic in the late 1940s. Both his parents played very important roles in forming his character, and from his father (right) he got his political beliefs. (CB)

Jack, recalls, Black Widow spiders living in the long grass. Downtown Weston reminded Jack of the sort of town he saw on cowboy films, with its Main Street shops fronting onto wooden sidewalks. Many of the streets were made of gravel with wooden duckboarding and open ditches on both sides. Each house had its own little bridge over the ditch. From time to time neighbours would miss the bridge with their cars, maybe coming in late, and in the morning Jack would be delighted to see the back ends cars sticking up out of the ditch. The surfacing was fine in summer and winter, but in the spring the melting snow turned the roads into quagmires.

The town had been created to provide the staff and infrastructure for the Weston food empire – which was, and still is, a huge concern in North America, and was best known in Britain for its 'Wagon Wheel' chocolate biscuits. George Weston, who began his working life as a baker's assistant at the age of twelve, had founded the company in 1882. In the 1890s he built his 'Model Bakery' and had salesmen riding in delivery wagons to ensure that no sales opportunity was ever missed. By the Second World War the firm became Canada's largest food processing and distribution company, and one of the largest in North America.

Apart from food production, Weston had also developed a name as a centre for light engineering, and Charlie worked in a bicycle factory. Betty took a job as a waitress to help contribute to the household funds. It's hard to say what took the Bruce family to Weston in particular, given that Charlie didn't work for the Weston company.

It was the food though that Charlie remembers to this day, 'There was still a lot of deprivation in Britain, but over there we just saw so much food we couldn't believe it.'

The emigration was supposed to be the beginning of a whole new life – one of sunshine, leisure, good food and fresh air; the Canadian take on the American Dream – but because of their parents' jobs the two boys saw even less of them. Jack describes himself as a latch key kid during that period, 'Except they wouldn't let me have a latch key.'

Jack was very happy in Canada; 'Weston had the atmosphere of a frontier town', he says, 'I had a great time. I loved the weather – it was either very hot or very cold. I can remember the snow ploughs pushing the snow up as high as the house in the winter, which was thrilling.'

Despite the difficulties they experienced as children, and the periods of financial hardship, Betty Bruce kept both her sons as smart and as well-dressed as funds allowed. Appearances always mattered. (CB)

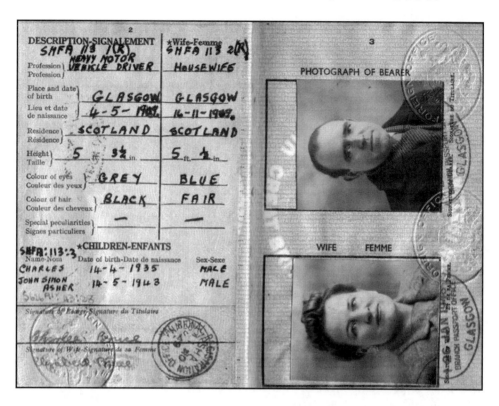

Jack's parents' passport, used for their epic journey to Canada in 1947. (CB)

The winters were bitterly cold but very dry. The Bruces had a furnace in their basement, and keeping it lighted wasn't a job to be neglected. The boys still spent a lot of their time outside, regardless of the weather. In the winter someone would simply turn on a hosepipe and in moments they would have their own ice rink.

Another fond memory, along with playing and swimming in the creek, was the start of his formal education. Canada had initiated kindergarten education for children under primary school age, which was then unknown back home. He recalls this as a delight, and he then started what we would know as infant school. It looked as if he would grow up to be a Canadian. As he puts it, 'If it had worked out for us we could easily have stayed there – and I'd have grown up to be Neil Young … or Joni Mitchell.'

Charlie Bruce's political activities continued – and did not go unnoticed. In August 1947 he attended the now-famous Communist-organised music rally at Peekskill over the border in New York State, where both Pete Seeger and Paul Robeson spoke and sang. The venue was a large lakeside picnic area. From early morning white supremacists and members of several right wing organisations ambushed those attending. There were sporadic fights and scuffles. The Westchester County police undoubtedly took sides, seeing the festival-goers as interlopers and troublemakers.

The violence increased as the afternoon wore on. The vigilantes were increasingly determined that the event would not go ahead. They called the festival-goers 'white niggers' and threatened to lynch Robeson. By nightfall the event had descended into something between a rural riot and a massacre. Agents of the FBI stood by, not taking part but taking photographs and making notes. Although it took place deep in the New York countryside, the event made headlines around the world. Aided by the unions, the music festival was held – but a few days later than originally planned.

Charlie was stopped at the border on his way home, and from that point on his allegiances and beliefs were known to the governments of both countries. Many liberal-minded people were politicised by Peekskill, and it would certainly have reinforced Charlie Bruce's thinking, and convinced him that the only answer was for the comrades to join together and stand firm in their opposition to the forces of the establishment.

Fear of Communism rapidly spread across the border from the USA, and it's probable that he was black-listed – especially as he was an alien, and would have been seen as some sort of foreign infiltrator infecting North American capitalism, intent on its downfall.

Jack's father was sacked from his job because of his trade union activity. He found it difficult to get another job, and it was his political views which were denying him and his family the Canadian Dream.

Soon the money started to run out, and, disillusioned, Charlie and Betty decided to return to Scotland. There was, Jack's brother recalls, an element of homesickness too, which seems almost incredible given the vastly better conditions they were enjoying in Canada. 'Our mother always convinced herself that if one thing could be made to happen then everything would be alright afterwards. She was a very strong woman and if she made up her mind to do something then that was it', Charlie Jnr says. She had decided that they were going to Canada and now it was she who decided that they to return to Scotland.

What equity they had in the house in Weston had been eaten up, as of course had the monies spent on the emigration. The family had just enough money to buy tickets home.

The contrast was considerable and the drop in their living standards immediate. The family lived in a succession of rented homes, most of which were at best far from attractive, and at worst truly awful – and were certainly far below the standard they had glimpsed in Canada. At first they were in a fairly desperate boarding house. When they could find a home to rent it was a primitive farm-workers cottage, empty because the agricultural labourers were again moving off the land and into the cities and towns –

and no one wanted their mean accommodation. The dream was well and truly in ruins and both the present and the future looked bleak.

Jack remembers one home which was better than the others. It was one of the previously-tied cottages on a corner of a farm outside Glasgow, back in Lanarkshire. The mines locally were 'strip mines' which left the industrial-scale excavations exposed and blighted the landscape in a way that would be almost unthinkable today. It also led to subsidence, the appearance of 'flash' pools and underground fires which could smoulder on for years.

Although getting to school was a long walk and then a bus ride, this particular cottage was far better than their other temporary homes, and it seemed that the family's fortunes might be improving once again. There was a railway running very close to the house, but even that didn't detract from its appeal. Jack had a pet, a hamster.

One evening though the farmer who owned the house arrived carrying a shotgun. He had discovered that Charlie was a Communist and, frighteningly enraged, demanded that they all get out immediately; 'We had to just take everything and leave. At that point we were totally homeless.'

Without a roof over their head the family qualified for a council-owned flat on a huge estate in Pollock. It was one of the post-War 'overspill' estates to which Glaswegians were re-housed from the city's tenements. It had a population of tens of thousands, but had no real centre and precious little sense of community. The whole development, huge as it was, hadn't included any provision for anything as basic as a pub. As Jack points out, no one owned cars there, and if his parents wanted to go out for an evening it involved making three different bus journeys in each direction.

All the moves meant that Jack went to several different schools, and his childhood friendships were often fleeting. In total he attended fourteen schools. He was a bright pupil and loved to learn, and as a result the teachers responded well to him. He was top of the class in English, was good at History, loved reading – and hated Maths. He was already good at Music, as a formal subject in the curriculum though, there was very little music to be found in his early schools.

Almost as much education was to be had from the wireless. Long before television was commonplace in the average home, and years before the Bruce family came to own one, the radio was a magical device; a door that opened to reveal hundreds of other worlds and stimulate the imagination endlessly. In one of the farm cottages Jack's bed was in an alcove off the living room, which was separated by a curtain at nighttime. There was classical music on The Third Programme, which Jack soaked up, long before he understood it at all. He also recalls lying in bed and listening to plays on the radio. One in particular was a drama about a nuclear war, and the eight-year old lay in terror, uncertain whether it was actually a play or was real life.

He had picked up something of a Canadian accent and as a result was picked on –
not bullied as such, but certainly picked on – by other boys. He had also come home
the proud owner of a parka, which was then an unknown garment in Britain, and certainly not a fashion item as it would be in the Sixties. Unfortunately it was deemed to
be effeminate; 'No matter how hard the winter, in Glasgow little boys were supposed
to go around in shorts and wellie boots. You were considered a sissy if you wore a coat
– let alone this parka thing. It was better to get bronchitis and pneumonia rather than
have your manhood doubted.'

As well as the long walk to and from the school in the morning and the afternoon,
Jack used to walk all the way home for lunch. Often his mother would come home
from her job, and he very fondly recalls these moments as 'my favourite time.' He
would sit with his mum, having her all to himself, as they ate and chatted.

Jack ended his primary education at Cardonald, where he was fortunate to be
taught by Douglas Burnie, who was one of those rare teachers who was truly and effortlessly inspirational. One day he brought a small record player into the classroom and,
without comment, played his class of forty-plus ten year-olds a recording of Louis
Armstrong, and then Mozart. He had a harmonica for every child, which he had probably paid for out of his own pocket, and he patiently taught his pupils how to play it.

His father was opposed to him going to the Senior school. He disagreed with the
process of selection, and wanted his sons to leave school as soon as they could and
join the ranks of working men. He wanted them to follow the traditional path, become
apprentices and 'get their papers' in a factory. By law a child only needed to complete
three years in either the Senior or the Junior, and then he or she was deemed ready to
step into the world of work. Part of Charlie's thinking might be so that his sons had
some security – you could always get a job if you had a trade – but was also a sense of
inverted snobbery. He wouldn't have wanted his boys to join the bourgeoisie, let alone
become bank managers and drive Rovers.

The working man's struggle was Charlie's life. He was greatly respected within the
Communist Party in and around Glasgow, and his house was often full of fascinating
people, political activists. Now-legendary names such as Willie Gallagher – who preaching Socialism with the Clyde Workers' Committee, had been imprisoned during the
First World War, was then a Communist MP for fifteen years, and finally advocated
anarchy - and Harry Pollitt – originally a boiler worker who, inspired by the Bolshevik
revolution of 1917, went on to become general secretary of the British Communist
Party - were often to be found sat at the kitchen table, arguing, debating, raising their
voices, singing. As Charlie Jnr recalls, 'There was always an argument going on – but
where would you be without an argument?'

In 1956 Kruschev denounced Stalin as a despot in his address to the twentieth

Communist Party Congress, and said that the former leader – who had died three years previously – had built his reputation on fear, suspicion and terror. This came as a terrible shock to idealistic Communists outside the USSR (and was to be compounded by the invasion of Hungary later that year). Jack can remember his mother in tears in their kitchen. To them he was paternalistic, benevolent 'Uncle Joe.' It was unbearable, unimaginable that this might not be the entire truth, and that it was being said by the new leader of the Soviet Union – who was by definition one of their brothers and comrades too. Jack, then thirteen, could hardly believe his parents' reaction. He thought someone must have died.

Betty had different ideas about her younger son's schooling, and Jack was sent to

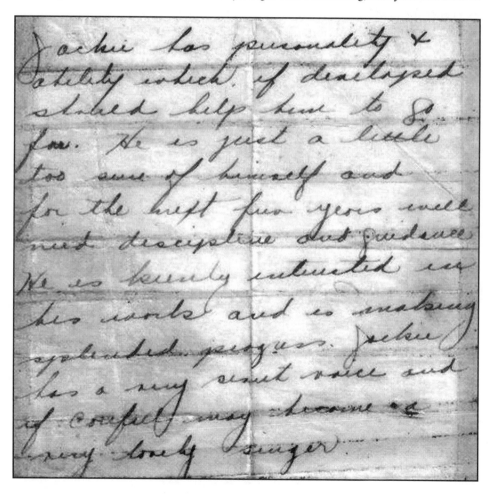

A page from Jack's school report, noting that he was 'a little too sure of himself.' (CB)

Bellahouston Academy. In theory his Quali grade wasn't good enough for the Academy but his mother disagreed, so Jack went to Bellahouston. The deciding factor was that anyone with a pass could enrol at the Academy if they agreed to learn Gaelic. It was a language that Jack came to love, and those were lessons he enjoyed.

The Academy had been founded as a private school in 1876, but it was a financial failure and was taken over by the Glasgow City Council just eight years later. It was housed in an unappealing high-Victorian building, all gables and towers, set just south of the Clyde in the south-west corner of the city. The school had a reputation as a progressive establishment though, and was highly regarded. In 1919 it had gained a swimming pool, which was unheard of at that time. Nowadays it is known as a centre of excellence for sport.

At Bellahouston he was fortunate to be taught by Douglas Burnie, who was one of those rare teachers who was truly and effortlessly inspirational. One day he brought a

In his Ballahouston Academy school uniform;
his mother's delight. (CB)

small record player into the classroom and, without comment, played his class of forty-plus ten year-olds a recording of Louis Armstrong, and then Mozart. He had a harmonica for every child, which he had probably paid for out of his own pocket, and he patiently taught his pupils how to play it.

Jack was overjoyed with the small, highly portable and rather exotic instrument, and was soon playing it with ease. Mr Burnie took a great interest in this particular pupil's progress. Having quickly discovered the limitations of his first mouth organ, Jack persuaded his parents to buy him a Hohner Chromatic harmonica. This offered all the notes of the chromatic scale and allowed the player to play in any key. The instrument's slide mechanism allowed Jack to alternate between the scales of C and C#, which was the same as alternating between the white and black notes on a piano. Nowadays such a harmonica costs £40, so it would have been a generous present for Charlie and Betty to buy their younger son.

Mr Burnie was delighted by the way his pupil took to the new instrument and encouraged Jack to try a wide range of musical styles, from jazz to the classics. His was the first positive encouragement that Jack can remember from his school days.

At about the same time, Betty Bruce, who was very fond of singing herself, arranged for Jack to have singing lessons. The staple diet was the songs of Robbie Burns. He went on to join a choir, and there he found a second mentor in the choirmaster, Jimmy Callan – who encouraged him to sing solos. Jimmy was also a Communist; the party enthusiastically promoted cultural activities for its members, and Jack sang for Paul Robeson at a concert. Robeson was a hugely important figure for the Left Wing. He was an American, which meant that not all Americans were wealthy warmongers, and he was black – at a time when the notion that a black guy could be successful, influential and a real political force was unheard of. Robeson was also a very brave man. He was undoubtedly a target for his political rivals, and his career suffered because of his Communist sympathies, but he never paused for even a moment. Born at the end of the Nineteenth century, he was a singer of operatic quality, and a genuine hero – of almost unparalleled status in Socialist and Communist circles.

He sang in Scotland at Left Wing events on several occasions, and at one of these Betty pushed her son forward to sing for him. In that company he was political aristocracy, and both Charlie and Betty must have been inordinately proud to see their son in such company. It's certainly a performance which Jack has never forgotten.

Chapter 3

J ack was soon competing at various singing festivals in and around Glasgow, where the repertoire was usually light classical music, such as the work of Schubert or Purcell. There would be set pieces, which every contestant had to sing, and then a second song, which could be of one's own choice. Jack got very nervous before the competitions started, not because he was frightened of performing or was awed by the occasion, but because he might not win. 'It wasn't any good to come second. You had to win.' He was already a very competitive and determined young man and never as much as in his music.

Talking of his abilities though, he says, 'Music was just something that I did. I was talented – a good boy soprano, but with a vibrato so that it sounded like a woman's voice - but no-one was saying 'Oh that's amazing!' or anything. I'm sorry that my voice wasn't recorded at that time.'

Despite the Bruce family's committed atheism he did go on to join a church choir, but that was 'for the money', as it was a church that paid its choristers. Similarly, he was paid for singing with the Carl Rosa opera company that visited Glasgow. He played a ragamuffin in 'Carmen.' He also sang on a young musicians' radio show broadcast from the BBC in Glasgow, which – as all their friends and neighbours could hear it on the wireless - must have delighted his mother in particular.

Jack maintains that there was no doubt that he was going to be a professional musician, even from a very early age – possibly even from his 'conducting' experience on the Franconia. 'I never thought of making a living as such, but this was what I was going to do. I just was a musician.'

He had found a wider pool of possible friends at the Senior school, and by the fourth year Jack and his colleagues could accurately be described as a gang. They became adept at playing truant from school, and distinguished themselves by wearing 'modern' hairstyles. At the local hairdressing college you could get your hair cut for free if you allowed the trainees to experiment on you, and the students preferred more

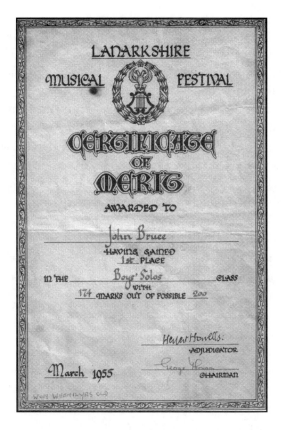

Urged on by his mother, Jack entered and won many
singing competitions in and around Glasgow. (CB)

interesting styles rather than the old 'short back and sides.' American-influenced rock 'n roll hair styles were the favourites, but were bound to lead to a telling off back at school: The teachers enforced a strict dress and appearance code.

Jack was always in awe of his elder brother's sense of style, and that of his friends. They were the Teddy Boy generation, but were much cooler – they wouldn't have stooped to slashing cinema seats, for which the Teddy Boys were, in the newspaper reports at least, notorious. Charlie and his mates favoured Tony Curtis haircuts and sharp clothes. As Charlie says, 'You didn't go out in casual gear. I wouldn't have dreamed of going out without a tie.' When Jack was twelve and his brother was twenty Charlie was undoubtedly something of an idol; something the elder guy was completely unaware of. One other reason for Jack being so impressed by his big brother was that Charlie had won the talent competition at school, with a hugely impressive piece of very fast boogie-woogie piano playing.

Although it was an achievement to pass for Bellahouston, Jack was, academically speaking, something of a small fish in a big pool. It was seen as a 'posh' school for the sons and daughters of the middle classes, and Jack felt ill at ease. He had been something of a solitary child since the return from Canada, and the social difference between him and the other children who lived locally, dictated by him going to 'the posh school', made him an outsider. He does argue that it might have been better if he had gone to the just opened comprehensive school, and been able to shine rather more brightly. His mother loved him being at the Academy. His father hated it.

One great advantage was that the school was blessed with an excellent music department, and this was both a great delight and a revelation. It was a well-equipped department, and was staffed by enthusiastic teachers who actively encouraged their pupils.

Jack had started composing music while still at primary school, and in his first year at the Academy he wrote a string quartet. One of his music teachers was Jean Dick, who Jack remembers as being 'very strict, very conservative' and who was a considerable force in the music world in the city. She had no interest in contemporary music at all; for her it had to be classical or nothing. The discipline was probably very good for her pupil, and she encouraged him to take his A-level examination in the subject and then go higher still. As he was the only pupil at that level he had the undivided attention of the music teachers.

Apart from Music the only subjects that held any interest for him were English and Art, and to a lesser degree, Gaelic. Nothing else on the curriculum mattered; his Science teacher ordered him to leave the class and not come back, 'That suited me. I was always the joker, always having to say something funny. He got tired of it.'

Having been excluded from Science, Jack used the time to play music. He had discovered a piano in the book store at the top of the building. He could sit there and play, no one knowing where he was, utterly happy.

The school offered to teach their pupils any instrument that attracted them, however charges were made for some instruments. The upright acoustic bass was free though. The school already owned one, and when he expressed an interest the school arranged for an elderly bass tutor to come in especially.

One problem became apparent immediately. Jack was very short, and simply wasn't tall enough to play the instrument. The tutor told him he would have to start again in a couple of year's time when, hopefully, he would be able to reach high enough to tune it. Jack was hugely disappointed, but Jean Dick suggested that he start by learning the cello – as a holding operation – and move on to the bass when his height allowed it.

She acquired an instrument, and also arranged for a dedicated tutor – who played lead cello for the Scottish National Orchestra. Jack's ability with the cello eventually brought him a scholarship to the Royal Scottish Academy of Music to study composition and the cello.

When he moved on to bass he fell in love with the instrument immediately; 'I think that all instruments are sexy when they are played well, but the bass is certainly a very sexy instrument for the person playing it. You push it into your groin and I used to get off on the vibrations. Very good for an adolescent male ...'

He remembers that A-level exam being very difficult, very advanced. Rather than going for the practical elements he elected to write pieces. He had to play the piano for the external examiners, as well as the cello, and sing. He had to know a huge amount about the history of classical music and be able to explain complex musical terms in layman's language. He was, he says, rather lazy when it came to practising, and his reading of music wasn't what it might have been. Jack found it easier – and more fun – to improvise, which of course wasn't always what his tutors wanted of him. In strictly academic terms he was better at English than at the aspects of music which didn't involve actually playing an instrument.

Thanks to an essay on the history of jazz he got his English A-level with the highest mark of any Scottish music pupil that year. This qualified him for the school's

Jack on piano accompanying his very glamourous looking mother as she sings at a party. (CB)

'David Orr Prize', which was the book of his choice. He asked for a copy of 'Ulysses' by James Joyce, which had been banned from publication until that year on grounds of obscenity. The headmaster decided that this was far from suitable and announced that, as Jack wasn't prepared to make another choice, no prize would be awarded. Jack decided to dig his heels in. He wasn't going to be told which book he could have, not by anyone. To take a rebellious stand against the headmaster himself was an irresistible temptation. It was the sort of gesture that would be more common by the late Sixties, but ten years earlier such defiance was unheard of. This self-assured, cocky youngster must have terrified half his peers, and to the others he must have been something of a hero. Eventually the headmaster relented, and presented him with the book - and Jack, proud of the prize and proud of his cussedness, has it to this day.

He was a member of the rock 'n roll generation – though was very selective as to which bits of it he wanted to sign up for. Bill Haley, the unlikeliest rock 'n roll star, had his first UK hit at the very end of 1954. During 1956, when Jack saw his thirteenth birthday, Elvis had all of nine singles in the top ten. With the exception of Chuck Berry and Little Richard, and especially Fats Domino, the early rock 'n roll stars didn't make too big an impression on him. The musicians he liked were edgier, slightly more dangerous and unpredictable – and they played an instrument; they weren't solo singers. They were also, usually, both American and black.

So far as British rock 'n roll was concerned, he was never a Cliff Richard fan, but thought Hank Marvin was terrific – perhaps unsurprisingly as his musicianship helped shape the tone and colour of electric guitar playing. At the very end of the decade though Jack says that he really admired the East London lad Adam Faith, who – unlike Cliff – was 'cool.' Jack saved his enthusiasm however for 'the musicians who swung.'

An early morning milk round before school meant that Jack was able to buy his first record player. It was, of course, a Dansette. It was something of a personal landmark too; the very first possession that he had bought with his own, earned money. Charlie Jnr was buying records too, all jazz – and he remembers a real highlight was Frank Sinatra's 'Songs For Swingin' Lovers', which re-established the teen idol as a serious, adult performer and made him the undisputed king of cool.

Jack bought all styles of music to play on his record player – mostly jazz - but he wasn't a great record collector. He preferred to play his own music.

Decades later, in an interview with The Guardian newspaper, Jack described his earliest influences as 'a very strange mix of Scottish folk, traditional jazz, modern jazz, classical and a little bit of rock n' roll.' He also surprised the interviewer by citing the classical singer Kathleen Ferrier as an early influence; 'She was a postmistress who was discovered and became a superstar. She was a contralto like nobody else - she comes from a time when music was simpler, and you could quite easily fall in love with her voice.'

He also mentioned Charles Ives and John Cage – one a classical composer and the other an ultra-modern minimalist composer: As eclectic a mix as it is possible to imagine.

The skiffle boom had started in the UK in 1954, and was at first almost entirely due to the work of fellow-Scot Lonnie Donegan - and Jack insists that band leader Chris Barber, who he has always admired greatly, must take equal credit. It was a branch of American folk music, and the songs were almost all about American iconography – mostly freight trains, it seemed. It was great music for joining in though, and very accessible, needing the most basic of instruments. The word itself had originally been used to describe those who were too poor to afford proper instruments. Many musicians who later moved on to other forms of music started in skiffle. Jack joined a skiffle group for a short while, though more for fun than for creative satisfaction.

He was as likely to be found playing boogie-woogie at the piano though. He describes himself as 'very rebellious, musically' – just as he was scholastically and academically. He hated Beethoven; 'Just three chords and stodgy with it', but adored the work of Mozart.

His teachers were telling him that serious music had died with Richard Strauss. His own researches brought him to Twentieth-century composers such as Stravinsky. He heard a concert by Stockhausen, which featured three orchestras, each with its own conductor, an electric guitar and the audience on the stage instead of the orchestra. Most music lovers neither liked nor understood his music. The work impressed Jack greatly. His was an intelligent, elitist rebellion.

There had always been some presence of jazz in the Bruce household; both Charlie and Charlie Jnr brought home jazz records. Jack's father often took him to jazz concerts in the city, and while still a teenager he saw and heard 'Jazz At The Philharmonic' with Ella Fitzgerald, Oscar Peterson playing piano and - Jack remembers particularly - Ray Brown on bass. Born in the mid-Twenties, Ray Brown had played with Dizzy Gillespie, Charlie Parker, Max Roach and Bud Powell. Ray had been married to Ella Fitzgerald, by way of further distinction. The vast majority of the audience at that gig would have been concentrating on Ella or Oscar; Jack was watching – and, even above the whole sound of the band, hearing - Ray Brown.

Charlie and Jack also saw The Modern Jazz Quartet, which had been formed in '52 and was recording with the then-young Atlantic label - to whom Jack would later be signed. The bass player with the MJQ was Percy Heath – who had played with just about all the biggest names in American jazz (and who died in April 2005). It was his performance that first fired Jack with the certainty that the bass was going to be the instrument for him.

Most of these concerts were held in Saint Andrew's Hall in the city centre, which was the city's largest venue. Jack remembers it as having very poor acoustics (it burned down in 1964, and The Mitchell Library, which backed onto Saint Andrew's Hall, expanded across the whole site. The complex now includes a new theatre, an art gallery, a bar and a restaurant). In the Fifties and early Sixties though it was a very traditional concert hall, and was large enough to attract the very best names.

Charlie also took his sons to see traditional variety, where you would get live music, comedians, magicians, dancers and maybe ventriloquists all on the same bill. These were at the music halls such as The Metropole and The King's – where Glaswegians had been entertained since Victorian days. They tended to be all-Scottish acts, and all-Scottish humour would have been completely lost on a visiting Englishman. Thanks to radio and, in time, television, a few acts did move onto a national stage – such as Jimmy Logan and Stanley Baxter – but the majority were very well known in Scotland and unknown anywhere else. The infamous Glasgow Empire, which was notoriously impossible for a performer if the audience took against you, was somewhat different in that it attracted international acts such as American singers and comics.

Glasgow, like Liverpool, thrived on music, and from the 1930s onwards when they first became available and affordable, almost every home had a record player. Lulu, who was the first Scot to make an impact on the national pop scene, recalls that although there was very little money in her household there were always new records appearing. They were rarely official imports – you simply didn't find this material in most other parts of the country – but were brought in by seaman and sold either to individuals in pubs or to small specialist record shops to earn a few bob. The sailors could get quite a few in a small space and they were – unlike cigarettes – unaffected by condensation or other conditions, and there was a ready market for them. It's no coincidence that Glasgow and Liverpool were the two main disembarkation points for boats coming from the USA.

The range of records that was available through this channel was tremendous. Any music which wasn't easily bought in the UK could be acquired unofficially. The ones her household acquired were mostly, Lulu says, blues and jazz; 'By the age of ten I was obsessed with Ray Charles and I sang every song he sang – though my dad would say 'That man's always fuckin' moanin!' My mother preferred the country and western songs, which we all thought was music to slit your wrists to. All my relations would go to one family's house or other, they'd put some records on, everyone would get drunk, and they all seemed to be great singers.'

One place where you tended not to get live music was in Glasgow's pubs. These were dedicated to drinking, and were strictly men-only places (if you wanted to drink with your wife you went to a better-decorated and more sociably-acceptable 'lounge' bar – less popular with men as landlords were allowed to charge more for drink served there). As Charlie Jnr says, 'You didn't sing in pubs. You'd be put out for singing.'

In Glasgow the pubs closed at nine in the evening, and the mission was to drink as much as possible in the very short time available. The authorities thought that shorter licensing hours restricted the working class's intake, but of course they probably added to it. When the pub was closing, the form was to buy 'a carry out', usually a quarter bottle of whisky wrapped in a brown paper bag, and a group of men would then retire to the home of one of their number to empty the bottles – and be told off by the woman of the house for waking the children.

Jack's parents didn't drink to excess; his father would drink more at parties, and his mother probably drank more than Charlie (her tipple was whisky and lemonade). Jack's memory is that the drinking just led to merriment and nothing worse. Once a few drinks had been taken the piano lid would be opened and the singing and dancing would begin.

Jack first tried to get served in a pub when he was fifteen. The effort was probably doomed to failure as he was particularly short and looked younger than his age. He knew that the men drank beer or whisky, but just to try and sound grown-up he ordered a gin and orange; a sickly combination of spirit and undiluted orange cordial. It was much more a ladies' drink, and was certainly not what a male teenager would have been drinking. The landlord, Jack says, stared down at him and said 'Ooot!'

The other very great form of entertainment was the cinema – 'the pictures.' This was extremely popular with Jack, as with most young boys of his age. He would go at least once a week; sometimes twice. Usually they would go as a family, or when Charlie Jnr was a bit older and had other forms of entertainment, as a trio – joining the end of an already very long queue. Jack particularly delighted in cartoons and animations; 'The mother dying in 'Bambi' made a big impression on me.' The best time to go was the Saturday matinee, which was like a big social club for youngsters; 'It was total pandemonium, and of course just one of us would pay to go in – and we'd open the emergency doors and let our mates run in.'

The Bruce family caught the first three-dimensional film, which required every member of the audience to wear specially made, cardboard-rimmed spectacles. It was basic technology but very exciting none the less. The effect worked pretty well, except in Jack's father's case. He complained loudly that he couldn't see properly and everything looked wrong. All was corrected once Jack had pointed out that he had the glasses on the wrong way round.

Jack remembers that his father always insisted on smoking his pipe through the film, filling the immediate area with acrid black smoke. Almost always someone sitting nearby would demand that he put it out, to which Charlie would reply angrily that he had paid for his ticket and would damn well smoke his pipe if he wanted to.

The family took holidays only occasionally. Jack can remember just two. One year they went to Whitley Bay, and another year to the great Glaswegian mecca of Blackpool. They went away by bus, which was a long journey on pre-motorway roads, taking the best part of a day.

At the famous Lancastrian resort it rained every day and they were at the mercy of the archetypical bed and breakfast landlady, who wouldn't let the children sit down for supper with the grown-ups. The children had to eat standing up at the sideboard – and their supper menu only consisted of Corn Flakes. The family had to leave the house after breakfast and, regardless of the weather, couldn't return until 6pm. Jack remembers it as great fun, regardless.

While still at school, Jack was also a pupil at the music college - and was also a member of the Junior Glasgow Schools Orchestra, which he joined when he was fifteen. In time he progressed to the Senior, which was a full-size ensemble of around ninety young musicians. Such was its reputation that it attracted top-flight conductors, and Jack remembers the standard of musicianship as being very high indeed.

They went on short residential courses, and at one the conductor was Norman del Mar, who was nationally famous and was regarded as the leading interpreter of the music of Edward Elgar. He was greatly admired as a conductor who could coax all the colours and subtleties out of an orchestra, and he too recognised Jack's talent and took a particular interest in encouraging him. Jack says, 'Somehow he could hear my playing through the rest of this huge orchestra.' He picked Jack out to play solos, and on one occasion when he overheard Jack improvising at a piano he went out of his way to compliment and, again, encourage him.

Jack's days at music college were numbered though. He was falling out with his tutors. They were furious with him for playing the blues or improvising. The atmosphere was too conservative, too restrictive.

While all this was going on and he was juggling these commitments to both school and college, he started playing professionally in a dance band. This created problems at the music college as students weren't allowed to earn from their talents while still being taught. You could pay your way by delivering milk, washing dishes or waiting on in a bar, but not by playing music - a rule which might take some explanation.

It was suggested to Jack that he either give up college or stop playing semi-professionally. It wasn't a hard choice; 'By then I wasn't learning what I wanted to learn so it was easy to just say bye-bye.'

Similarly his efforts at composition weren't appreciated or encouraged at college. That, he thinks, was to some degree a class issue – middle class people wrote music, working class lads didn't. Jack also had problems with the composition tutor, who was as openly homosexual as you could be in the days when such practises could result in a lengthy prison term. The man was a friend of Benjamin Britten, who was fairly widely known to

THE BRITISH BROADCASTING CORPORATION
Head Office: Broadcasting House, London, W.1

Broadcasting House, Queen Margaret Drive, Glasgow, W.2

TELEPHONE AND TELEGRAMS: WESTERN 8844

Reference: 11/KG   15th March 1956.

Dear Jack,

We are holding Children's Hour microphone tests
in the Glasgow Studio on Wednesday 4th April 1956, and
as you have applied for an audition, perhaps you
would care to come along at 3.30 p.m.   on that
date, and let us hear what you can do. Please bring
with you material suitable for Children's Hour, and
prepare several items.

We don't require a great many artists, so please
don't be disappointed if you are not chosen this time.

Please let me know by return if this is suitable.

I should like to point out that the BBC cannot
undertake to pay any expenses for people coming to an
audition.

Yours sincerely,

Kathleen Garscadden

KATHLEEN GARSCADDEN
Children's Hour Organiser

John B

Invited to a BBC audition just before his thirteenth birthday, Jack was warned not to hope for too much.
(CB)

be gay, and he wore the friendship like a badge of honour. He had ambitions towards Jack; 'He was obnoxious with it and was always trying it on. He didn't want to teach me anything; he just wanted my body.'

Back then it was quite unthinkable to make a complaint, formally or informally, and it reinforced Jack's thinking that it was time for him to leave. Apparently a pupil did later make some sort of complaint about the tutor's behaviour and it seems that he was required to retire.

Jack didn't need the milk round any more; at sixteen he was playing six nights a week. He was also earning more money than his father brought in. Charlie's wage was £14 a week – Jack was earning £16.

This was a considerable bone of contention. Charlie might have been delighted for his younger son at some level, but what he expressed was resentment. It could have been straightforward jealousy. It could have been that he felt he had never had the opportunities when younger and now his son's career seemed to be really taking off while he was still so young. It could have been that he was in some way being replaced as the principal wage earner in the household.

Charlie loved music but didn't think that being a musician was a suitable job for a working class lad. Somehow all that was middle class and effete; he still wanted Jack to learn a trade and work in a factory or a workshop. What he was faced with was something completely outside his experience, and therefore threatening. It didn't fit with his view of the world. Jack argued with him, pointing out that the jazz musicians they both admired were undeniably members of the working class, but his father wasn't to be convinced. Jack feels that his father maintained a bitterness towards him, which lasted until at least the mid-Sixties.

Everyone seemed to be telling the young man that he should 'know his place.' His brother says, 'If you were going to 'make something of yourself' as they said, you might be an engineer or even a doctor or a lawyer. That was what your parents would want for you. No one thought you could become a musician. I didn't think you could even aspire to be a musician.'

College pigeonholed him because of his background and rougher accent, and his father wanted him to move away from his roots. His mother pushed, and pushed hard – often far too hard – but that in itself wasn't enough. It wasn't going to be long before he would feel the need to leave all of this baggage behind.

Jack's commitments meant that when he wasn't playing music he was usually on a bus, or at a bus stop, on his way to or from playing. And of course he always had his big acoustic bass to carry around. He had lost his heart to a new double bass though. In McCormick's music shop in the city centre he had seen a Tarr bass. William Tarr worked in Manchester in the Nineteenth century and is known to have made over four

*His much loved bicycle; whenever he could he would ride
out of the city into the countryside.(CB)*

hundred basses personally, and there were many more made by his assistants. Nowadays his instruments sell for tens of thousands of pounds. The one in the shop window was, Jack says, the most beautiful, perfect instrument he had ever seen. It was far from affordable back then, but Jack decided that he could scrape together even the deposit that was being asked. After that it would just be so many hire purchase payments.

The moment he had saved enough he rushed round to McCormick's - but it was gone. The assistant could tell him that Ray Brown had been in and bought it for cash. Jack's disappointment was only tempered by the fact that it had gone to a very good home and was now owned by one of his heroes. Many years on Ray offered to let Jack borrow it, and he was certainly still playing it relatively recently.

Jack was soon playing with good bands, in sizeable venues. The dance halls were still very popular, and there was a strong circuit, though they would be turned over to pop concerts in a few years.

The band played an afternoon matinee for the dedicated ballroom dancers, but many of them disliked his bass playing. He was playing fast and trying new ideas, but the dancers wanted what they were used to. They wanted the rhythm to be simple and straight-ahead. It was a complaint that others would say of him in years to come. They didn't understand it and they couldn't keep up. Also, they didn't hesitate to complain to the bandleader and order that the young bass player be reined in. Jack tended to ignore them.

There was more going on in his life though; he also played in a Country & Western band, which had a large following – he played The Glasgow Empire with them, and they appeared every week on Scottish television. He also stepped into a recording studio for the first time; playing cello on a now-forgotten classical piece.

There were no barriers; no sub-divisions. The diversity was good – but irrelevant. It was simply music. He was in no sense a purist about the musical styles he played. What mattered was getting out there and playing. What mattered most though was his own composition. If pressed he would have said that what he saw himself doing with his life was writing music – becoming 'a serious composer' - rather than performing. How he was going to earn a living doing this was another matter, but then those practicalities don't matter when you're a teenager.

Asked what he spent his money on, Jack sums it up very simply; 'Cars and girls.' Talented musicians have always attracted the opposite sex, and Jack was intelligent, articulate, charming when he wanted to be, and quietly funny. He was also able to buy his round without digging too deeply into his pocket.

Both brothers seemed exceptionally popular with women – girls and women in Jack's case. Their parents started to be annoyed by the number of girls who came to their front door, trying to track one or other of them down. Often they were unwelcome visitors, and Charlie remembers one occasion in particular when Jack insisted that his brother answered the door – and that he wasn't at home to anyone. The girl who was standing on the front step was, Charlie recalls wistfully, absolutely beautiful. It was unimaginable that his brother was trying to avoid her affections. She was much more Jack's age, or even slightly younger, but despite that Charlie was sorely tempted to try and hijack her attention for himself.

Jack's love affair with cars had begun when he was a child. In Canada he had owned a much-treasured model of a Jaguar, but back in Scotland there wasn't much money around for Dinky toys. Almost no one in Pollock owned a car. Such an extravagance was close to being unimaginable. Jack can remember seeing just one in their street; a pre-War Opel owned by an elderly neighbour. He can recall his brother renting a large Ford Zephyr on one very special occasion, and eventually seeing a sports car for the first time. Now his income from music meant that, as well as paying for his keep at home, he was able to buy a car even before he was legally able to drive.

He drove his car quite illegally for several months, he admits, but he took and passed his test soon after his seventeenth birthday. He was driving himself to school every morning – at a time when few of the teachers owned cars, and the Headmaster travelled to and from school by tram. His red Sunbeam Talbot was something to be proud of, something for the neighbours to gossip about, and a very rare luxury for someone of that age in the late Fifties.

Over the years he was to find out which cars could and could not accommodate a double bass; for example, although you couldn't get the instrument in a Mini, you could get one in a (Scottish made!) Hillman Imp …

The orchestral course, which Jack had attended on several occasions, was held in Dunoon, a small coastal town on the north bank of the Firth of Clyde, which was popular with Glaswegians for day trips and week-long holidays. To reach it you had to go west by train, well out of Glasgow, to Gourock, and then catch the ferry across the estuary. Or, as Jack did, you could go directly from Glasgow on a paddle steamer – named 'The Waverley' after the Robert Louis Stevenson novels. It was on this ferry that Jack, aged sixteen, finally managed to buy his first alcoholic drink. He hadn't learned his lesson; he ordered a gin and orange – but this time he got it. It was, he says, horrible.

The summer after Jack had parted company with both school and college he was back at Dunoon, but this time he had a summer residency at The Pier Hotel. He was playing in the ballroom with a jazz band, and the orchestral course was held during his time there. He came across former colleagues, who were still playing concertos for fun while Jack was playing dance arrangements for money.

Just north of the town is a small inlet in the broad Forth. This is Holy Loch and was the main European base for the American nuclear submarine fleet. Prompted by the nuclear proliferation race between the USA and the USSR, the Campaign for Nuclear Disarmament had been founded in 1958 and had rapidly became a potent force on the left wing of British politics. The butt of its campaigning was much more America than Russia. Far more was known about America's armaments, as the USSR was an almost completely closed country. Also, like Jack's parents, the Left Wing still gave the USSR the benefit of the doubt at every opportunity, and in denial of the evidence.

It was a fashionable, almost 'trendy' campaign to be associated with, and no young writer, musician or artist would have dreamed of not supporting its aims. CND was also very much of its time; related to the Beatnik movement and a product of disillusionment with Harold MacMillan's Conservative government. It can be said to have led directly to the satire boom of the early Sixties, and as with the Communist party, it was a creative melting pot of artistic ideas as well as political thought.

Politically well educated by his parents, Jack was very aware of the issues, and unsurprisingly was a passionate supporter of the 'Ban The Bomb' movement. 1959 had seen the first 'Ban The Bomb' march in Glasgow, and in early '61 CND members had marched from Glasgow to Holy Loch, where the huge, hulking, dark blue-grey curves of the submarine sat low in the water – the same colour as the loch itself and the hills that rose steeply behind. In many conditions they were completely camouflaged, as was of course the intention, but when they could be seen they were sinister, almost eerie.

The protesters, like the holidaymakers, all arrived in Dunoon before making the short journey north. Corners of the town would have been heaving with radical activists. Be it clothes, haircuts, their implacable distrust of 'the Establishment' or music – trad jazz by preference - they were different. For Jack it must have been a different and highly attractive fresh take on his parents' politics; the same thing several paces further on.

The band was a curiosity in itself. It featured a one-legged trombonist, and a tenor sax player who was desperately ill – his colleagues had to go into long solos while he coughed his lungs up and then tried to get his breath back. It was led by Charlie Stewart, a classically trained drummer, who had previously been a long-serving member of the Scottish Variety Orchestra. He had, Jack says, been 'pensioned off.'

One duty for the ensemble was to perform on the beach accompanying the young hopefuls in talent contests. The popular hit that year was the ballad I Told Every Little Star and the majority of competitors chose that, and the band had to play it endlessly – while, just up the road, huge numbers of passionate campaigners were demanding that the Polaris nuclear missile should be scrapped.

Before he had been allowed to join the band for the season – the first time he had been away from home for more than a night – Charlie Stewart had been to see Betty and vouch for his son's moral welfare while he was to be away and under his care. This assurance didn't stop Jack chasing the dancing girls at the theatre next door, and embarking upon his first serious affair.

He was seventeen and she was in her mid-forties; a very grand lady

who lived in some style locally. Simultaneously though she was conducting an affair with an American officer at the naval base, a connection which Jack found 'a bit dodgy' as the Americans were very much the demonised enemy of The Left; the evil corruptors who brought their weapons of death to Scotland's quiet lochs.

Chapter 4

One night, in a break between sets at The West End Ballroom, Jack went down the street in search of a drink. He popped into a pub known locally as The Jungle, and was stood at the bar with his pint, minding his own business. The place had a reputation as the haunt of hard men, but if you kept yourself to yourself you were usually alright. He became aware of a man standing to one side, and the man caught his eye and said, 'Excuse me Jimmy, will you stand aside? I've got no argument with you.'

Jack didn't need telling twice, and he took a couple of paces back. The guy then pulled out a handgun and shot dead the man who had been standing on Jack's other side.

The outer suburbs might be polite and refined, and sherry might be drunk in nice front parlours, but many of the inner areas of Glasgow had a deserved reputation for violence. It was often extreme violence. The dance halls where music was played were also where the gangs met, and very savage fights were common. Murders weren't uncommon. The violence was so frequent that Jack was already thinking that he needed to get away.

The Glaswegian gangs were territorial and often had histories going back many years – sometimes hundreds of years. Partly it was also about religion – as with the Protestant 'Billy Boys' who were based in Bridgeton. They were named after King William of Orange, and in the '50s they were led by the notorious Billy Fullerton who boasted of murdering Roman Catholics and was much hated by the Left as he had received a medal for strike-breaking.

Glasgow has always been a sectarian city – like Belfast or Liverpool – and when the city fathers were clearing the slums in the Fifties and relocating families into the new towns, they tried to integrate the two groups. They went so far as to 'layer' blocks of flats with Protestants and Catholics. From an idealistic point of view it must have seemed like the right thing to do; in practice the forced integration made things worse.

The atheist Bruce family was Protestant by default, in that they weren't Catholic.

Primarily though the gangs' allegiance was to their own district of the city. Glasgow had been particularly infamous for its 'razor gangs' and the Glaswegian police were issued with reinforced leather neckwear to protect them from gang members' favourite move of slashing their opponents' throats. Ordinary citizens kept well away from gang members and certainly went out of their way not to cross them.

'If it had been Chicago or New York the violence wouldn't have put me off and I would have stayed', Jack reflects, but he had come to realise that he wasn't going to be able to take his career much further in his native city and it was time to go.

It was certainly the case that if you really wanted to make your name as a musician, and in many other vocations, you had to go to London. The music scene in Glasgow was very active, very vibrant, but it was only so big. You could make a good living in Glasgow, more so than in many of the larger provincial cities, but it wasn't where the record companies, the recording studios, the booking agents or the media were based. Everything that really mattered went on in London.

Jack had a growing reputation among the coterie of musicians and aficionados of jazz in Glasgow, and moving to London meant leaving that behind and starting again from scratch. He was young though, and while the culture shock was likely to be considerable, he had nothing to lose. His ambition, as he came south, was to play Ronnie Scott's famous jazz club in Soho. Nothing more specific or ambitious than that.

During the Sixties only one band and three individual musicians came out of Scotland and became nationally famous (there were many very busy local bands, among them Alex Harvey, but he wasn't to see broader recognition for years). All of them had needed to get to London before they really achieved a worthwhile level of success. The group was the five-piece Marmalade, who had established a huge following in and around Glasgow during the first few years of the decade. Indeed, they didn't play in England until 1965. They had been playing Cliff Richards and Shadows numbers, but found their own voice under the influence of composer and arranger Norrie Paramor, and became a safe, middle-of-the-road pop group. They didn't chart until 1968, but then they had a fair run of hits through to the early Seventies. Their biggest hit, their only number one, was their cover of the worst, toe-curlingly dreadful song that Lennon and McCartney ever wrote – Ob-La-Di Ob-La-Da.

Donovan Philip Leitch is three years younger than Jack, having been born in Glasgow in May 1946. He had a good run of hit singles, the first six or seven of which were fey, pre-hippie, pre-New Age whimsies.

He was just about the first musician in the UK to sing openly about drugs and to a large degree the more mainstream strand of psychedelic music trailed behind him. He was the dopeheads' first hero, but then he became rockier and heavier. He recorded an album track which was one of the precursors of progressive rock, and which should have been a huge single - Season Of The Witch. In 1968 he released Hurdy Gurdy Man, which was far more of an acid trip than a toke on a spliff. That was followed the next year by the brilliant madness of Goo Goo Barabajagal (Love Is Hot), with Jeff Beck playing a stunning guitar line. Donovan always suffered from very ill judged and unfavourable comparisons with Bob Dylan.

He was born and brought up in the suburb of Maryhill on the northern edge of the city. It was a working class area – his family and neighbours might almost have thought of Jack's upbringing as bordering on the lower middle classes – but it was far from being the worst part of the city. Donovan would have lived with trams rattling through the narrow streets, but a feature of the area was a large and delightful municipal park. And not far away were the large detached villas of the upper middle classes, from where lawyers and businessmen would commute to smart offices in the city centre. Also, when he was ten his family moved south, and he was brought up beyond that point in distinctly leafy surroundings in Hatfield in Hertfordshire. His accent lost its harshness and somehow he never had that harder edge which Jack's background had given him. He was softer both in terms of his perceived image and perhaps as a person.

Lulu and Jack had a lot more in common. She was five years younger (and was originally and rather extravagantly Marie McDonald McLaughlin Lawrie) and started singing professionally when she was still only fifteen years old. The same year she began fronting a band, first called The Gleneagles, and then Lulu And The Luvvers.

She was brought up in Dennistoun, which was very much a working class area of the city – though the local Senior School was highly thought of, and had a good reputation for preparing boys for well-paid jobs in the civil service. Her father was an offal dresser. This meant that he prepared the less attractive cuts of meat in the slaughterhouse. He started his working day very early, but would dash back home just before the children went off to school, with fresh meat for their breakfast – and for them to take for lunch, too.

Although he had a good, regular job (and, as she puts it, 'always had a bit of a scam on too'), money was usually tight. She remembers her mother going to the pawnbrokers' on a regular basis and, hopefully without the neighbours spotting her, would leave her wedding ring and get a small cash advance to see the household through until the next payday.

The Lawrie family 'lived up the close', which doesn't mean a tree-lined suburban cul-de-sac as it would in England. 'A close' was a tenement building, probably four or five storeys high, with a common stairwell. The one toilet on each level was out on the stairwell too, and having a bath meant filling a tin bath in front of an open fire. They were built as the cheapest form of human accommodation for Victorian workers, cheaper even than the 'back to back' terraced housing in the industrial cities of Northern England.

Lulu says that 'Glasgow was the whole world. There was nothing outside of Glasgow apart from on the movies. Now I realise that it was grey and forbidding place; not then – I didn't know there was anything else.'

At the age of seven she was singing with an accordion band. Like the Bruces the Lawries were Protestants and 'the Blue Noses' (supporters of the fiercely Protestant Glasgow Rangers football team) were forbidden from playing what were considered to be anti-Catholic, 'Orange' songs. Their answer was to create concert parties and disguise the Proddie anthems within ensembles such as accordion bands.

That aside, she and her colleagues simply sang on the streets; 'It was like in New York or the Southern states of America. Where people didn't have much money or much education they got onto the streets and tried to express themselves. These weren't people who stood around at cocktail parties having conversations about politics; they expressed themselves by playing music and singing. Jack and I were both born to it.'

She agrees that the gang violence was very real, and it affected her own family. There was a gang called The Tongs, who were one of a number which used derivations of the same name – including one gang purely made up of women. Their favoured weapon was the machete, which was light and fairly easy to conceal. It also inflicted the most terrible injuries.

Lulu also felt the compulsion to go to London in search of professional success. 'There's just where it happened. It's changed a bit now: Nowadays a band like U2 can live in Dublin and conduct their career from there. Back then it was go to London – or nothing'

The route to the London music scene for would-be professional musicians in the provinces was via the 'musicians wanted' section in the small ads pages of The Melody Maker. What caught Jack's eye was an advert for a ballroom band that wanted a bass player in a hurry. They weren't working in London though but in Coventry – an uninspiring town in the English Midlands, which was also still recovering from being comprehensively bombed by the Luftwaffe.

The ensemble had a Scottish name though; The Murray Campbell Band. Murray was a trumpeter ('a high note specialist', Jack says) who had previously played with Oscar Rabin's Orchestra. The advert asked for someone who was comfortable with Maynard Ferguson and Dizzie Gillespie arrangements, and demanded good technique.

A letter of application was sent off, and an invitation to come to Coventry for an audition was sent by return. Jack and his double bass went to Birmingham by train, where he could stay overnight with an auntie – where he would also be able to lodge if he got the job.

This was going to be the first truly professional job, and Jack admits that he was so nervous he almost didn't have the courage to go into the audition. It was held in the city's ballroom, where he found a really proficient, very professional eighteen-piece band playing. He listened to the previous auditionee, who was very good, and he started to doubt his abilities to get the job.

The piece he had to play was One Bass Hit, a Dizzy Gillespie arrangement on which Ray Brown had played a 'phenomenal' bass solo. The music had been transcribed and was put in front of each auditionee, and the intention was to intimidate them. Jack had been taught sight-reading at college though, and he could scan through it as if it was a page of text that he had to read. As soon as he saw the complexity of the music his self-confidence returned and he knew he could pass the audition. His run at the solo was, he says, 'amazing' and he was offered the job on the spot.

The band had a residency and they needed Jack to start immediately, which he said he could. The money was good, the music was great – he had four trumpets, four saxophones and a couple of trombones playing around him – and he had a great time. He commuted to Coventry from his relatives' home, where his paternal grandfather was staying too, so his first lengthy stay outside Scotland wasn't as much of a shock as it might have been.

The impression one gets of him at this time is that he was rather quiet, very private and slightly introverted – living a lot inside his own head – but also confident when he needed to be and always in control. Life was getting exciting, but he wasn't likely to be unnerved by that. He knew what he was good at, and what he was about. He didn't often suffer from self-doubt in the areas that really mattered to him.

He had very definite opinions. He knew what was right though; how things should be done. Also, he wasn't one of the hard men in any group or gathering; he didn't start fights or throw his weight around, he wasn't one for shouting and bawling. Nonetheless he was tough, and getting tougher. It was already apparent that he wasn't someone you messed around.

Jack had heard a lot of American jazz on record, but very little British jazz. The biggest thing that was around when he was young was Humphrey Lyttleton's Bad Penny Blues, which had been a hit in the pop charts. The British jazz scene in the late Fifties was centred on a small number of well-known individuals; musicians such as Humph himself, Ted Heath, Acker Bilk, Alex Welsh, Chris Barber and Terry Lightfoot. It was a busy, vibrant scene but it was dominated by these experienced, middle-aged men who were doing what they did – and were going to be doing exactly that forever.

After a while Murray Campbell was offered work in Italy and he had to put together a smaller band made up of guitar, tenor sax, piano, bass, drums, and him playing trumpet. Jack could hardly say 'yes' quickly enough when Murray offered him a place.

The band were being asked to play what was then thought of as r 'n b – 'Louis Prima stuff' as Jack describes it; 'Not really what I wanted to do.' It didn't call for exciting or innovative bass lines, but given the prospect of his first time abroad and getting paid for the privilege, he felt he could live with it.

In Milan they were met by a booking agent, who caught Jack's attention immediately; 'A really beautiful, slightly older Italian lady.' After a week spent playing conventional gigs they were required to move on to what was called cine-variety shows. The venues were cinemas and the programme consisted of a movie (often John Wayne Westerns quickly and badly dubbed into Italian) as part of a variety show. The band would be part of the mix along with jugglers, comedians and other speciality acts. In short, it was just like music hall shows back home, but with a full-length film in the middle.

The unfortunate element was that the band members were required to wear kilts. They were partly Scottish (though partly English too) but were billed as a Scottish group and therefore they wore kilts. It was what the Milanese expected. It was the only time that Jack has performed in national costume, and it is thought that no photos exist.

The band was lodged in accommodation which was part 'funky pensione and part brothel', near the cathedral in the city centre. The trip seemed to be going really well. Jack was having the time of his life. Then it all went wrong. The beautiful agent disappeared, taking the band's wages with her.

Murray Campbell gave the impression that he was going for help – and he disappeared too. The rest of the band was stranded in Milan, unable to pay their bills and with only a few odd coins between them. While they were wondering what to do, Jack was, as he puts it 'very well looked after by the ladies of the night' who worked out of the pensione; 'I wasn't much more than a little boy, but they adopted me. It was wonderful.' So it wasn't all doom and gloom. In fact Jack didn't want it to end.

To stop them leaving without paying the bill, the hotel owners confiscated the band's instruments and even their clothes. Eventually the British Embassy bailed them out and repatriated them. They were presented with rail tickets back to Britain, but when they reached Victoria station there were Foreign Office officials waiting for them – who confiscated their passports. The deal was they would have them returned once they had paid off the cost of their journey home. Some of their instruments went to pay the hotel bill, but the double bass wasn't among them. Probably just too big, and not as easily saleable as a guitar or a saxophone.

For the first time Jack found himself in London. This was where he had wanted to be for a long time, but the circumstances were far from ideal in that he had his bass but just about nothing else. He certainly had no money and knew no one. At that point though Murray Campbell mysteriously re-appeared and took Jack to his home on the south coast, in Brighton. He was sort of adopted again, but this time by an English family rather than Italian hookers – and was welcomed into a large and attractive house by the sea.

Together Jack and Murray went up to London to try and find work, and did what all musicians did: They went to Archer Street (known universally as 'The Street') first thing on a Monday morning. The form was that everyone who needed a gig simply showed up there and hustled for work. It was a long and illustrious tradition. It was like an agricultural hiring fair of the Eighteenth century, but for musicians. Business started, unsurprisingly, when the pubs opened.

The very first job he was offered was … in Italy. He was wanted to play in a band which had a residency on an American air force base. He had been in London for no time at all and was being spun round and sent away again.

The logistics were complicated. Jack was told that he would have to catch a train, then a ferry and then another train so far as central France. There he had to collect the rest of the band, and drive them and their luggage and instruments to the town of Aviano, not far from the Yugoslavian border. The route was going to take them right across Switzerland and over the Alps; 'It was a long bloody way.'

Jack was seventeen and had only driven in and around Glasgow, but he managed to give the impression that he was a lot older and had been driving cars for many years. The deception worked, especially as the booking agent very much wanted it to be true, and he got the gig.

He was given just enough cash to get as far as Paris, where he had to meet someone who would advance the rest of the money he needed to catch up with the band and the car. His contact was 'a black guy who you wouldn't have trusted with anything', and once Jack had tracked him down to a bar in Montmartre, he was presented with the directions – but no money. The contact said he hadn't got the money, and then disappeared. Jack was getting used to folk disappearing.

With his double bass in one hand and his suitcase in the other he trudged round the city before realising that he had no option but to throw himself on the mercies of British embassy staff once more. He was lucky. He was interviewed by a very sympathetic functionary – who was female, and in the way that women were already doing, she took a shine to the poor forsaken Scottish lad. She told him that he didn't qualify for help, though she might be able to get him back to Britain, which wasn't ideal. After a while though she lifted her handbag onto the counter, pulled out her purse and presented him with a fistful of francs of her own money – making sure that he had enough for food as well as the travel.

It was a stopping train, which came to a halt at every single station along the way, no matter how tiny, and was the slowest imaginable way to cross half a country. Jack eventually hooked up with his colleagues-to-be though. The line-up was a baritone sax, a pianist, a drummer and a very attractive female singer. The transport from there on was a large Mercedes Benz saloon car, which had been hitched to a trailer. It was a long trip, which lasted two days, with Jack having to remind himself constantly that he had to drive on the 'wrong' side of the road.

The band played every night in the Sergeants' Mess, which was a rung down from the officers' club but a way up from the 'other ranks' drinking halls. It was a purpose-built bar and restaurant, almost like a nightclub; 'It wasn't like the British NAAFI; the Americans didn't go short of anything. There was a proper bar with proper staff – and every type of drink you could ever want.'

The band played in the Officers' Mess on occasion but that was more formal, more restrained – and the lower ranks' bars were far less well appointed. Jack was very fortunate; the Sergeants' Mess was the best place to be.

The music was cocktail jazz, but it was pretty loose and they all had quite a bit of leeway in what they played and how they performed it. The money was simply amazing. Jack was being paid $200 a week and he was living on the base, in Bachelor Officers' Quarters. This accommodation was kept for unmarried officers who might be visiting from other units. It was truly luxurious, and Jack paid just $1 a day for it. Everything else seemed to cost a quarter or half a dollar, no matter what. A drink at the bar or a packet of cigarettes cost 25c. A full meal cost 50c. Cheap as the Miller Coors, Budweiser and Michelob were though, Jack never came to love American beer. His drinks were mostly spirits; Canadian Club or Whisky Sours. Off base he drank sparkling Italian wine, which was far too cheap for his own good.

The engagement lasted a full nine months, and despite any lingering political antipathy he might have felt towards American armed forces based in Europe – and heaven knows what his father thought of him 'collaborating' with the enemy - he was having the time of his life.

He lost no time in striking up friendships with the servicemen on the base, be they the NCOs he played for or the lower ranks. The Master Sergeants, he recalls, were older guys and were really interesting; 'They were professional soldiers and had been there all their lives. They were rough, tough, hard-drinking.' They were also the cornerstones of just about everything that went on within the base. They made no fuss but made everything work. They were good guys to know.

The other men he befriended fell into two groups, and could hardly be more different. The first were the sons of wealthy and influential parents who had arranged for their children to spend their obligatory national service in relative comfort. Actually, considerable comfort. The life of an Army grunt stationed somewhere in Asia was one thing; the life of a USAAF officer on a large and cushy base just outside Venice was very different. They tended to have jobs in weather reporting and the like. Jobs that wouldn't get you hurt. None of them were pilots, for example – though as Jack says, 'No-one hardly dared talk to the pilots. They were like gods.'

These guys seemed to have money to burn. They lived very well and didn't miss out on any of the things that young guys tend to be drawn towards. They all seemed to have sport scars – mostly shipped over especially from home – as well as local girlfriends, and endless energy. Jack was up for all of it, so they invariably took him along, albeit by guys this time. Yet again he was sort of adopted. It was becoming a habit.

One night they decided to go into Venice and get drunk. Having all piled into a big convertible they arrived at the famous Harry's Bar in the city, where Jack was surprised to see Spike Milligan, Peter Sellers and Michael Bentine drinking together – all The Goons except Harry Secombe. They were hugely famous to the wireless generation and were heroes to Jack. For someone of that age it was like running into The Beatles in the mid-Sixties. They overheard Jack speaking, and Peter Sellers, famous for adopting other people's accents and personas in an instant, suddenly became completely and convincingly Scottish. He stayed like that all night, as the two partying groups merged and got wasted together. In the small hours Jack and the Americans simply piled back into the convertible and roared back to the base.

On other occasions when Jack went into Venice it was for different reasons. He wasn't going to miss out on the cultural treats on offer, be it architecture, great art, or even high opera at La Scala.

Jack was still a good way off his twenty-first birthday, something like three years short of coming of age, and yet this path he seemed to be treading was taking him far beyond the experience of his family or any of his childhood friends; 'Venice is a magical, phenomenal place, and to be there at that age was wonderful.' He had the use of the elderly Mercedes Benz so he would set off in other directions, and often headed towards Trieste. This was a place of pilgrimage for him as it was where James Joyce had lived in poverty with Nora Barnacle in the decade before the First World War, teaching English. It was where he wrote Dubliners, Portrait Of The Artist As A Young Man, most of Ulysses, and the stage play Exiles. In 1909 he opened a cinema in Dublin but the business rapidly collapsed and he retreated to Trieste, where he and Nora raised their children. For Jack, to be walking the same Adriatic streets as Joyce was fabulously exciting

The other group of guys Jack connected with were very different from the first,. They were in the lower ranks and were mostly black. They greatly appreciated Jack's music, and many of them played too. They showed him a room containing just about every musical instrument imaginable and they simply started playing together. Tuesday was Jack's evening off, so that was when they dragged a few cases of beer into the music room and simply had a great time.

Later on Jack tried to initiate a jam session with these servicemen in the Sergeants' Mess but that was never going anywhere; the NCOs didn't want lower ranks in their bar and certainly didn't welcome blacks from the lower ranks.

He became particularly close to one guy, whose ambition was to become a profession jazz pianist; 'It was the sort of relationship you can have at that age. It was a very intense friendship, almost like a love affair – though obviously not sexual. We were really close. One night he was working near the Sergeants' Mess as I was going in for a beer, so I said 'Oh, come on in for a drink', and dragged him in." It was an innocent mistake but a bad one. The black guy was very rapidly expelled from the Mess – not for his rank but for his colour. Jack was greatly upset over the embarrassment and humiliation he had unwittingly caused his friend.

The other great asset on the base was unlimited access to the unit's record library. Everything that the servicemen could ever need was sent over from the USA, and this included records by the thousand. That was where Jack completed his jazz education. There he sat, a seventeen year-old Scot among thousands of Americans, a continent away from home, listening tirelessly to everything ever recorded by his musical heroes – and discovering ever more artists, and hearing new techniques and different ways of playing. Everything in life was absolutely perfect; better than he could ever have hoped.

After nine months it was becoming obvious that it was time for Jack to leave. He had begun an affair with a local girl. She came from a well-off family that owned a large knitwear factory, and while Jack thought of her as great fun, her feelings for him were rather more advanced. She wanted to get married. Jack very much didn't. That wasn't what he needed at that stage in his life – or indeed at that stage in his career.

The next development was that the girl's brothers appearing outside his accommodation on the base, suggesting that he was dishonouring their sister and that he ought to do the decent thing by her. These threats weren't to be taken lightly. All his alarm bells started to ring.

One particularly heavy night in the Sergeants' Mess Jack was really struggling to keep up with the older guys, who had far more experience with their alcohol. He was already smoking a lot, and late on in the evening he took out his cigarette lighter – a Zippo of course – to light up. The lighter was recently filled with fuel and the jet had opened itself wide. The sheet of fire set light to his arm – which, unfortunately, everyone else seemed to find hilariously funny. Despite being on a military base he struggled to get medical attention. He ended up having to be driven to an Italian hospital for even basic emergency treatment.

The burn stretched from his fingers to his shoulder; 'It was a real mess.' There was no way that he going to be able to play, so he simply left. It was the only thing to do. He flew to London – his first ever flight – and then on to Glasgow. It was getting on for a year since he had been back. He returned to the family home, where his mother nursed him for as long as it took.

His bass was still in Italy though and his job was being kept open for him, and he had rather lost his contacts back home. The only thing to do was to fly back to the base and hope that his woman trouble had come to an end of its own account.

It hadn't. His girlfriend was pregnant. Jack was faced with a crisis. In a fiercely Roman Catholic country this meant marriage. There was only one option. Jack collected everything he had and made for the railway station. He couldn't afford to take another air flight (let alone with his double bass), so he took a train and then a cross-channel ferry to London. He went home and didn't look back. He didn't go back to Italy for many years.

It must be assumed that the girl had the child, but what sex the baby was isn't known. Nor is what happened to her. It's possible that she had given birth to the child in secret and he or she was adopted immediately, as was so often the case. Illegitimacy was a huge social disgrace for both mother and child in the Sixties. It was bad enough in Britain. In Italy it would have been much worse. Both the Church and the State would have considered the child to have been conceived and born in sin. If the baby's existence were known it would have been very difficult for Wilma to have married – or even hold her head up in the street. It could have been very tough for both of them.

Jack has never looked back. Has never made enquiries. Surprisingly for someone who so focussed on his family and in particular his children, he has never wanted to know what became of either the mother or the child.

Chapter 5

Back at home Jack started the first non-musical job of his life. He became a window cleaner. It was an ad hoc arrangement; several musicians had got together to offer a window cleaning service. It was ideal in that individuals could drift in and out according to whether or not they were gigging. It was a way of picking up a few pounds without committing to anything, and it was a good networking and mutual help group. Whether or not they were particularly good window cleaners is open to question

On one occasion Jack was on the top rung of the ladder polishing the windows on the upper floor of a house in the select suburb of Rutherglen when the ladder slipped away from him. He fell to the ground and fortunately landed on something soft rather than hitting the paved driveway. As he lay there counting his bruises and checking for fractures he became aware of the lady of the house running out to him. Jack expected sympathy, a kindly word, and a cup of tea – if not in fact a glass of reviving whisky. He got none of those. The lady screeched at him, hands on her hips, berating him for having the ill manners to fall onto her herbaceous border.

Jack's other memories of that job include the popularity of cleaning factory windows – because they could climb up onto the roof and sunbathe out of sight in the vee of the roof. He also recalls making tea using water they poured into their billy can straight out of the bucket.

As a result of the contacts he made through the musicians' window cleaning collective he soon found a place in a trad jazz outfit; Jim McHarg's Scottsville Jazz Band. The Jim McHarg in question was no longer in the group. He had been both the leader and the bass player, but the other musicians had decided that they would be better off without him, so they fired him – but kept his name. It was a good move on their part; the band wasn't in the highest league but it was fairly well known and never short of a gig. Obviously they needed a new bassist in something of a hurry, and Jack slotted straight in.

Very soon afterwards the band had a series of engagements in London, during what Jack describes as 'the tail end of the trad jazz boom.' It was true; all roads led to London. This strand of jazz, the British take on New Orleans jazz, wasn't what he wanted to be playing. 'It was what everybody else had been doing. All the clichés', but it was a job. And a good opportunity to keep his eyes and ears open and see what else was going on.

This time he wasn't just passing through London. Jack and the band's drummer rented a flat – 'a dive' rather than a flat – in Willesden. He had the first place of his own, small and scruffy though it was.

That summer, 1962, they played a May ball at St John's College in Cambridge, which was a very smart black-ties-and-long-frocks event. Jazz bands were popular for these events as they smacked of bohemia and the music was easy to dance to. During the break between the two sets they were contracted to play, Jack went out for a smoke and a wander round. He was taking the opportunity to look at the girls in their very finest dresses mostly, but he could hear other music coming from a cellar. Best investigate.

A moody studio shot of a quiet,
shy but very talented young musician. (CB)

A year or so before his first brief visit to London, Jack, aged sixteen, had written to the already well-established saxophonist Dick Heckstall-Smith, completely out of the blue. 'I'd seen a picture of him in The Melody Maker', Jack says, 'And he just looked so hip. He had that Fifties look, with a carefully trimmed beard and no moustache. I thought he shaved his head but in fact he went bald very young.' That was all he knew of the man. He had never heard him play.

Dick replied with a friendly and encouraging note suggested that Jack look him up if and when he made the journey south, and offering to help him out in whatever way he could. He was nine years older than Jack – pretty well a member of a different musical generation, and was a formidable sax man, who was always working. Born in Ludlow in rural Shropshire, he was to play an important part in Jack's career.

There was no reason why a busy working musician should have taken the trouble to write back to this youngster – except perhaps that he too was from 'the provinces' and didn't have the strictly metropolitan mindset. Perhaps he recognised the passion. Perhaps it was simply that he was a really nice, generous-spirited man.

Receiving the letter was a small milestone in Jack's life. Here was proof that there really was a big world out there; it didn't just exist on the pages of The Melody Maker, and it was populated by real human beings. It's not difficult to imagine the sixteen year-old's thrill at reading the letter. The fact that he had received it was in itself warming and enlivening. Jack folded it up very carefully and kept it safe, and has it still.

The guy in the cellar at the May Ball, leading the quartet was Dick Heckstall-Smith. He was on tenor sax, Johnnie Burch was on piano, Maurice Salvat was playing bass, and Ginger Baker was on drums. It was actually The Bert Courtley Sextet, but Bert had cried off, and they were reduced to a quartet for the evening. It was a well-established band, with a residency at the Café des Artistes in Fulham, and Jack was greatly impressed: 'I was astounded by the music. They were playing a sort of modern be-bop. I was especially amazed by Ginger. I had never heard a drummer play like that. He had his cymbals completely straight and he was bashing the hell out of them. They were so good, confident and so loud – I'd never heard anything like it.'

As soon as that song finished, Jack, with characteristic self-confidence, walked up to Dick and asked if he could sit in on bass. There was no indication as to who this youngster was, Jack hadn't told Dick anything about himself, he just asked if he could play. It probably didn't help that Jack was wearing the tuxedo that was de rigueur with his band. He could have been a half-drunk undergraduate. No one was going to take him seriously. Jack retreated.

He wasn't to be put off though. He went back to where Jim McHarg's Scottsville Jazz Band were playing, and still on his break, grabbed his bass and carried it all the way back to the cellar. Down the steps, through the crowd, to the stage. He stood there with it until a very surprised Dick finally invited him up to play. Dick told John Platt, 'I said [to the band] let's do something really difficult.'

The first song they went into was a ballad, and Dick asked Jack to play the melody, where the chord changed every two beats on a very complex chord structure. If this young guy wasn't worth having on stage it would become very obviously very quickly. That was quickly followed with a faster blues; 'I played great. I just blew them all away', Jack says. 'He really kicked arse', Dick said.

He had to get back to his band though, and after those two songs he picked up his instrument once more and left just as he had arrived. No introductions and no good-byes.

Weeks later there was a knock on the door at Jack's place and it was Dick. He had been looking for the phantom bass player for weeks, and it had taken him that long to track him down. He didn't just want to say hello though; he had a gig for him. Dick had suggested Jack to fill the hole left by bassist Andy Hoogenboom's departure from Alexis Korner's band Blues Incorporated. There was an audition; Jack played after a piece by another bassist, who played electric bass. Jack listened to him and made a point of playing his acoustic double bass much louder. He was hired.

Jack's musical career can be seen as a long series of fairly equal steps, ever upwards, ever onwards, with most of them taking him that bit further yet. Joining Blues Incorporated was one of the biggest strides forward though; it moved him on from jazz and into the emerging r 'n b scene. Jazz was undoubtedly losing its momentum by the early Sixties. In contrast, moving towards r 'n b put him right at the centre of a music form that was just beginning to find its feet in Britain, and which would lead – in a remarkably short space of time – to the emergence of some of the best-known performers and biggest-selling records imaginable. It also brought him a new audience, both in the sense of the people who paid their money to hear him play, and almost as importantly, among the musicians who were creating the dynamic, thrilling British rhythm and blues.

At this point in his career Jack was very much a purist about the acoustic bass, and despised the very idea of an electric bass guitar. There were no real musicians playing the electric bass. No peers. No one to look up to and emulate. It wasn't considered a serious instrument. There was only one electric instrument which he considered to be any good at all – the Fender Bass.

In 1950 Leo Fender's company launched the first solid electric guitar to be made in commercially viable numbers; originally known as the Broadcaster and then the Telecaster. A year later Leo added a similar-looking four-string Bass model to the company's range. This was the Precision model, and it was rapidly adopted by, firstly Country & Western musicians, and then Jazz players. Jack wasn't a great fan of the instrument

In the early Sixties Jack was immersed in the London Jazz culture.
He and colleagues looked down on rock'n roll with scorn. (CB)

though; he felt that it had a 'nondescript' sound.

It wasn't until the Sixties that the electric bass gained respectability. The first electric bassist who made an impression on Jack was Monk Montgomery. He frequently played with his brothers, the guitarist Wes Montgomery and pianist Buddy, and was a contemporary of Jack's acoustic hero Ray Brown. Monk was an early advocate of the electric bass, but early in the Sixties he reverted to acoustic bass and stayed with it for many years. His style wasn't hugely distinctive though; he played fairly conventional walking, strutting bass lines.

The players who influenced Jack were still acoustic bass players. In the very early Sixties he was just becoming aware of Charlie Mingus, who was to become a great influence. Mingus was unusual in being a bass-playing bandleader, though he also played piano and composed. After his death in 1979 at the age of 56, The New Yorker magazine wrote, 'For sheer melodic and rhythmic and structural originality, his compositions may equal anything written in western music in the Twentieth century.'

Another was Jimmy Blanton, who played bass for Duke Ellington from 1939 until his death just three years later. He was one of the first bassists to take a worthwhile solo. In his autobiography Ellington said of him, 'Jimmy Blanton revolutionised bass playing. No one had played from the same perspective before. He played melodies that belonged to the bass and always had a foundation quality. Rhythmically he supported and drove at the same time.'

The bass on pop records in the early Sixties was understated and uninspiring. With one exception - which was Paul McCartney - the bass player stood right at the back, next to the drummer, and his work often got lost in the overall mix. They tended to play only the top two strings of the bass. There was one practical reason for this when it came to making recordings; too much bass could make the stylus jump out of the groove on a vinyl record.

One of the most successful British acts of the late Fifties and the early Sixties were The Shadows, who achieved a phenomenal number of instrumental hits (fifteen records in the top ten and five that went to number one) as well as those backing Cliff Richard. As Jack says though, 'Their bass player, Jet Harris, looked great – but he couldn't play for toffee.'

So far as American pop acts went, the only bass lines that made an impression were on Eddie Cochran singles, where Jack maintains that the melody was played on a six-string bass. The best example was 'Summertime Blues.' It wasn't rock 'n roll that interested him though.

'With jazz I had wanted to play as many notes as the saxophone could achieve', he says, 'I was pushing the limits, as many horn players or pianists would be doing. Yeah, when I was young I was showing off, but there had to be a reason to show off.

'I was most interested in contrapuntal music; lots of melodies that fit together to form a whole, to form a harmony. Above all I wanted to play melodically; to play within harmony. When I eventually played pop and rock, my job was to take the bass out of that functional, simple uninspiring slot.'

Although their time playing together was relatively brief, Alexis Korner was to be one of the most important figures in Jack's career – and you can say that about the careers of Mick Jagger, Charlie Watts, Paul Jones, Rod Stewart, Long John Baldry, and a host of other musicians, many of whom helped shape rock music in Britain and across the world.

Alexis had formed Blues Incorporated early in 1962 with harmonica-player and blues expert Cyril Davies, and the band soon gained residencies at The Ealing Club and at The Marquee in Oxford Street. Both these venues have become part of British music folklore, but The Marquee was the more important simply because it was in the city centre, a drum-stick's throw from Soho and Britain's Tin Pan Alley. It was the place to be seen and heard.

It was a fairly small club, but Blues Incorporated's regular gigs on Thursday evenings would often attract audiences of seven hundred or so (in the days before detailed fire regulations, and health and safety inspectors). On June 8 of that year the band recorded the album 'R&B From The Marquee' which took their music to a much wider audience, and was one of a small number of records which inspired a generation. It wasn't actually recorded in The Marquee, but up the road in Decca's West Hampstead studios; it was 'from The Marquee' in the sense that the track listing reflected their typical set list at the club.

When Jack first went to hear the band play he wasn't particularly happy. He was such a jazz purist that he considered Blues Incorporated to be 'a rock 'n roll band.' Nowadays he's appalled by the memory; 'I was so narrow-minded. If it wasn't free jazz - or be-bop to stretch a point - I wasn't interested.'

His scepticism was eclipsed by his admiration for their playing though, and he signed up. By the time the album was released Jack was a full-time member of the band. And they never stopped working. Interest in the album meant that there were now sizeable pockets of r 'n b fans all over Britain, and rather than being a metropolitan-only band, they were getting bookings to play in many provincial towns.

Alexis Korner and Cyril Davis were unlike in terms of their background, their music outlook and indeed to look at - but they shared a passion for rhythm and blues and pioneered it unceasingly. They also brought American blues and rhythm and blues players to the UK, and presented them with an audience - and a knowledgeable and ecstatic one at that.

Alexis was born in Paris of Greek, Turkish and Austrian parentage and grew up short and dark - and could look hugely sinister. For most of his adult life he had a mass of black curly hair and horribly long sideburns. His surname was originally Koerner and up to the age of twelve he was brought up in various countries across Europe. His parents settled in Britain just after war had been declared, and anglicised their surname.

His passion for black r 'n b came through the American forces radio in Europe, and he cited his earliest inspiration as hearing bluesman Jimmy Yancey playing on the wireless while he and his family where in an air raid shelter, hiding from a Luftwaffe bombing raid on London.

His first instruments were the piano and the acoustic guitar, in that order. He tried an electric guitar but the primitive pickups on the one he experimented with gave it a harsh sound and he returned to an acoustic instrument. He joined Chris Barber's Jazz Band within two years of the war ending, and then moved on to The Ken Colyer Jazz Group. He experimented with skiffle, indeed Chris Barber had very generously given Alexis a skiffle slot in the middle of his own set, but in 1954 he and Cyril Davies starting working as a blues duo; Alexis playing guitar and Cyril on harmonica. In '55 he and Cyril founded The London Blues And Barrelhouse Club.

Cyril was short, bald and plump, and came from the pleasant county of Buckinghamshire, in the English Home Counties. Utterly incongruously he worked as a panelbeater in a scrapyard. He too was originally a banjo player in a trad jazz combo. Like Alexis he was attracted to skiffle, but he then distilled his passion for black American music and flew the flag for r 'n b. Jack says of him, 'I can't express how great Cyril was. He was the real deal. When Muddy Waters was over and heard him, he wanted Cyril to go back and join his band. For a white guy to join Muddy Waters' band would have been quite something.'

Both men died too early – Cyril in 1964 at the age of 31, and Alexis twenty years later, aged 55. Cyril didn't live to see the huge impression that his beloved r 'n b made on the British music consciousness, but Alexis at least became a hugely-respected figure, both as a musician and a broadcaster.

Many musicians went through Blues Incorporated over the years, but the line-up when Jack joined was Alexis, Cyril, Dick, and pianist Johnny Parker – who had played the original piano part on Jack's much-loved copy of Humphrey Lyttleton's Bad Penny Blues. There was also a drummer; a reserved, thin-faced guy who had a wife, a steady and well-paid daytime job and a mortgage. He was called Charlie Watts.

Jack says that he thinks of Blues Incorporated as a fusion band; a melting pot. Indeed, they were the first band that fused Chicago blues with hard country blues, and 'crossed over into Charlie Mingus territory.' He had never felt so at home in a band as he was with Alexis; 'I loved that band. I was doing what I had always wanted to do. I was discovering the real blues.'

At The Marquee they were simply the hottest ticket in town. Even when the place was packed there'd be as many people outside still trying to get in. Jack adds, 'We had a lot of guests play with us too. There was a singer called Ronnie Jones, who was a great, sophisticated blues singer. On a Saturday we played in Ealing, and there was another singer there - Mick Jagger – he'd sit in a lot.' Mick didn't make a big impression on Jack, 'He was just some guy in a cardigan who got up and sang. I can't even remember what he sang. Of course he wasn't Mick Jagger then.' There's a photo of an obviously nervous Mick (wearing a shirt and tie, yes, and a cardigan) singing in front of Alexis, Cyril, Dick (who looks almost impossibly cool) and Jack – who seems to be on a different plane altogether. Keith Richard was there on occasion too, as Jack recalls, but he doesn't think he ever sat in with the band while Jack was also on stage.

Charlie Watts lived in Primrose Hill and was settled and married. Slightly less than two years older than Jack, Charlie was a Londoner through and through. His father had been a lorry driver for the railway company, and Charlie was born and brought up in the north-west London suburb of Neasden. Like so many others he was moving from jazz to this new r 'n b.

Alexis's band, Jack recalls, was 'very mellow – no friction, no egos – we all really believed in what we were doing.' He describes Alexis as very 'posh', very laid back and very polite.' He was also, Jack recalls, a truly dreadful car driver. They did a lot of travelling, to and from gigs, and Alexis always insisted on doing the driving – to everyone else's terror; 'One time it was very foggy and we were far into the countryside in the van, and Alexis was driving so fast in the fog that he obviously couldn't see anything. He took a wrong turn and we went through the grounds of a hospital. He didn't slow down; we just drove in and out at about fifty miles an hour. No one said anything.

'After Ginger had joined the band he always used to sit in the front passenger seat, riding shotgun, and on one occasion Alexis fell asleep at the wheel.' Ginger grabbed the steering wheel and the gear lever and tried to slow the van down and steer it safely onto the verge at the side of the road. Alexis woke up and very politely thanked 'Peter', as he always insisted on calling the man who everyone else knew as Ginger, for his trouble. 'It got so frightening that I stopped going to gigs in the van. My nerves wouldn't stand it. I'd catch a train instead.'

The only cloud was the looming split with Cyril. The popular thinking was that he was a drunk and that drinking himself silly was his mission. He also had a reputation for being difficult to get on with. Blues Incorporated played a lot of upper class, high-society parties like the Cambridge May Ball where Jack had first seen Dick. One was a debutante's 'coming out' ball ('coming out' socially, not sexually) in a huge house in Holland Park. Alexis, who was socially very mobile, asked Charlie and Jack to 'look after' Cyril and keep him out of trouble. It wasn't his usual milieu; it was a long way away from panel bashing. He was okay for most of the evening, but got more and more drunk – before vomiting all over a priceless Persian rug. Charlie and Jack had to get him home; 'He was very stroppy. He was a big, strong guy and we had to more or less carry him.' The truth was that Cyril knew he was dying. It wasn't time. He still had far too much yet to do.

Cyril was also unhappy when Graham Bond was drafted into the band to play sax (again Dick acted as headhunter). He hated saxophones, they were jazz instruments, not blues instruments. Jack says that he had tolerated Dick because he found his playing 'authentic.' He saw Graham's recruitment as a move away from the blues, which he was going to defend, literally, to his death. The change of personnel, with Cyril out and Graham and Ginger in, changed the band greatly, and though Jack says he still enjoyed the music greatly, he wasn't in love with the band quite as he had done.

Cyril left Blues Incorporated in 1962 and created The Cyril Davies Rhythm And Blues All-Stars with an impressive line-up of what had been Screaming Lord Sutch's backing band, The Savages. The band included Jimmy Page on lead guitar and the keyboards player Nicky Hopkins. Jack says, 'It was a great band, with a lot of energy. They had a great bass player – guy named Cliff Barton, who died very young.' Jack was to dedicate the piece Over The Cliff on his album 'Things We Like' to him.

Alexis and Cyril were the musicians who created British blues, Jack insists, and he adds that a lot of credit must go to Chris Barber too, even though the music for which

Jack playing double bass with Blues Incorporated; Alexis Korner is seated, playing guitar, and Ginger Baker is on drums. Dick Heckstall-Smith centre, on sax. (Public Domain)

he was best known was rather different: 'John Mayall has adopted this mantle as the godfather of British blues – especially in the States. That's crap. He has never done anything to say that that isn't quite true. [On www.johnmayall.net he is credited as 'the father of British blues' – thus moving into the direct lineage.]

'It was Alexis who saw John playing a solo blues set at The Twisted Wheel club in Manchester, and he advised him to move to London. It was Alexis who got John Mayall in. I've never read anything in a John Mayall article where they've said 'oh you're the father of British blues', and he's said 'no I'm not – it was Cyril and Alexis that started that whole scene off.' If you don't state things and keep stating them it gets re-written and the people who have the most commercial success get the credit that they're not really due. You get an inaccurate version and that really bugs me. I've got nothing against John, but I wish he'd credited them a bit more than he did.'

In an unlikely-sounding move – which would definitely not have pleased Cyril - the pop entrepreneur Ronan O'Reilly, who launched the pirate radio station Radio Caroline, became the band's manager. He was a man who made things happen – a Celtic outsider like Jack – and he dressed the band in smart suits and tried to give them an image and market them. It could have happened too, Jack thinks. They could have been 'the next big thing' – but The Beatles came along and took that slot, and for a seemingly long time nothing else but The Fab Four mattered. It took The Rolling Stones to really break the public's obsession with The Beatles every breath and twitch. Certainly Blues Incorporated's music was good enough, but perhaps it was too good. With the pure blues fading and more commercial r 'n b being injected, the mix was more accessible. It was still a long way from being pop for the masses though. And they didn't have the obvious sex appeal that seemed to be essential for world domination. They would have been a marketing man's nightmare.

The band was playing a Saturday night at The Ealing Club at the end of October 1962 when the Cuban missile crisis was at its peak. The American president John Kennedy and the Russian leader Nikita Kruschev were involved in a stand-off over Kennedy's insistence that the USSR remove the long-range missiles which the USSR had smuggled onto Cuba – less than a hundred miles from America's coastline. There was a huge feeling, especially among the politically aware, that this was 'it.' The superpowers were both going to press their red buttons and a full-scale nuclear was going to exterminate most of the life on earth. The British were geographically in the middle, which was bad enough, but as a close ally of the USA and with many of their bases here, the United Kingdom was obviously a prime Russian target.

It was just about the sole topic of conversation at the club that night, and Jack maintains there was a huge sense that this was going to be, if not their last night on earth, then certainly the last time they would share a stage in this world. 'It was as if the countdown had started, but we were still getting on with our lives', he says, 'I remember travelling on the Central line to Ealing with my double bass, and the whole train was hushed. We really believed that they were going to drop the bombs. We thought we were all going to die.'

It wasn't the end in fact. Kruschev backed down and removed the missiles from Cuba and life went on. For Jack this meant a steady routine of gigs, never out of work, and often playing the London clubs where the new music was being formed.

Jack's brother Charlie remembers seeing him play at The Marquee Club in Oxford Street, and was, he says, very proud of him. Seeing his little brother on stage playing the music which he himself loved – and obviously playing it exceptionally well – was a thrill.

He had seen Jack playing with Alexis at The Ealing Club, where he remembers Jack discussing whether or not he ought to be moving away from jazz and towards all this newer music. Although jazz was Charlie's passion, he thought that it was never going to a big thing again. He advised him to move on.

Charlie also recalls hearing The Rolling Stones at Ealing, but they weren't suited to either man's taste. 'At that time they seemed to just be doing Chuck Berry covers', Jack says. They certainly didn't have a huge following; 'We used to follow them onstage at The Flamingo Club and the place would be half empty when we came on. To be honest though, it was only like that for a matter of weeks. They had a hit [with Come On, a cover of an obscure Chuck Berry track] and that was that.'

Charlie Jnr had become an electrical engineer and was often in London on training courses. He and Jack would meet up for a few pints. The elder brother was starting a career with what became British Telecom, and then BT, and his life was shaping up very differently from Jack's.

Jack wasn't much changed by the breadth of his new horizons and the considerable range of experience he had already seen. He still looked youthful, fresh-faced, and boyish. He was definitely maturing though; becoming more worldly-wise. Because of the difference in their ages they had never done a lot of things together. Now there was a reason for Charlie to look up to Jack, instead of the other way round.

On the USAAF base Jack had tried every drink the bar could offer, but certainly wouldn't have considered himself to be serious drinker. Soon after arriving in London though he found a chemical combination that seemed to suit him ideally; 'I had a secret chemical mix. It was my formula and it never failed: One Dexedrine pill, one pint of bitter and one spliff. I'd be wonderful for the whole evening. If I had any less or any more it didn't work.'

Jack had discovered the stimulant Benzedrine when he was on the base, and as it was a well known 'jazz drug' he was delighted to come across it. Like many others he had great romantic images of heroes such as Charlie Parker and Billie Holliday doing their best work on drugs; hitting heights which they would never have been able to achieve straight. 'Musicians did say that it wasn't good and you only think you play better, but it couldn't be true because they all did it', Jack says, and given the USA/USSR nuclear stand-off which was becoming even more intense and threatening, they didn't expect to live to see their thirtieth birthday anyway, so why care about their longer-term health?

The hipsters thought of drugs as part of their culture. It may or may not have improved their appreciation of the music, but it was simply the thing to do. And as London was still a large port and ships still traded with the old Empire countries, it was easy to obtain and fairly cheap.

Their American peers did it, the Beats did it, it was perfect. As Jack says, 'We used dope to isolate ourselves from the mass of humanity. Ordinary people didn't know about drugs. It gave us a feeling of being an elite.'

Chapter 6

In 1962 Janet Godfrey was a 15 year-old schoolgirl living in Swiss Cottage with her parents. Her father was in the rag trade and, coincidentally, was also involved in Left wing politics. Together with a group of friends, Janet used to go to The Marquee club every Thursday night. They would walk all the way from north-west London so they would be able to afford the entrance fee, and they often ended up having to walk all the way back too. Their mothers would have been horrified. They had discovered the new and dazzling British blues scene and were hooked on it. They didn't go looking for boyfriends or to compare handbags; they went for the music, and to be part of one of the most exciting and exclusive scenes in London at that time.

'The place was always absolutely packed', Janet remembers. 'The sweat was mixing with the condensation. It was brilliant.' She insists that she and her friends went for the music, and weren't interested in the musicians. She would hardly have recognised any of them outside the club. The scene was very exciting, she adds, but very innocent. In time she started going to gigs with Blues Incorporated's pianist Johnny Parker, but they weren't an item. Johnny might well have had ambitions in that direction, but it wasn't to be.

On day, visiting Johnny's tiny flat she discovered Jack, who was living there and was sleeping on the couch. Johnny wasn't at home so she and Jack just passed the time, chatting. Before that, she says, she hadn't really noticed him. Except once, in a pub, when she had been with Johnny. She had been on a school trip to Russia, which was very unusual then, and she had a Russian badge on her lapel. Jack spotted it straight away and asked her about it. He was very impressed that she had been to the USSR, and they connected immediately on the level of their families' politics. She had been seen talking to Johnny and Jack by the older, trad jazz guys, and they had warned her off, saying that the musicians who played modern jazz were bad news – all druggies, every last one; they all want to be Charlie Parker, that's their problem.

Later that same day she and Jack went out together – but only to buy a small paraffin heater. It was winter and there was no form of heating in the flat. The cold had become so severe that Jack could stand it no longer and had decided to do something about it. It was at this point, as Jack decided what model heater he needed, and they struggling to get it lit back in the flat, that Janet realised that there was a certain chemistry between them. She was falling for this shy, boy-ish Scot. It was inevitable from that point on that they would begin a relationship. He was nineteen and by then Janet was sixteen.

Janet found Jack to be delightfully romantic, and very caring. At night he would slip little notes through the letterbox at her home, for her to find in the morning. That meant a huge amount to her, and she has every one to this day. She and Jack were very close; they were rather more than just boyfriend and girlfriend. He was her first love; undoubtedly the great love of her life.

He was quite shy, she says, and music was simply everything to him. It was his whole life, and all his friends were in the London music scene, so of course they became her friends too. She was more than happy with that; not only had music played a big part in her upbringing, but she was happy to have crossed the line from merely being in the audience to being 'with the band.' The band were playing just about every night of the week, and Janet often accompanied him and the band to the gigs – certainly the ones that were either in London or within easy reach. She had joined the inner circle, and was, albeit peripherally, a part of the team which created the music she adored.

There was about to be a very important shift in Jack's career though. One that was initiated by drummer Charlie Watts making a decision which was to be momentous both for him and for the history of rock music.

Charlie had a good job in the drawing office of an advertising agency in the West End. He wasn't like all the other guys on the scene; he had prospects in the straight world. It was with great misgivings and after much persuasion that he left his job in early '63 to join The Rolling Stones on a full-time basis. In retrospect that move of Charlie's was crucial to Jack's career. Dick Heckstall-Smith still had his great talent for putting the right people into the right bands, even though they weren't his bands. He'd suggest a name or even turn up with someone and they would be exactly right for that group. In this role of recruiting sergeant, he introduced Ginger Baker to Blues Incorporated as Charlie's replacement. The man who would become one of the greatest bass players of his generation was about to become professionally involved with the man who was to be one of the most-admired and respected drummers of all time. Maybe Jack and Ginger would have worked together at some other point, but it was Charlie's move to The Stones, and Dick's 'man management', that made it happen right then – at what can be seen historically as exactly the right point in the careers of both men.

Ginger Baker - originally Peter Baker - was born in Lewisham in south London on August 19 1939 within days of the Second World War being declared. He was brought up in a working class home in New Eltham. Money was always tight, and his earliest years coincided with the worst years of the Blitz, when the city of London and the inner suburbs were being heavily bombed almost every night.

As a young teenager his passion was racing cycles, and he spent every penny he could find on his bike. He spent hours either riding or working on the machine, trying to make it faster still. He was completely and utterly competitive. He didn't race to take part. He raced to win. Even then he had something to prove. It was a rare day when someone got to win while Peter Baker was around.

He joined the Air Training Corps and started playing trumpet, but soon began drumming instead. When he was fifteen he crashed his greatly loved bike and decided that it was time to make a decision between bikes and drums. He spent the money that would have bought him a new bike – all of £3 - on a drum kit and taught himself to play it.

He pestered a trad jazz band for a chance to sit in with them, and kept on at them until he had worn down their resistance. He then saw an advertisement placed by The Storyville Jazz Band, who needed a drummer. In his book 'Disraeli Gears', John Platt recounts how Ginger took his kit, which was a child's toy, all the way from his home in New Eltham in south-east London, to the audition in north-east London. He told them that his usual kit had been damaged, in some unspecified way, and said that he was just using the toy kit until it was mended. That must have sounded highly unlikely, but his playing was so good that they gave him the job regardless.

Having become a permanent fixture he was now on wages, and with that income he soon bought a new and far better kit. He was able to spend £12 this time, which wasn't a small sum of money in the mid-Fifties, especially for a sixteen year-old. Now that he had the tools of his trade, Ginger got a full-time job with a trad jazz band. From then on he was on the road almost constantly. As with Jack, there was never anything else under consideration; he was always going to be a drummer and nothing else mattered.

The jazz band was led by Bob Wallis, who had begun his career as a cornet player with a Salvation Army Band, based in the notoriously windswept seaside town of Bridlington. He discovered New Orleans music though, and after touring Denmark in 1954 moved to London. He joined The Storyville Jazzmen and went on to play in Ken Colyer's Omega Brass Band before starting his own band.

Bob was an important figure in Ginger's early career. He encouraged him and indulged his eccentricities – such as wearing a bright green suit on stage – and most importantly he introduced him to his huge collection of early jazz records. On one of these Ginger heard a drummer who was to become one his first heroes; Baby Dobbs, who played with Louis Armstrong. Later in life Ginger said, 'I fell in love with what he was playing. Baby Dobbs was the link between western military drum techniques and African drummers. He was the man who first successfully married the two. He was the first jazz drummer.'

Ginger went on to play in some of the best-known trad jazz bands, including those headed by Acker Bilk and Terry Lightfoot. Trad jazz was enjoying considerable commercial success at that point. The music was being played on the radio, and records were selling well. Some recordings, such as When The Saints Go Marching In were very popular hits.

Terry Lightfoot found Ginger's adventurous style irritating, and he didn't need a drummer who had a furious temper. It wasn't what he wanted and he said so. Ginger responded by simply walking out. He spent some time gigging in Europe, and then returned to his mother's house. He made the best of this period of unemployment by playing the drums throughout the day, almost non-stop, completely immersed himself in learning every technique and every nuance there was. One feels for his mother.

One of Ginger's heroes was Max Roach, and Ginger started to emulate his be-bop style, and also began to re-style himself according – getting smarter in his dress and having his hair cut in a slick 'jazz style.'

His own style was emerging, but as he says, 'In those days I played like a madman and got emotionally involved in the music. I was always accused of being a rock n' roller.' What was happening was that he was moving from trad jazz to Modern jazz, as were many of his contemporaries. It was a seismic shift, and it was about attitudes and edge as much as the music itself.

In 1960 Ginger met Phil Seamen, who was to be the biggest influence on both his playing and his lifestyle. Phil drank very heavily though, and was also a heroin addict. Ginger, who wasn't averse to the first of these, rapidly joined him in the second.

Having seen Ginger play at the May Ball, and been blown away by his drumming, Jack was keen to work with him. After Ginger joined Blues Incorporated he and Jack rapidly became good friends, and in fact Jack moved from Charlie's sitting room to Ginger's. His new couch was in Braemar Avenue in Neasden, a couple of miles north of Ealing and not far from Wembley Stadium.

'I was very close to him. He was like an older brother to me', Jack says. Ginger was impossibly thin, with a stark, gaunt, almost skeletal face and a mass of ginger hair – though he wore that slicked back severely, so that he looked like a jazz musician should. He was good looking in a rather sparse way, and he was a sharp dresser when he wanted to be. Jack found him 'a very romantic figure', and adds that he learned a huge amount from him, especially in terms of rhythm and tone. He remembers Ginger and

Phil Seamen sitting in the band room at The Flamingo Club, tapping out the most intricate rhythms on the tabletop. Jack says that, for him, that room was the most thrilling place to be. He could hardly believe that he, almost always the youngest person there, was in this creative milieu with these worldly and far more experienced musicians.

Ginger and Jack became a very tight rhythm section immediately. They were a two-man team, for hire as a hot rhythm section if the gig was interesting and there was cash on offer. As well as working with Blues Incorporated they played with the Johnnie Burch Octet, and they also played the Friday-to-Saturday All-Niters at The Flamingo with the other young jazz guns-for-hire such as Georgie Fame and Johnny Mumford; 'We weren't welcome in Ronnie Scott's. We were the young Turks', Jack says, 'We pooh-poohed the establishment, the older generation. We felt that they had no balls. We looked down on them.'

A lot of this difference in attitude was about confidence in their music, and how they saw themselves. These youngsters thought that the British jazz scene didn't have enough confidence in itself and its music. The older guys were in thrall to their peers in the States, while the young bucks thought that they we were as good as anyone in the world, and could certainly compete on equal terms with the Americans. They were, Jack admits, arrogant – but says that it was a vice that simply had to have. They were never going to displace the old guard without the self-confidence of the young, even if it was ratcheted up more than a few notches.

With these other bands Jack felt happy to try out some of his own music. It was the first time he had played his compositions with a band. He had a residency at The Plough public house in Ilford, in Essex. These were pretty informal gigs, held every Tuesday night, and it was no problem to include quite a few original compositions. The very first piece of his own which performed for an audience was called The Immortal Ninth. Another was HCKHH Blues, which eventually ended up being recorded for Jack's 'Things We Like' album. The late Ian Dury, famous Essex resident, frequented these gigs, and was later to cite them as having been a real inspiration to him.

He maintains that he was very introverted at this time, and would hardly ever say anything to anyone. He agrees with Janet that he was very shy; 'I only lived for playing.' He was undoubtedly self-assured to the point of arrogance with regard to his music, but he kept his own counsel - kept it all to himself.

Beneath that façade though he suffered, as he says he always has, from extremely low self-esteem. He doubted his own ability constantly; doubted that he could live up to his own high musical standards. It seems incredible to anyone who knew him, or knows him, but the veneer of confidence was both thin and delicate. It was this that made him seem arrogant; 'But I wasn't arrogant, I was shit-scared.' He tried hard not to have to speak in public. He thought that the best thing he could do was to try and take everything in, but say as little as possible so as to not make a fool of himself. He didn't want to be ignored, but he definitely didn't want to draw attention to himself. He was, he says, a very late developer.

He was dressing like a jazz musician now, with Dick and Ginger as his role models. His hair was short and neat, and from time to time he would grow a 'jazz' moustache, pencil-thin and intended to send out the same cool message as Dick's carefully trimmed, moustache-less beard. He bought his clothes at Austin's in Shaftesbury Avenue. He didn't have a lot of spare cash to spend on clothes, but his favourite look was an Ivy League jacket, a button-down shirt, and a thin, dark tie. The look was of a jazzer, a hipster – but it wasn't that far away from the style which the Mods were evolving at the same time.

In the same way that Dick's style had impressed Jack even before he had heard the man's music, Graham Bond made a similar impact. The first time Jack laid eyes on him he just thought he looked 'so sharp', in a beautifully cut suit; 'He looked like a white Cannonball Adderley, and he played like that too. A phenomenal guy with so much energy.'

When Cyril Davies left the band Graham stepped in, first as tenor sax player and then moving to Hammond organ – as and when Alexis allowed him to do so. The line-up was Alexis, Jack, Ginger, Dick and Graham.

Graham was a hugely talented and innovative musician who was also to die young. There is all too little of his work still in circulation, but he provided one of the pieces of the jigsaw that created the picture of British r 'n b of the Sixties. Born in Romford in Essex in '37, Graham had played the piano as a child but had taken up the saxophone as it was good for the breathing difficulties he experienced, being an asthmatic.

By the late Fifties he had completely immersed himself in jazz and played alto sax for band leaders Terry Graham, Goudie Charles, and Don Rendell. He toured extensively with Don, as part of a quintet, and had frequent gigs at London very best clubs - The Flamingo, Ronnie Scott's and The Marquee. They became only the second British jazz outfit to record for an American record label.

It is said that Graham was the first person in Britain to own a Hammond organ. He is also credited with being the first person to use a Mellotron, a precursor of the synthesiser. Graham said of it, 'The Mellotron uses pre-recorded tapes of other instruments. Every note in the register of a trumpet is recorded, and I can play it on the organ keyboard, getting the real sound.' Previously only Alexis had sung ('He didn't sing, he growled') but Graham started singing too.

He joined Blues Incorporated in 1962, after a stint with the Johnny Burch Octet. Soon Jack, Ginger and Graham started to perform in interval slots during BI shows, while the rest of the band were having a cigarette and a beer. The three of them soon realised that they were really starting to gel as a trio, with Graham very much the leader of this ad hoc ensemble. What Alexis didn't realise what that he was unknowingly allowing an independent unit to form within his band.

None of these line-ups were an exclusive arrangement though. It wasn't unknown for Graham to play with Johnnie's Burch's band, Blues Incorporated and the Bond, Baker, Bruce trio on a single night.

By February '63 Jack, Ginger and Graham were vaguely thinking about leaving Alexis and forming their own band, but took matters no further. They had played one very successful gig together at The Twisted Wheel club in Manchester, and had worked out that as trio they each earned significantly more than with either Johnnie Burch or Alexis.

Graham then forced the pace. Jack turned up for a gig and saw Alexis looking very upset, as he had never seen the famously affable and relaxed guy before. Graham had told him that the three of them were leaving and Alexis saw the group, which he had put together so carefully, and which had been so well received, falling apart overnight. He was heart-broken, which Jack didn't at first understand. He had no idea that Graham had made the decision, let alone announced it to Alexis and thereby handed in their resignations. Alexis barked at Jack and stormed off. Though he was deeply unhappy at the time, Alexis – characteristically – soon came to terms with the decision and gave them every encouragement.

Initially the line-up was just bass, drums and alto sax, and they played jazz clubs as a jazz trio. They then decided that the group ought to be a four-piece and recruited guitarist John McLaughlin, and Graham moved over to play organ. The work started to come in rapidly and the band began to get an enthusiastic following. It seemed that they always playing. John was soon fired though; partly account of his inability to turn up for gigs on time, and partly because of his musical time-keeping – Ginger always insisted that the guitarist kept speeding up and slowing down, and couldn't maintain a steady beat.

Dick had been invited to join what became The Graham Bond Quartet, but at first declined. They approached him again after John had been expelled, and by September '63 he was in the band full-time. With Graham on organ it was a great fit. Although they thought of themselves as jazz musicians, they were moving away from the form in many ways, just as under Alexis's tutelage they have moved away from the blues. The band's name was definitely very jazzy and rather old fashioned, so it was changed to the more distinctive and quirky Graham Bond Organisation.

Their music was very much the sum of the musicians' talents. As Bob Brunning – the original bass player with Fleetwood Mac - says in his book 'Blues: The British Connection', Dick described the music as 'Unclassifiable.' It was heavily jazz influenced but

Dick's presence broadened the base; 'It was me joining that settled the thing into a group sound. You couldn't label it r 'n b and you couldn't label it progressive, but whatever it was, it was a solid group.' Dick's presence disciplined the band and the long jazz solos, which were starting to become its trademark, ceased. His playing and his personality had a very positive effect on the other three.

There was one fascinating way in which The GBO stopped being a jazz band. Purist jazz connoisseurs were, above all else, cool. They listened to music utterly devoid of physical movement, save for the occasional click of the fingers or appreciative nod of the head. It was rock 'n rollers, with their patently inferior music and absence of musical virtuosity, who bounced around and generally screamed and got sweaty. At a GBO gig though, everyone danced; the joint was jumping when they played. They were playing wild jazz-based music, but the audience wasn't sitting there with brows furrowed and a finger held to pursed lips. They danced and danced. It was the first hint that something else was coming into the music, and audiences weren't then to sit cross-legged and respectfully rapt again until Pink Floyd came along.

Jack regards it as having been a truly great band, and there was hardly a night when they weren't working. The GBO played well over three hundred gigs through 196. These were all in the UK; the band never played abroad. Jack says of this schedule, 'I've never had to practice my instrument again. I did all my practising on the road with Graham.'

There was a particular highlight in August '64 when The GBO played the fourth National Jazz & Blues Festival in Richmond. An r 'n b group called The Yardbirds were also on the bill, and during a long on-stage jam, Jack and Ginger played along with their hot-shot guitarist, Eric Clapton. It was the first time that the three of that shared a stage, crowded as it was.

Janet describes The Graham Bond Organisation as 'a weird-looking band.' They didn't look like anyone else. They weren't casually dressed like the blues bands and yet they weren't all in matching suits like a pop band; 'When you saw them walking down the street people would back away. Jack was the most presentable, but Ginger was pin-eyed and scary. Graham was ... well, Graham'

The band criss-crossed Britain – very slowly - in a succession of weird and terrifying vans. The first was a converted Daimler ambulance with blacked-out windows. Three guys could sit up front thanks to the long bench seat, but it was Jack, as the 'kid' in the band, who had to roll about in the back with the gear. There wasn't even a seat for him; he had to arrange everything as best he could, and he found with trial and error that the least uncomfortable thing to do was to sit on one of the rear wheel arches.

The band played the dance halls which graced every town of any size, and simply kept working. They built up a huge following. They weren't a pop band that released commercially orientated singles, let alone ones that they got to play, or mime to, Top

From left: Jack, Dick Heckstall-Smith, Ginger Baker and Graham Bond – the remarkable line-up of a very remarkable band; The Graham Bond Organisation. (Public Domain)

Of The Pops. They weren't to be seen in the pages of the just-starting-to-emerge teenage girls' magazines. They were an exciting live band who showed their audiences a damn good time. They never played to half-empty halls. The GBO was a great band, Janet says, 'They were an amazing band. It wasn't a mainstream pop group but they had hard-core followers, and there was always an amazing atmosphere at their gigs.' She does make the point though that they were always a much better band live than they were on album.

Across the winter of 1964/5 they were booked onto one of the broad-appeal pop package tours. Jack was still, just, playing acoustic bass. These package tours illustrated how the guys in the pokey and smoky offices in Tin Pan Alley thought. The concept was a hangover from variety shows, where the audience demanded the largest number of acts, each of which performed only for a few minutes. It was the way television producers, many of whom had come up through the variety theatres, thought too.

A package tour would comprise one big name and a supporting cast of half a dozen or so other bands and solo artists. They would tour the country by coach, always to the most frantic of schedules, working in obscure market towns as well as the big cities. Some provincial towns visited by these tours haven't seen well-known live bands since the package tour went out of fashion towards the end of the Sixties. In many cases, of course, the venues don't exist any more.

The headline act was Chuck Berry, with The Moody Blues close behind him. During the tour, if a band had a chart hit, it could easily leapfrog over the main attraction, which would find himself or themselves relegated instantly to the second division. That happened on this occasion; The Moody Blues epic anthem Go Now went to number one in the second week of December and was the biggest song around for quite a while. Very many kids in the audience must have come to see them, and didn't even know who Chuck Berry was. 'Suddenly there were all these kids screaming for The Moody Blues', Jack says, 'And it became their tour. Chuck wasn't very happy about it.'

There was also the r 'n b band The Downliners Sect, who played frequently at Eel Pie, Marquee Club-regulars The Five Dimensions, and the greatly-admired r 'n b singer Long John Baldry, who was very much a part of the London blues scene. Further down the bill was the four-piece band Winston G (fronted by guitarist Huw Lloyd Langton, who went on to play with Hawkwind and The Pretty Things), and singer Mike Patto – who opened the show, strangely, by singing several Chuck Berry songs, and then acted as Master of Ceremonies. It was a very curious mix, but if you were a teenager living in Launceston or Louth – let alone Liverpool or Leeds – you'd have killed to get a ticket.

As well as the more popular evening shows, the bands also played afternoon matinees. These were populated by school children in the main, and on occasion the audience would be a bit thin. Chuck Berry would come on stage once his band had struck up, doing his famous 'duck walk' and brandishing his Gibson. Halfway across the stage he would scan the audience and if the house wasn't full enough he'd carry on duck-walking – straight off the other side of the stage, leaving the band wondering what on earth they should do. Chuck Berry's star had faded since his big rock 'n roll tours of the Fifties (and these youngsters certainly weren't his real audience – there wasn't a Triumph Bonneville or a black leather jacket between them) but no one had told him, and he wasn't going to play to anything less than a capacity crowd.

Jack watched from the wings, amazed. He had seen Chuck on the film 'Jazz On A Summer's Day' – a documentary made at the Newport Jazz Festival. His place on the bill was highly controversial at the time as he was very much rock 'n roll and not a jazz musician at all. Jack says that he wasn't hugely interested in his music, but admired him and liked his lyrics. He was, he says, in awe of his imperious star status. 'He didn't give a shit. He was pretty unpleasant to us. He would never look at us, never say 'hi.' He was travelling with his sister – at least, that's how she was described.'

After the last gig of the tour the other bands decided to try and repay his indifference. They told him that they knew a really great, really famous restaurant, and told him they would love him to be their guest for dinner. They managed to persuade him to abandon his chauffeur-driven car - his black Austin Princess, the choice of Lord Mayors and secondary members of The Royal Family - and join them on the bus for the trip to the restaurant. Once he was captive on the coach and they had set off, they went out of their way to be rude to him, and started singing him the rudest songs they knew, or could make up, all to the tunes of his songs.

The restaurant they took him to was called The Blue Boar, which meant nothing in particular to him, but was in fact one of the very first service areas on the then-new M1. At that time it was the only stopping-off point on the motorway, and was notorious for being one of the nastiest, greasiest dives imaginable. They ignored that fact and acted throughout as if it was a high-class joint serving cordon bleu cuisine. It was a long time before Chuck realised that he was being sent up.

The promoter and pop manager Robert Stigwood had put the tour together, and it was Jack's first contact with a man who would have a considerable impact on his life and work through the rest of the decade.

The GBO recorded a live album in June 1963; 'Live At Klooks Kleek' –that being one of their regular venues, a small club in unfashionable West Hampstead. In August '64 the Organisation recorded several tracks which were released on the 'Rhythm And Blues' sampler album. Their first full album was 'The Summer Of '65', which – incredibly – was recorded in just three hours. As Jack points out, you should never put a date on an album name because it, well, dates it. It was a mixture of American standards and original compositions.

Record Mirror' said of it, 'We're urging those not 'in-the-know' to grab a copy of this exciting album. Raw-edged, almost all the way. Brisk. But musically - that's above all else. Great tenor sax from Dick Heckstall-Smith; spasms of exciting harmonica. A first-rate album.' 'Disc' magazine's reviewer wrote, 'It sounds like nothing else I've heard, and is really musical in spite of the raw instrumental sounds achieved. Drummer Ginger Baker contributes one of the best solos I've heard on disc.' Meanwhile, the venerable New Musical Express opined, 'Way-out blues sounds, weird at times, but always fascinating. Plenty of wailing harmonica and raving vocalistics (sic).'

Around half the tracks were r 'n b or blues standards, such as Hoochie Coochie Man, Neighbour Neighbour, Got My Mojo, and Traintime – which was to become Jack's masterpiece with Cream, at least so far harmonic playing was concerned. There were an original Jack Bruce compositions; Hear Me Calling Your Name. He now had one of his own compositions on record. The vocals were dubbed on later, and this was the only song on which any additional work was done; everything else was played as live and simply recorded. The rest of the band wasn't hugely helpful with regard to his compositions. Granted, time in the studio was tight, but they allowed him just twenty minutes to cut all three tracks. Now he had his own work on vinyl though; songs he had written, on which he sang, and on which he played.

Jack was still far from familiar with the recording process. It was still the case that the producers – who were employed directly by the record company and were dependent for their career progression on pleasing their bosses – wore white shirts and conservative ties. They spoke the Queen's English, drove Triumph Heralds and Singer Gazelles, or commuted in from Cobham on the train. They looked as George Martin did at that point, though very few others had his imagination and appreciation of the music they were working on.

The engineers wore brown overalls with pens in the top pocket, and the musicians were looked down on as a necessary evil. They were at best patronised. When a track had been recorded it wasn't played back to them; it was played back for the benefit of the producers and the record company executives. There was a class element to all this, which Jack of course hated; 'It was them and us. The studio was the shop floor.' The decisions were made in the management office and their diktats were announced over the foldback speaker. At much the same time there was the famous upper class, middle class and working class sketch on the television programme 'That Was The Week That Was', with John Cleese, Ronnie Barker and Ronnie Corbett, and that was the structure in the recording studio, and to a large degree – despite the efforts of independent mavericks stretching from Joe Meek to Andrew Oldham – in the rest of the industry too.

Somewhat surprisingly, the band also recorded a Lennon & McCartney song at the same session. The Beatles, who were absolutely enormous worldwide by then, hadn't yet recorded I Saw Her Standing There, and it was offered to Duffy Power, who was also on the EMI label. Duffy had been one of the boys in Larry Parnes' stable (hence the characteristic Parnsian name) but had escaped and become a highly respected r 'n b singer. Many of his singles were cover versions, including Bobby Darin's Dream Lover and Jerry Lee Lewis's Whole Lotta Shakin' Goin' On. He occasionally sang with the GBO.

A Graham Bond song, Farewell Baby was to have been the A-side, but the EMI execs thought differently and turned them around. The record was released in May '63 and the following month the single was reviewed by 'Beat Monthly' magazine, which gave it five gold stars and said, 'Top side is penned by those Beatle Boys Lennon & McCartney, but though Duffy and his friends perform it well, I don't think the song is suited to an R&B outing: still it's worth a buzz from the Graham Bond organ grooves, and Duffy's vocal escapades could make the lower deck of the charts.' It didn't. By then it was the opening track on The Beatles first album, which had gone straight to number one. Jack rather liked their version of it, and still has his copy.

Jack was still leading a semi-nomadic life, always in 'digs' – when he wasn't sleeping on sofas – and though he was earning steadily, he was spending with ease. He was getting by though, perfecting his craft and simply enjoying his life. Everything moved on though when he, Graham and Ginger played a freelance session for the Jamaican jazz guitarist, Ernest Ranglin, who was one the true pioneers of ska and reggae. He had originally been a ukulele player, and had only recently been brought to London to play on My Boy Lollipop, which was an energetic number two for the singer Millie.

Ernest's producer was insistent that Jack play electric bass for the recording (which was eventually credited to Ernest Ranglin & The GBs), which – ever the jazz purist - he was reluctant to do. He didn't like other people telling what he should do, but the money was good and his attitude was rather 'what have I got to lose?' He hadn't touched a bass guitar before, but he had to acquire one for the session. There didn't seem to be much point in buying one, as he was never going to touch it again, so he persuaded a shop to loan him one. Foote's bass shop in Golden Square, on the northern edge of Soho, was easily the best place to buy both acoustic and electric basses – 'a wonderful place' – and Jack is fairly sure that this first electric instrument came from there. It was a semi-acoustic Gretch with 'horrible' black nylon strings, which sat high off the fret board. It wasn't what you'd think of a rock star's guitar. He felt comfortable with it though because it was so large, and therefore felt slightly more like what he was used to.

It was a leap in the dark, but it worked. He loved every moment of the session, and felt as if he had been playing electric bass for years; 'I'd never even touched one before but I fell in love with the bass guitar. It was instantaneous; I just knew that was my instrument.' The other advantage was that by turning a knob or two he could really gain volume. His ambition had been to play louder than Ginger, and the Gibson allowed him to do exactly that. He was delighted.

All of a sudden he could go to gigs in a Mini. It was liberating physically as well as musically. It was the one truly pivotal shift that he had to make. It would probably have happened at some other time and in some other way, but as it was it was almost thrust upon him.

At this point, Bob Brunning points out, 'Jack was really only known to the serious club-haunters, but his consummate skill was very quickly recognised. He went on to be great electric bass player, but he was a great double bass player – which is a whole lot more difficult.'

Chapter 7

The first bass guitar Jack actually bought was a cheap Japanese-manufactured Top Ten, which was a vague copy of a Fender. He plugged that into a Watkins Pick-A-Back amp, the name being a distortion of piggy-back. It was two separate units, the amplifier in a smaller case and the single 15-inch speaker in a matching larger unit. They were handsome things, covered in black leather-effect fabric and with a silver grille across the speaker. They were badged 'WEM' (for Watkins Electric Music) and 'Power Bass.' There was one jack plug input, a mains indicator light, and four black Bakelite control knobs.

He also had a fifteen-inch Grampian speaker, and in these days before roadies, bodged everything together himself, simply twisting the bare wires together. This casual approach to electronics almost killed him. The band was playing at The 100 Club and Jack stepped forward to the microphone to sing one of his regular vocal spots, First Time I Met The Blues. He made the mistake of touching the microphone, and completed the circuit. All the power going through the club's electrical system re-directed itself through his body.

The current snapped his hand into a claw, gluing it to the mic, and the power arced between the guitar and the microphone. It was a moment before the rest of the band realised what was happening, and even then they failed to react. Jack managed to kick off the mains supply himself. The power through the guitar strings had burned four deep channels in his right hand, and the air smelt on burning flesh.

Several guitarists have been killed in this way, the best-known being another Glaswegian, Lesley Harvey (brother of Alex), who was electrocuted during a gig in 1972 while playing with Stone The Crows. The following year, John Rostill, longest-serving bass player with The Shadows was found dead in his home studio, having been electrocuted by his instrument. An ex-colleague of Eric Clapton, Keith Relf was found dead in 1976, again electrocuted by his guitar. The Rolling Stones bass player Bill Wyman once received a similar electric shock on stage, but like Jack, survived.

Eventually, and with the current safely turned off, the other members of the band carried him backstage. The shock had left his body absolutely rigid, so much so that they laid him on the top of an upright piano. Meanwhile, someone had asked from the stage, in the very best tradition, if there was a doctor in the house. The 100 Club was just round the corner from a medical school, and there was a virtual stampede of assistance. Jack was told that apart from the burns to his hand he was fine, and was in no further danger. However he was, he says, 'Literally buzzing for days.'

The cheap Japanese guitar had melted, so some good had come of the experience. Jack decided to go looking more seriously for a bass that really suited him. He took his time. He shopped around. He decided on a Fender Bass VI, 'Which is basically a big Fender Jaguar. It's just a six-string guitar, but an octave lower. I thought that would be great – we didn't have a guitarist in the band and I thought I'd be able to play guitar solos.'

It is said that in designing the Bass VI. Leo Fender was thinking that it could be 'a baritone guitar' as well. It's a traditional Fender shape, with the upper horn much more pronounced than the lower (unlike the equally-sized horns on Stratocasters), and was usually seen in a three-tone sunburst finish. It uses three pickups and a tremolo arm, so if nothing else it was a great thing to puzzle the audience with. It had a short, thirty-inch scale.

The instrument has been described as 'a jack of all trades and a master of none.' A specialist bass guitar reviewer described it as, 'A very different beast; not a guitar, not a bass, six strings and looks like a Jag. The first time you play it it's an out of body experience. It feels like a guitar, then a BOOM comes out. [It has an] interesting and different tone, and six strings means you can do some interesting things.'

Both George Harrison and John Lennon were to use a Fender VI on the 'White Album', 'Let It Be', and 'Abbey Road' (though Paul McCartney stuck to his Hofner, Rickenbacker and 4-string Fender Jazz Bass). Peter Green has recorded with one, as has Robert Smith of The Cure.

The strings run very close together on the VI, which makes it difficult to play – and certainly very difficult to play at speed or with great intricacy. This would have appealed to Jack though; it was a way of impressing and confounding anyone watching him play. This is a man who likes to keep his fans on their toes. The attitude would have been best expressed along the lines of, 'Okay, now watch this.'

Although the band, with that line-up, worked almost non-stop, there never seemed to be much in the way of remuneration. Graham was 'just terrible with money', and as he was the band leader that was a problem. 'You'd see him after the gig, with the place empty, at the other side of the room, getting paid by the promoter', Jack says, 'And by the time he'd walked over to the rest of the band the money would be gone. I still don't know how he did it.'

Jack and Janet on their wedding day; London,
September 26 1964 (Janet Bruce)

Graham had other problems too. The police were often looking for him with regard to non-payment of alimony, and on one occasion he was actually hauled off stage by officers who had a writ for his arrest. He still had a day-job selling infra-red ovens, which pre-dated microwaves. Whenever the band were playing in a pub, or absolutely anywhere else that served food, he would disappear and try his sales patter on the manager. He didn't like to leave a venue without having both played a storming gig, and sold them a catering-level infra-red cooker.

On September 26 1964 Janet and Jack got married. She had simply walked out of school halfway through taking her A-levels, much to her parents' understandable unhappiness. Her father was very upset, but her mother was more pragmatic. She didn't like it but she decided that she could live with it. Janet wasn't interested in her education any more. All that mattered in her life was the music scene and her relationship with Jack.

Jack had to be brought round to meet his parents-in-law to be. That went well though and the necessary arrangements were made. The marriage was held at the old Hampstead registry office. The guest list comprised close family from both sides. Janet describes her dress as 'Very nice, cream, Sixties but a bit more dressy – knee-length. Jack was in a formal suit with a shirt and tie. Janet remembers them both being terribly nervous. She was nineteen and he twenty-one. The wedding reception was held at Janet's parents' home, but before hand Janet and Jack dropped into the pub next door, where they had a brandy each. A real treat. Janet's parents paid for a hire car, and they drove to Broadstairs in Kent, where they had a three-day honeymoon.

Once Jack had relaxed in their company he got on very well with his in-laws, but Janet had problems. She was very fond of Jack's father and brother, but there was a difficulty between her and Betty. Betty still thought of Jack as her youngest and dearest. She had difficulty letting go, and no girl was ever really going to be good enough for him. She came to stay quite often; indeed they saw more of her than of Janet's parents – despite the fact that they lived quite close by. Janet always felt that she was being inspected, which of course is not an uncommon situation. Janet was still young, but she knew she was going to have to deal with it. Janet had gone straight from living with her parents, as a young girl, to being a married woman and having to forge very different relationships. She says that she was intimidated by Betty. As Janet says now, 'She was a very strong woman, and she always had a huge effect on Jack. It was difficult for him to break away.'

Life was good. They were very much in love and were also each other's closet friend and ally. The couple played tennis on Hampstead Heath, and caught all the latest films as soon as they came to the cinema. They played harmonicas together. Very much of that time, Jack had decided that his wife wasn't going to work. He would be the breadwinner and she was to be a housewife. Her job was to create a home for them both in their first home of their own, at Bracknell Gardens in Hampstead. At first, immediately after the wedding, Janet had moved in with Jack, who was by then living with John Mumford in West Hampstead. That was an awkward situation though, and soon they rented into their own flat. On the other hand, he handed all his earnings over to Janet and she handled the domestic budget, and gave him 'gig money' for cigarettes and the odd beer. Neither of them drank much, though Jack did introduce her to smoking dope, which was freely circulating in their circle. He smoked a lot, but soon reduced his intake when he realised that the drug really didn't suit him. She says that she because more of a dope smoker than him, but their consumption was never great.

Janet found herself on her own a lot. If she didn't go to the gig with the band there wasn't a lot else to do. She used to do the household chores when Jack wasn't around. She discovered an all-night launderette and taking the washing there and watching it spin round became a small event in itself. She did have a friend who worked in A&R for Decca. They had famously turned down The Beatles, and the company was desperate not to miss whatever or whoever was going to be the next big thing. The two of them went to gigs, on expenses, and eventually reported back on the potential of the bands they had heard. The executives probably took their recommendations very seriously, but Janet thought it wasn't much more than a bit if fun.

She started writing lyrics for The GBO, of which she says she's 'not exactly proud' now, in fact she says that they embarrass her. It was an exciting time. Anyone – even a girl, a wife – could end up writing the lyrics for a song, and see it performed and recorded. Everything was suddenly opening up. 'We had come out of what seemed like a black and white world, the Fifties and early Sixties, and everything had been grey. Clothes were dull, cars were dull; everything was dull. Then there was a very positive atmosphere and you felt encouraged to do things, creatively. And some of the barriers were down,' she says. Some of her lyrics were distinctly racy, and were hardly the sort of sentiment her mother, or indeed mother-in-law, would have recognised or admitted to, but Janet was in love, she says, and just about anything was possible and permissible. On the other hand, Janet found that there was often an oppressive atmosphere around the band, and for all the moves into the Technicolor Sixties, and she felt she had to keep quiet in their company more often than not. It was still very much a man's world. On sight, all women were immediately split into one of two sorts by the guys in the band, 'The nice women and the good-time women. It was very unfair to women really.'

Janet says that she was never at ease with Graham, and always kept him at arm's length; 'We never had much to say to each other. I didn't like him as a person but I loved the music.' She says that when it came to giving them a wedding present, Graham had burgled his first wife's house, and presented the happy couple with the blankets off her bed. A little while after he came round to the flat and asked if he could have back that bed linen they had borrowed. '

Graham was always immaculately dressed, somewhere between a jazzer and a mod. He also had a settled domestic life, with a wife, children and a nice home – a respectable semi-detached house back in Romford. As a result of his inability to hang onto money long enough to pay the others; Ginger decided that he was going to take over the running of the band, which Jack agreed with completely. Graham had been a strong, almost domineering character, but he was no match for Ginger once the drummer had decided he was going to replace him as bandleader. It's possible that Graham saw it as a relief.

If nothing else, they weren't getting paid, and Ginger, who had a wife and a child, simply took matters into his own hands. He made everything more business-like, booked the gigs, got everyone there on time, and looked after the cash. However he also quickly assumed that he would have the last word on all subjects.

Ginger has always had a reputation as a man you did not contradict lightly. He seemed to be absolutely certain that it was him against the world, every second of every day. Bob Brunning recalls playing a club in Liverpool alongside The GBO, and when they came to set up they found that there was almost no room left on the very tiny stage because Ginger already had his kit in place. Bob made the mistake of suggesting to Ginger that he might like to move his drums – the biggest kit Bob had ever seen – which brought the response, 'I ain't movin' my fuckin' drum kit for anybody.' Bob was left in no doubt that further discussion was out of the question; 'You knew where you were with him', Bob adds, sardonically.

In the summer of 1965 Jack got his first real taste of pop television when the band played on the wonderfully-hip 'Ready Steady Go.' They were playing their new single Lease On Love, which was well reviewed but again didn't sell well. A writer for New Musical Express, who didn't have the best command of the English language, said of it, 'The soloist has an inherent r 'n b feeling, and this is particularly noticeable with the persistent blues riff behind him.'

Jack describes the music they were playing as 'hard-driving r 'n b; cutting edge for its time.' It was the first band to cross over from jazz to what would be seen as rock, and they were therefore the first band to bring the jazz concept of personal virtuosity to rock music. By and large, with a few exceptions – such as Hank Marvin within The Shadows – bands played as a single entity, and individual ability wasn't what was wanted or needed.

The Flamingo Club was their favourite venue. It was popular with black GIs stationed in Britain, and it had the most responsive audience. No one sat quietly on their hands at The Flamingo. It was also where other musicians tried to take them on: A lot of Americans who were visiting the UK used to come to The Flamingo Club and ask if they could sit in. As Jack says, 'People like Cat Anderson, the trumpet player from Duke Ellington's band used to come and sit in with us, but we scared them off. It was a great band for the time; there hadn't been anything quite like this; really powerful, really intense.'

Pete Brown, who was to become Jack's song-writing collaborator, was part of the New Departures jazz/poetry group, which had a residency at The Marquee at the same time as Jack was playing with Alexis's band. Pete worked on Tuesdays, but got in free anytime during the week, so he became very familiar with Jack's playing. He was a great fan of The GBO; 'I just thought they were the best thing around. They were to musicians what The Beatles were to the public. They were incredible musicians and they were innovators. And because they weren't beautiful, weren't pretty, they gave hope to a lot of people who wanted to become musicians.'

They fused British inventiveness, he explains, with American soul and jazz. He regards them as one of the few really great British bands, and musically can be regarded as the forerunner of Cream; 'The GBO was one of the most creative things to come out of this country, and people are still trying to figure out exactly what they did.' There was a gulf between bands whose main medium was television, and the rest, who

From left: Dick (kneeling), Ginger, Jack and Graham. Everyone agrees that The GBO were a very weird-looking band, but live were one of the most exciting groups of their time. (Public Domain)

depended on playing for live audiences. Which is why a huge number of people had heard of The Dave Clark Five, and relatively few knew of The Graham Bond Organisation – vastly better musicians though they were.

The GBO released a single in January '65, while they were still on the Chuck Berry tour. Tammy – Jack's arrangement of, amazingly, a Debbie Reynolds song (of which he is still rather proud) - didn't chart. There were other singles, none of which made any impression on the charts, and then in December '65 the band's second album – the cheesily-named 'There's A Bond Between Us' was released. Again it was a mix of old and new, with the old including their version of Ray Charles' What'd I Say, and the blues classic Have You Ever Loved A Woman? There were no Jack Bruce compositions on the album, in fact most of the songs were credited to the whole group. One song – Baby Be Good To Me - was co-credited to Janet Godfrey.

This record was well reviewed, but it's interesting to see that Jack's name was never mentioned in the press. Ginger, Dick and of course Graham were all pulled out for particular praise within their own disciplines. No one mentioned Jack though, important as he was to the band's overall sound. It didn't help that he was, at this point, very much the quiet one who stood at the back (he was later to say that he felt an affinity with George Harrison in this respect, but while he was self-effacing in The GBO, The Bluesbreakers and Manfred Mann, that was hardly the case in Cream).

There wasn't really a bond between them. It was time for Jack to move on. By the time the record was actually released in 1966, Jack was gone. Ginger, in his role as bandleader, fired him. Jack reacted by refusing to go. He had been there since the band's inception and Ginger had no more right to fire him than Jack would have had to try to dismiss Ginger. 'I regarded it as collective, a co-operative band. He decided that he could fire me though.'

Ginger's reasoning was that Jack's playing was 'too busy.' A rock critic has since written that Ginger 'had problems with Jack broadening the range of the bass parts.' Jack says, 'I was experimenting, trying to take the bass in a melodic direction. Ginger thought that the bass should be in the background going plunky-plunk.' Pete Brown says, 'Ginger always reckoned that Jack's timing wasn't that good, but if you listen to the records now you can hear that it was Ginger's timing that was out.' He also says that arguments over 'musical differences' were perhaps a smoke screen for their high levels of competitiveness. Pete Brown says, 'There was always so much conflict going on – conflict that rose out of competitiveness. It wasn't unique to them, but it was always there.'

The two men, both of them very determined, very stubborn, dug their heels in. Jack simply refused to accept that he was being fired and turned up for gigs as if nothing had happened. As well as going along to hear the music, people used to turn up to see whether or not there'd be a fight between the two men.

Graham and Dick, meanwhile, had no say in it all. Ginger was livid with rage; his newfound authority was being challenged almost nightly. He tried to ignore Jack, but Jack would have arrived under his own steam, and would have set up his amp himself – and he proceeded to play. Eventually Ginger pulled a knife, prodded it into Jack's guts and said, 'If you turn up at the next gig this is going right in.' Jack had no reason to disbelieve him, and from that moment on he was no longer any part of The Graham Bond Organisation.

Dick, who greatly enjoyed playing with Jack – and who regarded him as the only guy to work with so far as the bass was concerned – was greatly disappointed by Jack's departure. Being the guy he was, he wasn't going to try and stand up to rough boy Ginger though.

In August 1965 Ginger left The GBO and was replaced by Jon Hiseman, who had been playing semi-professionally for several years, but who now took the opportunity to give up the day job and become a professional jazz drummer. The jazz scene's old guard were still smarting from the direction that 'their' music was taking; two 'eminent' jazz musicians went to see Jon and pointed out that in joining Graham's band he was wasting his talent and throwing any chance of a career. Like Jack he had been brought up on classical music, and had played every style of music imaginable – from modern jazz to old time music hall (and including a spell in the band in a circus big top) - and didn't think to label music and stick it in little compartments. The approach shocked him. He decided to ignore them.

A year or so previously Jon and Jack had played together a couple of times in The Mike Taylor Quartet, but only sitting in during rehearsals. These, Jon's remembers, were on Jack's very rare nights off from the Organisation. Jon was to return to play with Jack at towards the end of the decade, post-Cream.

In 1966 the Organisation toured with The Who, and in the Seventies The Who's drummer, Keith Moon, recruited Graham to play the saxophone - and indeed play the saxophonist - in the film 'That'll Be The Day.' In 1968, Graham moved to the USA. He was there for just under two years and it was a very creative time for him; he released three albums of work composed in America – 'Love Is The Law', 'The Mighty Graham Bond', and 'Solid Bond.' He returned to the UK and played a very poorly received show at The Royal Albert Hall, which dispirited him greatly. He then joined Baker's post-Blind Faith band, Airforce.

His style began to change dramatically. The suits were discarded and were eventually replaced by flowing robes. He became very interested in, and all too involved in, various forms of magick (always with a 'k') and mysticism. He began to wear a large pentagram over his robes - he was a very large man - and with his black goatee beard he looked the complete warlock.

He formed two occult-heavy bands; firstly Holy Magick, and then Magus (with folkie Carolanne Pegg). These interests filtered through into his music, and in conjunction with his wife, Diane Stewart, who was also heavily involved in witchcraft, he recorded 'We Put Our Magick On You.' They co-wrote most of the tracks, and the sleeve notes explained the magical theories behind the record - and assured listeners that playing it would cast a protective astral ring around them. In the dying days of The GBO, Graham negotiated three different exclusive publishing deals on the same day.

Graham's drug of choice was heroin, which eventually took over his life. When he couldn't get hold of heroin though he downed bottles of Collis Brown cough medicine instead – which, amazingly, had a heavy morphine base. Whenever he moved house he would leave behind cupboards full of empty cough medicine bottles.

The best work of these later years was his collaboration with Pete Brown, which led to the album 'Two Heads Are Better Than One.' By this time however he had money worries and was largely disillusioned with the music scene. He was also taking drugs at a dangerous level, and suffered a nervous breakdown, which resulted in a month in a psychiatric ward.

In May 1974 he was killed when he fell under an underground train at a north London station. There have been suggestions that he was pushed, but it is more likely by far that it was suicide. Jack still has Graham's pentagram, with its ruby set in the middle, and treats it with great caution; 'I think it is powerful. It's hidden away.' He also has a Peruvian war axe which Graham owned and which he believed had magical powers. Graham used to carry it around, hidden under his robes.

Jack was to work with Dick Heckstall-Smith many more times over the years, and when Dick died in the autumn of 2004, Jack wrote, 'When I first came to London in the early Sixties Dick took me under his wing. I looked up to him as an older brother and he introduced me to many aspects of music that changed my whole life. Indeed it was Dick who got me my first important job with Alexis Korner's Blues Incorporated, and it was Dick who first played me the music of Bob Dylan and The Beatles. He turned me on to great writers I had not known, like Joseph Heller and Malcolm Lowry.

'If it had not been for his encouragement and guidance, I might never have been a part of the blossoming London scene. Dick introduced me to Ginger Baker and told me to check out a brilliant new guitarist called Eric Clapton!

'Dick never received the recognition he deserved. He was without doubt the world's foremost blues saxophonist. His ability on tenor and soprano saxes (sometimes both at the same time) was unsurpassed in his chosen field.'

A short while before Jack left the GBO, they had worked as Marvin Gaye's backing band for his first UK television appearance. Meeting him had a great effect on Jack, and the American was very generous, and made no bones about the fact that he was greatly impressed by the young Scot's playing. After the TV show Jack had invited him back to his flat, and was stunned when he agreed to come along, and the two of them sat up all night, talking and swapping stories. It's a tiny detail, but one thing about him which impressed Jack was his 'amazing green boots.' He scoured London looking for an identical pair of green boots so that he could look like Marvin Gaye – at least from the toes to the ankles.

Marvin was endlessly encouraging, and even asked Jack to return to the USA with him and join his regular band. It wasn't a viable proposition, but his encouragement and appreciation gave Jack the determination to persevere with his music. He had been considering simply giving up and going back home. Jack was still young – he celebrated his twenty-second birthday in May 1965 - and he was still vulnerable and sensitive. Ginger had hurt him badly. In fact it wasn't to be long before he was re-united with Ginger in a new band, but the relationship between them would never again be what it was; the antipathy and mutual suspicion that has lasted for four decades began at that point. He had looked up to Ginger, and had developed a great respect for his musicianship, but if he couldn't communicate his thoughts and ambitions to him, then what could he do? If it had not been for that one night spent talking to Marvin Gaye in a tiny flat in West Hampstead, sat on furniture almost literally made out of orange boxes, Jack might well have sold the electric bass and retreated from the London music scene.

Chapter 8

In October 1965 Jack joined John Mayall's Bluesbreakers – but at that exact point it was a blues band without a lead guitarist. Eric Clapton had been in the band since the previous April, having left The Yardbirds because they were straying too far from the purist blues high ground – and were even having Top Ten hits. He had set off on a hare-brained adventure across Europe, and John had cast round for a replacement. He tried John Weider (who went on to join Family, and nowadays plays with The Manfreds), John Slaughter, and Geoff Krivit, but finally gave the job to Peter Green, who was one of the very few guitarists who could have stood in Eric's shoes – certainly so far as the fans were concerned. A short while later Eric re-appeared, impoverished and chastened, and asked for his job back. Peter was out and Eric was back in.

Eric had been a fairly frequent guest at GBO gigs, and was a big fan of both that band and – as he told Jack later – his vocal abilities. It was at exactly this point that Eric's reputation as a guitarist was really taking off, really going out beyond the pure cognoscenti.

Like Jack – and indeed Ginger - Eric Patrick Clapp had a difficult childhood, but the reasons were very different. His wasn't a poor or deprived upbringing – his home was a comfortable lower middle class house in Surrey. The difficulties were more psychological.

Eric was born on March 30 1945 and was brought up by Jack and Rose Clapp in a very warm and loving environment. At some point though, when he was still at primary school, he discovered that Jack and Rose weren't his parents but his grandparents. His mother was Patricia Clapton; Rose was her mother and Jack her stepfather. Eric had been born to Pat when she was just sixteen, and – given the social mores of the time – she had handed him over to the older couple, who very generously offered to bring him up as if he was their own son. Patricia then disappeared out of their lives.

This discovery undoubtedly had a devastating effect on him, but not so great as when Patricia turned up at the Clapp's home. She had been living in Germany, but returned to the UK and suddenly arrived in Eric's life. He was nine. While she stayed Patricia was passed off as his elder sister, for the benefit of the neighbours, which must have further added to his confusion.

She left as suddenly as she had arrived, and it was to be many years before mother and son met up again. Jack and Rose tried to carry on as if nothing had happened, but the meeting scarred Eric. He had been a shy, reserved boy, but now he retreated even further into his own thoughts, and began to display a distinctly rebellious side. At question was his identity, and he needed to place himself within the world. As he is quoted as saying in Michael Schumacher's biography, 'I wanted to be different from everyone else. I sensed that I was, so I developed the philosophy of flaunting it, but not in an outgoing way. I was very introverted.' He failed his eleven-plus despite being a bright child.

Eric was quiet and self-possessed, but it was probably exactly these aspects of his personality, which allowed him to immerse himself in music. He wasn't a team player. He wasn't captain of the football team. He was happiest on his own, playing records, and trying to master his £14 acoustic guitar.

As a young adult he was still thoughtful and aloof – in a way that was easy to take exception to; when he was first playing with bands he looked superior and slightly sneering – very much set apart from his colleagues and peers. At least he could communicate through his guitar, and that was his saving grace.

John Mayall was much older than Jack or Eric. He had been born in Macclesfield in Cheshire in 1933 and so was a whole decade older than Jack. He wasn't any sort of an elder brother figure though; he was a notoriously fierce disciplinarian. He was teetotal himself, and wouldn't stand for excessive drinking among his band members – and they were very much members of his band. The Bluesbreakers was never a musicians' collective. He had served in the army during his National Service, including a tour of duty in Korea, where East faced West with great suspicion. He rather ran his band as a sergeant might run his squaddies. 'He was very stingy to work for', Jack says, 'The wages were very poor – barely a living wage. Yet we were touring all the time, going to places like Aberystwyth and back.' He also makes the point that the band crisscrossed Britain's 1960s A-roads in an old Commer van, and everyone was jammed up in the front, apart from John, who had had a full-size bed built into the back for himself 'and whatever bird he had picked up.' The others had to take turns sitting on the cowling over the engine.

In summary Jack says, 'I've never admired John Mayall's music, and I've never admired the way he treats his bands.'

While he was with The Bluesbreakers, Jack made a solo single, on which he both played and sang. With I'm Getting Tired on the A-side and Rootin' Tootin' on the B-side, it wasn't typical of his style. He describes it as 'sort of folk/rock', but when it came to recruiting other musicians for the session the only names he knew were from the jazz or r 'n b scenes. The drummer was a free-form jazz musician, John Stevens – who he had worked with in Johnnie Burch's bands, and who probably wasn't the best man for the job. The producer on the session was Robert Stigwood, and this was the first time that Jack worked directly with the man who was to play so large a part in the story of Cream.

Jack had joined The Bluesbreakers as the replacement for John McVie, who had been in the band since its formation in 1963. Mayall fired McVie, who was fond of the odd pint, for being a touch too merry on stage. Eric returned to the band in November 1965, and Jack and Eric shared a stage as members of the same band. The only gig that Jack remembers vividly, with both him and Eric in The Bluesbreakers, was at Heathrow Airport.

Bob Brunning says of that, albeit brief, line-up, 'Jack was far more creative than John McVie. That band really was like the forerunner of Cream – because Eric and Jack really get off on each other's music.'

It was a short-lived liaison though. Jack decided that John wasn't paying him enough, and left. He had been with the band just over six weeks, from late October to December. John Mayall then recorded a track called Double Crossin' Time, apparently aimed at Jack and his very inconvenient departure from The Bluesbreakers. Although bands picked up and lost members fairly casually, John considered Jack's departure to be an act of disloyalty – though it must be said that John himself was never backward in firing musicians. Line-ups weren't sacred.

John was only to have a few months of stability though; Eric left The Bluesbreakers the following May. 'After Eric had left' Jack says, 'It wasn't one of John Mayall's finest bands.'

Everyone, it seemed, had to go through The Bluesbreakers at some point or other, though Jack was in and out in no time at all. Mayall had no option but, after trying John Bradley, to bring McVie back into the band.

In November the band recorded a single for the Immediate record label, Sitting On Top of the World, which Cream would completely re-define and make their own. Over the summer of '66 Jack and Eric made some interesting recordings together. One was the album 'Primal Solos', which wasn't released for another twenty years.

Along with vocalist and harmonica player Paul Jones, drummer Pete Yorke and keyboards player and singer Steve Winwood, they also recorded three tracks which appeared on a sampler album, recorded in June 1966 and released on Elektra. Paul Jones and producer Joe Boyd had got the project underway, and the thinking was simply that it was time for some of Britain's best young blues musicians to come together on vinyl.

The three cuts on 'What's Shakin'' were Memphis Slim's Steppin' Out, S McLeod's I Want To Know, and Robert Johnson's Crossroads – which of course Eric and Jack would return to and re-create as one of Cream's greatest moments.

These tracks were credited to Eric Clapton and The Powerhouse, and were slotted in, rather incongruously, between songs by The Lovin' Spoonful, Al Kooper, Tom Rush and The Butterfield Blues Band – all American of course, and all unlike the music coming out of the British r 'n b scene. The front cover featured a shot of The Lovin' Spoonful and the names of the other artists were run far smaller than theirs. The Lovin' Spoonful had seen a run of good-time poppy hits in both America and Britain, and the record was sold on the back of those. One of their biggest hits, Daydream, went to number two in the UK charts, but stalled there behind Pretty Flamingo. Which is interesting because Jack played bass on Pretty Flamingo.

Keyboards player Manfred Mann, who had been born Michael Lubowitz in South Africa in 1940, met drummer Mike Hugg when they were together in the Ken Goddard Quintet. At that point they were playing piano and vibraphone respectively, and they spent the summer of 1962 at Butlin's holiday came at Clacton-on-Sea in Essex, where the band had a residency playing lounge music.

By March of the following year they had become an r 'n b band with a debut gig at The Marquee, and had added vocalist Paul Jones (then still Paul Pond), guitarist Mike Vickers, and bass player Dave Richmond. Paul was terrifically good-looking, Manfred was groovy as could be, and they were a dead cert for chart success. They were soon playing all the right venues, and through 1963 they developed a sound which was far more commercial than just about anything emerging from the scene at that time. They specialised in very catchy, sellable singles which were pop without being cheesy. Some were written especially for the band, but the majority were songs that Manfred had found. Sometimes they were Dylan tracks (and later Manfred would turn minor Bruce Springsteen album tracks into big hits, long before Springsteen was really famous), but often they had been minor hits in the USA and he found them and reworked them. No matter what they had played though, the talent and sheer grooviness of the band would have shone through.

They were also doing the right thing at exactly the right time. They were perfect for television, both in terms of their sound and their image. Pop music television was just starting to really happen, and the contrast between Manfred's studious jazz cool and Paul's mischievous boy-next-door look was perfect. Manfred never smiled; Paul rarely stopped.

The big breakthrough in teenage television, the show that alienated your mum and dad, and wouldn't have had Kathy Kirby on even if she had joined The Beatles, was 'Ready Steady Go.' With the by-line 'The Weekend Starts Here' it was completely informal, and its presenters were almost self-consciously amateur. Bands played against bare studio walls, with the camera cables and lighting rigs in shot, and the studio audience really looked as if they belonged there: The Top Of The Pops audience looked as if they were rented from the junior range at Rent-A-Stiff. The RSG crowd looked terrific, danced well, and were perfectly cool. It was exactly what Swinging London was all about.

The show initially used The Surfaris' Wipe Out as its theme song, but then asked Manfred to write them a new one. 5-4-3-2-1 was perfect. It fitted the show, it was a great r 'n b/pop single and Manfred, cleverly and cheekily, even name-checked his own band in the lyrics. This started the group on a run of great singles, all of which had reasonably solid r 'n b credentials, but were also commercial pop which were bought in their hundreds of thousands by teenage girls who didn't know their rhythm 'blues from their elbows. It was what Spencer Davis did, it was what The Yardbirds did – but Manfred did it as well as anyone, and for longer.

Tom McGuiness had replaced Dave Richmond, but in late '65 he switched over to play guitar as Jack joined up. Tom and Manfred saw Jack playing with The Bluesbreakers at The Flamingo Club and approached him straight after the show, asking him to join the band. Jack had no hesitation in saying that he would. He was on the point of getting married and the promised wages were a lot better than with John Mayall's band.

Seen in retrospect, the move doesn't fit with his progression through the serious blues and r 'n b ranks, and in reality it wasn't his sort of music. 'I wasn't a fan of their music', he says, 'but I thought it might be a laugh to be in a successful pop band.' He was particularly impressed that The Manfreds had expanded and now featured a two-man brass section; Henry Lowther on trumpet and Lynn Dobson on tenor sax. This wasn't what mainstream pop bands did, and it was indicative of an open mind and non-pop thinking. It helped too that the band had good r 'n b credentials, to counter the shame of Top Ten hits. Jack got on very well with both Henry and Lynn and greatly respected them as musicians. In his own mind he saw them and himself on one side of the fence, and the other band members on the other; the real musicians versus the rest. When they came to get paid, there was one rate for the members of the band, and other for the side-men, Jack, Henry and Lynn. He was in that band just for the money, but their presence allowed him to feel that he wasn't abandoning his musical credibility completely.

With his ears and eyes open though he learned a lot. Image and style hadn't really mattered in the bands he had been with up until then. He wasn't there for long but what he saw around him was instrumental in how he saw Cream evolving if they were going to see really worthwhile commercial success. Everyone was in search of the Holy Grail; selling millions and millions of records to spotty, impressionable kids, but still retaining the creative integrity and the respect of those musicians whose respect was worth having. Herman's Hermits sold huge numbers of records but they weren't gods to their peers in The Marquee.

Jack is defensive about his time with Manfred Mann, 'Music is my living and I haven't always been able to choose what I do. I didn't join out of choice, but out of necessity. It was a gig. Bach had to do things to pay for the family or to get married. The people in the band weren't as interesting as the people I'd be working with before. The guys I'd be working with before, apart from being superior musicians, were much more fun to hang out with. Crazier.' Jack describes Manfred Mann as a 'middle class band', which is a term of mild abuse in his vocabulary.

The GBO looked like cool hipsters, but that was recognised only by a very small number of the record-buying public. Manfred Mann spread cool across a much broader horizon, and for every single that The GBO had sold, the Manfreds sold a thousand.

His first gig with the band was in a dance hall in Stevenage in Hertfordshire – and at that point he hadn't even met the other members of the group, let alone rehearsed with them. He just busked through the whole thing. Thereafter he never listened to the records to hear how his predecessors had handled the bass parts. He just started again with his own bass parts; 'To be honest, it was very simple.' He also claims that he despaired of guitarist Tom McGuinness being able to play in tune – and used to tune his all-steel National guitar for him when he wasn't looking. Jack has bumped into Manfred Mann several times over the years, and when they met at a television studio in Germany recently, Manfred said that he had been a bit in awe of Jack, who he considered to be 'too good for the band.'

In May 1966 Pretty Flamingo went to number one in the UK, and was in the singles charts for three months. It was Manfred's second number one; Do Wah Diddy Diddy had gone to the top in the summer of '64. Jack had played on a Top Ten hit. Every week the band whose single was at number one played last on the BBC Top Of The Pops television show. Even then it was an institution, and it was a sort of certificate of success (in some cases very brief) – like being on The Ed Sullivan Show in the USA. For British pop musicians it was a rite of passage, and it meant that everyone who had been a school with you, known your mum, or once met a cousin of yours, now knew you were not just famous.

The British pop industry was still trying to crawl out from under the influence of the old-style Variety form of entertainment, and quite inappropriately the band was booked into a residency on the pier at Blackpool. It's a moot point whether or not the booking agents noticed that the audience was made up of teenagers rather than middle-aged holidaymakers. The band suffered from a scaled-down version of Beatlemania, with young girls screaming out their performances on stage and besieging their cars and hotel rooms.

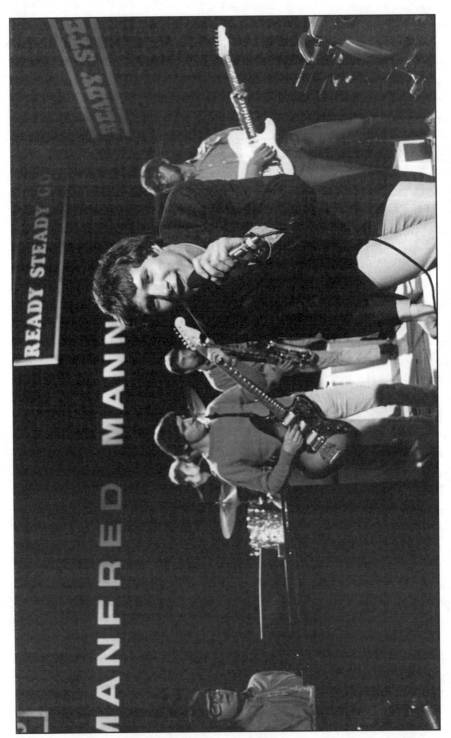

The gig that Jack is least proud of - playing with Manfred Mann in 1966 (3rd from left) (Redferns)

Jack also remembers a less successful gig at a very traditional working men's club in South Wales; 'Before we went on it was very quiet. We were wondering what was going on, and the moment we went on stage the whole place filled up. Then they started throwing pennies at us for some reason – and then a fight broke out. Then this huge fight seemed to be directed at us; they had decided they were going to kill the band. We had to run away.' Manfred says that he found Jack hiding in a cupboard in the dressing room, and had to drag him out before persuading him to jump through a window – with a long drop on the other side.

The band's travelling arrangements were somewhat better than John Mayall's in that they also had a car and a van, but the band got to travel in the car while the equipment went by van. It was often decided that there wasn't enough room in the car though, and Jack, as the newest member, would be relegated to the slower, colder, noisier van. This did mean that Jack was unhurt when the car crashed on its way back from a gig. The roadies stopped the van at a service area and Jack bought a paper – only to see that the fact that The Manfreds had been in a car crash was not just news, but was already there in print. The van was that much slower. They drove round to the hospital, and as he says, 'It was difficult not to gloat.'

Jack describes himself as 'very much a side-man' with the band, but he did undertake a lot of arranging for them in the short while has was a member. His classical education was invaluable, and he turned his abilities to creating a Manfred-style arrangement of The Rolling Stones' Satisfaction, and four instrumentals for the Extended Play record 'Instrumental Asylum.' It still rankles though that he only received £30. Something else that wasn't popular with Jack was the hip uniform they were required to wear, 'I couldn't stand the check flares, and the polo-necks were very itchy.'

Interviewed in Melody Maker, Manfred said, 'Jack is an invaluable asset. He plays wonderful bass guitar and has a ridiculous sense of time. Jack is the most forceful personality of the new guys. He's got a great wariness against being had, but he's most co-operative when he's willing.' It read like a schoolmaster's end of year report, but was a very accurate portrayal of the man. Manfred also let everyone know that he had stolen the ace bass player from John Mayall, which was a good bit of one-upmanship – suggesting that his band was a better prospect for a talented and ambitious young musician.

In July both Jack and Paul left though – Paul to begin his solo career and go back to a more authentic, though not boorishly purist, blues style. Jack and Janet were good friends with Paul and his wife, and they knew in advance that Paul intended to leave the line-up. Paul was replaced by Mike D'Abo, and the band had another half dozen Top Ten hits before morphing into Manfred Mann's Earth Band and seeing three more hits in the UK Top Ten. Jack remembers Manfred as a genuinely nice guy, who was very kind to him just as his career was really taking off. Jack was replaced on bass by Klaus Voorman, who says that even then he was a great admirer of Jack's work – though there was no feeling that he had to 'live up' to his playing. His first job was to set about making the bass lines simpler; he has some sympathy with the notion that Jack's playing is 'busy', but shrugs and says, 'But everyone is different.'

Chapter 9

Ginger Baker was undeniably the driving force in the creation of Cream, though this did lead to him believing it to be 'his band', which is a notion that soon went out of date. These two other guys were very much his equals, but he decided that when it came to making decisions, he was in charge. It was never going to be the sort of situation where there was a bandleader and a couple of sidemen. That was old thinking; jazz band thinking. This wasn't Chris Barber and his band, or Humphrey Lyttleton and his band – that wasn't how rock bands worked. The Beatles wasn't John Lennon or Paul McCartney's band, just as The Rolling Stones wasn't Mick Jagger's band (much though he might have wished it was). This was to be an endless source of friction. One of several.

It was Ginger though who came up with the idea of the band, and who pushed to make it happen. Working with Eric had been in his mind since the jam session at the '64 Richmond Festival, and that had moved up a gear or two when Ginger had seen Eric playing with The Bluesbreakers at Oxford in April '66, and had then sat in. He had the idea that it was time for a small, tight super-group, but he also wanted to work with Eric. Jack says, 'Ginger was very impressed by Eric's playing – we all were – he was streets ahead of anything else we had heard. Even in those early days Eric had an authority which was quite astounding.'

Eric agreed that it was a great idea as soon as Ginger suggested it to him, but immediately said that the bass player had to be Jack. He also said, quite specifically that Jack also had to be the singer. He didn't say that in any absolute sense; it wasn't 'Jack or no band', but it was obviously a very firmly held opinion. That wasn't what Ginger wanted to hear after the anger that surrounded Jack's departure from The Graham Bond Organisation.

Ginger decided that is was worth trying to heal the wounds though, which can't have been easy for him. Like Jack he was, and is, a very proud man, and very certain of himself when he believes himself to be in the right. He made contact and Jack agreed to a meeting. This was to take place in Jack's parents-in-law's home – a council-owned flat in Boundary Road in St John's Wood. Jack doesn't remember why there, but it's not hard to imagine that he wanted to keep Ginger at arm's length until he was certain of how things were shaping up.

Ginger made a good first impression. He arrived in a new Rover 2000, which was an impressive car in 1966 – a brand new model and a dynamic design inside and out; radically different from anything which the very staid manufacturer had produced previously. Any owner of a Rover 2000 was ultra modern; an avid reader of Colour Supplements. If Ginger was hoping to impress Jack, then he succeeded. Also, it wasn't a cheap car – it cost £1,300, almost the price of bank manager's Mk2 Jaguar – so he was obviously making good money. This meant that he wasn't coming begging. Whatever else, it wasn't going to be an embarrassing conversation. (In fact Ginger had bought the car out of the royalties he had earned from a B-side, which he had written.) Thanks to Ginger's exuberant driving style though the car was written-off just a few months later.

They took tea together, from his mother-in-law's best china cups, and Ginger explained his thinking for this still-unnamed band. Then he simply asked Jack to join. It was very hard for him to do. Jack says, 'I don't know how he managed to do that. I think he saw the possibilities of that three-piece line-up. It must have been so important to him.'

Jack wasn't surprised that Eric had wanted him in on bass, but was surprised and flattered that he also wanted him to sing. He certainly didn't think of himself as a singer; 'I used to sing a couple of songs in a set with Graham, but I only sang back-up vocals behind Paul with The Manfreds. The only big thing I'd sung was the harmony of Pretty Flamingo.' Eric must have seen the man's potential as a vocalist, as well as his obvious and more immediate talent as a bass player. Jack didn't have any objection to the plan; 'I just said 'Yeah, great."

There was one condition imposed on Ginger by Jack and Eric. They told him that if the band was going to go ahead, let alone be a really worthwhile project, he had to give up heroin. It wasn't an ultimatum that he liked, but he did so, there and then. There was a lot of dope around, Janet says, though they weren't 'obsessive' about it. Apart from uppers that was about it. Heroin wasn't good for the band; wasn't good for business – though both Eric and Jack would come to it in time.

The next step was for the three guys to go round to Ginger's home in Neasden, and start playing together. They set up the equipment in the house's tiny sitting room and simply began jamming. It worked immediately, and for all of them; 'It was great, right from the word go.'

Eric and Jack have always given Ginger credit for being the dynamo behind the formation of Cream, and it is something which he doesn't want people to forget. Writing

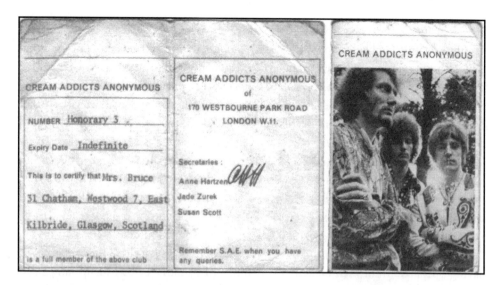

Jack's mother, Betty, was the third (and honorary) member of the Cream Addicts Anonymous fan club (CB)

in The Daily Telegraph in 2005, albeit about his passion for polo, he mentioned music very briefly, saying, 'I founded Cream. I'd like to be remembered for that, not just as 'Clapton's drummer' – it's very frustrating when people call me that.'

From suburban Neasden they progressed to Eric's flat in Ladbroke Square, just north of Holland Park Avenue in Notting Hill. In the middle of the square there's a communal garden to which the residents have access but the public do not, in fact it's the largest private square in London (and can be seen in the Hugh Grant and Julia Roberts film 'Notting Hill'). It was here, on a glorious spring day, that Jack, Eric and Ginger laid plans for the new band. None of the passers-by or sunbathers knew it – indeed they didn't themselves - but what they were planning was to become, within months, one of the most exciting and most important bands of all time.

One of the items on the agenda was whether or not Cream should be a quartet, and it was suggested that a keyboards player was needed to supplement lead guitar, bass and drums. There was one immediate choice – Steve Winwood. He was still only eighteen years old but had a strong reputation as an organist, singer, and - to a lesser degree – guitarist. He was in The Spencer Davis Group, which had seen a run of highly respected r 'n b-influences hit singles in recent months. In October '66, a few months after the formation of Cream, and with Gimme Some Lovin' in the charts, Steve and his brother Muff left to join Traffic. That band concentrated on albums rather than singles and these were well received by the cognoscenti.

Graham Bond was also considered, but his erratic behaviour in recent times unnerved them, and once Robert Stigwood was involved with Cream he took a very firm line against Graham being in the band. He was right; Jack, Eric and Ginger struggled with the rigours of Cream; Graham most certainly would never have survived it.

Jack was dead set against the idea of a keyboards player though. He wanted, he says, 'a powerhouse.' That meant a trio, though trios in pop and rock were very rare. There was The Big Three; a pre-Beatles rock 'n roll band that was known for its unruliness. They have been described as 'the loudest, the most aggressive and visually appealing act on the Liverpool circuit.' Despite being signed up by Brian Epstein, they didn't have any commercial success – their 1963 single By The Way only reached number twenty-two. They shared a bill with The Graham Bond Organisation at Klooks Kleek, and Jack held them in very high regard; 'They were good, really good.' He cites them as an influence in the thinking behind Cream, at least in his mind.

Jack describes The Who as 'a trio with a yodeller', but even there the dynamics of having a separate front man made it a very different band. Pete Townshend sang a certain amount - and John Entwhistle sang one, or at the most two, songs in a set – but if Pete had been responsible for all the vocal work it would have been a different beast (Jack's not backward when it comes to being rude about The Who; he describes Pete Townshend's playing as, 'All show and no substance. I can't stand Pete's stuff. It's all twee and twaddle. We all know there are three chords, and it's up to the rest of us to use them more effectively than he does.')

Pop bands, and the emerging groups who could be described as rock, were all four or five-piece outfits. The first hint that Cream was going to be radically different came with this one element; they were to be a trio. It was perceived wisdom that you needed four or five guys to create a band. Just about everyone fitted into that mould; the best-known quartet was The Beatles, followed by The Kinks, and any number of groups from The Fourmost to Plastic Penny. The biggest quintet was The Rolling Stones, as were thousands of other bands - such as The Hollies, Herman's Hermits, and everyone between The Animals and Dave Dee, Dozy, Beaky, Mick and Tich. Every band on the planet was primarily a quartet of lead guitar, rhythm guitar, bass and drums – with one guitarist who sang, or with a freestanding front man taking the numbers up to five. That was the formula.

Jack's thinking was that going out as a trio was the 'brave' option. If they're the very best musicians around then three is more than enough. In fact, anything more than that is too much. Also, he says, 'There's a magic in the number three. Musically you have classical Indian musicians who work as trios. And in jazz groups my favourite line-up was playing with just a drummer and a horn-player. The starkness, the bareness was great - and you had to cover a lot of areas to make the music interesting. You couldn't just plonk about. You had to be really listening, and working very hard.' He wasn't looking for an easy option.

Jack does think that Eric was never particularly happy with Cream being a trio, at least early on; 'Cream developed into two different bands - the studio band and the live band.' He says that the fact that they could over-dub, in the studio, even minimally – working originally with just four-track recording equipment – made a huge difference and moved them away from the purity of the three-man format.

In May '69, post-Cream, what might have been the four-man Cream was formed when Steve, Eric and Ginger recruited ex-Family bass player Ric Grech to found Blind Faith. They recorded one album, which went to number one – perhaps filling the vacuum left by Cream, and selling to Cream fans – both in the UK and the USA. It featured a remarkable and controversial sleeve showing a photo of a naked pre-pubescent girl holding a distinctly phallic model airplane. Many teenage fans had to hide it from their mums. Blind Faith collapsed later in the year, and after joining Ginger in Airforce, Steve returned to Traffic – which was by then was a trio. Their first move was to record the innovative, landmark album 'John Barleycorn Must Die.'

Jack says that he never gave any real thought to the style of band Cream were to become, or the sort of music they were going to be playing. There wasn't, he says, any sense in his mind that they were going to be a 'jazz-rock-blues' fusion band. It has been said that Eric thought they were starting a blues band, while Ginger though it was going to be much more a jazz outfit – and it would be reasonable to expect Jack's position to be nearer to Ginger's. Not so, he says. Eric described their music as 'sweet and sour rock 'n roll', but Jack's thinking, even before they had started rehearsing or playing their own material, was to have 'very light vocals with a very hard backing. I wanted the guitars and drums to be really working hard and the vocals to be hovering above them.' It was an ethos that was maintained through the band's life, and it's a hallmark of much of their music. There are many songs which are underpinned by very hefty powerful instrumental lines, contrasting with much lighter, often ethereal vocals. The instruments also often run far faster than the vocal part. The first Jack Bruce and Pete Brown composition, I Feel Free, set the tone, and this distinctive and stylish contrast can be heard again on songs such as Dance The Night Away, World Of Pain and – perhaps most effectively of all – on We're Going Wrong. Even on the jokey Pressed Rat And Warthog, Ginger speaks the lyrics slowly while a monstrous juggernaut shifts in and out of top gear behind him.

As he says of this technique, 'I think that's partly responsible for the band's success – particularly in the States. People hadn't heard anything like that. The band's famous for long improvisations, but what made the band was the songs and the fact that they had this tension between the music and the vocals. That's what made them interesting and commercial.'

What delighted him most was that this was an obvious chance to write new music.

This ambition had stayed with him since his teenage years, and above all else – above even playing an instrument – he wanted to compose: 'It was a great opportunity to write music for great musicians and have it heard by a larger audience.' Jack wasn't expecting the band to be selling albums by the million, and he certainly didn't expect them to be playing sell-out gigs at Madison Square Garden or The Royal Albert Hall. The formula seemed right though, and his artisan days in Manfred Mann aside, it looked as if this new band might be the biggest thing he had played with so far. Jack might not have had any sense that this band was going to be The Next Big Thing – the next Rolling Stones or whatever - but in the area of the music business in which he was comfortable, people simply didn't think like that in those days. A pop manager might put together a group with nothing but commercial success in mind – investing in the musicians just any businessman would in any new project. Musicians who had come out of a straightforward love of the music, be it a passion for the blues or rock 'n roll or whatever, merely wanted to get in front of an appreciative audience as often as possible, and hopefully get their work onto vinyl.

'Everyone talks about the Sixties as some kind of amazing time, and there were amazing things going on, but there was dross just as there is now', Jack says, 'There were manufactured pop bands in the Sixties: There were terrible bands and a few really good things. The difference between then and now is that then it was a small business and now it's a huge business.'

Jack credits Eric with coming up with the band's name almost before the question is asked. Jack isn't sure, but he thinks that Eric suggested it during that first jam session at Ginger Baker's home; 'We weren't blasé about it, we were very excited about it, and Eric said something like 'It sounds like the cream.' They didn't discuss any other possible names, the decision was immediate, and was 'organic.'

This could sound like insufferable arrogance, but Jack insists that there was a difference – and the difference was defined by the absence of the definite article. It wasn't 'The Cream.' It was simply 'Cream.' And that made a very subtle difference, though for a long time promoters, used to bands having the definite article in front of their names, couldn't cope without it. It was certainly a good indication of the three men's estimation of their own talents – none of them were lacking in musical self-confidence – but it wasn't them setting out their stall for the world by saying 'We are the greatest band that has ever been.' Jack describes himself as 'naïve', which many would doubt, but all three of them were too bright to make a mistake like that. The way it fell, without the 'the' was perfect; 'it didn't do us any harm', as Jack admits.

The band then rented rehearsal space in a school in Kensal Rise in north London, where they played for the amusement of an elderly caretaker and a troupe of Girl Guides. Rock journalist Chris Welch was invited to hear them, and in his book 'Cream' he recalls the Brownies (the junior arm of the Girl Guides) listening in, and a group of young girls hanging around outside, thrilled by the presence of real live pop stars. Chris was greatly impressed by the music, even at that early stage, on their third day of rehearsals. He also realised that this band was going to be ferociously loud. Despite having his ears torn off during one of the first ever renditions of NSU, Eric told him that they only had a sixth of their amplification in place. He also said, 'Most people have formed the impression of us as three solo musicians clashing with each other. We want to cancel that idea and be a group that plays together.' Yes and no, as it turned out.

Janet Bruce knew right from those rehearsals that the new band was going to be huge. 'From the moment they played it was magic. The chemistry was there. It worked', she says. Janet goes on to say that there was a lot of excitement around, but it was all for the music itself. The thought that they were going to be creating new music was what fired their enthusiasm. There was no thought about the commercial possibilities of what would soon be christened Cream,. 'It was all for the sheer joy of what they were doing. There was a sense that this was rather special, rather powerful.'

There was a small news item in The Melody Maker dated June 11, no more than a dozen lines, unofficially announcing the new band, but in the issue of Melody Maker dated July 30, Chris Welch let the cat out of the bag in no uncertain manner. His piece began, 'A thunder of blues in a church hall complete with Brownies and caretakers was the bizarre setting for the first tentative creations of The Cream – Britain's most exciting new group, featuring star instrumentalists Jack Bruce, Ginger Baker and Eric Clapton.'

There were hints that that the three members were looking at the new band from slightly different musical angles. Eric was quoted as saying that 'jazz is definitely out.' He went on to say that what he wanted to play was 'anything that people haven't heard before.' He also predicted that Pete Townshend would be writing for the band, which is hilarious in retrospect – especially given Jack's antipathy towards him. Jack pointed out that there was a lot of original material of his that he wanted the band to try out. He added that although they had only been rehearsing for a few days, they were 'fifty percent ready' to go in front of the public. Mind you, they seem to have been pulling Chris's leg mercilessly; they assured him that they were going to be playing with a live turkey on stage, as a Dadaist statement. No known fowl would in fact ever have survived the volume.

The band's first gig was at The Twisted Wheel club in Manchester on Friday July 29 1966. The date had booked to Joe Tex and His American Showband, but he had cancelled and Stigwood – by then in place as the band's manager - had decided on a fairly low-profile shakedown gig for the new band. There was no local publicity for Cream, so the audience had no idea what to expect. Originally an unlicensed coffee bar, The Twisted Wheel had moved to larger premises in the city centre and become an unparalleled venue for live rhythm 'n blues. It wasn't a big place but it attracted its audience from all over the North-West, the Midlands and East Yorkshire. They weren't like the folk in the equivalent London clubs though; they were Mods, with no interest in artiness and jazz. The club booked the biggest American r 'n b names, who otherwise struggled to get good gigs in the UK. It was the birthplace of what eventually became Northern Soul, and was also the best place to buy a pair of Lambretta side-panels – freshly liberated from someone else's scooter.

Robert Stigwood had organised a large American Ford Galaxie estate car to get them and the gear to Manchester, but it broke down on the way – which wasn't a good start. He had also employed an old friend of Eric's, Ben Palmer, to be their roadie, and as it turned out, mediator and all-round calming influence. No-one had told him what duties he was supposed to fulfil as the roadie, and having driven the band to the gig he went for a pint – leaving them to set up their own gear, until very firmly told otherwise.

Jack had played the Twisted Wheel almost on a monthly basis with Graham Bond, so it was familiar territory. It was part of their circuit. It wasn't, he says, 'a posh place', and for Cream's unannounced, first ever performance, it was only half full.

Had it not been for the date at The Twisted Wheel the band would have been launched from cold at the high-profile Windsor Festival on Sunday July 31. The warm-up gig was definitely a help. They mostly played blues standards, and also tried out a set of less well-known known blues, almost all of which had been suggested by Eric. They were songs he had heard, mostly only on record, over the years and had been longing to try. Most blues bands played things like I Got My Mojo Working, and the audiences had heard them time and time again. Whatever happened, Cream was going to be different. As they had announced, they were going to play the unexpected. Several of the songs they tried out at The Twisted Wheel were Robert Johnson compositions, which Jack found 'pretty obscure.' The band also played the first song Jack had written for Cream, NSU.

Melody Maker came back to 'the Cream' (still with the definite article but now with a lower case 't') after that first big gig, which took place just two days after they played in Manchester. Reporting on the previous weekend's Windsor Festival the paper noted that although the whole event had been cursed by terrible weather, Cream's performance was one of the highlights of the festival. They had shared the extensive bill with big names such as Geno Washington's Ram Jam Band, The Stan Tracey Big Band, The Who, The Move, Jimmy James and The Vagabonds, Chris Barber, and Georgie Fame and The Blue Flames – something for everyone in fact.

Cream played on the Sunday, and as the paper reported, 'They kicked off with

Spoonful and Sleepy Time and Jack Bruce's harmonica and vocal feature Train Time (sic). Eric's incredible guitar playing induced the audience to shout and scream for more, even while he was playing more! And Ginger's solo using two bass drums said everything. Called The Toad (sic), it sent the crowd potty.'

It might be thought that the band came as a surprise to this new audience, but though they can't have been certain which direction Cream was going to take, Jack believes that they gave them what they were expecting. It was a jazz and blues festival, with the latter having grown in relation to the former over recent years, and apart from NSU the band played a solid blues set.

In the bar afterwards Jack and Robert Stigwood had a drink with Chris Welch, who had delighted in their performance, and Jack thanked him for being so kind about them in print. Stigwood, he recalls, kicked him hard on the shins for being so uncool.

The band played Klooks Kleek, close to Jack's home, on the Tuesday following their appearance at the Windsor Festival, and through the rest of the August they played a handful of gigs. These were all in and around London, apart from a surprising booking at The Town Hill in the smart seaside resort of Torquay in Devon. Towards the end of the month they went into the recording studio for the first time, and began the sessions that would lead to the release of 'Fresh Cream' at the end of the year. In the meantime they were still gigging, playing the sort of venues Jack had played with The Graham Bond Organisation. Some were ballrooms and civic halls, but as many again were still the small clubs that made up the London circuit – be they part of the accepted jazz/blues circuit, such as The Marquee, The Flamingo or The Ricky Tick in Hounslow – or, even, incredibly, the village hall in Hoveton in Norfolk. And that must be that hamlet's only claim to rock fame.

Right from the start they were a phenomenal live band. Cream was about musical virtuosity and massive levels of attack. Bob Brunning, who saw them live several times in London clubs, says, 'It was just the sheer ensemble power of their playing. I'd never seen a band that shoved so much into their performances. Other bands, no matter how good they were, tended to coast occasionally, or catch their breath with a couple of more laid-back tunes.

'Cream was like a power station. You turned the power on and they just went. They were fiery young killers with the most amazing energy levels.' To some degree this full-on force frightened the British, but it was a large factor in their success in the States.'

Bob adds, 'What they were saying, was that you could play anything so long as you were very good at it. They weren't a soul band, they weren't a blues band, they weren't a rock 'n roll band – but they could be all of those things in one evening. The message is don't close your ears to the possibilities.'

In October the band released its first single, Wrapping Paper, with the vastly more interesting Cat's Squirrel on the B-side. Wrapping Paper was a great surprise, and indeed a big disappointment. It wasn't even a good pop song, and it certainly wasn't rock, and it wasn't Cream. It sounded like something that The Temperance Seven might have recorded. The New Vaudeville Band was enjoying a hit with the breezy, 1920s-style Winchester Cathedral when Wrapping Paper came out, and anyone would have been forgiven for thinking they were related.

It was the first song that Jack and Pete Brown wrote together, and Jack says that they issued it 'because there was nothing else that could have been a single.' He makes the point that, like Sunshine Of Your Love, Wrapping Paper is at heart a blues-based song, 'But I was trying to be too clever.' Pete adds that although it was a blues-based piece of music, he wanted to tell a story – 'weird Hollywood dream images' - rather than write a simple blues lyrics. His verdict on the song is that 'it turned out peculiar. It didn't really work but it was a surprise.' Melody Maker called it 'weird', and another review said 'the musical content is nil.'

They played their first session for BBC radio in late October, and made their first television appearance on November 1, on Ready Steady Go, of course. Anyone watching them perform the song on RSG would have been thoroughly confused about this new supergroup's musical intentions. Manfred Mann watched the band perform from the side of the RSG set and shook his head. Cat's Squirrel – almost an instrumental – was much better; a fast blues featuring some excellent harmonic playing by Jack. It should have had rather more vocals and been the A-side. Cream weren't about singles though, they were an albums band, but they didn't know it yet. Wrapping Paper peaked at number thirty-four.

In 1966 what mattered to a band was how their 45s fared in The Hit Parade. More than anything else, their placing defined a band's success. That's what got them headlines and made them money. Everything else followed on from that. If you had a Top Ten hit, let alone a number one, you could cobble an album together off the back of it and sell that, and the kids would pay to see you play live. Yet again it was The Beatles and The Rolling Stones who were turning everything on its head, but Cream came in very close behind them. Just two years later, when Led Zeppelin formed, they could eschew singles completely. Albums were what mattered now, and what made the real money.

Cream recorded their first album through the autumn and it was released in December. Seen retrospectively 'Fresh Cream' wasn't their strongest album, and in some ways it seemed that they hadn't quite found their feet.

It was recorded very quickly, as things were in those pre-Sergeant Pepper days, but Jack says that wasn't necessarily a problem. In his opinion all Cream's albums were cut too rapidly and that was certainly frustrating - but it did give them an immediacy, and

*Jack playing with Cream in Sweden, on the band's first
visit to Scandinavia in November 1966.
He hadn't quite got into his sartorial stride. (MK)*

certainly the lack of post-production let the fans know exactly what the band were about. In the Seventies, especially as more advanced recording techniques were introduced, the process itself could easily get in the way of the music and became a hurdle, albeit of their own making, which the musicians had to get over. Pete Brown makes the point that there was another advantage to the speed at which they were required, and that is that it simply didn't allow them any time to disagree – let alone fight. A band can't afford to develop the notorious 'musical differences' if they're looking at the clock every couple of minutes.

Of all the band's albums it's 'Fresh Cream' which Jack wishes the band could have spent more time on, though he says that it did put down a strong marker in terms of both what the band was capable of, and what he personally was trying to move towards. Running through the track listing makes Jack smile. The band's greatest moments were still ahead of them – there wasn't going to be the traditional problem of the 'difficult second album' – and this was undoubtedly a record to be proud of. It went to number six in the British album charts and number thirty-nine in the USA.

Wrapping Paper didn't make it onto 'Fresh Cream', but there were four songs with Jack's writing credit on the album. As well as I Feel Free, which opening the record for the American market at least (it wasn't included on the British release) and NSU, which followed it, there was Sleepy Time Time and Dreaming – all four running as a block at the start of side one.

Sleepy Time Time is a very sophisticated piece of music, mixing a jazz rhythm with a blues lead guitar. It summed up what the band was about and how the trio differed in their influences – and yet could bring them together in a previously unattempted fusion. These four tracks made up about a fifth of the running time of the album, but they hung together as a single entity, and they laid a pathway for the listener – which led on to five pieces of solid blues, all introduced to the other two by Eric. These new interpretations of authentic blues tracks would have been less accessible without that route in. The Bruce tracks, with and without collaboration, were what opened the door and invited the listeners in.

Jack describes Dreaming as an attempt to write a mainstream pop song, and he adds, 'It didn't quite come off - but it was a brave attempt.' It's less than two minutes long, which is short even for a pop single, but it works well as an album track. It's too accomplished to ever have been a pop single, with its interwoven lyrics and fascinating, complex drumming. This was music of quality, and quality often sat uneasily in the Top Ten, as it always had and always will.

Chapter 10

Before the formation of Cream, Jack had only rarely played harmonica or sung. There was no particular reason for the former, except that the harmonica was never a jazz instrument, and so far as r 'n b was concerned, Jack has been quoted as saying, 'I never dared pick up a harp [harmonica] until Cyril Davies died.'

The reason for the latter was a snooty feeling in the jazz world that a singer wasn't really a musician. He or she was either just a pretty girl to get the audience interested, or a disposable front man. And the bass player certainly didn't sing. In pop – and what become rock – it was very different though. The singer is hugely important to the group, be he or she a front man out on their own (like Mick Jagger), or an instrumentalist who also sang (like both John Lennon and Paul McCartney).

'It wasn't my choice to be the singer in the band', he says, 'Eric had heard me singing my couple of things with Graham Bond and he just thought that I should be the singer. I was very nervous about it.

'I hadn't thought of myself as a singer and I still hadn't found the range of my voice. I thought I had a really low voice – I didn't know that I had this other range. I think I became the singer by default.'

It's relatively rare for a bass player to be the lead singer in a band; if there isn't a front man then usually it is the guitarist who sings. Having said that, Sting, Phil Lynott, Flea from the Red Hot Chilli Peppers, Lemmy of Motorhead, reggae musician Lloyd Parks and Suzi Quatro all play or played bass and also sing lead vocals. Paul McCartney shared vocals with John Lennon of course. Singing and playing the bass at the same time has been compared to 'trying to pat your head and rub your stomach at the same time', because it's usually the lead guitarist who plays the melody line, and the bass player is putting out a rhythm line. Therefore the bass player would be playing one thing and singing another.

Mo Foster, who has played bass for a huge range of people – from Cliff Richard to

Jeff Beck and from Gil Evans to Phil Collins, says that he is simply in awe of people who can sing and play bass at the same time; 'I think that Jack, McCartney and Sting are just geniuses. Jack goes all over the bar line with his voice, but his bass is immaculate. Always in the right place.'

Bob Brunning agrees, 'I think that someone like Jack must be able to separate two halves of the brain, with one half singing and the other half playing bass. I've always been impressed by Jack doing that.'

David Hadley Ray, who plays bass for Pete Brown's band, agrees that somehow or other Jack manages to separate two halves of his brain to both sing melody and play rhythm, and he attributes his ability to having learned to master the piano. If he can cope with playing melody with the right hand and rhythm with the left, it's so much easier to go on to sing and play bass. David adds, 'I think that if Jack had had Jaco Pastorius's technique that would have been detrimental, because if you're going to sing as well, you can disconnect.' David used to do both, but says that both disciplines suffered as a result, and the only thing to do was to stop trying to sing and concentrate on playing bass.

Musing on the thought, Suzi Quatro says, 'It's not easy for a normal person to play bass and sing lead; they are totally contradictory. You need to be able to separate out different parts of your body. When I play, my hands go onto automatic pilot so that I can sing.

'It definitely helps being classically trained. I trained both as a classical pianist and percussionist, so I became used to two hands and two feet doing different things.' Much like Dick Heckstall-Smith being able to play two different melodies on two saxophones, or a sax and a clarinet, simultaneously; simply beyond belief for mere mortals. Pete Brown's opinion is that it needs a precise, indeed mathematical skill to do it successfully, and that if Jack hadn't led the way, it's possible that no one would ever have done it.

Jack has admitted he had considerable difficulty singing is Born Under A Bad Sign. He makes the point that the rhythm of the bass riff crosses the rhythm that he sings. The same thing occurs on Politician, but of course that presents less of a problem because Jack has written both lines, and written them to suit his playing and singing. He's never been happy with the recorded version, and has only been able to sing it to his satisfaction in recent years.

It soon became time for Jack to add another bass guitar to his surprisingly modest collection, and he decided on a cherry red, double cutaway Gibson EB3. Once again he could play this instrument like a lead guitar. It too has a short, thirty-inch scale and Jack could bend the strings, and he used lighter La Bella strings to make this easier still; 'Eric would be bending strings and I'd be bending strings. I wanted to play a bass guitar but I wanted the emphasis on guitar rather than a bass which just happens to be a guitar.' Also, he says, ever the thrifty Scot, 'it was cheap.' In fact he paid £40 for it.

Gibson were best known for their traditionally-styled semi-acoustic instruments, though it was a highly innovative company – having produced an electric double bass back in the Twenties, and in 1958 introduced the stunning Flying V. The solid-bodied EB series of bass guitars was introduced in 1961. They were distinctively wide-waisted, with short, sharp-ended horns. Many bass men found them difficult to play on account of their broad and rounded neck. It's very versatile though as far as its sound is concerned; 'You can make it sound like Duane Eddy or the deepest double bass', Bob Brunning points out. 'It says something for his skill, because they're not easy to play.' It's not quite true to say that only someone who had trained on an acoustic bass would instantly be at home with the EB3, but it's certainly a great help in feeling comfortable with the instrument. In 1969 and 1970, as a direct result of Jack's use of the instrument, Gibson's sales of the EB3 tripled.

In their 1965-66 catalogue Gibson described it as 'The ultimate in an ultra thin, hand contoured solid body Gibson Electric Bass. The delicately balanced design automatically adjusts into a natural, comfortable playing position with or without a strap.' The blurb boasted that the instrument featured a 'new extra thin, custom contoured, double cutaway body design, with chrome-plated metal parts, and a new, extra slim, fast, low-action neck which joins the body at 17th fret.' The guitar had a one-piece, adjustable neck, made of mahogany, and an adjustable truss rod. The fingerboard was made of rosewood, with pearl dot inlays. The sound was collected by 'two Humbucking pickups for greater tonal range.' Jack's EB3, serial number 333147, had an extra 'baritone' switch setting for the neck pickup. During the 1968 Farewell tour, Jack replaced three of the four volume and tone knobs with white Fender knobs. These were switched back to the regular Gibson knobs later.

The red EB3, which Jack played for many years, and can be seen in the 1968 Royal Albert Hall concerts, was stolen in the late Seventies. However a fan brought it to him before a gig in New York in 1984, and Jack immediately gave him another of his basses in exchange. He used it for a couple of songs that night, but then put it aside, saying that it felt too short by then and he had lost his sense of affinity with it. His drummer, Bruce Gary, asked if he could 'baby sit' the instrument, and Jack agreed. A little later he offered to swap it for Bruce's Chapman stick (a curious stringed and fretted instrument with a wide fretboard and no body, designed by Emmett Chapman at the end of the Sixties). Although the Stick had cost him £2,000, Bruce agreed to the exchange, and only sold the EB3 many years later when he received an irresistible offer from a specialist collector. It was said to have been auctioned on eBay some time ago but didn't meet its reserve despite going up to $28,600.

Jack also owns a 1960s Thunderbird IV, original examples of which are now also very rare. Made by Gibson from 1963, it has a prominent lower horn with an elegant Thunderbird logo on the scratch-plate. For years he has used SIT strings – the acronym standing for 'Stay In Tune', which he says, 'actually work.'

For a while he used a Danelectro Longhorn, which bass expert Dan Armstrong 'doctored' for him. As Jack told an interviewer from Vintage Guitar magazine, 'Dan had a place just opposite Manny's Music Store on 42nd Street in New York City, and we would take our guitars to get them souped up. There was a Danelectro in his shop that he'd been working on, and I bought it. It was useful for some things, but I didn't use it much. I did use it on some tracks. It had a very interesting sound, more like a piano, and it was quite twangy.'

The most satisfying bass to play though is a fretless instrument, which has none of the parallel divisions running across the fingerboard, guiding the left hand. Cliff Barton of The Savages (which became Cyril Davies's backing band, renamed The Cyril Davies Rhythm 'N Blues All-Stars) was the first musician Jack saw playing fretless bass, and he recalls that he didn't see another for a long time.

With a fretless bass guitar you can, Jack says, 'Pitch your own notes. That is very important on a bass. Intonation and pitch is what gives character to the playing. For instance, the appeal of Miles Davis, the wonderful Miles Davis, comes from his intonation – and basically he just plays a little bit flat all the time. It really draws you in.' He goes on to make the point that if you are singing as well, it's a great help to be able to adjust the intonation very slightly to suit the vocals. Needless to say, playing fretless bass is far from easy, and only a very good and highly intuitive player can make a success of the instrument. Mo Foster is renowned as one of the most accomplished fretless bass players. He says that it took him twenty years to master it though; 'It's so different to an ordinary bass. It has a 'rise' and it seems to sort of growl a bit.'

Jack's all-time favourite bass guitar is his fretless Warwick. It's a 'real' instrument, he says; a fretted guitar is a 'non-instrument.' It follows on more naturally in terms of musical progression from his early training with the cello and his years playing double bass; 'I can play a fretless bass completely in tune because I had that early training. It's difficult for a lot of people to pitch their playing, but for me it's natural.'

He has one fretless Warwick, which is more than twenty years old, and which suits him better than any other bass guitar he has ever played. This makes it a very early model as the company was only founded in 1982. 'They keep making them for me and I say 'thanks' and then I go back to the old one.' Nowadays, playing his own material with his own bands, he always uses the fretless Warwick. Otherwise he finds that, 'the frets get in the way now. They're a hindrance.' He switched to the Warwick halfway through the reunion concerts, to play Stormy Monday, and stayed with it for the rest

During the Cream years Jack bought his father an electric
ukulele. It's not known if Charlie ever mastered it (CB)

of the gig, playing music on the fretless which was previously always played on a fretted bass.

The first fretless he bought was a Dan Armstrong Plexiglas bass. These had trans-
parent bodies and looked astonishing on stage; the instrument would catch the light
but it looked as if there was nothing there apart from a fingerboard and headstock. It
was said that the Plexiglas 'eliminates unwanted vibrations and frequencies while producing tremendous sustain.' They were designed by Dan Armstrong and made by
Ampeg, or rather The Ampeg Bassamp Company, which was founded by acoustic bass
player Everette Hull in the late Forties. The fretted version of the model was re-intro-
duced in the late Nineties and even then cost £1,500. In July 2005 a dealer was offering a fretted Plexiglass bass for sale, apparently signed by Jack, for £900.

There are, Jack says, two original fretless Plexiglas basses in the world; Jack still has
his and Paul McCartney has the other. 'It might be worth a few bob to somebody', Jack
adds, grinning, 'But I'd never sell it.'

On reflection Jack doesn't understand why he didn't start playing fretless instruments earlier, and wishes he had. One of the very first to do so, and who then played fretless bass to devastating effect, was Jaco Pastorius. It's a rare bass player who doesn't mention Jaco as an influence and an inspiration. He is best known for his work with Blood, Sweat and Tears and Weather Report. Less than modestly he dubbed himself 'The World's Greatest Bass Player.' Peter Erskine, who played with him in Weather Report, has written, 'The fact that Jaco started off as a drummer when he was young, and was an avid and astute listener, gave him an understanding of the beat that few bass players will ever match. His innate and studied sense of time, as well as his rhythmic execution, was the clearest and best articulated imaginable.'

Sadly, Jaco, whose real name was the rather more prosaic John Francis, was also a manic depressive who refused medication and lived the last years of his life in a state of utter destitution. He tried to re-enter a nightclub in his hometown of Fort Lauderdale in Texas, from which he had been banned, and then started a row with a doorman - who promptly beat him into a coma. He never came round and was pronounced dead ten days later, aged forty-six.

Fretless basses weren't readily available in the early Sixties though, and Jaco did what many others would do later and take the strings off the instruments and then laboriously pluck off all of the frets, one by one. That left slight depressions behind though, which wasn't satisfactory, so the only option was to fill these in with the epoxy wood filler - and then sand them down until the neck was absolutely smooth. If Jack had been able to get his hands on a fretless when he first went electric he would almost certainly have picked one instead of a fretted bass – and everything he ever did with Cream and in the earlier years of his solo career would have sounded different.

When Mo Foster first tried to emulate Jaco and found that he couldn't simply walk into a music shop and buy a fretless bass, he got in touch with the bass-maker Neville Whitehead and commissioned him to make one. He took the ebony neck of an upright acoustic bass and shaved it down to the shape of a bass guitar. Given the density of ebony that must have been a long job; he certainly went through three plane blades, Mo says, and a lot of perspiration. That was then fitted onto Mo's existing Jazz bass. At that point he says he had a lovely bass guitar, and 'not a clue how to play it. At first the pitching was awful.' He then had to comprise and have lines drawn across the neck to give him some sort of guidance; 'I love it now though. I've kept it and used it on most of the stuff I've done. It's melodic, it can swoop, it's bluesy. It's my voice.'

David Hadley Ray was already an experienced electric bass player, and when he decided that he wanted to move on to fretless bass, he went to college and learned how to play an acoustic bass before then going on and playing fretless bass guitar. Once he had moved on to fretless he played it every day, hour in, hour out, for three weeks before playing it for a paying session. Describing what it is like to play, he says, 'You can never really relax. You're aware that if your intonation is wrong then everything is thrown off. You don't have the same level of comfort – you don't have the margin of error that you have with a fretted.' He found that it was certainly worth persevering with: It is, he says, just so much more expressive, and much more fun.

The instrument does have its limitations though; playing with Ringo Starr's band he found that songs like I Get By With A Little Help From My Friends simply doesn't work on the fretless; 'You can play the notes but that really nice McCartney bass part only sounds good on an old bass, so I use my Gibson EB1. It was the first bass guitar they made, back in the Fifties, and it has that old sound that works well for those tunes.'

The EB1 was made to appeal to acoustic bass players, which was a tall order in the Fifties. To help out, and hedge their bets, Gibson supplied a chrome-plated peg, which could be screwed into the bottom of the guitar, where the rear strap button would normally be, so that the guitar could be played vertically, like a double bass. It's likely that very few players did that.

Only around 550 of the violin-shaped EB1s were made, at a rate of about fifty a year. A good one, even without star provenance, can easily go for £10,000. Jack's model, which he used for the first half of the reunion shows, would be worth considerably more.

Between the EB1 and the Warwick he reckons that he's got just about everything he needs. Warwick has brought out a limited edition bass to honour the Cream reunion.

Many bass players use effects, and Jack went through a period in the Seventies when he tried several. Nowadays he has no time for anything that intrudes into the true sound of the instrument; 'Effects might be right at the time, but I find that they date things very quickly.'

In the Sixties there were very few effects on offer. Just about the first Jack encountered was the Watkins Copy Cat, which used a loop of quarter-inch recording tape to produce artificial echo. As the tape went round it recorded the sound, and moments later played it back – using ordinary tape recording heads for both actions. This gave a basic echo effect, and slowing down or speeding up the motor driving the spools could vary the effect. The tape was then erased and round it went once more. The inherent problems were that the tape stretched or broke, and the sound quality rapidly deteriorated as the tape loop was over-used. It was the sort of toy that you would play with a few times and then discard.

That effect was followed by delay, reverb, and the fuzz box (as used by Eric on I Feel Free), but then came the wah-wah pedal, and that made a much greater impact.

Eric and Jimi Hendrix were the two great exponents of wah-wah, and Jack has a high opinion of the effect – so long as it used with skill. The wah-wah effect was first used on country 'n western records at the end of the Fifties, but this was achieved by the guitarist working the tone knob. Some guitarists did the same thing with the volume pedal on Fenders, which was particularly popular for use with steel guitars. The first commercial units were made by Vox and appeared in '66; then Dunlop brought out their Cry Baby model. Jack tried it and at times he and Eric would both be putting their sound through Vox wah-wahs. Nowadays he is dismissive of the notion of wah-wah on a bass.

The other element within Cream's sound was their choice of amplification. When Jack had been playing with Alexis Korner, everything had gone through just one 50-watt amp. That wasn't going to be anything like enough for Cream.

Both Jack and Eric used 100-watt Marshall amplifiers with a 200-watt PA system, all fed through two sets of speakers, each fitted with four 12-inch speakers. These amps were highly thought of, and gave a clean, solid and unfussy sound – but did distort the sound. In theory distortion should be a bad thing, every musician's enemy, but some distortion can be good – especially if it gives the right overall sound. As Mo says, 'The sound of those guitars going through Marshalls was novel. No one had ever heard that before. Amplifiers hadn't been in pain before. Jack's bass was massively over-driven. It wasn't a clear sound at all. Marshalls distort very easily – but pleasantly. The EB3 is a very high output bass, much higher than a Fender, so the overdrive was much greater on the input stage.' Which means that there was a lot more going into the amps from an EB3 than there would have been from any other bass guitar – let alone a lot more coming out.

'The set-up allowed Jack to arrive at his incredible fart sound', Mo adds, 'It was like blowing a great big raspberry all the time. I loved it.'

Of course in the Sixties there was always the temptation to turn up the volume on your own amplification – one which was hard to resist as a band like Cream resorted to audio warfare. Nowadays there's a sound engineer at a £50,000 mixing desk thirty rows back, and he controls the volume, not the guitarist or bass player.

Marshall had only started making amps in 1962, and they were very keen to hear the opinions of professionals who used their equipment. They weren't slow to associate themselves with rock stars either, and were happy to provide custom-made units. The factory provided Jack with a 200-watt amp, which was used in all but the smallest venues, and which fed through twin speaker stacks. There were now two slight figures on stage, bookended by these towers; both of whom had massive power at their fingertips.

'We were very much influenced by The Who in terms of using Marshall stacks', Jack admits, 'Being a trio we wanted a lot of sound.' There was rivalry between Cream and The Who, who also used Marshall amps. In search of ever more power, Pete Townshend had asked Marshall to make him the first 100-watt amp. Jack was never heavily into the technology but his move to 200-watts came suspiciously soon after The Who's bass player, John Entwhistle, had commissioned the Marshall factory to make him the first ever 200-watt amp. Speaker cabinets designed for bass guitar were larger, to allow the cabinet to develop the volume. Marshall bass amps were also available with 15-inch speakers, and bass speakers had much stiffer cones. The extra power did lead to distortion, but that was acceptable in the search for massive impact.

When Cream undertook their two US tours early in '67 Robert Stigwood didn't want to pay for the cost of shipping this huge rig over – it would of course have had to go by air – and they used far less powerful Vox and Fender equipment. When they went back a third time they took everything; Jack had two 200-watt amps and a 200-watt PA system. The Americans were used to volume, but when everything was cranked right up even they didn't know what had hit them.

Before the 2005 reunion concerts Jack mused about using Marshall stacks, but in the event he used two identical Hartke set-ups, one for his Gibson and the other for the Warwick. Jack's guitar technician, Baron Troy, made sure that he had back-ups for everything, including a spare fretted Warwick as well as a spare fretless

Talking about Jack's style of playing, Mo Foster makes the point that he doesn't really use 'true' vibrato; 'That's left to right, rotating the hand, like a cellist would. When I was playing a session with an orchestra I used to quiz the cellists to see how they did it. He does it as a guitarist would, by pushing the string – or slide up and down.'

As Mo adds, 'There's only one trick in playing bass. If something's going wrong you have to glare at the guitar player as if it's his fault.'

He doesn't agree with the thought that Jack might be a frustrated guitarist; 'He plays roots and first diversions and plays harmony. He is a bass player, very firmly. He plays fast runs, which I'd say are Motown-inspired – but there's also Bach in there as well.' If he was asked to nominate his top bass players of all time there is no doubt, he says, that Jack would be included; 'There'd be Jack and there would also be McCartney, Jaco, Stanley Clarke, Carol Kaye and then the double bass players, Ray Brown and Ron Carter.'

Almost above all else though, Mo adds, it was energy and drive that made Jack a great bass player; 'He doesn't race though. His timing is always impeccable. He plays fast little connecting lines and off-the-wall harmonies.' It's certainly very true to say that in every performance he has ever played, Jack has simply given everything he has.'

Philadelphia-born David Hadley Ray has played with Pete Brown's band for many years, and as Pete usually includes a couple of his and Jack's Cream songs in his set, David has been required to recreate the work of one of his heroes. He first came across Jack's playing as a teenager; he heard White Room and loved it but was only able to get it on a K-Tel compilation, where it was sandwich between bands like 1910 Fruit Gum Company and The Monkees. He doesn't find playing Jack's bass lines too daunting though, except on the odd occasions when has been Jack is in the audience, staring at him and watching his every move. David says, 'It's all blues-based, and if you have any kind of blues background it's easy to figure that out, though they changed it up a bit! Jack has theoretical knowledge from his piano studies, and that's the mother of all music theory.' His mission has always been to take what works and make it a touch funkier. 'Technically, anyone can get through it, but the important thing is to get the right attitude into it.' The important thing, he says, is not to over-play …

David played with Pete Brown And The Interoceters at The Rockinbeerfest in Huntingdon in August 2005, where Ray Minhinnett's Cream'd were also on the bill. Cream tribute bands are rare, and Cream'd are probably the best known. Their bass player is Ian Ellis of Savoy Brown. Whereas Pete's band play funkier, extended version of Cream songs – with keyboards, percussion augmenting drums, and two backing singers – Cream's play it straight, and as a trio. The problem though is no matter how accurate they might be in reproducing the music, no other band can include Jack's singing, and capture what that brought to the originals.

As early as 1966 Jack was voted Best Instrumentalist of the year by the readers of Beat Instrumental magazine. Bass players didn't often get recognition of that kind.

Interestingly, Suzi Quatro loves Jack's singing but is less sure about his bass playing. She tends towards Ginger's opinion of more than forty years ago that his playing is 'too busy.' 'I don't overplay', she says. 'That's a big sin in my book. The bass should hold the whole thing together. I don't like bass players who are actually frustrated guitar players – like Phil Lynott – it misses the whole point.'

Equally intriguingly she and Jack share a bass-playing hero in Tamla Motown's stalwart James Jamerson; 'He was an original member of the Funk Brothers and played on all those wonderful early Motown hits. He was just the best. He used the same Fender Precision, never changed the strings, and – I believe - only played with two fingers.' It has been pointed out that Jimmy's playing is often confused with that of his lower-profile colleague Carol Kaye, who specialised in playing very fast conga-style parts, but always used a pick.

Bob Brunning quotes Cream as one of the greatest influences in his musical life, and says that he was bowled over by this terrific bass player – who also had 'a wonderful, expressive voice.' However he too thinks that he was 'too busy for the band's good, too messy. Jack was becoming not just the bass player in the band, but a solo artist who just happened to play bass. He could have been a guitar player.' He also thought that the music was sometimes simply too loud for its own good.

Bob's philosophy about bass playing could hardly be more different from Jack's though. He always wanted his playing to be 'invisible – in the sense that the bass and drums should be seamless and solid. You know that they're there, and you'll know if they're no good – but you'll almost not notice them.'

That's a good definition of how things had always been, and to a large degree still are; the bass man as team player, tucked away at the back. It wasn't Jack's modus operandi either musically or personally though. He needed to be out there on his own, fighting his way to the front. That was equally true of Ginger and Eric. They hugely appreciated each other's talents, but when they were together their single-minded mission was to out-play the other two. Volume helped of course, but the key criteria were simple technique, over-layered complexity and originality. Each was intent on letting the audience know that they could play their instrument better than anyone else on the planet, but there was also a well-developed sense of each of them also trying to establish their musical superiority over the other two – either one at a time or both simultaneously.

Amateur psychologists might feel that they could establish this as a basic – almost psychopathic need - and trace it back to the three men's earliest years and upbringings. If their different but equally difficult childhoods had left them with a highly-developed – highly over-developed – competitiveness, no-one would be at all surprised. Each was probably the crème de la crème within his own discipline, but the idea of relaxing and resting on laurels was unthinkable. They had to re-establish their dominance every time they played.

They were always a team of sorts - a team of three combatants who were pretty well at war with each other a lot of the time, as well as with a common enemy. In his biography of Eric Clapton - Slowhand - Harry Shapiro describes the three as 'working together like a team of bomb disposal experts.' The Sunday Times put it rather well, 'It was a creative tension that worked an improbable magic.' They were often moving in different – but never opposing – directions. It's amazing that it didn't all fall apart; indeed it's to their very great credit. Out of conflict came brilliance.

In the early Sixties pop music did begin to uncover some interesting and highly creative bass players. Tamla Motown, Jack says, used melodic bass when most people thought the bass line should just be a simple line in the background. Often the bass was more complex and more fundamental than the guitar part. Of Jimmy Jamerson, Jack cites his bass work on Standing In The Shadows Of Love or on Stevie Wonder's I Was Made To Love Her as the most brilliant examples of his art, 'There's a lot of notes – and a lot of grace. Motown songs were often just a top line with vocal harmonies and a very chordal thing like a piano or vibes playing four in the bar, or a guitar playing chinky chords. Then there's the bass ... playing melody.' Jamerson wasn't 'just' the guy who played bass. As Jack said to Bass Guitar magazine in 2003, 'I wanted to be playing melodies rather than just root notes. That kind of polyphonic idea appealed to me, as opposed to just a supportive role.'

Interviewed in Record Collector magazine in 2005, Jack is quoted as saying that of the three musicians in Cream it was he who had to adapt his style the most in order to dove-tail into the band's sound; 'I had to change a lot, to simplify in some ways and become interested in new things. Eric was very good at teaching us both, introducing us to people like Robert Johnson or Skip James. We all had to compromise in a musical sense, but we were all learning.' Jack admits that he had only a limited knowledge of the blues, and knew very little about Delta blues, which was Eric's speciality. He's played dance band music, country and western, lounge jazz, trad jazz, modern jazz and r 'n b; now he had to become a blues bassist too.

Bob Brunning has an interesting thought regarding the line-up of Cream. He thinks that the band might have benefited from a fourth member; not a guy on keyboards player but another bass player. He would have had someone playing conventional, 'invisible' bass alongside Ginger, disappearing into the rhythm, and allowing Eric and Jack to alternate lead and rhythm guitar down the front of the stage. They would have had equal musical status and could have slipped easily between their two roles and the music demanded. It would have worked like Keith Richards and Ronnie Wood – except that one guy was playing a bass, albeit, on occasion, one that looked like a guitar.

In the way that there is often a close musical relationship between a singer and a lead guitarist – as in Robert Plant and Jimmy Page, or Steve Tyler and Joe Perry – and a similarly strong bond between rhythm and lead guitarists – Keith and Ron – there has often been a fascinating, intertwining relationship between bass players and drummers. The example that comes to mind first is Mick Fleetwood and John McVie. Those two men know each other's musical instincts inside out, and can predict what the other is going to do without giving it a moment's thought. They are a true team, the rhythm section indeed, and they play almost as a single organic entity.

Somehow Jack and Ginger never had exactly the same empathy. They weren't always on the same side, facing in the same direction – and certainly neither was happy for their sound to become wrapped up in the other's. They greatly appreciated each other's playing but they played as individuals and were never two talents beating as one. Jack – ever the lone wolf – puts it very simply, 'I think drummers like to play with me because I make them sound good.'

Chapter 11

Born in Surrey – not far from Eric - but brought up in Golders Green in North London, Pete Brown started writing poetry when he was a teenager, and had seen his work published by the time he was eighteen. He was also a huge jazz fan and had been haunting the local trad jazz clubs since he was thirteen.

Like Jack, Pete had both music and politics woven into his upbringing. His father sang with Jewish choirs, and via his uncle, who was a communist and 'an East End radical', he performed with The Communist Theatre. His day job though was selling shoes on a market stall.

Pete had a romantic dream of being a travelling poet, and in 1960 he formed a poetry duo with Mike Horowitz. The two art forms, jazz and poetry, slipped together easily, and Pete started reading at jazz performances. He was to become well known for his writing, but not so much as a poet but as a lyricist. He has had enjoyed very long working relationships with Phil Ryan, and – until his death – Dick Heckstall-Smith, and he and Jack have been working together for almost forty years. It has been stormy but very productive relationship. They haven't always got on, to say the least. In between bursts of great creativity they have had often lengthy periods of animosity; at the time of writing, in the late summer of 2005, the two men were not on speaking terms.

Jack remembers Pete as just having been around 'the scene' forever, and not long after Jack arrived in London for good he visited 'the famous house in Primrose Hill where Pete lived, where people lived in cupboards.' They were aware of each other but hadn't worked together, apart from Jack playing acoustic bass at one of Pete's jazz/poetry gigs, though Pete had been working with Ginger at poetry readings for some time.

As often as possible Jack, Eric and Ginger used to declare 'party night.' The venue was usually Jack's home because he had a piano in the flat; shades of his parents' drinking and singing in their parlour in Glasgow. It was an opportunity to make some noise, smoke some dope, drink some booze and generally have fun. 'We used to play mad things. Somewhere I've got tapes that I made at the time, on an old Akai – they're hilarious.

Everyone would join in – Ginger would be playing the spoons.'

One party night Ginger brought Pete along, with the thought that the two of them would try writing songs together in the midst of all the madness.

That was his first introduction to the trio as a band, and shortly after, Ginger phoned him from their recording studio in Chalk Farm and said that they were struggling with a particular track. Pete went over and set to work on the lyrics, and Wrapping Paper was written almost as it was being recorded. Within minutes of the lyrics being written, the song was on tape.

Meanwhile, Jack had been trying to swap ideas with Janet – with whom he had already written the appropriately dreamy Sleepy Time Time. She had thought up the lyrics on one of her long walks into central London from Swiss Cottage). During the first rehearsals, up in Willesden, she walked to the church hall from their home in Hampstead, and it came on to rain very heavily. By the time she arrived she was soaking wet, but as she walked into the hall and the guys saw her, they went straight into Sleepy Time Time; 'It was my little song, that I'd made up, and that moment was really special.'

Ginger and Pete wrote one song together that is best described as early World music, as it was based on a Polynesian tune that Ginger had found. Neither combination was really working though, so they decided to swap partners, and the two songwriting teams were born. Ginger and Janet wrote Sweet Wine that night, which appeared on 'Fresh Cream', and Jack and Pete went on to create some of the most original, important and lasting rock songs ever heard.

Jack knew Pete only slightly from his poetry/jazz fusion work, but what mattered was that their complementary talents dovetailed perfectly when it came to song writing. 'Pete was quite mad - but I suppose we all were. He was also very hairy. But he could write words.'

NSU was the first song Jack wrote for the band; their first completely original piece. He sang lead vocals and he and Eric shared the distinctive, high vocal harmonies. Having written NSU on his own, Jack decided that he wanted to work with a lyricist; 'NSU was just something that came into my head. It was simple but subtle; the phrasing comes from Otis Redding – the phrasing is syncopated between the beat. My lyrics were never very good, but I was very pleased with that.

'Writing music is an inspirational thing for me. It's not something that I can sit down and work at. Some things I write on my own take years. I might not be happy with it and I'll put it away, and then suddenly it'll re-appear and I'll finish it. One song I wrote the words and lyrics for, Life On Earth, I dreamed. I woke up and had the whole thing, complete. I can't chip away at lyrics.'

This process was new for both men. In the past Jack had written music for existing lyrics, and Pete was – to say the least - much more a poet and a performance artist than

Poet lyricist, performer and producer Pete Brown has written the lyrics for the majority of Jack's songs over the past forty years – including all the most famous compositions. (MK)

a pop lyricist. The greater leap was on Pete's part. He had had his work published and well reviewed by the critics, but in a very different sphere. His world was cerebral and intellectual at a time when pop lyrics very definitely were not. Looking at his pre-Cream work it seems ludicrous to suggest that he might have become a pop lyricist. The likes of Have I The Right or Concrete And Clay wouldn't have fallen from his pen. Even the work of a more creative lyricist such as Graham Gouldman, who was still a teenager when he wrote For Your Love for The Yardbirds and Bus Stop for The Hollies, simply can't be compared with Pete Brown's lyrics.

The timing was crucial. Bruce and Brown were part of a movement. The mighty Jagger/Richards and Lennon/McCartney song writing teams had begun moving into far more interesting areas in the preceding months. The former had written 19th Nervous Breakdown, Paint It Black and Mother's Little Helper in 1966 – while at the same time John and Paul moved a thousand miles away from Love Me Do and I Wanna Hold Your Hand, and created Paperback Writer, Eleanor Rigby and Tomorrow Never Knows. Together with Pete Townshend they undertook the utter and very timely destruction of the sickly 'moon in June' style of pop song. And it all happened in 1966. In the future, others would still sing soppy love songs (indeed Paul McCartney would too, unfortunately), but they would never sound modern and important. Pete Townshend started the year with the very first real and confident anthem of teenage rebellion, My Generation, and followed that with the confusing Substitute, the nostalgic The Kids Are Alright, and I'm a Boy – a song about enforced transvestism. He didn't do soppy. He didn't do love songs. Nor did The Rolling Stones. Nor, after I Feel Free, did Jack Bruce and Pete Brown. Lust, yes, but that's rather different – and much more rock 'n roll. The new thinking swept everything else away – teenage tears, pining for parental approval and the limited ambitions that had satisfied an older generation.

Jack describes Pete as 'very undemanding' and says that working with him must have been 'maddening' for the lyricist; 'He would come up with these really good lines and I'd be saying 'no, that's not it. I'm very definite about some things that I want.'

They worked together on most of their songs, in the same room, trying out things and rejecting a couple of dozen ideas for every one that they used. Theirs was never Elton John's style of song writing, where he would tinkle at the piano in Windsor while Bernie Taupin, on the other end of a phone line in southern California, then added the lyrics.

A lot of their joint compositions went through huge changes and the finished article would have been unrecognisable from what they started with: I Feel Free was originally about bicycling through France, foe example. Incredibly.

Most of the songs that carry a Jack Bruce writing credit are co-compositions with Pete, though there are exceptions, such as Dreaming on 'Fresh Cream' and We're going Wrong on 'Disraeli Gears.' The latter was simple inspiration; 'I wrote We're Going Wrong walking down a street near where we lived in Hampstead. I'd just had a row with my wife and the whole thing just came to me as I was walking along. The lyrics and melody just appeared together, which is the very best thing that can happen.'

Pete makes the point that they worked very quickly. The ideas flowed and the two men sparked off each other. Slower writers wouldn't have been able to keep up with the band's schedule, and as with the speed at which the songs were recorded, the speed at which they were written probably gave them immediacy and an urgency. There was simply no time to go back and polish.

Cream adopted the full-on Carnaby Street look with enthusiasm, and looked great in the clothes … most of the time (Redferns)

On almost all occasions the music came first and Pete fitted the lyrics around the musical framework. One exception was Politician, where Pete had written the full lyrics quite some time before, and Jack wrapped the melody around it. Cream played it on a BBC session, where, he says, he improvised the riff and the lyrics were 'a bit ruder.' Only later did it get ironed out and have its edges tidied; 'It became darker and felt like a New Orleans marching song.'

'Pete's lyrics were very important', Jack says. 'Very clever. Very poetic. Pete was always more of a poet than a lyricist; there's a very definite but very fine distinction between the two.'

Of the entire Cream canon, Jack's favourite is I Feel Free; 'I had a definite idea of what I wanted to do, and I think I achieved it. I wanted to write a single that was very distinctive, and not like anything else. Also, I always wrote songs out completely – in fact I've still got the manuscript for I Feel Free. It makes me feel good.' Pete Brown describes it as the only true pop song they ever wrote, and thinks of it as something that The Beach Boys might have recorded.

Its power, he says, lay in the band's ability to create a contrast; 'The very complex, soft, lyrical vocals, and underneath that you had the most incredibly powerful, driving rhythm section that anyone had ever heard at that point.' Pete describes Jack's contribution to that song as 'genius', and makes the point that the arrangement he wrote for it was so comprehensive that the track was 'producer-proof'; 'It was like a big band score. It's all inter-related and you couldn't take anything out of it. Everything was there and there was nothing you could change.'

He goes on to say that the one 'which has been best to me' is unsurprisingly Sunshine Of Your Love. That's the song which has brought in more royalties than any other – split between Jack, Pete and Eric as it was credited three ways.

Jack gives the impression that he thinks that many of the songs he and Pete wrote after Cream are better than the earlier ones. It was easier for them, post-Cream; a lot of the pressure was off, there was more time for everything, and there was less input – for good or ill – from other people.

After they had written a song and were both happy with it, the next step was to play it to Ginger and Eric. Jack never made demo tapes of the raw material for the other two, but where they needed demos for the record company they would cut a track or two in a tiny studio in Chalk Farm – in conditions, and with recording quality, which would be laughable today. The results could be good though; 'A lot of good things happened that way', he says.

Jack often had problems getting his musical ideas across to Eric and Ginger though. He could write the music out, but that was a classicist's way of communicating. He had to explain his thinking as best he could, but without seeming to tell Eric or Ginger what they ought to be playing. Usually he would end up by playing the parts on his bass 'and stamping my foot.' He wouldn't ever dare to suggest, he says, how Ginger might add a drum line. The most he would offer is where he thought the drums might come in. He says that for Ginger's benefit he simply described the beat on NSU as being 'a bit like River Deep, Mountain High' and left it at that.

What he was trying to create were 'complicated songs which sounded simple. They had to sound natural. I wanted things that didn't exist that often in pop and rock songs; subtle chord changes and things like that.'

All his life Pete has had what he calls 'a symbiotic connection' with Glaswegians in particular and Scots in general. It stems, he thinks, from his teenage hitchhiking days, when he often seemed to end up in Glasgow and he discovered that he liked both the city and its people. Something else which Jack and Pete shared was a love of the surreal humour of the radio series 'The Goon Show', which had run from 1951 to 1960. There was a great British traditional of nonsensical humour, but The Goons were quite unlike anything else that had been heard, and were to Pete and Jack's generation what the television series 'Monty Python's Flying Circus' was to the next generation. Hipsters and jazzers adored the modernity and the originality, and the song-writing team identified with that sense of humour. Pete cites it as a great influence on their work, and it is there – but not to the fore. They both insisted that the blues shouldn't be taken too seriously, as Eric perhaps would, and they were, on occasion, vilified by blues purists for mixing jokes into blues phrases. Pete's response was that there were terrific humourists hiding among serious musicians – be they Mose Allison or Screaming Jay Hawkins.

Many of their Goon-influenced songs were never recorded, including the one about selling fridges to Eskimos. The same sense of humour is more obvious on other Cream tracks, such as A Mother's Lament, and on Ginger's Edward Lear-like track Pressed Rat And Warthog.

Pete puts that sense of humour first when listing the elements that have always drawn him and Jack together, and follows it with, 'creativity, romanticism, a love of jazz and blues, and four decades of shared experience.'

He considered that he was just helping out on Wrapping Paper, and that the writing of I Feel Free was a one-off. It didn't occur to him that this was a major career development – a whole new creative medium for him to explore. Part of the problem was that he going through a very difficult time in his life, experiencing severe panic attacks and drinking heavily. He was also speeding a lot, and the combination of that drug with alcohol exacerbated his nervous condition. Jack persevered though. It seems that he could see the value of the partnership and he wasn't going let Pete spin off.

'We weren't doing it to make money', Pete insists, 'The money was a surprise. I had some skill and Jack had an enormous amount of skill, and we put that skill into the work.

All Cream songs had distinctive, dramatic intros, but it was an aspect that Jack was especially keen on. He always wanted to come in with a bang, and a distinctive bang at that. The songs are recognisable from the very first note or two, and they open with utter self-confidence. And yet no two sound the same. 'It was always very important to me that there was that distinctive quality to the music. I wouldn't ever want to sound like anyone else,' Jack says. He was always gripped with the desire to be different. No song of his, indeed no Cream song, can be said to sound like the work of any other band. Jack's need for uncompromising originality came from the standards set by his jazz heroes. He makes the point that you can tell that you are listening to Jelly Roll Morton or Duke Ellington or whoever from just about the very first note.

Jack grew up with, on the one hand, the standard repertoire of jazz, and on the other, with a very broad knowledge of classical music. Plus he was always listening to new music and listening again to his favourite music – and listening critically, so that he was always learning. Given his musical education he never had any trouble incorporating elements from other musical forms into his own compositions. Pete came from poetry, which he describes 'a very intense, very technical form of writing.' They were both working through distinct disciplines. Individually they were just about unique; there was no one else composing pop and rock music who had Jack's background, and the other poets who worked in contemporary music were the members of the far more esoteric Liverpool Scene, and the very commercial Scaffold, who wrote schoolyard ditties.

Pete makes the point that what they were striving for was the opposite of the planned obsolescence of just about all the pop music being produced at that time. They weren't trying to be fashionable or keep up with what else was going on; 'We weren't trying to be commercial. We were trying to do something interesting and say something. Jack wanted to explore certain musical shapes and I wanted to explore certain subjects.' On occasion Pete felt that his role was translator, and his job was to put Jack's musical images into words. Sometimes it didn't work, but when it did, the pair were unmatched; 'Jack and I could deal with all sorts of things, both British and Transatlantic. Take It Back is sort of about the American draft and Vietnam, and Dance The Night Away is about semi-psychedelic experiences in Britain in 1967.'

Jack and Pete had rapidly become a very well established song-writing team, and during the Cream years they wrote far more songs than were recorded. Some of these were to sit around for years before seeing the light of day. As we've seen, they wrote Hey Now Princess very early on but it didn't surface on record until 'A Question Of Time' was released in 1989 (Cream's demo cut of the song wasn't released until it appeared on a compilation album in 1997).

It's an understatement to say that the two men haven't always got on. A graph of their personal relationship across the last forty years would show a line first rising, and then crashing back down, then rising once more – before plummeting even lower. Sometimes the song-writing process worked well, Pete says, and at other times it has been 'hell.'

There have been times when they had to put any personal problems to one side because they needed to create new music. They had to take a coldly professional stance and get on with the job. You don't have to like your creative partner, just as you don't have to like a commercial partner – though it helps. In many ways, Jack and Pete have been like a married couple; sometimes getting along okay, sometimes rowing terribly, sometimes sulking and swearing that they'll never speak to each other again. In the way that couples often decide that though the situation is far from perfect, they have to stick together for the sake of the children, these two have stuck together for the sake of the music.

Chapter 12

J ack and Ginger first met Robert Stigwood when he came to a GBO gig at The 100 Club. Jack recalls that Ginger was very excited about his presence, and described him as 'a big-time manager.' Stigwood, born in Adelaide in Australia in 1934, had come to the UK in the Fifties and had drifted into the music business. He had seen some success managing John Leyton, who was originally an actor and starred in a television adaptation of the Biggles adventures. He had two big hits - with the all-strings-and-girlie-chorus singles Johnny Remember Me and Wild Wind, which were produced by Joe Meek. His pop career was short and he returned to acting, but the experience gave Robert a credible base upon which he could build a career as a pop entrepreneur.

Like Meek, Robert was one of the early mavericks in the music industry, who refused to accept what their peers told them, and certainly wouldn't work by the principle that 'it must be the right way to do it because that's how we've always done it.' When they decided to turn John Leyton into a pop star it certainly didn't matter to them that he wasn't blessed with much of a singing voice. That would have been everything to the industry's grandees; what mattered to Robert was that he was good looking, knew how to move, and photographed well.

Robert made two important changes to British pop thinking early on. Acting as the middleman between the artist and the record company, he set up an innovative distribution system, which gave him a high level of control. Secondly, unlike many others, who scoured the lower reaches of the US charts for songs that their bands or solo singers could cover for the British market, Robert went looking for home-grown songwriting talent. That was a distinct plus in that the writing and publishing royalties didn't go straight to America.

The 1965 package tour with Chuck Berry headlining almost broke him, but although he called in the receivers, he maintained his extravagant lifestyle and bluffed his way through. Rock manager Simon Napier-Bell said of him, 'He became fascinated by [the pop industry]. He loved its trickery and tease, and the apparent ease with which money could be made. What made Robert Stigwood different from his predecessors is that he expanded laterally. He didn't remain simply a manager or an agent. He moved into music publishing as well, and into pop concert promotion. He was in every way the first British music business tycoon, involved in every aspect of the music scene, and setting a precedent that was to become the blueprint of success for all future pop entrepreneurs.' It's telling that Robert was the promoter for The Rolling Stones' first big UK tour, in 1964. They played seventy-two venues and he took 40% of the gross income. Bill Wyman says that at the end of the tour his personal bank account was in credit by just £39, and in the band's opinion Stigwood had £12,000 of their money as well as his own cut.

Stigwood became The GBO's manager, with Ginger as his main advocate within the group. Jack says that he thought it was 'a great break' for the band when he took them on, but he soon started to have doubts.

There was a clash of opinions as to whether or not he should be Cream's manager, with Ginger insisting that they needed him, and that without a good manager – and Stigwood in particular – they didn't stand a chance. Jack's position wasn't just that he didn't want Stigwood, but that he thought that the band didn't need a manager at all. His thinking was that they needed an agent and an accountant, and that was all. To this day he bitterly regrets that wasn't how it worked out, but as he says, 'Ginger was the boss.'

When Ginger had phoned Chris Welsh with the news of the band's creation, he had been more than a bit ahead of himself and the other two weren't particularly pleased. Old nervousness about Ginger re-surfaced in Jack's head, but it didn't go any further. It didn't help that Jack was still employed by Manfred Man and Eric was still with John Mayall.

So Stigwood's first job at the manager of Cream was to ease Jack out of his existing contract with Manfred Mann. Ginger's announcement made his job a lot more difficult, and potentially expensive, but Manfred took a gentlemanly stance on the matter. There are many rather sharper men in the music industry who would have rushed straight round to the lawyers as soon as they realised how successful Cream became. John Mayall's anger at losing Eric, again, was assuaged by recruiting Peter Green once more.

Stigwood then set about promoting the new band. He told the press that they had a five-year contract with his recording label and had received an advance of £50,000, which was a massive amount of money. The by-line for his publicity campaign was 'The first is last and the last is first, but the first, the second and the last are Cream.' No one knew what it meant but it sounded appropriately portentous.

Bands had always had managers; that was the natural order of things. They were often more important than the groups themselves and they earned more. Again, that was just how things were. It cannot be said that The Beatles would ever have broken through without Brian Epstein. Had he not poured almost his lifeblood into promoting them and getting them a recording contract, the face of pop and rock music worldwide would have been very different. Given that no one had experienced success on that scale, and that he was ill-prepared to deal with the strains on a personal level, many of the decisions he went on to make can be criticised. Others quickly learned from those lessons; the value of merchandising and licensing was never under-estimated again, and inspired managers such as Peter Grant knew that focus was everything. Older managers, still locked into the Variety way of thinking, always felt that they needed a stable of stars in case one act faded – incredibly, in retrospect, Epstein did, as did managers such as Don Arden, who followed him. Peter Grant realised that it was putting all his energies and passions into one truly talented band was what paid dividends – as Led Zeppelin's massive success testified.

The first crack in the protective wall around the concept of pop industry management came when The Rolling Stones fired Andrew Oldham. Andrew had been very important in, firstly, the band's recording success, but perhaps more importantly still, in developing their own talents as musicians – and Mick and Keith's abilities as songwriters. Then they decided that they could move on without him. Mick Jagger is one of the most astute men ever to walk across a stage and seize a microphone, and he knew that they could go further and make more money without him. They replaced him with an accountant and a booking agent, and these men worked for the band – not the band for them.

It was an important moment. A rock group had realised that they had power, and had used it. It would have happened at some point, and it needed to be a big-earning singer or band that did it. The fact that it was The Stones meant that it was going to work, and that everyone else was going to sit up a take notice.

Cream could have been as big as they were without Stigwood, and Jack makes an argument that they could have been bigger still – and been together for much longer if he hadn't been part of the equation. They weren't fresh-faced and impressionable kids, just arrived in town. They knew who was good at what, and were bright enough to ask around when they didn't. On the other hand, he describes Eric as having always been 'very sophisticated', but says that he and Ginger – despite Ginger's self-image as a canny businessman – were very innocent.

Robert Stigwood's sexuality is relevant to his relationship with his bands, and especially to Jack. For intelligent, gregarious and often rather sharp gay men, the music industry was a safe haven. Like television, the theatre and the entertainment industry generally, it was a safe place to be at a time when homosexual activity meant a prison sentence and social disgrace. Like Meek, Epstein and Stigwood, Simon Napier-Bell is gay, and among other theories expounded in his book 'Black Vinyl, White Powder', Simon discusses what he sees as a gay, and often Jewish and gay, cabal within the music business. Writing in the gay magazine 'Attitude' in 2005 Simon argues that the music business in the Sixties was about sex rather than music or business. He claims that all the sexiest and most memorable moves made by straight musicians were as a result of suggestions from their gay managers.

Interestingly, the artists themselves, with a few exceptions, weren't gay – it was the guys who didn't appear on stage, the managers, the agents, the producers, who were (although brave and clever souls like David Bowie had played with the idea of bi-sexuality, those few exceptions were very successfully hidden until the late Seventies, when Tom Robinson put the issue right at the top of his agenda). Jack says that he was uncomfortable with Stigwood in this regard.

Before, during and after the career of Brian Epstein, the first pop manager whose name was known across the world, it has always been suggested that one of the main motivations for these usually-older and more worldly gay men was the availability of the handsome, skinny-hipped artists. It wasn't hard for them to define the exact appeal which they were selling to adolescent. Some may have gone along with this as the price of their manager's skills, but there are far more stories of advances being rebuffed. Jack was most certainly not interested. He was perhaps an obvious target, being young, good-looking and charming. Sure, when he didn't want to know you, he kept you at arm's length, but when he was smiling and joking he was a very attractive young man. He was utterly happy when women recognised this, but guys who fancied him could forget it. This had been on offer before, and it wasn't welcome – not from anyone, and certainly not from Robert. Even Janet noticed their manager's attentions, and the fact that it made her husband very uncomfortable.

Stigwood had cut a very canny deal in 1966 by paying The Who's managers, Chris Stamp and Kit Lambert, for the right to become that band's booking agent. Using this leverage he coaxed The Who away from the Decca recording company and onto his own label instead. The Who's first single for Reaction was Substitute, which wasn't the best thing they had ever done but was a big hit. The financial implications for Stigwood's new company must have been considerable. It was a Machiavellian move on his part, but the band members were involved in the sense that they knew that they could use this as an opportunity to break away from the producer Shel Talmy, with whom they had foolishly signed a five year contract.

This was important to Cream, because Stigwood's muscle now allowed him to couple the new band with The Who for an American residency, which began in March

1967. They were going to New York, where The Who were big enough to draw sizeable crowds. The band's image was super-hip, arty, and distinctly superior, and the Dutch art collective was asked to paint Jack and Eric's guitars. They had been discovered by The Beatles, and who had painted John Lennon's piano and his Rolls Royce, as well as George Harrison's Mini (and, curiously, a bungalow) as well as the band's London boutique - to paint psychedelic designs on Eric Clapton's Gibson SG and Jack Bruce's Fender VI bass. Jack's Gibson was finished in blues and orangey-yellows, but Jack found it 'sticky' even when dry, and rarely played it after that. It looked like an illustration for Strange Brew; very much of its time. Jack gave it to Leslie West and is now on show in The Hard Rock Café in Los Angeles.

Surprisingly Robert didn't tour with the band. He popped up occasionally – Jack says he went along to the prestigious venues, New York and Los Angeles ('I don't remember him coming to South Bend, Indiana …') - but it wasn't a wise move not to be there all the time. Although Peter Grant's position with Led Zep was very different and the two situations weren't exactly analogous, Grant was always there. Always. That meant that he knew what was going on, he knew where the money was going, and he could look after his musicians, pamper to their every whim and insulate them from the demands of the outside world. Stigwood would have been wise to have paid as much attention to the three individuals as he did to the aesthetic look of their guitars.

Song writing teams often write on the road – in the tour bus, on the plane or in the hotel room in the early hours – but Stigwood never let Pete Brown go on tour with the band. It was a lost opportunity, and Pete doesn't understand it. He makes the point that as a freelance lyricist Stigwood had no control over him; the manager didn't pay his wages. Pete was offered an exclusive publishing deal with Stigwood's company, but he shrewdly turned it down. From Stigwood's point of view that wasn't a good situation, and his attitude towards Pete was always civil but very cool; 'In fact I think he hated my guts.

'He was an authority figure with a bad reputation. Offering me an exclusive deal was like offering me, as a vegetarian, a hamburger. Anyway, the commercial reasoning behind the hamburger was something I didn't want to accept in my life.'

Another of Stigwood's business deals, which had an immediate and highly advantageous effect on the band, was moving all his recording contracts to Polydor. A new Managing Director had been appointed to head up Polydor, Roland Rennie, who was a friend of Stigwood's and who he had previously worked with. Rennie gave Stigwood an excellent deal for Cream to record with Polydor. They didn't just get high percentages on sales, but also generous up-front funding to cover recording costs. This was how Stigwood managed to set up a recording session for Cream in New York and with Tom Dowd, Atlantic Records' very talented engineer, in charge. They would probably have shone in a British recording studio, with a British producer ... but what matters is that what they did with Dowd was sheer brilliance. And it made the trio feel very good about themselves. They weren't lacking in self-confidence, but for a still-new band from the UK to be working in that studio, with that team, must have felt good.

Ahmet Ertegun founded Atlantic records in 1947 and it rapidly developed its own distinctive 'house' sound and became one of most important independent labels. Ahmet – whose father was the Turkish ambassador to the USA - was a passionate music lover, and as a direct result of his influence the company had a policy of seeking out, fostering and nurturing new talent. One of their first great signings was Ray Charles, and his jazz, blues, r 'n b sound – though still accessible and commercial – was entirely typical of Atlantic.

During the Sixties, soul music followed onto the lists, and Atlantic further increased its reputation as one of the USA's most respected labels. Ahmet was a good judge of talent on the other side of the glass too; he recruited the producer Jerry Wexler (who had the foresight to buy into the company in 1953), Tom Dowd and arranger Jesse Stone. Atlantic also had a back room of terrific session men, who weren't in the business of making a poor record good, but could make a good record great

At first Atlantic wasn't sure what to do with Cream and weren't at all keen on them being virtually foist upon them. They wanted a single focal point, and were keen to put Eric centre stage and have him sing lead vocal, despite the fact that Jack was obviously the better singer. Ahmet had seen Eric playing with John Mayall while he was on a trip to London, and he recognised both the man's great talents and the fact that the audience adored him. So, thinking along uncharacteristically conventional lines, he imagined Eric as the front man, with the other two as his backing band. Ahmet rarely made mistakes like that, but fortunately the band didn't see it that way.

In January 1967 Stigwood tried to buy Brian Epstein's holding company from him. When The Beatles heard about it they were furious. They loathed Stigwood and felt that it was an act of betrayal of Epstein's part even to be talking to him. Epstein backed away quickly, but to everyone's surprise he did agree a merger between the two companies. No one knows why; Epstein was, in theory at least, in a far stronger position that Stigwood. It's possible that Stigwood never had the money to be able to complete on the outright purchase, but it would have been very much his style to give the impression that he could afford it several times over. Epstein, a sensitive and tortured gay man, probably felt at ease with Stigwood, and saw him as an ally, not a threat. It's also true to say that he wasn't the sharpest businessman ever to grace the pop and rock world.

The merger turned Stigwood into rock management royalty overnight. For him it was nothing but wonderful news. He placed all his commercial assets into Epstein's

NEMS company, and in return received a reciprocal shareholding in the enlarged NEMS. He also got a very generous a salary, and an executive position as co-Managing Director. Most importantly for Cream, he now had access to huge financial reserves, and NEMS' organisational resources. He could bankroll projects at almost any level, and without either consulting anyone else or going out with a begging bowl.

Chapter 13

I n the autumn of '66 Chas Chandler, previously the bass player with The Animals, brought the then unknown Jimi Hendrix to London. He had recognised a prodigious talent and decided to move from performing to managing so that he could make this young guy a super-star.

Less than a week after arriving in the UK Chas got him and his newly-recruited sidemen, Mitch Mitchell and Noel Redding, a gig supporting Cream at The London Polytechnic. Jimi was impressed enough by the band to want to sit in with them. This was unheard of; this wasn't a casual jazz combo where any half-decent musician could get up on stage and jam with the band.

He asked Jack during the band's break, and Jack said it was okay by him but he'd have to ask the others. He found them in the pub, and Ginger said 'no' but Eric said 'yes', so that was a majority decision in his favour. Jack went back and told the shy, diffident and slightly nervous American that it was okay for him to play with the band. Jimi plugged his guitar into a spare input on the bass amp and was away.

Writing in Rolling Stone magazine, Roger Waters of Pink Floyd, who was a student at the college and was at the gig, said, 'The curtain drew back and the three of them started playing Crossroads. I had never seen or heard anything like it before. It was an astonishing sight and an explosive sound.

'Two-thirds of the way through their set [Jack] said, 'We'd like to invite a friend of ours from America out on stage.' It was Jimi Hendrix. He came on and did all that now-famous stuff, like playing with his teeth. The ticket cost a pound or so. It might have been the best purchase I ever made.'

Cream's roadie, Ben Palmer, said later, 'He was the first person to ever sit in with Cream, and the last.' Eric was noticeably shaken. He was supposed to be the undisputed king of the hill, but here was this unknown guy, just off the plane, playing guitar in a way that no one had ever seen before - and stunningly well. Eric realised that Jimi was to some degree a threat, but that the world was big enough for both of them, and his respect for his fellow guitarist's virtuosity overcame any nervous envy. Jack has said that even the very next day Eric was copying some of Jimi's licks.

Chas had taken Jimi to Carnaby Street and outfitted him in the essential Swinging London style. This was exactly how Cream dressed too. Eric had previously taken a more formal, more sartorial approach to what he wore on stage, but once Jack and Ginger dropped their jazzer styles and started dressing to suit their achingly up to date music, Eric joined in too. If one was going to be a peacock then they all were.

The style had developed out of the early Sixties Mod style; the full, extravagant madness of velvet jackets, bishop-sleeved shirts in huge paisley prints, silk scarves and cummerbunds and trousers – in any colour you liked – which were ferociously tight down to the knees and then flared out from there on. The style wasn't proto-hippie, it was far too smart and fastidious for that. Hippies made a point of looking different, but their bottom line was that they didn't care about how they looked and were anti-materialistic. The Carnaby Street style was proudly materialistic.

Men hadn't dressed as flamboyantly since the Restoration. Even Regency dandies had been more restrained; in fact they looked positively Puritan compared to these popinjays. Jack, Eric and Ginger were all handsome young men, and they had the slim frames and skinny hips that made the styles work. They also had the money – or Robert Stigwood provided the money – because until similar (but less well-made) clothes were produced for the mass market and it wasn't cheap to be as exuberantly dressed.

Both Jack and Ginger moved on effortlessly from their jazz styles, and adopted the rapidly-emerging Swinging London fashions; indeed they were almost a test bed for style – they could get away with sartorial extravagances for which a teenager in Swansea or Scunthorpe would have been mocked in the street. Eric had always taken great care with his clothes. When he was with The Yardbirds he had gone for a preppy, Ivy League look. Now he too bought up everything that the most trendy, groovy boutiques offered, though he tended to be a touch more restrained than Jack. Jack jumped in with great enthusiasm. Given the choice, Ginger went for clothes with an ethnic slant – and was years ahead of his time in doing so.

They looked damn good and they knew it. Those were the days when bands tried hard not to look like their audiences – they were set apart and they wanted everyone to know it. It was also a huge contrast to the old fashioned stage wear which some performers still wore. It wasn't that long ago that The Beatles had been obliged to wear matching suits (with jackets featuring 'Beatle collars) and matching shoes.

Very few bands actually dressed as well, as fastidiously even, as did Cream. Or took the look quite as far. Like the music itself, this set them apart from the herd. In their way they were as conscious of their image as any other band. It didn't always work though. There is footage of the band playing Strange Brew on Ready Steady Go, and they are considerably over-dressed. They look awkward; as if the clothes are wearing them rather than the other way round. Eric is wearing an exaggerated hunting stock round his neck, and a high-collared jacket – and he looks as if he's struggling to move his head in any direction.

The other band which dressed very much the same was The Jimi Hendrix Experience. Jimi looked great in these clothes, and knew how to wear them. He wasn't a conventionally handsome man, but he was certainly the right shape, and was the perfect clothes horse for the era. That was far from being the only similarity between the two bands. His first single was Hey Joe; a brilliantly produced song, which had the same power as The Animals' similarly modern re-working of the traditional House Of The Rising Sun (the common denominator being Chas Chandler). That song, and the follow-up, Purple Haze, which Jimi wrote, established his reputation in the UK – a process that took weeks rather than months.

Here was a second power trio, and though Jimi dominated The Experience in a way that no one person dominated Cream, his sidemen were very skilled musicians – and the band shared with Cream the fundamental power and attack.

'The first thing that springs to mind when you think about about Cream and The Jimi Hendrix Experience is the similarities', Bob Brunning – who missed his first gig but saw Hendrix's second show in London, at The Marquee - says, 'Jimi looked so exotic. He wasn't pretty but he was obviously very sexy, and he wore these wild clothes – and the scene in The Marquee was still London Mod at that time. But as with Cream, you had beautiful musicianship and a beautiful voice in a busy sort of band. Jimi's rhythm section didn't hold up alongside Cream though – Mitch and Noel were a much more standard rhythm section, which was how Jimi wanted it. They proved again that if you've got a trio where everyone is superb, it's okay.'

Comparisons between Jimi and Eric on a personal level have never rung true. The fact that they were both highly skilled guitarists in just about as far as it went; when it came to style and technique they were very different. Jimi was wild and sensual whereas Eric was precise and controlled. Eric's work was based in the blues whereas Jimi was a rock guitarist – heavily influenced by the blues, but as influenced by r 'n b, soul and other black American styles as well.

Jack comes down very definitely on one side of the argument. He maintains that Eric is a better guitar player than Jimi ever was, 'Jimi was Jimi, and he could have played the Indian nose flute and it wouldn't have mattered. But in an instrumental sense I would argue that Eric was at least as good as Jimi, probably better.' He goes to say that Jimi suffered to a degree because the musicians he usually shared a stage with 'didn't kick him up the arse' – didn't stretch him. He says that he's not having a dig at Mitch Mitchell and Noel Redding, but they were very much Jimi's side men. The implication is that Jack would have given Jimi a real run for his money.

If comparisons between Jimi and Eric don't really work, then perhaps a more valid comparison can be made between Jimi and Jack. Both men were the singers and the principal song-writers in their bands, and both played their instruments in an innovative and exciting way, utterly disregarding how the instrument had been played before – indeed deliberately avoiding musical precedent in order to make their mark. Both played with undisguised passion - where Eric played with detachment and emotional control.

These two men, together with their bands, were crucially important in contemporary music suddenly maturing, as it did during 1967. Before then just about everything was pop – popular music engineered for the largest possible market and therefore tending to the lowest common denominators. Music existed to sell as many records as possible, and make as much money as possible – for the industry, that is, not necessarily for the musicians. It was the way the business thought and everything was geared to that formula, from Johnny Ray to Adam Faith to – most obviously – The Beatles. Looking right was more important than sounding right, and if you didn't fit the mould you could forget it, which is why bands like The Graham Bond Organisation were so successful as a live band, and yet had so little success in terms of record sales.

The Beatles, to their enduring credit, were one of the first band's to kick the traces and simply do what they wanted to do; write and record far more intelligent, more adroit, more worthwhile music. They wanted to test the limits of their own abilities and they ended up testing the limits of the whole industry. They weren't alone of course, but they were the most important. Both Cream and Hendrix cannoned in immediately after the landmark which was Strawberry Fields Forever, which built on the adventurousness of 'Revolver' and paved the way for 'Sergeant Pepper.' The timing was coincidental, but it was perfect. There was a huge wave of new music; intelligent, highly skilled and appealing to an audience which was older, more aware musically and itself gaining in maturity. Rock was being born out of pop, and without Cream, and in particular the ability of Pete and Jack to take song composition to a higher level, its face would have looked very different, and probably have progressed less far.

Cream had come out of British blues and jazz, and Jimi's background was primarily American r 'n b, but it soon stopped mattering where the musical influences originated as a whole new dynamic entered the music. In total their work was vastly greater than the sum of the parts. With the exception of The Rolling Stones and The Beatles post-Strawberry Fields Forever – who were in their own two-band Premier League – Cream managed, almost more than anyone else, to combine a stunning and united image, immaculate cool and massively respected musicianship. And the other band who did the same thing, and at the same point, was that one other peerless power trio – The Jimi Hendrix Experience.

Chapter 14

The cover of 'Fresh Cream' was a fairly conventional affair, with a single photo on the front, showing the three members of the band against a flat black background – albeit with a blue gel on the lights on one side and red on the other. Jack is wearing a leather flying jacket, helmet and goggles – for no apparent reason. It's not a good photo of any of them. On the back they were show in negative, and there were brief biographies of all three. Obviously the record company felt that they had to explain who these guys were. Of Jack, the unfortunately comma-free text read, 'Jack is a fiery musician of great feelings and the sounds he produces from his six-string bass and harmonica are quite revolutionary.' The cover was designed by Stigwood's publicity and public relations company, Mayfair Public Relations.

The cover of the next, 'Disraeli Gears', was very different.

The album was recorded over a ridiculously short five-day period in the early summer of 1967. The title came from a mis-hearing of the words Derailleur gears when Ginger Baker was talking about racing cycles. Whereas 'Fresh Cream' was recorded in London, the new album benefited from Stigwood's Atlantic connection.

In March '67 the band recorded seven tracks by way of a demo tape, and this was the first thing played to Atlantic. These tapes were to be the subject of some controversy; they were lost – perhaps deliberately – and then turned up again when it suited management for them to do so. Four of the songs were eventually recorded by Cream; Take It Back, We're Going Wrong, Blue Condition and SWLABR, but two – The Clearout and Weird Of Hermiston were taken no further by the band, and were eventually re-cut by Jack for his first solo album. The last song, Hey Now Princess wasn't to re-appear for a generation.

The first album had seen Robert Stigwood credited as producer, which Jack says was stretching the facts more than a little. Pete Brown describes him as 'the worst producer in the whole world – with no musical knowledge whatsoever.' The personnel on the latest recording were to be very different.

Tom Dowd, had unparalleled status within Atlantic as both a producer and an engineer. He had worked with just about all of the label's artists but was particularly respected for his productions with Aretha Franklin. He had made Atlantic stereo as early as 1952, and had designed their studios himself. As well as producing and engineering some of the best r 'n b records ever made, Tom had also worked with Ray Charles, Ornette Coleman, Charles Mingus and John Coltrane. He was one of the very few people on the other side of the glass who the band, and Jack in particular, would be impressed by.

With his background in blues and r 'n b, Tom was a perfect choice to work on the new album, and it's surprising that he wasn't the producer. That job went to Felix Pappalardi, who was a regular at Atlantic, for the simple reason that he happened to be in the building when Ahmet was casting around for someone to take control off the sessions.

He was born in the Bronx in New York City in 1939, and studied at the Michigan Conservatory Of Music. Like many of his colleagues in the very early Sixties he was into folk music and he gravitated towards the clubs and bars of Greenwich Village. His first professional engagement was playing bass for Tim Hardin in the Village. That was his preferred instrument, but he soon started to gain a reputation as a producer. As well as Hardin, in the period between '63 and '66 he worked with Ritchie Havens, Tom Rush, Tom Paxton and Richard and Mimi Farina; the hippest of the hip New York folk crowd in fact. There is a story that having found an import copy of 'Fresh Cream', possibly even before it was released in the States, Felix told a friend how stunned he was by their music – and said that one day he would produce an album with them. Felix was to also contribute material for the album; he co-wrote Strange Brew (with Eric Clapton and Gail Collins, his wife) and World Of Pain (just with Gail).

As soon as you saw 'Disraeli Gears' in the record shop you knew it was something very different. The cover was like nothing else you had ever experienced, with its fantastic, day-glo front and its acid trip montage back. There were no formal photos of the band and hardly any type at all. The two sides almost didn't hang together; the front was full of motion and huge blocks of disorientating colour, while the back was static and deliberately bitty – the largest single image being an eye, looking out at the viewer from the middle of the sleeve.

It was designed by Martin Sharp, a friend of Eric's who was also heavily involved with the underground magazine OZ, and created several of its most memorable front covers. It's not enough to employ a cliché and say that he broke all the rules; he worked as if there were no rules and there never had been. 1967 was the year of the great breakthrough in album design. Before then a simple photo of the band was pretty well enough, but the thrilling eruption of creative expression in Britain at that time turned its attention to the album sleeve, and transformed it into true pop art. In the days when album covers were almost worn as a sign of one's music cred, and you wait-ed for the impact and the ensuing compliments as a chum leafed through your record collection, Martin Sharp's designs led the field.

His work on this album was a very happy accident though. The original plan had been to use shots of the band taken by rock photographer Bob Whitaker on Ben Nevis. The band journeyed to Britain's highest mountain along with Janet Bruce, and at the bottom of the mountain they proceeded to get absolutely out of their skulls on phar-maceutical acid. Eric, Ginger and Jack were in their full, Top Of The Pops fab gear, and all five of them set off for the summit. Three-quarters of the way up, their paths crossed that of a party of serious, properly-dressed and equipped climbers, who were understandably startled to see anyone out on the mountain without the correct equip-ment. Although the band had gone up the 'easy' route, velvet cloaks and snake-skin boots still had to catch on among mountaineers. Then they recognised the members of the band, and – two and a half thousand feet above sea-level – asked for autographs.

They didn't quite reach the summit, but settled on a plateau not far from the top. There they took in the view and wandered in and out of their individual mystical expe-riences. It was always said that the one female who accompanied them on this lunatic trip was Charlotte Martin, Eric's girlfriend, but it was in fact Janet. It was Jack who switched the identities during a newspaper interview years later, possibly because he didn't want her parents to know that Janet had used LSD, albeit only a couple of times.

When they finally decided to descend, they thought it might be a good idea to run all the way down, either along steeply vertiginous tracks or by simply cannoning down the loose scree. More climbers are injured, or lose their lives, coming down mountains than going up. It's quite beyond belief that no-one even experienced cuts, abrasions or concussions – let alone lost their life.

Bob Whitaker hadn't been ideally equipped for the assignment. He had been told that Cream was going to do a tour of the north of England and Scotland and that shots were needed for publicity, so he had just jumped in a car and headed north. A few days later he took what he had to Martin Sharp's studio, he was startled when Martin pro-ceeded to cut up the expensive prints with a pair of scissors. The artist simply cut out what he wanted, stuck them to a twelve-inch square, and started colouring in with the latest graphic innovation, Day-Glo paint. The process took moments.

The Bruce/Brown tracks on the album were Dance The Night Away, SWLABR, and Take It Back, while Jack alone wrote We're Going Wrong. There was also, of course, Sunshine Of Your Love, which is probably the best-known and most-played Cream song of all time – with White Room (from their next album) not far behind.

Famously Jack and Pete wrote Sunshine Of Your Love in Jack's flat very early one morning, having worked through the night – Pete scribbling away in a notebook and Jack trying out lines on his acoustic bass. 'We'd got nothing despite working all night and we were a bit despondent. Pete was looking out of the window, and I picked up the acoustic bass and played de-de-de-de-dum-dum-dum-de-de-deee, and he said 'It's getting near dawn.' It sounds contrived but that's exactly how it happened.' That bass riff became the would-be bass players equivalent of Smoke On The Water or Stairway To Heaven; in just about every music shop all round the world, some youngster – or oldster, for that matter – has tried out a new instrument by running through that same phrase.

The song wasn't completed immediately though; 'I had two parts of a twenty-four-bar blues and I didn't know what to do with it. We had a rehearsal and I played it for the guys and it was Eric who made it work by writing the turn-around – the three chords at the end of the chorus.' Which is why Eric received a song-writing credit, along with Jack and Pete.

When they first played it through at Atlantic studios, Ahmet Ertegun hated it and said that it wouldn't work, and if it did, it wouldn't sell. Ahmet had always had problems understanding Cream. He had heard Eric play in London in 1966 and been hugely impressed, and what he had expected was more like The Experience – Eric and two sidemen.

Fortunately there were other people around at Atlantic, and they had other opinions. One was Booker T Jones, who was wandering around the studio complex, either on their own business or simply checking up on the British interlopers. He disagreed. They told the band it was going to be great. Needless to say, in the band's thinking he out-voted Ahmet easily. He might be the boss but what did he know compared to Booker T?

It's a very tight, very precise song, and it said everything that needed to be said at that stage about Jack's singing and bass playing. It's also a song which he has returned to again and again over the years. It was the strongest element on a very strong album, and came to define the band in the public's understanding. At the time that label might have been given to the dreamy Strange Brew, but that song hasn't stood the test of time quite so well and soon sounded dated.

The Cream music which doesn't sound fresh in the twenty-first century, leaving aside jokey tracks like Mother's Lament (credited to all three band members) and Pressed Rat And Warthog, were more fey than the Bruce/Brown compositions; a bit hippy, a bit pre-New Age – such as Blue Condition, World of Pain, Those Were The Days and Strange Brew. The originality of Jack and Pete's work, together with the precision of the production on those songs, has made them immortal. They will still be played in the twenty-second century.

The other Bruce/Brown tracks on 'Disraeli Gears' were Dance The Night Away, SWLABR and the least successful and enduring of their tracks, Take It Back. The glorious We're Going Wrong was written by Jack alone, and again was very much his song in every way. There were no old blues numbers on the album, for good or ill, and Jack and Pete had been responsible to some degree for six out of the eleven. The album was a glorious success, and is rightly regarded as one of the twenty or so greatest albums of all time. The Daily Telegraph's arts correspondent, Charles Spencer, has described it as, 'A masterpiece, an entirely successful fusion of blues and full-on psychedelia.'

'The jump from 'Fresh Cream' to 'Disraeli Gears' was a very great one,' Pete says, 'They had found their producer. When I first heard the album I thought it was magical. Felix really knew what to do with them in studio. First and foremost he was a musician, and recognised their musical potential. He had a very strong sense of arrangement and structure, which Jack had too, but Felix helped him articulate it in the studio. He knew how to get the right sounds out of the band.'

Jack plays down Felix's role in the recording process, saying that he himself was more responsible for the production. ' He was never obtrusive. He was there but he never tried top change your mind, or say 'You've got to have this' or 'You've got to have that.' He wasn't trying to mould me into what he thought I should be.' He adds, 'With the exception of songs like Strange Brew I gradually I took over and became the producer of the band, with Felix as an assistant. Even down to arranging and finishing Ginger's material.'

Felix and Jack became very close, but they were also very competitive, just to confuse the dynamics further; 'Felix wanted to be Jack', Pete says, 'He was jealous of Jack, though he was very talented and could play a lot of instruments and produced some great things.'

Strange Brew had been released as a single in the UK earlier that year (with Tales Of Brave Ulysses on the B-side) and had gone to number 17. 'Disraeli Gears' was released in November '67, almost a year after the release of 'Fresh Cream.' The album went to number five in the UK and one place higher in the States – but was in the Billboard album charts for all of fifty weeks.

During that time they were gigging regularly, but for the first few months of '67 were still playing surprisingly small venues. They were booked into clubs and the occasional student union. In mid-December '66 they had played in Paris – but only in a club. In early March they played two shows in Northern Ireland, and a few days later they flew to Scandinavia for two gigs in Sweden and one in Denmark.

At the end of February '67 they played two nights at The Star Club in Hamburg – five years after The Beatles had learned their craft there. At the end of March they got their first taste of the USA. It wasn't a stadium, let alone a cool club, but it was New

York. The DJ Murray The K presented a review, which he promoted himself, called Music In The Fifth Dimension. The venue was the RKO Theatre in central New York.

Maurice Kauffman was a radio DJ, who had declared himself to be The Fifth Beatle as soon as The Fab Four landed in the States for their first US tour. He was such a self-publicist, and so shamelessly presented himself as being on the same level as the musicians, that many Americans thought he had discovered The Beatles. Shortly afterwards he managed the same trick with the Rolling Stones.

He was, in American parlance, a jerk – he wore a Beatles-style wig to hide the fact that he was going bald – but he had considerable influence. The musicians tolerated him because of this, but also teased him. He had been running big multi-name music shows every Easter for several years. 1967 was to be his biggest show, with eleven acts billed. Cream was alongside The Who – both bands billed as being 'direct from England – so that ensured a party. Jack was delighted to be sharing a stage with Wilson Pickett, but the soul singer wasn't impressed by the British bands' behaviour off-stage, which he described as 'unprofessional.' Smokey Robinson was billed as appearing but in fact he never showed up.

Janet Bruce went with the band, and she remembers that they were collected at the airport and driven straight to the theatre. There was no opportunity to have a look around or go sight-seeing. Then, all the musicians were locked in. There was no escape.

Cream played five shows every day, one a matinee which was very thinly attended – and then only by quarrelsome, bemused youngsters. In each show Cream were allowed just eight minutes, which hardly did them justice – to put it mildly. Murray The K's wife was far more interested in the dancers than the bands, and she managed to get the music element shortened even further so as to leave more time for the choreography. Eventually Cream was allowed just one song per show. The bill got so crowded that some bands were paid not to go on. After every show Murray The K held a post mortem and discuss how everything had gone. This included commenting on and criticising the performances. It wasn't a good idea.

They had played for nine days solid, and it wasn't an inspiring experience – indeed Eric later described it as 'a bit like being in a concentration camp.' At least they had played in the States though. On their return to the UK they played at a tiny jazz club in Redcar on the North Yorkshire coast. May, June and July were fairly thin months so far as live gigs were concerned, with only seven live appearances during May – one being the New Musical Express's Poll Winners' Concert at The Empire Pool, Wembley, and by contrast, another being at a dance organised by the German Jaguar drivers' club.

In August they played the Sunday night at the Windsor festival again, this time for an audience of 20,000 – who now knew exactly who they were, and what a treat they could expect. A week later the band left for the USA. This was their first big American tour, and while the venues weren't huge they were pretty good places to be seen; through September they played The Fillmore West in San Francisco, The Whisky A Go Go in Los Angeles, and The Psychedelic Supermarket in Boston. The Americans knew what the band was capable of and most shows were sell-outs.

Across August and September 1967 the band played eleven almost consecutive nights at The Fillmore, and Jack regards this as the zenith of the band's career. The band was still young and the three musicians were still fresh – and equally importantly The Fillmore had the best in-house PA system they had ever used. It was here, too, according to Janet Bruce, that the band really started to realise that there was something quite enormous going on. They were always met with enthusiasm by British audiences, but here in San Francisco it was a different world and a different vibe. Here they saw the first clues that they were reaching a truly broad audience, and their talents were being fully appreciated. They came out of the hotel one morning to find that adoring fans had covered their limos in flowers during the night. It was a bit hippy, so far as gestures went, but it rocked them. Hippy though, so far as it went, was still a real movement, coming up from the streets and the radical underground. Business interests hadn't spotted it yet and started to turn into a commercialised parody of itself. It was good; the right people were becoming passionate about what Cream was doing.

Quoted in Chris Welch's book on the band, Jack says that it was at The Fillmore in '67 that they started extending songs and adding improvised sections. They received a hugely enthusiastic response from the audience, who were used to Big Brother And The Holding Company and Jefferson Airplane, so were already on the right level for Cream's music.

The Americans were musically very literate, and appreciated quality and virtuosity. It didn't even matter that every one of them was out of their heads. As Jack said, 'The audience were all so out of it, so laidback, and they'd shout 'Just play!' We started jamming and that's what we became known for.' He also says that Eric would play solo for a very long time, often alone on stage, and the result was 'some incredible stuff, quite amazing.'

They had spent three days in the Atlantic studios straight after the Murray The K shows, and they peppered the US tour with recording sessions too. Over two dates, in mid-September and early October, they recorded White Room (so they were recording tracks for 'Wheels of Fire' before 'Disraeli Gears' was released). They returned to Britain and by contrast with playing the likes of The Fillmore, played a tiny club, Magoos, in Glasgow.

November was very busy, with more than a dozen live gigs, here and in Scandinavia, as well as several television appearances. December was quieter, though there were three dates in the States immediately before Christmas – one being a huge private party in Chicago.

During '67 Jack had found time to return to the jazz scene to work on the recording of the album 'Trio' with Mike Taylor (who had co-written songs with Ginger Baker for Cream) and Jon Hiseman. Ron Rubin played bass when Jack was unavailable.

On some tracks Jack played the acoustic bass with a bow to create a haunting bass sound, which suited the eastern influences which Mike was introducing into his music. The session must have been a great pleasure for Jack after the rigours of touring with Cream. He was completely unchanged by being part of a super-group, Jon says; he arrived at the studio without any fuss or pomp, and simply got down to giving the very best performance he could, just as he would always have done. Mike Taylor never saw the broad recognition his music deserved, and he died in 1969 aged 31, almost certainly having taken his own life: Jack and Jon were among the musicians who played at a tribute concert for him in June of that year.

Things started getting a lot busier in February. Again they were playing live and performing for television in Scandinavia, followed by a trip to the New York studios, which lasted ten days. From there it was straight out onto their second US tour which was to last until the middle of June – and then it was back to the Atlantic studios for more recording work. On this tour there were still a few modest venues, but in the main they were playing auditoria, big ballrooms and convention centres.

In the autumn of '68 Jack had a change of pace – and a few days of very authentic blues. An old friend of Eric's, Mike Vernon, was producing an album for blues singer Martha Velez, and had put together a stunning line-up of musicians, including – among many luminaries - Mitch Mitchell, Christine McVie, who was singing with Chicken Shack, jazz-rock keyboards man Brian Auger, and Jim Capaldi from Traffic. He asked both Jack and Eric to complete the team, and the album was released in 1969, entitled 'Fiends And Angels.' It remains a sadly little-known but hugely impressive work.

'Wheels Of Fire' was released in August 1968, and was a double album – which was a talking point in itself (though it was also, confusingly, available as two separate single albums, and over the years, in several other formats too). The first disc was recorded in the studio, and the second was live. This was a nod towards the theory that Cream was a different band live and on record. The cover was again designed by Martin Sharp, and was printed in just two colours, black and a metallic silver. It looked far more sophisticated than 'Disraeli Gears' and had even more visual appeal.

The first disc opening with the stunningly powerful White Room, with Jack keeping time like an atomic clock, Ginger thundering through patterns more complex than had ever been heard on a rock record, and Eric showing that he was the absolute master of wah-wah guitar. Jack's singing moved so effortlessly into his upper, treble range that some thought there were two singers duetting. It was a hugely impressive introduction to the album. In many ways it is the perfect Cream song; perfectly structured and ordered, meticulously produced, and with not a note too many or too few. Some of the most interesting musicianship comes in the fade-out; Jack allows himself to run into a lovely jazz bassline.

Jack composed the music for White Room long before he played it to Pete, and the lyricists first reaction was to write 'a psychedelic Cinderella story' (Pete still has the lyric, and any Creamologist would sell their granny for it). It simply didn't work though, and Pete's imagination was then fired by the song Red Room which had been written by a friend. It was a very different sort of thing, but Pete was actually living in a white room – in a flat off Baker Street, near both Marylebone and Euston stations – so red became white. He started off writing a rambling eight-page poem, which eventually turned into the lyrics after a massive drinking binge - which had seen a girlfriend run off in terror because Pete insisted on talking to the furniture. He says that another inspiration was movie imagery, and indeed the song sounds like odd frames from unrelated films which somehow join up to make a complete image.

Pete has very rarely written about himself when working with Jack. Over the years Pete has found it important to write lyrics which were very much created to fit Jack's personal landscape; you can't sing as passionately about someone else's cares, concerns, fantasies and ambitions as you can about your own.

Like Sunshine Of Your Love, White Room doesn't sound at all dated, forty years on. Pete says that he and Jack were trying, consciously or semi-consciously to avoid writing disposable pop. Coming out of their classical and jazz backgrounds it was understood that music was created to last, which wasn't exactly how Dave Dee Dozy Becky Mick and Titch worked. A lot of music of the time, be it Strawberry Fields Forever, Pinball Wizard, House Of The Rising Sun or Let's Spend The Night Together sound as good today as the day they were recorded, but the total is still a minority of the great mass of overtly commercial music being pumped out. Consciously or semi-consciously, Jack and Pete were writing music that would last; music which would still be heard and still sound good in years to come. In that there were extraordinarily successful.

At much the same time Pete was giving up both drugs and drink, having been a prodigious user of both for a dozen years or so. He was suffering from anxiety and panic attacks, indeed his enjoyment of Cream live was greatly marred by the terror which was brought on by the excessive volume. He stopped using stimulants completely, which left him with extreme claustrophobia for about a year, but also gave him an informed perspective as Jack's intake of both alcohol and drugs increased.

Cream: Jack with Gibson EB3, Ginger, and Eric uncharacteristically with an acoustic guitar (Redferns)

Politician was unlike anything else they wrote in that it dealt with a single, obvious subject, and actually told a tale. It's cynical and satirical, and at times Jack almost sneers the lyrics. The words could only have been written by Pete Brown, just as the bass line could only have been written and played by Jack Bruce.

As You Said doesn't fit comfortably on this album. It's much more the sort of music which Jack came to after Cream had disbanded, and it belongs to a different thought process. It's very classically influenced, without a hint of blues or rock. Jack played two cello and two acoustic guitar tracks, which were mixed with Ginger keeping time on the hi-hat. Apart from that percussion it was performed solo. On Pressed Rat And Warthog he played the recorder as well as injecting a second melody with lightning-fast bass.

Deserted Cities Of The Night is less distinguished, though Jack played a fairly conventional but very powerful bass throughout. He also played guitar and cello on the track, while Felix played viola. The song's real treat is the break, which sees Eric lay a solo over a typically fast and complex Bruce 'n Baker foundation.

The first record included only two re-worked blues numbers; Chester Burnette's Sitting On Top Of The World, and Born Under A Bad Sign - which was a recent recording, written by William Bell and Booker T Jones, and which Felix brought to their attention. They stretched Willie Dixon's Spoonful to nearly seventeen minutes in all, which was a fair representation of how they improvised at great length when playing live. On that track Jack displayed just how much vocal power and soul he was able to inject into a song.

Of the other three tracks, one was Ginger Baker's masterpiece Toad, where bass and guitar led him in and then drop away to give him space for a lengthy and stunningly adroit drum solo. Slightly too lengthy, some said. The other was Jack slamming down his visiting card with Traintime. He plays dynamic, swooping, Ferrari-fast harmonica over Ginger's impermeable, concrete-cast drumming, and manages to articulate the lyrics almost as he plays. It's a seven minute-long work of genius; a terrific achievement. Once again it was as if Jack was saying, 'You want to know what I can do? Listen to this!'

On the record it sounds as if Traintime is woven into Toad, but in fact the two songs were recorded at different times and in different auditoria. The first three tracks were cut at Winterland in San Francisco over a two-day period, and Toad was recorded at The Fillmore West.

The second disc opens with one of the band's all-time classic tracks though - their furious, brilliant, manic version of Crossroads, on which Jack's bass playing was inspired and incandescent. To really understand the track you have to go back and listen to the Robert Johnson original. Being able to make such a leap, to take the song from where it started and position it where they did was a prodigious achievement. The blues had come a long way. It's the perfect example of Jack, Eric and Ginger battling it out to the very last breath, and the results have delighted music lovers for almost forty years.

This was the first double album to ever sell a million copies, which earned the band a platinum disc. In time-honoured tradition, Jack's is hung on the wall of his downstairs loo.

There were major problems within the band now though. There was still a large degree of animosity between Jack and Ginger, and they rarely came to blows, but they could hardly be in the same room together. Their relationship made everything difficult; working together in studio, being on the road, working on new music. Eric usually found that the best survival technique was simply to keep out of their way. Certainly his hopes for the band were not being realised. Musically it was still great, but he was sensitive man, and didn't have the rugged self-defence systems the other two had built up. He couldn't handle the aggression. He wanted to play great music but he needed a more stable and far less tempestuous environment in which to live and work.

The other factor was that all three band members were simply exhausted. They hardly ever stopped. The workload was terrifying. Nobody in management realised that the musicians needed time to relax, unwind and re-charge their creative batteries. Playing venues like The Fillmore was great, but there were far too many smaller gigs which were stuffed into the diary, and which only served to further stretch the band's energy and strain the dynamics between them. Also, Cream never had the back up which bands started to gain in the Seventies, and which are taken for granted today. No money was spent on guarding the investment; there weren't enough assistants let alone a band masseur and physiotherapist.

By the time 'Wheels Of Fire' was released though, the decision to break up the band was already four months old, and they were planning their farewell tour.

By way of a diversion, in 1968 Jack had also played on the single Lily The Pink recorded by the trio of Liverpudlian poets who made up The Scaffold. It was a cross between novelty record and a Penny Lane-style slice of Scouse whimsy, but it caught the imagination and was an unexpected hit. It wasn't really true that anything coming out of Liverpool at that time could get into the charts, but Lily The Pink went to number one – and that's Jack playing bass on it.

Chapter 15

The financial rewards started to flow in during late 1967, and the money was from both live gigs and record sales – particularly album sales in the States. Pete Brown can identify the moment exactly; he had been earning £20 or £25 a week on the jazz and poetry circuit and was living in one room. By the middle of '67 the song-writing royalty cheques were worth tens of thousands of pounds – he remembers that just one cheque was for around £40,000. He bought an elegant house in Montagu Square, just north of Marble Arch, and started spending money – including investing in his own band.

The division of royalties was always a sore point with Ginger. His argument is that he brought enough to all the songs to at least get some cut out of the revenue they generated. While Pete always got on well with Eric, he and Ginger have always kept each other at arm's length. Pete doesn't have a lot of time for Ginger's thinking, arguing that these songs – such as White Room, I Feel Free and Sunshine Of Your Love - served to greatly enhance the band's profile, so Ginger earned well off the back of them, albeit obliquely.

Pete had one advantage over Jack and the other members of the band: His royalties came to him through the established music publishing system, with no one in the middle making deductions. The band had long lists of expenses re-charged to their accounts before they saw any cash, and that was one of many ways for the unscrupulous to take fiscal advantage of artists. Pete would also have been paid promptly. Jack had to wait for whatever level of remuneration he ended up with. He is firm in his belief that where there was always a delay in the band getting paid, huge sums were being made by management, by investing the money for a few months before advancing it. Jack would then see the cash, but not the interest that it had generated. As Pete said, 'Strange things happened to the money. But then it did for a lot of bands in those days.'

It's highly likely that Jack didn't see all the income due to him, but that doesn't mean that was badly off. The days of small flats and small cars were over. It was now big houses and Ferraris.

In Pete's opinion the success did start to change Jack, but it was brought about by the adulation rather than the money. He was, Pete points out, still very young; 'He was playing to 20,000 people and 10,000 women were trying to rip his trousers off. It must change you. Before that happens you can't have any concept of what it would do to you.'

Janet deliberately keeping a low profile, and was quite happy with that. Nowadays they would be a celebrity couple, but in 1967 it was just becoming acceptable for pop and rock stars to admit to being married. John Lennon's marriage to Cynthia was kept strictly secret for a long time, and when it was revealed, a million girls around the world went and wept into their pillows. Similarly, Charlie Watts and Bill Wyman had to pretend that they were available bachelors. In the Manfred Mann days, Janet recalls, Paul Jones's wife was forbidden from even letting on that she was with the band when she went to a gig. For a sex symbol like Paul it was assumed that admitting to having a wife was commercial suicide.

Of his huge success with Cream, Jack's brother says, 'In a way I think I saw it com-

A study in style; Charlie wears a plain T-shirt, while Jack goes for the full Carnaby Street effect (CB)

ing. I wasn't surprised. I thought he was going to be a big thing. Mind you, for a while I had no idea how big Cream had become. It took a while to sink in to my consciousness.' He was still a jazz aficionado and what Cream was doing was beyond his immediate experience.

'When Jack introduced me to people he'd say 'This is my brother and he's very critical' because if I didn't like something I'd tell him. I was tactless. I realised it came from a blues background though and it was easy for me to like it when I got into it.' Jack always gave his brother a copy of his latest record. Charlie's over-riding criticism is that they played far too loud.

Charlie felt nothing but delight for his brother's obvious success; 'I was never jealous or anything. It obviously wasn't going to be me doing that. I was very happy to bask in the reflected glory!' He also gives him credit for working very hard indeed at mastering the bass and going beyond the conventional thinking. He remembers, fairly early on, seeing calluses on Jack's fingers inflicted by the heavy strings. 'He practised and practised and practised. Someone who knew of the connection once asked me what it took to break in as a professional musician. I told that from having watched Jack there were two things he had to do – go to London and work on the instrument every hour you could.'

Charlie saw Cream play on several occasions. One gig he attended was back home in Glasgow and he went to their hotel. His impression was that they all looked so youthful, and that both drink and drugs were openly available. He recalls Eric being very quiet, and says of Ginger, 'Just looking at him you knew that you didn't want to get too close to him. Especially after they had played!'

Charlie remembers the Ferraris too. On one occasion he was arriving back at Heathrow with two trade union colleagues and Jack offered to come and pick them up. He roared up in his latest Ferrari, everyone was squeezed in and they set off back to London on the A4 at a speed Charlie remembers vividly to this day.

At least once Jack went home to Glasgow in a Ferrari. This was a car which cost just short of £7,000, which was the price of a sizeable house – perhaps the equivalent of £500,000 now. You could get fourteen perfectly acceptable mid-sized saloon cars for the same money; even a Jaguar E-Type, very much an exotic and fabulous car, was around a quarter of the price. A new Ford Cortina was a possession to be very proud of. It had four cylinders and could manage 80mph from a 48 horsepower engine. A Ferrari of the same year had twelve cylinders, generated 300 horsepower and was capable of an unimaginable 160mph.

Exotic cars would still have been rare sights in Pollock (though by this time his parents had now moved out to East Kilbride, and the quality of life was undoubtedly better), and for his old friends and neighbours in Glasgow this value was as much as they might earn in total in a lifetime. It's hard to imagine what they made of it, but the reaction was probably one of pride rather than envy though. At least one of their own folk, something they actually knew, was enjoying real success. Unlike now there would have been no fear that anyone would have tried to vandalise the car.

Charlie also recalls one day when he was outside his own house working on the second-hand Minivan he owned. Vans were significantly cheaper than cars as they attracted a lower level of Purchase Tax. Family men who bought them would fit seats into the back to turn them into very basic, windowless estate cars. Charlie was struggling with a metalworking saw, trying to complete this job in the very cramped rear of the van when Jack arrived. He was in another Ferrari, a newer model, and the roar came down the street ahead of him. Charlie couldn't help but note the difference in their respective circumstances.

Riding in a cab through the streets of San Francisco with Robert Stigwood, during the Fillmore residency, Jack insisted on taking a closer look at a car in a dealer's window. It was a Chevrolet Corvette Stingray convertible, a stunningly aggressive sports car that stood alone as America's most powerful and most expensive sports car. With just a few optional extras it cost $5,000, and it wasn't at all hard to nudge that price up to $6,000. The Ford Mustang was a hugely desirable sporting car, but you could buy two of them for $5,000, and get change. The Corvette had a 427 cubic inch motor, which produced 435 horsepower. It was enough to tear your head off. It was the car that The Beach Boys and Jan and Dean revered.

Robert asked Jack if he'd like it, which was rather unnecessary, but added to the drama. Robert told him they'd come back tomorrow with the takings from that night's gig, and so they did. Robert led him inside the showroom – enjoying it as much as Jack - summoned the salesman, and proceeded to count out the cost of the car, as it was on the tag hanging from the interior mirror, in dollar bills. Jack was completely stunned, and delighted beyond words. So was the salesman. The salesman spluttered, 'Jesus Christ', as the pile of notes grew bigger on his desk, 'I'm not even going to count it. Here's the keys.' Jack drove them back to their hotel, revelling in the V8 roar and the unmatched acceleration. A few days later he drove the car down to Los Angeles, from where it was to be shipped back to the UK, 'And I got stopped by the police a lot.'

Back home he made the mistake of driving the Sting Ray on English roads, in the wet, and trying to go round corners. Wet bends were European concerns, and hugely powerful American cars weren't made for them. Corvettes were simply terrifying in those conditions. Jack then decided that he would use the car for a touring holiday of the West of Scotland. A less appropriate vehicle can hardly be imagined. He took it across to the Isle of Arran on the tiny, open ferry, and it must have looked curiously incongruous. He sold that car privately and the new owner blew it up in Regent's

Street. Never mind, time for a Ferrari.

There was another side to the buying of the Corvette. It was a revelation. It started Jack thinking about money – or rather, started him thinking that there was probably a vast amount of money around, but very little of it was in his account. As he says, 'I'd never really thought that I was rich, that I had money.' It may well have been Stigwood's act, smacking of braggadocio as it did, that got him thinking about the cash that the band was earning.

He went through a number of other makes of supercar before alighting on Ferraris; 'I wanted a really great sports car and eventually I just sort of settled on Ferrari.' He forgets exactly how many he has owned, or what models, but he reels off an impressive list - and a few moments later remembers another, and several minutes later yet another. Close to the top of that list is the 330GT 2+2 (which was a concession to the arrival of his first son, though getting even a small child into the back would have required a very supple spine). There was an e-mail on his web site recently from a guy in New Zealand who recalled hitchhiking with a friend in Scotland in the late Sixties. A guy in a Ferrari drew up and gave them a ride all the way to their destination at very high speed. Jack was the driver, and the correspondent has never forgotten being shoved in the back and spending the journey curled up like a half-closed penknife

There was also a 365GTC, in which he slid off the A6 while on his way up to Scotland. At high speed. Again he had picked up a hitchhiker, and though they both walked away, the car was wrecked. It wasn't his fault; a suspension component had sheared off. Jack's Ferrari dealer got in touch with the factory, who swore that such a thing simply could never happen. They continued to deny the possibility of such a failure – but also offered him a new Ferrari Daytona, on the understanding that they could take the other car away. Discreetly.

Janet got to drive one of the Ferraris – just once – when they were living in East Anglia. Jack fell off a moped near the house and caught his hand between it and the gravel. This wasn't just a painful injury, it was obviously a potential disaster. With his hand bandaged as well as possible, he got into the Ferrari and Janet drove him to hospital in Colchester. He was treated, and was told it would heal perfectly well given time. On the way home though, seeing a line of stationary cars ahead, she went for the brake pedal. It wasn't the brake though. She says that she remembers the front of the car lifting as it accelerated forwards. The car they hit wasn't too badly damaged, but as she says, 'For some reason it really badly damaged the Ferrari.' Fortunately Jack was too preoccupied with his injured hand to care – 'He must have been in shock. He didn't scream at me' – but she never again drove one of his Ferraris.

Nothing ever really worked properly on his Ferraris, and the Daytona in particular gave him a lot of problems, 'The heater never worked, and the lights never worked properly – you couldn't see properly at night at all. But you forgave it everything. That car was phenomenal.' He says that he can't define the attraction of the marque, and falls back on 'If you've ever driven one you'll understand.' Ferrari's great rivals, their near-neighbours Lamborghini, get very short shrift from him because they made their name manufacturing agricultural tractors – and because they dared, outrageously, to try and take Ferrari's crown as supreme Italian sports car manufacturer.

The Daytona, registration number APG 11H, was the car on the cover of his album 'Things We Like.' It was, he says, the most wonderful car he has ever owned.

All three members of Cream were car fanatics. Ginger bought a Jensen Interceptor, which was made in the less sunny and romantic surroundings of West Bromwich. It was a very rare and exotic car though, and was also powered by a monstrous American V8 engine. It cost him £4,000 – three times the price of a Mk2 Jaguar. Ginger's car wasn't just an Interceptor though, it was the FF version which had four wheel drive – at a time when only Land Rovers had such a thing – and an electronic anti-skid braking device, many years before ABS first became available. It was fabulously exclusive, only three hundred were ever made, and that was of course ever so important.

He was in very good company with the Jensen; Frank Sinatra had an Interceptor – though not an FF - as did Matt Busby. Other rock stars went for them in the Seventies, including Mitch Mitchell, drummer with The Jimi Hendrix Experience, and Jon Bonham, drummer with Led Zeppelin (in fact he owned several), folk singer Barry McGuire, and Cliff Richard. Curiously there was also a band called Jensen Interceptor. Ginger was as ferocious a driver as Jack. Jack once allowed him to drive from London to the house in Suffolk; 'He drove so fast, I hated. He was just trying to scare me – and he succeeded very well.'

Eric was as one with Jack. He also went for Ferraris. Jack says that Eric was a terrible driver. He remembers him owning a particular rare and hugely desirable Ferrari Berlinetta – and watching him repeatedly hitting the pavements on both sides of the street as he tried to turn it round; 'I'm sure he's a very fine driver now ...' When Britain's rock aristocracy all went to the Isle Of Wight in 1969 to see Bob Dylan play, they hired a luxury coach for the trip. Eric refused to join in, and insisted on driving them himself in his Mercedes Benz 600SEL limousine – the car of choice for despotic dictators.

Jack's fleet included such contrasts as a Morgan, a couple of Mini Coopers ('everyone had them'), an AC Cobra and a Rolls-Royce Phantom III. The Rolls was a massive car, dating from the Thirties. It had elegant, sweeping lines and a huge 12-cylinder engine - the same engine that powered Spitfire fighters, as Jack points out with pleasure. It had belonged to Dame Mirabelle Topham, who owned Aintree racecourse. The car was painted in royal livery and was used to transport the Queen every Grand National day.

'I really could park that car anywhere. I used to park it on the pavement in central London and no one ever complained. It seemed like a good family car ...'

The Rolls could hardly have been more different from his line of sports cars – especially as the engine was almost completely silent and free of vibration at any speed. It was good for about 80mph, rather than the Daytona's 170mph.

The most radical car he bought was a Lola, which was really a race car, and which shouldn't have been let out on the public road. They had originally been built for long-distance races such as Le Mans, Sebring and Daytona, and were powered by a massive Chevrolet V8. It looked like a more radical version of Ford's GT40 (which Jack considered – but decided against). The company offered a small number to the public as part of a homologation programme (a specified number of cars had to be offered for public sale before the car was allowed to race). You could have any colour you liked so long as it was white. You added the race stripes yourself.

The songwriter Jimmy Webb had bought the first of the road-legal versions, and Jack got the second. To get in you had to turn a key and then slide back the Perspex roof – and climb in as best you could; they were the lowest road cars ever manufactured. The seats lifted up on electric motors to aid access, and then lowered you into the very depths of the car. 'It wasn't a very good car', Jack says, 'But it looked very good. It looked amazing.'

One day Jack met Ahmet Urtegun at the Robert Stigwood Organisation offices in Brook Street. It was snowing, so he didn't want to be out in the weather. That wasn't a good enough reason to ask Jack for a lift though. When they got out to the street though, the car was nowhere to be seen. The world's lowest car, covered in snow, was utterly invisible. Jack uncovered it, Ahmet got in, and Jack drove him to his hotel – at his usual speed, in a race car, in central London, in the snow. There was never any question of Ahmet asking for a lift ever again.

Jack was running another road-legal race car, a Lotus 47, when his first son was born. The birth was obviously imminent and the obvious thing for Jack to do was to drive his wife to hospital. The Lotus wasn't much easier to get into than the Lola, and while it was a struggle for her, a full nine months pregnant, to get in, it was an even trickier job after the blissfully short drive to the hospital.

It was the era when, suddenly, young men who looked as if they couldn't afford a Triumph Spitfire, were dropping into the country's most exclusive car showrooms and just taking their pick of what was on offer. Jack wasn't the first, but he was very much in that mid-Sixties wave, to whom money simply didn't matter. If he wanted the blood red Ferrari in the window then he was going to have it. It wasn't just rock stars; it was photographers, actors, designers and even hairdressers. Rock stars probably had the highest profile though, and it wasn't long before the artists' parking compound behind a venue would look like a Motor Show in itself. Nowadays football training grounds look the same. He recalls meeting Rod Stewart at a gig at The Oval; Rod was arriving in his new Lamborghini Miura and he was in the Daytona. They traded insults about each other's cars. It was a wonderful time to be young and wealthy.

As well as his everyday cars he still owns a Bristol 412 - a quirky, boxy 2+2 made between the mid-Seventies and the early Eighties: Another British-made car running a large American V8 engine.

'I had a BMW M3 convertible a couple of years ago and it was the first good, modern car; the first I'd been impressed by. I wouldn't trust myself in a real sports car now. My days of sports car are over.'

Part of the income from the reunion concerts is going to fund a couple of new cars, but Jack is worried that buying large-engined cars is no longer socially acceptable. A Bentley's W12, six-litre engine makes a considerable impact on the environment and has one of the tiniest miles-per-gallon figures. He considers this for a moment, but the thought passes. Yes, he's going to get a Bentley – and possibly an old Ferrari too, just for the glorious hell of it. 'I've always been a bit mad with cars', he adds, perhaps a little unnecessarily.

'I've always been a bit mad with cars', he adds, perhaps a little unnecessarily.

Success didn't really change Jack though, in Charlie's opinion. 'Jack has a lot of my father's characteristics. He's assertive, dogmatic and argumentative', Charlie says – but having said that he adds that he's not that dissimilar himself. Success made these traits appear stronger.

Charlie says that his parents were very proud of their younger son. Their mother in particular was delighted with his success. He's not certain that he entirely agrees with Jack's opinion of his father's resentment – though by then, perhaps inevitably, the two brothers were drifting apart. Their lives had become very different.

Janet was close to Charlie Jnr and his family, and when the break-up occurred it was she that notified the wider family. By that point, Charlie says, Jack was unreachable both physically and emotionally. The process of estrangement accelerated. 'Whether he didn't want to know me or whether it was the drugs – I don't really know. I couldn't have a conversation with him any more.'

It was Jack's illness in 2003 that brought the two brothers back together. Charlie had been to a couple of his gigs and they had exchanged greetings, but when his second wife Margrit phoned him and told him about Jack's condition Charlie decided that getting together once again was well overdue. It was Margrit, he says, who engineered the reunion.

'I'm not uncomfortable in his company these days, but he still has the traits. There's still a lot of our father there. He's not backward at coming forward. He can be very affable but he needs to be approached cautiously.

'I do think that Margrit has been good for him … mind you, I thought Janet was good for him! I'm very proud of him though.'

There was a moment in a trade union meeting in January 2005 when the Cream reunion was mentioned and Charlie made some sort of comment, which could have suggested knowledge of the band. Another committee member spotted this and asked him why that was. Before he could answer a colleague said, 'Don't you know? Charlie is Jack Bruce's brother.' The questioner sat there absolutely open-mouthed, looking like a guppy. 'He nearly fell over onto the floor.' Charlie enjoyed the moment.

'Mind you, when I've heard people say that I'm his brother I have corrected them and said 'No, Jack's my brother.'' Charlie adds.

He was very surprised to hear about the reunion concerts – 'astounded' is his word. 'All three are real characters in their own right, but Ginger and Jack were like oil and water. They both had very strong opinions about the way things should be and they just picked at each other automatically. They just didn't like each other.'

Chapter 16

During October and November 1968 Cream played eighteen Farewell gigs across the USA. These were at some of the biggest venues they had ever played, and it was ironic that they did so to say goodbye. Their audiences were ecstatic for the moment but disconsolate for the future. The fans simply didn't understand the decision. They felt robbed of their musical future.

To whatever degree though, the band had done what its three members set out to do and the break-up was inevitable; Jack says, 'We had just wanted to be recognised for being a great band. We never wanted to bring down society or anything; we only ever wanted to make good music. That's all we wanted to do. All the other stuff people attached to us was because of the times in which we were playing. We just wanted people to listen to us and have a good time.'

The band's last American gig was at The Rhode Island Auditorium on Monday November 4. They then had a three-week break before they played their Farewell show at The Royal Albert Hall – or rather, shows, as they actually played two gigs at the hall on Tuesday November 26.

The BBC commissioned film-maker Tony Palmer to make a 45-minute documentary of the Farewell concert for the Omnibus arts programme, which was broadcast the following January.

It was a schizophrenic work. Palmer used the new-fangled zoom lens to give an impression of psychedelic modernity, but the structure, and in particular actor Patrick Allen's commentary, were very old-fashioned; the latter sounded as if it belonged to a 1950s documentary produced for the good of the nation. Along with a greatly overused zoom effect, with the image swishing in and out, Palmer also, inexplicably, showed us a medium close up of a youth in the audience for an infuriatingly long time. This guy was shaking his head fairly wildly from side to side, and, infuriatingly, the camera returned to him again and again. At the point where you really wanted to see what your musical heroes were doing, all you were allowed to see was this lad treating

Coming to the end of the road in 1968.
By then had been two years of almost non-stop recording and gigging (Mitchell Kane)

his embarrassed and annoyed neighbours to a dandruff shower.

The film was shot over both performances the band played that day; the give-away is the fact that for some numbers Ginger was wearing a dark green, embroidered African smock, and for others a blue satin shirt. The band were a sartorial delightful to the end; Eric wore a red and gold cowboy shirt – very country and western, while Jack was in a mid-blue shirt with a slightly fey ruched collar.

Interviews with each were cut into the film, which slowed the pace, and were obviously filmed quite a long time before the gig (the give-away here being different hairstyles and in Jack's case, the presence of a somewhat scrawny moustache). The interviewer's questions sounded as if they were written on another planet; indeed his questions were almost certainly dubbed on afterwards. In his interview, Jack – wearing a big-brimmed leather hat with a large feather stuck in it – railed against his classical music education at length, but then felt he had to establish his musical credibility, and said, 'Bach is the ultimate bass player.' It was a culture slot, after all.

Palmer said of the film, 'It's rough; raw would be a better word. It's often clumsy.

But it does have the extraordinary energy of the occasion. I don't think I've ever seen another recording of a concert in which the atmosphere is so exactly as it was on the night.' It wasn't hard to agree with the first sentiments and disagree completely with the last.

The band had never had that sort of exposure on British television, and it introduced a lot of people to their music, and ignited interest in others who might have been stirred by hearing a couple of their singles. Hearing the band was one thing, but seeing them play confirmed their virtuosity and energy – particularly the phenomenal force that Jack and Ginger put into their playing. In those pre-MTV, pre-The Tube, pre-The Old Grey Whistle Test, pre-Later days there were very few chances to see quality music on television – and seeing them miming on a mainstream show wasn't quite the same. It's just a shame that it was all posthumous.

Cream was supported at The Royal Albert Hall by the progressive rock band Yes, and another trio, Taste - which was fronted by Irish blues guitarist Rory Gallagher, who was just twenty years old. He played alongside bass player Eric Kitteringham and drummer Norman D'Amery. It was the highest profile gig that Rory had played at that point and proved to be a very useful platform for his talents.

Their last full album, 'Goodbye', was released in March 1969, and the single taken from it, Badge (with What A Bringdown on the B-side) was released the following month. These were the band's parting shots. They themselves were long gone. The cover shot showed the band in silver frock coats, with silver bow ties, silver top hats and cans, doing a Variety Hall-style 'thank you and goodnight.' It was horrible.

Several songs, which had already been heard on record, were revisited on 'Goodbye'; an exhilarating, riotous, nine minute-long version of I'm So Glad, the ominous Politician, and the dark and moody Sitting On Top Of The World were all live recordings made during the final American tour. Badge, Doing That Scrapyard Thing and What A Bringdown were recorded in studio in London just a few days before the Albert Hall shows. There was a composition by each of the band members; Badge – which was a posthumous hit in the singles charts - was written by Eric (with George Harrison), What A Bringdown by Ginger, and Doing That Scrapyard Thing was a Bruce/Brown composition. It's a flimsy song, and one of their weakest; a nonsense song that doesn't work – whereas What A Bringdown is a nonsense song which works far better. And it's a rare day when a Baker song is better than one by Bruce and Brown.

Soon after Cream announced that they were to split, The Jimi Hendrix Experience was scheduled to play on The Lulu Show. Her early evening programme featured some of the best musicians in the world. As she says, 'We had great guests on that show. We'd had Aretha Franklin, Wilson Pickett and Stevie Wonder - but no one did what Jimi did.'

Although Lulu had known Eric since she first came to London, she hadn't met Jack until he joined Cream. She was blown away by the music, and in particular his singing. She says, 'I loved I Feel Free. It wasn't the blues, it wasn't r 'n b, it wasn't rock 'n roll – it was just so new. Each of them was a great musician, and of course the three of them thought they were in three different bands. But the fusion was what made it so enormously successful.

'They knew they were good at what they were doing. I know they were trying to beat each up with their instruments – but that's true of a lot of bands. You have to have that ego, or be stoned. Or both. They just went into the zone and became as one.'

Jimi started off his set on her show by playing his own music, but stopped in mid-song. Then he announced that was going to play a tribute to his favourite band, and started playing Sunshine Of Your Love – a characteristically wilder, less focussed but brilliant cover of the song. At a time when just about every word uttered on television was scripted, this was unheard of. And the band didn't stop playing when they were told to. Lulu recalls, 'It was unbelievable; I didn't know he was going to do that – I don't think that he knew he was going to do it – but I was just thinking what's he doing? Oh my god!

'This was the BBC, and live. You couldn't go to a commercial or anything. I thought the poor Floor Manager was going to have a heart attack.

'Afterwards Jimi came up to me and apologised. He was so well mannered, such a gentleman. He was genuinely upset about Cream breaking up.'

Jack says that the speed at which everything was required to happen was ultimately responsible for the break up of Cream. They never had the luxury of time. Everything was stuffed into too short a time-span. For this he blames Robert Stigwood.

His opinion is that Stigwood was never aware of how good they were as musicians, how good the band was as an entity in itself. He was looking, he says, at short term gain rather than long term investment and return; 'Like so many managers at that time, he was just trying to milk it. Their thinking was that it wouldn't last, and often it didn't last because of their shortsighted and selfish attitude.' The number of live shows they had to play, and the haphazard way they were organised and timetabled, meant that there was never the luxury of time to try out new ideas in the studio and refine their music. With some obvious exceptions, Stigwood never hustled them into the right venues, he says, and obvious opportunities were missed; 'We didn't play the Monterey Festival', Jack says, 'We didn't do Woodstock – we didn't do anything like that. Which is a great, great pity.' The band toured America incessantly, he says, bringing in cash, but not playing the best venues, the historic festivals, or getting in front of the right people; 'We never went to Australia, we never went to Japan, we never went anywhere apart from America. The only European things that we did were as the band was beginning.'

Pete Brown makes the point that many people in the music industry were still certain that pop and rock were merely passing fads; 'They thought people were going to go back to wanting sixteen-piece dance orchestras. Management's attitude was to grab a piece of this while it was happening, and the fuck off. For years it was pot luck with management, and as a result you got some very bad decisions.'

Jack argues that the band couldn't write new material together – either with each other or with their preferred writing partners - because there was simply never enough time. Going somewhere, anywhere, together during 1967 and having a couple of months to try new material would have made a huge difference to both their musical strengths and their individual relationships. He was very ambitious as a songwriter and composer, he says, but certainly not to the exclusion of the others. He regrets not having been able to write more with Pete for Cream, though he wouldn't have wanted their work to dominate either an album or the band's live set-list. There should have been enough time for everyone to have contributed, in whatever way was best for the band.

Robert Stigwood certainly provided the band with a launch pad, but having done that he had them playing in front of tiny audiences at poor venues, often in the most obscure places. As late as July 1967 – with both 'Fresh Cream' and 'Disraeli Gears' having gone into the top twenty in the album charts - they played a tiny venue in Elgin, in north-east Scotland. Three or four years previously that would have been understandable, but events had moved on very rapidly in that time, and a manager of a band like such as Cream could have justifiably been far more confident and adventurous.

Pete is at one with Jack about Robert Stigwood's lack of vision; 'It wasn't Beethoven or a cure for cancer or something, but Cream made very good, serious, popular music with genuinely artistic elements. They were to music what the better side of Hollywood is to the movie industry; somehow or other good things do get done, and it's an uneasy relationship between art and commerce but art does break through.'

Jack also agrees with commentators who have said that Stigwood was seemed more interested in The Bee Gees, because the commercial opportunities they offered were more obvious. It's likely that he better understood what The Bee Gees were about. He was too old to be a Cream fan, too much a popularist who didn't understand the appeal of walking down a suburban street in an ex-RAF greatcoat with the right album sleeve under your arm. Robert liked to live well; he wasn't at home in hard rock venues.

Although they were all born in England, Maurice, Barry and Robin Gibb were all brought up in Australia, like Robert – and above all, they were the sort of straight forward pop band which connected with his experience and taste. They had no rock ambitions, no desire for their records to be played late at night by John Peel, or be considered musically important by the cognoscenti. They played catchy pop songs and made a lot of money, and that was great.

Andrew Oldham was an anti-establishment rebel who delighted in shocking, and he channelled that into exactly the right sort of promotion for The Stones. Brian Epstein was a far more conventional figure, and more conservative in business, but he had both foresight and an understanding of what The Beatles were capable of. If Cream had been fortunate enough to have the management they deserved, management that focussed on their development to the exclusion of everything else, and never lowered its standards, the band would have been even bigger than they were, and would have been playing and recording for much longer.

Jack is passionate in the explanation of his thinking. These are thoughts with have obviously been hovering in the back of his mind for nearly forty years; 'He had absolutely no imagination. What if the band had gone on? Think of what Eric has done, think of what I have done in my own way – not commercially so successful – but musically perhaps more successful than what Eric has done. Think if we had gone on...'

To most of their fans they could hardly have been more important or have connected more directly, but the short span of the band's career was certainly a great disappointment to many. Another school of thought, working through the 'what if' theories, suggests that the band did what they did supremely well and then got out before they went stale; got out while they were at the height of their powers.

After 1968 The Beatles went into bitter decline and endured internecine horrors that soured the happy memories for many fans, and left them angry and perplexed. The Rolling Stones however did not. As a result of the complex strengths within the band and the unflagging ability of Mick and Keith to write some of the best rock songs the world has ever heard, they simply stayed doing the job. The graph went down as well as up, but the fact that more than four decades after their formation that one of their tours will attract audiences totalling millions tells its own story. On the other hand, death brought an end to both Led Zeppelin, following the death of drummer John Bonham, and to Jimi. Led Zeppelin was in existence for a full ten years, but Jimi's span was not that much longer than that of Cream.

Cream could have followed any of these paths. Given the strength of the personalities in the band, and the absolute self-confidence and certainty of each one of them, they might have ended up like The Beatles. They might have harangued one another publicly in an unseemly fashion and launched legal actions against each other on a daily basis. The band might well have come to a natural end with the death of any one of them. The odds against all three being alive today – against them being alive to play the reunion concerts – must be enormous. One of them might have stuffed his supercar into a wall at high speed, or – more likely – succumbed to their drug and alcohol intake as Jimi and Jon did. It's highly unlikely, given that there was no one dominant voice in the band, but rather than the three of them were constantly pulling in three or more different directions, that they could have had a career similar to that of The Stones.

Jack has a different 'what if' though, and a very intriguing one. Having established the trio as the core of their music, the band could have moved on with an almost infinitely flexible approach. They could have expanded and contracted as they wanted, and used Cream as a format within with which the three musicians could have exercised their individual passions.

There are four core members of The Rolling Stones, and beyond that a more or less constant crew of another five or six musicians and a trio of backing singers; these others all on wages and hired in as needed. Jack's thinking is an extension of that thought process. The Stones only play their own music, but Jack can imagine Cream playing their own music, old and new, and then being joined by sidemen as they moved into other areas. Ginger could have gone further, under the Cream umbrella, exploring world rhythms and in particular African music. Eric could have had a blues set within any given gig, while Jack could have taken a jazz/rock route. If they'd had a star keyboards player, say, such as Steve Winwood, he would have headed up a run of his own songs before being merging back into the mix.

Pete agrees, and makes an analogy with The Police – with a format very much modelled on Cream's - who went on to use horn sections, string sections and keyboard players; 'Cream would have thrived on that. It would have been a great idea.' He also thinks that Jack would have found a broader canvas much more fulfilling as a composer; there's only so much you can do for one guitar, one bass and one drummer, no matter how talented those musicians were. Quite apart from the music, the trio became very claustrophobic, and a broader spread of personnel would have helped dilute the tensions between them.

Again though, that's not what pop bands did. The line-up in a pop band was sacred; if it was John, Paul, George and Ringo, then that was how it was – it was the complete, immovable package. The most that happened was that lead singers left to go solo – Paul Jones left Manfred Mann, Wayne Fontana left The Mindbenders, and Brian Poole left The Tremeloes (and in all three cases the bands saw greater commercial success than the singers who had embarked on their own careers). Until Brian Jones died in 1969 there were no changes in personnel in any of the famous pop and rock groups, and the notion was pretty well unthinkable. That was the way the pop world worked, but Eric, Ginger and Jack had come out of the jazz and blues worlds, of course, where the band name lived on forever, but the personnel might change on an almost weekly basis.

Cream was different, largely because of the different background of its members. They hadn't been a bunch of teenagers sweating away in a suburban sitting room, moulding themselves into a single entity and trying to break through to the big time. Cream was three individuals, all very experienced and respected in their own right, who just happened – at that time – to be working together. For the same reason, and it was radical thinking for the pop world, they could simply stop. A rhythm guitarist with a pop band never really thought of a career beyond his band; he was part of a team – he needed the band. And as long as you were enjoying any degree of success you kept on keeping on. Cream didn't think like that. When they'd had enough they simply said so – and stopped. It came as a huge shock to their fans, especially those who weren't of the older jazz/blues generation. It wasn't what bands did. It wasn't how bands thought.

Certainly it was what they felt they had to do at that point in time, but there could have been alternatives to the band simply disintegrating. As Jack argues, 'Cream could have been like a huge review. We wouldn't have been this trio endlessly touring the world. We could have had time separately to do our own things and then come together. How fabulous would that have been?

'It's incredible how shortsighted and selfish Stigwood was. That's what destroyed the band.'

Jack says that he has never been jealous of any of the other bands that came after Cream and can be said to have capitalised on their work. Led Zeppelin found a huge, ready-made audience eager for quality blues-based rock, and to a very large degree Cream and Jimi Hendrix had created it – and left the vacuum which Led Zep and others filled. That's the natural order of things; new bands build upon the successes of their predecessors. What Jack is envious of is their management. The conversation comes back to Peter Grant; if they had been blessed with a manager with his strength and dedication, he says, the history of the band would have been very different – and certainly much longer. Peter Grant was ambitious for his band, and wasn't ambitious for himself – let alone only for himself. 'If we had had a Peter Grant, or better still, Peter Grant, it would have been a different story.'

Jack wasn't left isolated by the break up of Cream though. Far from it. He had his own plans, and was hardly going to pause for breath. Ahmet Ertegun advised him to recruit a couple of sidemen and start recording and touring with material that was at the very least Cream-like. Ahmet wanted him to put the other musicians on wages and, he said, Jack could earn himself a fortune. 'It simply wasn't what I wanted to do', Jack says. The idea that Jack could have run two careers in parallel, with a commercial band on one side of the equation and his own more original and creative work on the other, doesn't make any sense to him.

He did receive three serious offers to join other bands, and they were three very different – dizzyingly different - groups.

The least surprising approach was from Led Zeppelin. They had begun working in

October 1968, and the following spring they made their approach to Jack. Their bassist, John Paul Jones, came round to see him – and how it would have worked having two bass players involved is now rather lost. It might even have come back to Bob Brunning's idea of Cream having two bassists. He and Jack discussed the idea, and John followed up with a letter. It was a serious approach.

It wasn't what Jack wanted though. He would have been playing, to a very large degree, their music rather than his own – and anyway, he'd just left all that endless-tour madness; 'I'd done that. I didn't want to back on the road with some mad band.'

From Led Zeppelin's point of view he would have been a great addition to the line-up commercially. He would have brought a huge number of Cream fans to the new band immediately, and his profile was far higher than any of them at that moment. It would have been a very interesting coupling, to say the least, and Led Zep would have become a different group. From Jack's point of view though it was a non-starter. Which is almost a shame, not just from a music fan's point of view, but also so far as the Ferrari dealers of England were concerned.

The next offer was from Crosby Stills & Nash. The band had been formed by Stephen Stills in 1968 following the break up of his previous band, Buffalo Springfield, David Crosby who had been with The Byrds, and Graham Nash – who was still with The Hollies. They released their eponymous first album in June '69, which was to stay in the American album charts for two years. With a big US tour booked they had to fill out the stage, and it was at this point that Stephen asked Jack to join.

Jack had liked the album and was very interested in the idea. He assumed, understandably that his job would be to both play bass and sing, and he thought that the mix of voices – all three founding members sang – would work really well. Stephen wrote to him however, emphasising that they wanted him to play bass, but singing wasn't part of the job description. Jack could see that he might be joining up as a sideman, and perhaps it wasn't going to be Crosby, Stills, Nash & Bruce. That was definitely not what he wanted and he declined the offer. Jack had no regrets; Stephen wasn't his favourite person, he says. By the end of the year SC&N had become Crosby Stills Nash & Young after Neil Young had been recruited.

The job offer that was most surprising, and which delights and amuses Jack to this day came from Hank Marvin. The Shadows had been formed in 1958 out of Hank's Newcastle-upon-Tyne-based skiffle quintet The Railroaders, when Cliff Richard's manager was on the look out for a band to back the singer. They were to become a phenomenally successful group, not just with Cliff but in their own right too. Under their own name the band had made five number one singles through the Sixties, and had only had one single not make it into the top forty. Their instrumental style, with Hank out front, always smiling and playing utterly distinctive guitar on his bright red Fender, had a huge effect on that generation. They dressed immaculately and did a little synchronised dance in time to the music – which was, along with the sound of that Fender, their trademark. The Shads can truly be said to have launched a thousand rock 'n roll careers.

In 1969, when he was trying to put a new line-up of the group together after a lay-off, Hank phoned Jack and offered him the post of bass player to the Shads. It was an incredible offer – a chance to join a very British rock 'n roll legend – but that sort of music wasn't Jack's thing. He wouldn't have been happy in the smart uniform, let alone playing someone else's bass parts on three minute singles. The culture clash is beyond imagination. Anyway, he says, he didn't know the steps. Very nice to be asked though.

Chapter 17

Jack and Janet finally bought a house of their own in early 1969. It was just off Regents Park Road, between Chalk Farm and Primrose Hill, and it cost £19,000. She had Liberty's make the curtains, and everything she wanted to create the ideal home was ordered without a second thought. She had a kitchen in the lower ground floor, which had every modern convenience. It was straight out of The Observer Colour Supplement. People passing by often glanced in, and then stopped and peered through the window, amazed by the modernity. Jack had a state-of-the-art recording studio built at the top of the house. Not quite at the top in fact; above that was a roof garden, complete with an astronomy-standard telescope for looking at the stars.

Charlie Bruce adds; 'I had no idea how wealthy he really was. It just all appeared. Janet and he moved in to the house near Chalk Farm, and it was a huge terraced house on four floors. The way it had been done out ... it wasn't ostentatious or lavish, but heavens you could see the money.' Janet says, 'I had all the money that anyone could want.'

A lot of their wealth was illusory though. Band's managers made sure that they controlled the purse strings at all times. If a band member wanted something, he only had to mention it to management and the object of their desires materialised – as if by magic. From management's point of view it helped to insulate their charges from the real world, which was very much in their interest, and they also kept the accounts. If something was bought, or if a limousine so much as turned a wheel, the cost would be re-charged to the artist's account. These accounts were being frequented debited for expenditure real or imaginary. Few musicians had any idea what was going on, and if they ever saw the accounts – which was almost unheard of anyway – nobody could remember what on earth they had spent money on six months previously. When it came to the cash, everything, money in and money out, was loaded in the management's favour.

Janet remembers Jack as being very generous. He often bought her expensive jewellery, and in the working class phrase 'she wanted for nothing.' One year he bought her a Morgan sports car for her birthday.

Jack and Janet's first child, Jonas – usually known as Jo - was born in February 9 1969. Jack remembers pacing the corridors of the hospital in Hampstead for hours and hours, waiting for news of a birth. It seems that the nurses forgot him though; 'After hours after a nurse came up to me and asked me why I was still there. I told her I was waiting for news and she said 'Oh, you had a son hours ago.''

Jack now seemed to have everything; a glorious home, a son, fabulous cars, money, international fame and the respect of his peers. He was also planning his solo career, but, Janet thinks, the demise of Cream left him deflated in some way. It's not difficult to imagine him feeling that whatever he now did, he had to at least keep up with whatever Eric and Ginger achieved. No, not keep up – he had to better whatever they did. It was at this point that he should have been relaxing, getting his life back under control and enjoying their child. What happened to spoil it was heroin.

The first guy Jack knew who was a user of hard drugs was the drummer Phil Seamen, who Jack regarded as a genius and 'the greatest jazz drummer ever to come out of this country.' Phil was a registered user of both heroin and cocaine. He was a lot older than Jack, having been born in Burton-on-Trent in Staffordshire in 1926.

Ginger Baker was probably the second user he knew. Both Phil and Ginger guarded their secrets carefully and kept the much younger and less experienced Jack away from their activities; 'That idea that junkies try to turn other people on is simply not true ... they want all the drugs for themselves!' On rare occasions Jack would help Phil administer his heroin, simply because he wasn't able to do so himself. His veins had gone completely and he needed help in tightening a tourniquet further up a limb than he could reach himself, so that he could find a blood vessel which allowed him to inject the drug. Both users warned Jack off using hard drugs – which, he says, only made him want to experiment with the magical substances. These two older guys were heroes of his, and in many ways role models, and had unmatched abilities as jazz drummers. Something was obviously going right for them – maybe it was this.

Jack had also been influenced by a book that he had read while he was still at school, 'Second Ending' by Evan Hunter. He was a prolific author, and this book, published in 1954, was his tenth work under his own name since he was first published in '52. (He also wrote very popular crime novels under the pseudonym Ed McBain. He died in July 2005). His best known novel was 'Blackboard Jungle', which was made into the film of the same name.

'Second Ending' concerned the rapidly increasing problem of drug use in the poorer areas of New York, which he knew about from first hand experience. The main character is jazz trumpeter Andy Silvera, who is hopelessly addicted to heroin. In his last days, he's still full of promises to kick the habit and get back into shape for a job audition. At the start Andy was a rather shy boy, just starting a career in music. The plot follows him as he discovers jazz, women and drugs – and it's the latter which destroys his promise. It's a serious book, not a slice of the shock-horror pulp fiction which came later, and in a pivotal moment in the book his friend Bud tells him, 'All the advantages of being alive will simply disappear. You will not want a girl, or a car, or clothes, or movies, or beaches, or talk, or music, or anything but H. That is it. You will slowly and surely and without doubt sink into the gutter with your gorilla on your back.'

If all this was supposed to discourage young men from following the same path, it didn't work. Jack had no trouble identifying with Andy Silvera. He says that he became hooked on the idea of heroin just by reading the book. He says that he was very much taken by the romanticism of the story, and, being a fifteen year old he closed his mind to the terrible descriptions of withdrawal which were also recounted. He's not entirely serious, but not completely joking either, when he says that another reason for leaving Glasgow was so he could take drugs, which seemed to be completely unavailable on Clydeside.

There was a lot of cannabis around the jazz and blues scene. It was still a fairly rare drug in that any narcotic was rare, and the police had very little interest in it. It was equated in their minds with the Afro-Caribbean communities in London, and so long as it didn't go beyond that area, which was pretty much closed to them anyway, they didn't really bother with it. Most dope came in from India or Africa, but there was a West Indian connection via the famous Q Club in Praed Street, where ska and bluebeat music was being pioneered.

In the popular press, where the subject surfaced occasionally, marijuana was portrayed as a threat to the very fabric of society – capable of turning even the most mild-mannered teenager into a raging, sexual-charged monster. Many youngsters tried it because of the newspaper coverage, and were sorely disappointed.

Jack's first experiment with dope took place in John Mumford's flat in Berwick Street, between Oxford Street and Soho. After a couple of inhalations of the joint, Jack was 'so out of it.' A switch was thrown in his mind and he immediately snapped into paranoia. Terrified of the reaction, he went into the bathroom and lay motionless on the floor, hoping that normality would return sooner rather than later.

That was the effect that dope was to have on him. His Benzadrine, beer and spliff formula was better, but a joint on its own made him fearful and suspicious. He says now that cannabis was obviously totally wrong for him, and he simply shouldn't have gone near it. There would have been no telling him that when he was that age though: 'I would have been a much more outgoing person if I hadn't used dope, and a lot of

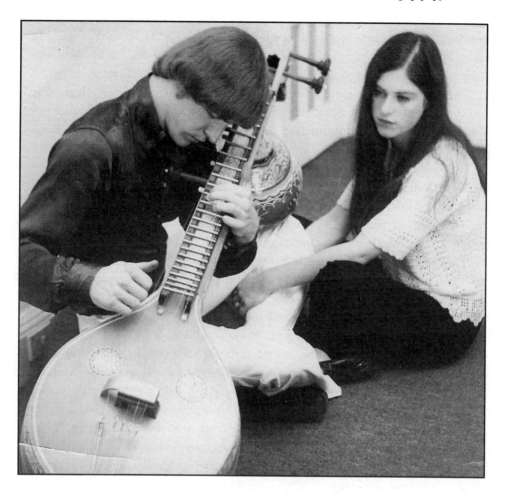

A Sixties scene: Jack explores Eastern musical techniques while Janet looks on (JB)

the problems I had through all the Sixties and into the Seventies were to do with the fact that I smoked a lot of dope and it didn't really suit me.' Janet Bruce says, only half jokingly, that things might have been better if he had got on with cannabis ...

He persevered though, and he makes the point that the drug itself was very different to what you see nowadays; 'There was a lot of very fine grass around, very strong stuff, and it wasn't just 'grass' to us – you'd know exactly where it came from.' And there was just so much of it about. It was simply so easy.

The drugs looked different too. When you scored some dope it wasn't unusual to get the whole flower, just wrapped up in newspaper. There was also kif (pronounced keef, which is cannabis in crystalline form, shaken off the best buds). That came ready sorted out for you, like a processed pipe tobacco such as Old Holborn. You could just scoop a portion into a pipe and smoke away. Kif was 'an everyday smoke.' Nowadays, Jack says, you have to go to Jamaica to find anything as pure and as strong.

There were, he says, quite a few musicians who had no interest in drugs; 'But I don't remember many of them.' It's slightly surprising that he doesn't because they would have rather stood out from the rest of the guys. It was all so much an integral part of the scene.

Jack maintains that drugs have been important in the development of music since the Nineteenth century, and not just in the blues or rock or pop; 'Debussy played a certain kind of music, and then he obviously discovered dope – and the music changed.

'Dope does let you hear music separately. You hear lines separately and more clearly. You develop the ability to hear music in that way anyway, but it was a short cut. It also gave you a tremendous desire to play.

'I don't think it was all bad – in fact I don't think it was very bad at all. Someone like me, who was possibly verging on being nuts in those days anyway, shouldn't really have smoked it. But I did – and here I am.'

The Graham Bond Organisation's van was always filled with a dope fog, and if they were travelling out of London they always had to take their own supplies. Scoring dope in a provincial town in the early Sixties was either very difficult or simply impossible. On the way to one gig they realised that they were lost, and having seen a policemen walking the beat as they once did, drove over to him to ask for directions. As they opened the window a great fug of dope smoke must have rolled out. The policeman either didn't notice or didn't know what he was smelling – which is far from incredible. He told them the way, they played the gig, and only thought later that it was perhaps a dumb thing to do.

It wasn't in any way a drug culture, as it would be thought of today. It was a music culture, of which drugs were a fairly integral part. There was no violence (that they were ever aware of, at least) associated with drug dealing. By the end of the Sixties it would be a very different scene. In the early Sixties the authorities saw no correlation between drugs and crime.

Drugs in general and dope in particular by-passed the lower and middles classes, but was far from unknown in higher society. It was racy, sexy and smart – as it had been in the Twenties. Those folk didn't score their own though; they tended to have socially mobile dealers who could be buying supplies in Brixton or Notting Hill one night and discreetly passing it on in Mayfair or Belgravia the next. Within the music scene no-one seemed to deal as such; it was just there and was passed round in exchange for small denomination bank notes such as the small, brown ten shilling note.

Jack was, he admits, drawn to the whole idea of drugs, for largely romantic notions.

He also worries that, now that drugs are so much a way of life, the process is repeated by generation after generation. There was a clique within the jazz scene, which included Tubby Hayes, Dickie Devere, Chris Thompson and of course Phil Seamen and Ginger Baker, who were dedicated heroin users, and were widely known for it. Many other musicians, including those who used dope, were very unhappy about the presence of the harder drug and kept these guys at arm's length.

LSD had been created in laboratories only a few years before, and began to enter a broader consciousness in the mid-Sixties. Unlike many others, and despite appearances and what their sleeve art might lead you to think, Cream wasn't really an acid band. They did take trips together but it was an infrequent occurrence. One took place in the countryside, possibly in rural Cheshire, as they were travelling to a gig in Liverpool. They had made a diversion to Bakewell in Derbyshire because the band felt that they had to try Bakewell tarts from their source, and during the next stop they took acid together. Everything was fine; perfect conditions for a great trip – but that changed when they started to drive through the glum suburbs of Liverpool. By then they were coming down a bit and everything started to crowd in and become dark and threatening. They went for a Chinese meal, which made matters worse, and by the time they arrived at the venue they were completely strung out.

Jack began using heroin while he was still living in the house in Chalk Farm, at the very beginning of the Seventies. It was very easy to score as the drug was widely available and very affordable. As it became known that he was a user it became even easier to score; there would be pushers sitting in cars in the street outside the house, or simply knocking on the door when they felt like it, offering him more and more. If he wanted to score he just had to walk over to the window.

Hard drugs were seen as a very different thing from soft drugs like dope. Many users were middle-aged women who had been prescribed morphine-based pain killers. Heroin users simply registered with a doctor and had the drug prescribed for them. This was usually a private doctor rather than a general practitioner, and in London there was a network of professionals who specialised in hard drug use. This was quite legal, though they did operate on the edge of their profession, and weren't popular with their peers. Some doctors actively tried to get their registered users to cut down their use with a view to weaning themselves off drugs completely. Others were simply operating a commercial concern, and saw addicts as customers. There was an outcry when one medical practitioner – Lady Frankau, sitting in the more respectable end of the market - was found to have prescribed the huge total of six kilograms of heroin during 1962. These doctors charged for the prescriptions, so he was probably buying a new Mk2 Jaguar. Or with that amount, even a reasonably-sized detached house.

Users passed the drugs, or just the prescriptions, between themselves, but there was no real black market. Boots The Chemists in Piccadilly was a well-known haunt of hard drug users simply because it was so central, and because it was open (very unusually back then) all night. You handed over your prescription and got your heroin. There is a suggestion that some cannabis users switched to heroin because you could be arrested for possession of dope, whereas if you had a prescription then possession of heroin was entirely legal. The situation in Britain was so liberal that users would jet in from North America just to score their heroin, and jazz musicians who used the drug would schedule their European tours so that they dropped into the UK first, for exactly the same reason.

There was a tiny number of registered heroin addicts in the whole country; in 1960 it was a couple of hundred. Many of these were surviving ex-servicemen who had developed morphine addiction while being treated for wounds. The total reached 1,000 in the middle of the decade.

The scene came to the surface in 1967 when Lady Frankau died, and addicts were scrabbling round trying to find another highly sympathetic doctor. One was John Petro, who made no secret of his work, revelled in being a celebrity doctor, and even discussed his work on 'The Frost Programme' on television. In 1968 doctors were stripped of their power to prescribe heroin, which the former Chief Inspector of the Home Office Drugs Branch described as 'an unmitigated disaster' as it led directly to an increase in drug-related crime and bad heroin cut with just about anything that came to hand.

It was a 'tragedy' that the way users of hard drugs were both processed and regarded, Jack believes. His rationale is that what was seen by the authorities was the use among the upper classes. He points out that cocaine was fashionable before dope and heroin – Cole Porter sang about it as if it were alcohol – and before that opium was in wide use. Many grandees in the Nineteenth century, and even back to the Eighteenth century, lived on laudanum, which was opium suspended in flavoured alcohol. It was a particular favourite of poets and writers of course.

Jack believes that as a direct result of the black consciousness movement that erupted in the Sixties, the American government instigated a secret policy of introducing drugs as feely as possible into the black community. The intent was to distract black youngsters from politics and sideline their ambitions. And, he says, it worked; 'It was a deliberate policy to pretend to be doing something about it [the drug problem] but in fact not be doing anything at all – and in fact encouraging it.

That first heroin user of Jack's acquaintance, Phil Seamen would have claimed that he only ever dabbled with heroin, but he was deceiving himself as to his control over the drug, as opposed to its control over him. As soon as he first took heroin, he was he says 'complete.' It gave him the feeling that there had previously been something lacking in him as a human being, something not right – but heroin made everything alright and made him whole.

One day he was on a train, on his way to a gig, and, staring out of the window as the landscape flashed past, he began thinking seriously about the effect the drug was probably having. There seemed to be two options; to give it up and live a longer life or to use the drug and accept that he was almost certainly going to live a much shorter life. He wrestled with this thought for a long time, and then made his decision. He decided to go with the heroin. It was his choice. He died in October 1972 aged 44.

It might have been thought that the death of a man he was so close to, one of the first musicians he had met when he came to London, would have pulled Jack up. That wasn't the case though. 'I thought that Phil had had a great run, given the way that he had lived', Jack says, 'We missed him very much, but that's what happens if you decided to live that way. Plus, I was young, and when you're young that all seems so far away from you.'

Despite his own excesses over the years Jack claims to never had any sense of his own mortality. He contradicts what appears to be the obvious in saying that his lifestyle was never so extreme that it was life-threatening. Many others disagree with that. He adds, 'I had my moments, but I never thought of myself as a Keith Richards-type character. Maybe I should have been. Maybe I'd be more pickled than I am – though actually I think he looks even worse than I do!'

Heroin is a product of the opium poppy, which is processed into morphine, and is then adjusted chemically to become morphine. Once it is introduced into the body it converts back into morphine; heroin is a way of carrying the morphine into the body.

It is the strongest painkiller known, and it works on both a mental as well as a physical level. In use the drug represses the respiratory system, so that it slows down the heart and breathing rates. When people overdose it simply means that everything has slowed to the point of shutting down. The drug also acts on the chemicals in the brain to produce a sense of euphoria. It's very seductive for people with problems in that it simply makes them go away, or so it seems.

Heroin isn't particularly bad for the body, and is certainly more benign that alcohol; the big problem is that the effect diminishes with every use, and users are constantly searching for the high of their first hit. Eventually users will be feeling less and less effect and will be taking the drug for the negative reason, which is to avoid the illness brought about by chemical void within the brain, which exists before the brain's natural pain-killers can re-assert themselves. Thus users need to carry on taking heroin to avoid the withdrawal systems, not because it produces the wonderful sensations they had known once. Dependence on the drug overtakes everything in one's life and the necessity of securing a supply of the drug is paramount – over family, relationships, job, everything. There's only one problem in your life and that's getting the next fix.

For the first eighteen months or so of the decade Jack was an occasional user of the drug. He dabbled. By the spring of 1972 though he was addicted. He was a junkie, and it wasn't a secret. He was taking intravenously and the quantities were getting greater almost day by day. He was soon outstripping the use by his jazz heroes; 'Ray Charles just dabbled with it compared to me.' He also liked to combine heroin with other drugs. One of his favourite mixes was to take cocaine while on heroin

Jack has no illusions about what he was like at this time. 'I was a horrible arrogant little shit. You wouldn't have wanted to know me then. I didn't want to know myself, and nobody else did.'

The drugs, he admits, had become just about the most important thing in his life. There was music, of course, but no other focus apart from that and drugs. And frequently the drugs crowded out absolutely everything else.

'That was my very worst period as a human being. There were very few redeeming aspects to my character. I could afford to be like that, but there are no excuses for being that way. I was not a good person to know.

'It took me a long time to become that horrible, and it took me a very long time to stop being that horrible.'

He admits that he tended to use people, in the way – he recognises now – that junkies usually do. He goes further and says that he was probably worse than the average junkie. For the simple reason that he could be. He didn't need to steal to pay for his habit, but he knows that he certainly would have done had he needed to.

In describing how he feels about those days now, he uses the word 'ashamed', but then retracts it and tones down the self-criticism, saying, that it's not a time in his life that he is proud of.

Pete Brown describes Jack's use of heroin as 'one the most gigantic habits of all time.' Then, after a moment's thought he adds, 'Plus his alcohol consumption has been spectacular at times.'

Chapter 18

Late in 1969 Jack bought the island of Sanda – two miles from the mainland, and south of the Mull of Kintyre – which had been for sale with an asking price of £100,000. 'I just fell in love with the idea of having an island', he admits.

A short while earlier Jack had tried to buy a house in the north-west of Scotland, near Oban in Argyllshire. He had seen the advert for the property in a local newspaper while on holiday further north in Wester Ross. The house came with a private beach, its own mountain and even a stop on the branch line off main west coast line, which only serviced the house. Jack decided that he not only wanted it, but that he wanted it now; 'I screamed down there in my Ferrari. It was summer and the roads were full of caravans. I was such a mad driver in that car. I got there in super-record time. The house was amazing. A beautiful fortified house. I thought 'this is for me!' I drove up to front door and the lady there said 'Who are you?' I told her I'd come to buy her house, and she said 'No you've not. You're not buying my house!' She wouldn't even show me round. Maybe I was too scruffy; maybe it was because I had a Glasgow accent. She wasn't going to sell me her place.' Jack was appalled and hurt, but there wasn't a lot he could do about it. He got back in his Ferrari and drove away.

Sanda had to do instead. It was one mile from north to south and about a mile and a half from east to west, and comprised around four hundred acres. Paul and Linda McCartney had a home just across the very choppy stretch of water that separated Sanda from the Mull. To get there the Bruce family had to fly to Glasgow and then catch a small plane to the military base at Campbeltown.

Although it was home to several hundred sheep and a lighthouse (known as The Ship, perversely), the island's history dated back to the very earliest Christian times, and the chapel on the isle, St Ninian's, may be the oldest Christian settlement in Scotland. In 1093 the island was invaded by Vikings, lead by the splendidly-named Magnus Barefoot, who killed everything he found there and razed every building. There is a legend that Robert The Bruce's brother, Prince Edward, used Sanda as a look-out while Robert was escaping from the English in 1306. A cave on the island might even have been the site of the mythological moment when Robert The Bruce watched the spider patiently building and re-building its web, and he decided that he too should never give up. Jack admits that he very much wanted it to be the place where that happened, especially given them having the same surname, of course. The island's appeal for Jack is fairly obvious.

There was just one habitable house on the island, apart from a working lighthouse; that was on the south side and it was a half hour walk across to the house on the north. Although they came and went in their own boat, mooring at a jetty by the house, the Bruces were usually dependent on the lighthouse supply ship for just about everything they needed. Once a week they would walk to the lighthouse to order the groceries, and then back to collect them. If they needed to make a phone call they had to trek there too – and because the line had to be kept open in case of emergencies, it was only available to them between five minutes to noon and five minutes after.

Sanda's attraction for Jack was the sense of space and the simple beauty of the island. He says that it's not a beautiful landscape as such, but is 'More like an Irish landscape. It's very green, and not rugged as most of Kintyre.'

Jack bought Sanda as a place to relax but not as somewhere to work. It's surprising to learn that he doesn't regard a sense of place as at all relevant to his work as a songwriter. He can work as well, he says, in a hotel room as he can in his music room at home or in a Scottish cottage. He has been known to compose a symphony during a train journey. In the Eighties he lived in Germany for six years, but he denies any suggestion that living in a completely different culture had any effect at all on his music. It seems that the inspiration has never come from any external source but purely from within. He frequently alludes to living and working completely inside his head. There was never any chance of him building a studio on Sanda.

Janet remembers it as a wonderful place, but very hard work. They had no mains electricity, so used a generator – which was only ever in use for a couple of hours each evening. In 1970 the family spent the whole summer there, but Jack was away for part of that and she was alone there with a small child, and was pregnant with another. One of her memories is of having to get up at five in the morning to boil water for nappies, using a Calor Gas stove, and then being up to her elbows in water at a stone Belfast sink. She says it was like living in a working museum – and that she would probably enjoy it so much more nowadays.

Tony Palmer, who had made the film of the Farewell concert, was commissioned to make a documentary about Jack. Called 'Rope Ladder To The Moon', it included filming on the island, complete with a curious scene in which he and Pete Brown – who

By the early Seventies Jack was a very well-established and greatly-respected musician.
Above all he was fulfilling his longest-held ambition - to compose new music. (John Levicke)

Jack had insisted was involved – jumped on to dry land from a boat, pretending to be Magnus Barefoot and one of his Viking raiders. Then they were all required to go out on the tiny walkway that goes round the very top of the island's lighthouse. The sixty foot-high lighthouse was situated on a narrow promontory, above the hundred and fifty foot-high cliffs that rose up out of the foaming surf (and below which, at low tide, could still be seen the wreck of the Byron Darnton, which had come to grief as recently as 1947). It makes you giddy just looking at the photos.

Jack was filmed walking round and round, with the cameraman and sound recordist walking backwards in front of them, and Pete walking backwards behind them, trying hard not to be either trampled or knocked off the gangway. Pete remembers that experience as absolutely, understandably terrifying, and describes the film itself as being 'absurd.' He says, 'It was a terrible, empty film. Tony Palmer was besotted with Jack. He had this full Oxford thing and he thought it was great that Jack had been working class but now he was piloting aeroplanes. Jack loved it at the time because it was so flattering.' There was an antipathy between Pete and Palmer, as he explains; 'Tony hated me because I came from the same background as him. We were lower middle-class Jewish, but he now had the posh voice and everything. Instead of talking like that he should have been talking like I do.'

Jack's Scottish identity is important to him, though – somewhat surprisingly – he plays this down. He will enthuse about the lyrical abilities of Robbie Burns but does think of his own nationality as British rather than the more narrow Scottish. He would argue that race is an irrelevance, indeed that it's nothing but a destructive force, and that he is a citizen of the world.

Like the English, the Scottish don't look on success very kindly. For every person in Scotland who is proud of the achievements of Billy Connolly and Sean Connery, at least one other resents them their wealth and fame. There must have been some element of that in the past, but nowadays Scottish music lovers are very proud of Jack. For many in their forties and fifties he is a hero, while for those somewhat younger he has been an inspiration and has proved that you can come out of the far north and walk on an international stage.

An old Scottish friend of Jack's agrees that he plays down his Scottish identity, but insists that it very important to him in reality. He adds, 'He's very Scottish when he's in Scotland!'

Jack sold Sanda in 1976. It is now a holiday destination, and is marketed as an ideal location for weddings and hen and stag nights (a pub was built there in 2002 – Jack missed out on that). One of Jack's ambitions is to take his youngest son to see Sanda, driving from East Anglia – so long as it's 'in a good car.'

After he had purchased the island, Jack bought a thirty-foot motor cruiser, and invited Pete Brown to come up to Scotland and have a play with it. A limo took the two of them to Heathrow, and they then flew to Glasgow. As they were being driven to Heathrow, a large black bird hit the windscreen of the car and ended its days in a bloody mess. Pete announced that this was a portent, and that the whole trip was doomed. He was nearly right.

Jack has always had an astonishing facility to teach himself how to do all sorts of things, and, Pete says, he proceeded to learn how to pilot the boat simply by doing it. They sailed towards The Isle of Arran and moored off Brodick on the island's east coast. They didn't get into the harbour, but moored off shore. Pete wanted to make some phone calls, so they got into the boat's tender and set off for the town. By the time they were ready to return, a storm was brewing, and the boat was dragging its anchor and going round in ever-decreasing circles, pivoting on the anchor. Unwisely they set off in the dinghy.

They didn't get that far though. Somehow or other Pete managed to capsize the dinghy beneath them and both men were thrown into the sea. Pete wasn't a bad swimmer but Jack couldn't swim at all. Jack got on top of the smaller boat, and Pete tried to swim to the cruiser. Then things began to get desperate in the very cold northern water. After a while, half in and half out of the sea, Jack – who wasn't in the best physical shape at that time - was getting tired and very cold and was struggling to maintain his grip. Pete eventually reached the motor boat, but then found that he couldn't get aboard; the sides were simply too high. He swam around the boat to find the ladder at the stern but struggled to climb it.

Pete believes that Jack wasn't far away from slipping away, and that he would have followed him shortly afterwards. Pete certainly couldn't have swum to shore. Quite by chance though someone on the island spotted their predicament – which is quite incredible as they were a fair way out. A rescue boat arrived, and not a moment too soon. Jack had very nearly joined the surprisingly long list of rock stars who have died by drowning. Once back in Brodick, Jack joined the rescuers in what Pete remembers as a particularly heavy drinking session.

In the early Eighties Jack bought a house in a village in Wester Ross, on the coast, north of the Sound of Raasay which separates the north-eastern side of Skye from the mainland. It was originally a holiday home, but Jack and and his second wife lived there for a while later in the decade – firstly just the two of them and then with their daughters. Jack's reluctant to talk about it now; it's too special to him, he says, and 'It's relatively unspoilt and I don't want to say where it really is. Places get ruined. I don't want people to go there!'

He had done all the things that rock stars are supposed to do. He had bought the huge country house, the string of fabulous motor cars, and had added a few toys of his own choosing to the list, such as Sanda. He had a lot of amount of money coming in and there was no reason not to enjoy some of it. Jack was now able to indulge his passions, and indeed find new ones. It's what all his peers did. It's what anyone would have done. As Janet says, 'Everyone expected you to have all these things.'

He had been very generous to both his family and Janet's. He paid for foreign holidays and bought cars for both sets of parents and Janet's brother. It's impossible to know how wealthy he really was, but he certainly had access to huge amounts of money if and when he wanted to go shopping. He tried a lot of different things, as anyone in his position would.

With the money came the fame. He adored the stardom and the adulation; he liked being recognised and people shaking his hand or wanting his autograph. He still does. On the other hand, he had a need to be quiet and private, and there was still a level of shyness beneath the veneer – admittedly a thick veneer – of self-assuredness. He had the great advantage of not having the level of personal exposure of, say, John Lennon or Mick Jagger, so the attention was neither as great as it might have been, nor as constant. Plus, his fans weren't the sort of teenies who screamed and fainted and wet their knickers. People who appreciated his music and might recognise him in a public place were older, and rather more civilised. That's not to say that they wouldn't intrude, but they were easier to deal with, and non-threatening.

Fame was easier in the Sixties and Seventies than it is now. His photo would often have been in the music press, and of course he had been on television many times, but there wasn't the all-pervasive celeb culture that has developed over the past decade. There weren't any of the all-consuming magazines that turn over every aspect of the lives of the famous, nor did celebrities have to collude with such an industry and fear alienating them. For Jack it was easier, it was better.

He had never needed any help when it came to getting to know members of the opposite sex; but if he had, then his fame would certainly have solved the problem. As it was, being very talented, very wealthy and very well known - added to his still-slight frame, his boy-ish good looks and his charm – made him pretty well irresistible. It was a combination of factors that he didn't hesitate to put to good use.

It is true to say that he was still developing as a musician, and was a thoughtful and sensitive artist, and he needed space within his life to let his imagination run free and be able to marshal his thoughts.

Heroin and alcohol aside – and those were, for a lot of the time, very big shadows over him - life was good. Not only did he have all the material possessions he could want, but he was composing and playing great music – which was being very well received by both the music lovers and the music press. Above all, he was in the satisfying position of being greatly respected by those whose opinions were worth hearing.

Although Jack often worked with musicians he knew well, such as Dick Heckstall-Smith and Jon Hiseman, there were a lot of other musicians, engineers and producers he knew he would enjoy working with: Fame and the success of Cream had opened doors. Now he could get hold of just about anyone he wanted to work with.

However he was still locked into The Robert Stigwood Organisation, as it became. He had seen enormous success with The Bee Gees, on top of Cream's achievements, and had diversified into films and theatrical productions. Like Eric, Jack was contracted to Stigwood for any work beyond Cream, so he had no option but to continue as a part of his operation. It was an all-encompassing contract, covering management, agency rights, publishing – everything. It was a long time before Jack was free of it, and a lot longer still until he finally received anything like the royalty payments due to him in an out of court settlement.

This meant that he didn't have quite as free a hand in recording his post-Cream albums as he might have liked. It didn't necessarily mean that compromises had to be made, but it did mean that quite unnecessary battles had to be fought before he could go to do exactly what he wanted.

Chapter 19

'S ongs For A Tailor' was simply revolutionary', says bass player and author Bob Brunning, 'I bought it the day it came out and it was an obvious development of Jack and Pete's songwriting skills. There were some very difficult bass riffs on it, in fact I think some of Jack's finest playing ever is on that album.'

The album, with Jack looking intense, unsmiling, and Byronic on the front, was a personal and professional triumph. What on earth do you do after being in a band like Cream? Where do you go? Jack went to Pete and to Felix, and they created a body of work which combined new songs with several that had been recording by Cream but not been released as Cream recordings. Taken together, they created a very successful continuum from what Jack had done with Cream. In 2000 it was voted one of the five hundred most influential albums of all time.

It was, he says, an album that he had to make so that, post-Cream, he could get on with his career; 'I had to get away from Cream and make a record that was lots of little songs of mine. There was no improvisation; just little statements.'

Jack now had a large degree of creative freedom of movement. He had the power that success and money can bring, and he had the great luxury of time and space. He didn't have to do the one thing that he has always feared and avoided with a passion - make compromises.

Some of the songs on the album had been written during Cream's existence, but hadn't been taken up by the band for whatever reason. Theme For An Imaginary Western, for example, was one of several songs written during the Cream days, some of which were cut as demos by the band, but strangely 'lost' (a few, but not all, did reappear and have been included on Cream box seats). The first time Jack had played it for Eric, he had been told that it was rip-off of what The Band (who both Jack and Eric greatly admired) were doing – although it had been composed as early as 1964.

It is one of Pete's favourite songs, and he was glad that it appeared on 'Songs For

A Tailor' rather than being released by the band; 'It needed a more dramatic treatment than the trio could manage. It's a big canvas and it needed keyboards at least.' Other songs had been started during the band's life, but not finished. Just a couple post-dated Cream completely.

It was undoubtedly a wise move to bring in Felix to produce the album, to act as Jack's foil. It is to his credit that he didn't try to make it sound like 'Disraeli Gears' or 'Wheels Of Fire.' There are echoes of Cream of course, but then it would be strange if there were not, but the album was fresh and vibrant. Musically it owed very little to what had gone before, except for the magical Bruce/Brown style of songwriting.

Again though, Jack says that the credit for production should really go to him rather than Felix Pappalardi. Jack had written out all the parts in his studio at home (except for George Harrison, who didn't read music – he was just given chord progressions), and, he says, 'There was no real production. All of the songs were arranged by me and then recorded the way they were written. No matter what Jack says about the level of his contribution to the overall sound, Felix certainly understood what Jack was trying to achieve, and they communicated well on every level. Jack was not to work with Felix again, indeed he had already decided that what he needed was a skilful engineer, and in future he would be his own producer. Certainly he knew both what he wanted to achieve and how best to reach it, and in theory at least any other set of opinions would only get in the way and create a barrier between him and the music.

There was an argument though, one that might not even have occurred to Jack, that a really gifted producer could actually add something more; that were colours beyond his palette which an empathetic sprit could help him reach. It wasn't a question of gilding the lily or of trying to fill any inadequacy on Jack's part – his abilities obviously weren't in doubt – but another brain might have brought new ideas. Maybe Jack would argue that it wouldn't be his own music, but while compromise was definitely out so far as his own recordings were concerned, perhaps a working relationship with a producer might have been a valuable collaboration. Pete Brown says, 'The problem with Jack's work after Felix is that he never found the right producer, either because his ego wouldn't let him, or because he just didn't find him.'

The album wasn't recorded anywhere exotic, such as Atlantic's New York headquarters, but in the Morgan Studios in Willesden in north London. Just a couple of miles north-west of Jack's home.

Pete wrote some of his greatest lyrics for this album. Some songs were straight forward and direct, such as The Clearout (which was recorded by Cream and was slated to appear on 'Disraeli Gears'). Ministry Of Bag was brilliantly funny – Pete at his most anarchic and mischievous. For the rest, he created mosaics of images and ideas, with which he skilfully built up an atmosphere. It was abstract impressionism in music. Or rather, he gave the listener the colours and the outline, and left him or her to paint their own picture. No one ever really knew what the individual songs were about, just as nobody felt they had to. The lyrics were intelligent, inventive, and fantastic - in the true sense of the word.

Overall, it's interesting to note what is absent from this album – and this is, simply, many of the elements that made Cream so famous. There are no showy, self-conscious guitar solos, no searing virtuosity, no scorching blues licks. Similarly, the drumming is restrained and supportive; there's no flamboyance, no wild colours. Everything has changed, including Jack. Jack has evolved.

It would have been a brave soul who predicted what Jack's first solo album would sound like, but as soon as you heard it, it made perfect sense. It moved the listener on in a straight line from what he had done with the band. Now though he could write intricate, carefully structured arrangements, which discreetly hinted at his classical background and his years spent playing jazz – despite that fact the record itself, with moments of blues, r 'n b, folk and even soul, defied categorisation. Above all, he succeeded in the one criterion, which had driven him throughout his career; the music sounded completely fresh and original. It didn't sound like anything he had done before, let alone anything that anyone else had done before. The music was utterly and distinctively his own.

He had his choice of musicians too, of course. George Harrison played guitar on the opening track, Never Tell Your Mother She's Out Of Tune (which Jack describes as 'a twisted soul song'). Jack thought of George because he had been so impressed while working with him on Badge, and was very pleased when he readily agreed to guest on the track.

Jack chose Chris Spedding to play guitar throughout the rest of the album, having been introduced to him by Pete; at that time Chris was with Pete's band Battered Ornaments. Jack specifically didn't want a well-known 'guitar hero', whose work might detract from the impact of the songs themselves.

Chris is more specific, 'I think he was looking for someone who didn't sound like Eric Clapton. Also, I got a lot of work around that time because I could work with both jazz people and rock people. Apart from John McLaughlin there weren't many guitarists who could do that.' Jack says, 'He was absolutely the right guitarist for that record.'

Jon Hiseman played drums on all but one track. John Marshall played drums on Rope Ladder To The Moon. Jack employed his old Manfred Mann colleague Henry Lowther to play trumpet where brass was required. He was joined by Harry Becket, John Mumford and, of course and quite rightly, Dick Heckstall-Smith. In both Chris and John it seemed that Jack was looking for the antithesis of Eric and Ginger. Both men were straight-ahead, uncomplicated and if anything understated musicians. Jack equated John's style with Ringo Starr, who was far from being a fiery exhibitionist like Ginger.

It was a remarkably talented roster. Jack had been able to create an eclection of some of the musicians he admired most, and who were best suited to create the new music he was trying to capture. It's also true to say that Jack was comfortable with musicians he knew well, and because he knew them well he could work more quickly, they were well suited to his style, and he knew that they were capable of the parts he was writing for them. Without the two and a half years of Cream that would not have been possible; Cream was both an end in itself, and in other ways, the means to an end. Pete says that he was able to try things on 'Songs For A Tailor' that he could never have got near with Cream.

The way Jack worked in studio came as a surprise to Chris and John. Every morning they would get to the studio before him, and when they arrived he would play them the song on the piano, and would play Chris what he wanted from him. They then laid down their parts and eventually left. They didn't hear the whole thing, indeed Chris says that he would have played slightly differently if he had been able to. Jack knew what he wanted though, and he was there to give what was required of him.

Chris described the work on the album was being 'very concentrated.' He says that he at least was always nervous about what he was going to be presented with, and from one day to the next didn't know what to expect. There was no doubt that Jack was in charge; he wasn't tyrannical and he didn't throw his weight around, but he wasn't going to be either messed around or distracted either.

When Jack toured in support of the album he wanted to play the new material, of course, but confounded his fans by refusing to play anything from the Cream years; 'I was going through a phase of not wanting to play all that stuff. Quite rightly. I was trying to get away from it.'

Now though he had his own voice, and with 'Songs For A Tailor' he opened a door - and everything that he has done since has followed the path that led on from there. He had put down a marker to show this huge new audience that Cream had brought him that he wasn't merely one third of that band, and that he had a lot more to offer. He was a singer of great range and expression, he was a hugely creative and accomplished bass player, he could competently play just about anything else he needed to put into the mix, and he was a very skilled arranger. Above all though, he was the composer he had always wanted to be.

Jon Hiseman's opinion is that Jack's solo work made less impression than what he did with Cream precisely because he was in charge and there was no one there to contradict him. Creative conflict often produces the greatest art, and that was the case so far as Cream was concerned. The theory is that you need the aggression and the edginess; the competition and the sideways glances. If you eliminate the hard times and opt for an easy life, you rarely achieve as much. Doesn't feel like it at the time, sure, but Jon argues, "Songs For A Tailor' was a truly fantastic record and is my favourite of all the records I've played on, but it lacked that dangerous element which people will always pay to come and see.'

The record was recorded in April and May 1969, mixing was finished in June, and it was released in September. It received rapturous reviews from the rock critics, and the album went to number six in the British album charts. Jack celebrated his twenty-sixth birthday while the album was being recorded.

One person who was greatly impressed by 'Songs For A Tailor' was Paul McCartney. He phoned Jack and asked him to take a copy to the Apple headquarters and play it to the rest of The Beatles. George had played on it but hadn't heard the whole album. Jack relates 'playing it for the guys' with understandable pleasure; 'That was nice', he says, with a touch of under-statement.

As for the apparently obscure title of the album: On the morning of May 12 1969, while the record was being finished, the folk band Fairport Convention was returning from a gig at Mother's club in Birmingham. Their Ford Transit crashed on the M1 just coming into north London at Mill Hill. It is most likely that the roadie who was driving simply nodded off. The van hit the central reservation, somersaulted, and then ran right off the motorway and came to a halt on a golf course. Guitarist Richard Thompson's girlfriend Jeannie Franklyn was killed outright, and drummer Martin Lamble died shortly afterwards in Stanmore hospital.

That violent death should hit a band whose image was so soft and fey seemed impossibly cruel. Jeannie Franklyn had been a highly regarded young fashion designer. She had run a clothes shop on Santa Monica Boulevard and had designed and made clothes for Jack. Her sense of style had been a considerable influence on Jack, and he was so moved by her death that he dedicated the album to her.

With guitarist Larry Coryell, ex-Hendrix drummer Mitch Mitchell and keyboards player Mike Mandel, Jack Bruce And Friends played the Lanchester Arts Festival in Coventry at the end of January, and a single gig at the Lyceum in London the following day, before heading to the States. It was a short tour, surprisingly, given that they were promoting a new album which was very important to Jack, but they did play some of the best venues. These included the Fillmore East in New York, Fillmore West in San Francisco, the Electric Factory in Philadelphia, and the Eastman Theatre in Detroit. By early March the band was back home.

'Songs For A Tailor' wasn't the first solo album he recorded. In August 1968 Jack had recruited Dick Heckstall-Smith, Jon Hiseman and John McLaughlin and had gone into IBC studio in London to cut the album 'Things We Like.' This was a rather different beast though. It was a jazz album, and in a way was Jack flexing his muscles while Cream was still breaking up around him. And having fun.

It wasn't to be the album to come back with first though. Jack wanted a much more personal record as his first solo release; 'I wanted to make a statement. I didn't want to release something that was so different from what I'd done before. I wanted to hold on to the jazz album until I'd released a 'proper songs' album.' If 'Things We Like' had been the first release after Cream it would have looked as if Jack was going back to his jazz roots and turning his back on what he had achieved with Cream – which would have been a very false impression. The two musical forms could run in parallel in Jack's mind but both his fans and the critics would have confused; the thinking is that one musician can only wear a single label. Accordingly the release of 'Things We Like' was held back until 1970.

The jazz critic of the London magazine Time Out (which was A5 in size and still a black and white agit-prop rag) didn't understand this subtlety, and started his review with a rant against the delay. Misunderstanding the thinking, he said 'There's certainly nothing very avant garde or fearfully freaky about it.' He went on to give away his background by writing about 'cryptic but attractive themes written by Bruce himself', and adding that '[they] never stray far from a finger-snapping beat.' Overall, he liked the album and recommended it to the readers, but concluded by saying that although Jack was 'more than competent on the string bass fiddle', he had come to prefer him on his electric bass thanks to what he had heard on 'Songs For A Tailor.' So that was one jazzer converted, at least.

Its presence meant that the jazz world was both confused and delighted. Those who had sneered that he had sold out and gone over to rock 'n roll were bemused. The more open-minded appreciated the fact that, despite his success in the rock world, he was still passionate about jazz, while the less open-minded struggled to cope with the fact: These no more entrenched opinion than that of a music purist who had made his mind up.

With his well-respected band Colosseum, Jon Hiseman has often revisited Jack's work. The group played jazz/rock with a touch of the blues, and for many years included Dick Heckstall-Smith in the line-up. Their music veered towards the edge of progressive rock occupied by The Nice, and it was a wonderful live band (and still is, especially on the strength of their performance at the Dick H-S tribute concert in the summer of 2005). The singer was Chris Farlowe, and on their covers of both Theme For An Imaginary Western and Rope Ladder To The Moon, he showed by default just what a great sense and a precise sensitivity Jack had as a singer. They're very difficult songs to sing really well, and being more of an r 'n b singer Chris sounds awkward and strained.

On Imaginary Western he's three-quarters of the way towards sounding like Arthur Brown.

Jon Hiseman remembers a moment of kindness and praise during the 'Things We Like' session which changed the way he thought about his playing. He says that he had always been wracked by self-doubt about his abilities. While they were listening to one track being played back Jack praised his drumming on a slow song which Jon had found particularly challenging, and told him that there was no one else in the world who could achieve exactly the same playing. 'That changed the way I thought about myself and what I did', Jon says, 'All I had ever heard before were what I thought of as the mistakes, but all he heard was what I was playing. He didn't know what I was trying to do, he only heard the result. Jack was important to me because he was the first person who ever said anything like that to me.'

Jon has always performed set-piece drum solos of monumental, Toad-like length, and anyone who was ever tempted to think a drummer is a drummer is a drummer, only needs to listen to Jon's The Time Machine and hear how radically different his playing is from Ginger's.

Chapter 20

Jack and Janet's second son, Malcolm, was born in London on September 7 1970. Malcolm arrived very suddenly, a couple of weeks early. Once Janet realised that the birth was actually imminent she told Jack that he was going to have to act as midwife. The doctor wasn't answering his phone and there was no chance of an ambulance getting there in time.

He hadn't been present at Jo's birth; fathers were actively discouraged from being in the delivery room, and were expected to do the cliché thing and pace the corridor, chain-smoking. It was a quick birth. Janet remembers being on the bed naked, with all the windows open – and having to persuade Jack that it wasn't necessary for him to cut the umbilical chord himself.

A short while later the wonderfully trendy, over-size magazine Nova was putting together a feature on this startling new trend for fathers to be present at the birth of their children. As Jack had been so, albeit not exactly from choice, they asked if they could include him. Janet recalls that the magazine sent a man and a woman to interview him – and only him. She brought in the refreshments, served the tea and biscuits, and the conversation didn't re-start until she had left the room. Jack and the boys can be seen in the photo; Janet isn't there. The feature was titled 'Father and baby doing well.' Jack says in it that he was so moved by the birth that he was going to write a song called Beautiful Placenta, though thankfully the world has in fact been spared that. The newspapers then picked up the story – and at least Janet got into the photos that time. She was peeved, but seethed in silence. Such were the days.

Janet admits that during this period she was preoccupied with her new son; that she became a mother to the exclusion of just about everything else. A new mother gets very tired very quickly, and just about the sole object of her attention is her child. That's how the maternal instinct works, and has to work. Perhaps Jack felt shut out; it's a common enough thing once the husband is over the thrill of the birth (particularly of the birth of a son). They certainly weren't doing things together as they always had.

Janet began to notice that Jack wasn't around as much as she expected.

In the spring of 1971 Jack decided that the family ought to move out of London. They were going to live in the country. It was a surprising thought as both he and Janet had lived all their lives in urban settings. Janet in particular thought of herself as a Londoner through and through; the countryside might as well be a foreign country. Jack had always yearned for more open horizons though, and had never forgotten the joy of his boyhood bicycle rides out of Glasgow. For him the move wasn't simply what rock stars are supposed to do – having made some money, buy a mansion in the country and fill it with juke boxes and coats of armour, and build your own pub. It was a search for space, the beauty of the landscape and a better quality of life for himself and his family. Nowadays he didn't need to be near London all the time, constantly reminding people of his existence, as musicians tend to have to do, and hustling for the next gig.

Also, Jack was aware that his home had become a magnet for pushers. They were like vultures, and a wealthy, high-profile heroin user was like a fresh corpse to them. They haunted the street and it was very hard to avoid them, so the level of temptation was great. He had recognised that he had a problem, and it was out in the open – so that the couple could discuss it and tackle it together.

A lot of people were doing the same thing, and moving out of London. The attractions that the capital had enjoyed through the Sixties were starting to pale. The city was changing and many of those who could do so moved further out. As he says, 'London had lost its romanticism, its idealism. It became a hard place. London suddenly became a place not to be in the Seventies.'

The couple started house-hunting, driving out around the city to just about every point of the compass. There's a very long tradition of newly-wealthy Britons moved out to beautiful houses in the country as soon as they've made some money, and it should have been a joy. There was almost no limit to what they could spend on a new house, and they could re-locate to anywhere that took their fancy. There was to be a new life among open fields. For many couples it would have been a dream come true.

It wasn't what Janet wanted though. The house in Chalk Farm was her dream home. It was more than she could ever have hoped for, and she had put her heart and soul into re-decorating it and making it into a real home. It was also exactly where she wanted to be; close to her friends and family and within a short ride of central London. Jack, however, saw a move out of London as a necessary step in getting away from the supply of heroin.

Having toured the Home Counties, they fixed their attention on Essex and Suffolk. The area where the painter John Constable lived and worked – now inevitably known as 'Constable Country' – could hardly be more typically English; a gently rolling land-

Jack with Malcolm (left) and Jonas at home in the kitchen at Le Mote (JB)

scape with small fields edged with ancient hedges; narrow, winding lanes running between picturesque villages; ancient market towns with broad high street, elegant town houses and quaint shops.

They bought a house called Le Mote Hall on the edge of a pretty village. It was a large and very elegant Georgian house, built on the site of a much older dwelling. It was very much an English manor house, set in its own formal gardens and lush parkland. It stood well back from the road and was exactly the sort of house that you see on a full-page advert, facing the inside front cover of Country Life.

Jack was very happy at Le Mote – and his contentment was undoubtedly good for Janet too. They had a productive kitchen garden and Jack's piece de resistance was making leek soup using freshly-picked, home-grown vegetables. He loved the Suffolk landscape and had no problem making friends, perhaps better described as acquaintances. The pub and the church were the two centres of life, and Jack ignored the latter and became a regular at the former. It was one of the best ways to become admitted into local life, but of course Jack wasn't like anyone else. He was a famous, wealthy rock star. He might spend long and pleasant evenings drinking with the farmers and tractor drivers, but he didn't really fit in – which was a fact he was entirely happy with. He wouldn't have wanted to be mistaken for just another local bloke; he had spent most of his life distancing himself from the mass, safe in the knowledge that he wasn't just like everyone else. He had a broad circle of drinking friends. It's not difficult to imagine a degree of resentment though; he was still not yet thirty, he was never short of money – to say the least, and he lived in the mansion on the edge of the village and flashed through the lanes in his Ferraris.

They had staff who lived in – though Janet insisted that she, as the woman of the house and the boys' mother, always did the cooking. They had a gardener to keep the four acres of garden trim.

Jack had the ballroom turned into a huge music room and studio. One of Janet's greatest delights in those days was to simply be around while Jack was composing music. He now had every instrument he could want – including acoustic guitars but never an electric guitar. What wasn't immediately to hand was at the end of a phone line, as was as the latest recording technology. He spent a lot of time playing the piano – he has always said that playing the bass is work but he plays the piano for fun – and, apparently from nowhere, a melody or a chord sequence would emerge, and new music would grow organically.

They were to live at Le Mote for eleven years, but Janet says she was never truly happy there. She was cut off from both her friends and the lifestyle she was used to. She also had nothing in common with her neighbours. She was very cautious about people who wanted to be her friend because she was a rock star's wife, and wisely so. Her friends tended to be the wives and girlfriends of whichever musicians he was working with, but if they moved on to other projects then the women went to, and Janet tended to lose touch. It was difficult but it was part of the life.

Although Janet apologies in the explaining, and says that it sounds like a small point, she had no one to talk to about bringing up babies; no one to turn to for advice about how to handle a demanding toddler. She felt isolated, and that she was having to deal with all this on her own. For her, Le Mote was always a house and never really a home.

Nowadays the area is far wealthier and more mobile; people commute into London on a daily basis. Thirty or so years ago it was deeply rural though. When she tried to make friends with other young mothers she found they were nervous of the people from 'the big house.' If Janet had acted the role of lady of the manor, she might have been admitted into the upper reaches of county society and been able to take tea with the rural dean, become chairman of the Women's Institute, and host smart dinners for the local gentry. That wasn't what she was used to, and certainly wasn't how she saw herself.

Malcolm remembers the Bruces being regarded as the family who lived in the big house and had money. Their lifestyle contrasted sharply with many of their agricultural neighbours; 'It was us and them. We were the rock star's kids, living in a big house.

From left; Malcolm, Jack and Jonas go cycling together in the lanes of East Anglia (JB)

My parents weren't snooty but people did treat us differently. We had a Ferrari and a Rolls-Royce, they had an old Ford and a tractor.'

Both boys attended the small primary school in the village, and weren't without friends. Malcolm says that he thinks he has blanked out the more unfortunate memories, and has only happy memories – such as riding his bike through what was then a very quiet and largely traffic-free village, and playing with a chum, whose father had a farm – one big, free-to-enter adventure playground.

Janet still travelled a lot with Jack, and if she didn't she would often get calls from management asking her to fly out to him; 'They'd say things like, 'He's in a state. You've got to get a flight.' That kind of thing. He was upset and not dealing with things. It mightn't be the drug issue, but that might have something to do with it', she says, and then adds, 'I do understand the difficulties of touring, of people watching your moves, of not being able to trust people. Wondering if they really my friend or are they not.

'Jack would be in a mood and I'd have to jump on a plane in the middle of the night – have to leave my children. He always came first. Maybe it was the old-fashioned thing that he was the bread-winner ...'

Occasionally family holidays would be scheduled alongside tours or foreign studio sessions – which is how the boys got to see tourist attractions and theme parks at a time when that was a very rare treat for British youngsters. They often took holidays abroad, as well as going back to the Scottish Highlands, the isles off Scotland's west coast and the beaches on the east.

The Bruce family went to the Caribbean a number of times; to Barbados and Jamaica in particular. For one holiday they stayed in Sandy Lane in Barbados – a five-star destination for the very rich – and both Jack and Janet had real problems with the fact that the local people who worked at the resort were very much treated as second-class citizens; the staff were all black and the guests were all white. On the other hand, these were considered to be plum jobs to have, and within their communities they would be seen to have secure and well-paid jobs, and would be much envied. And neither party would welcome a guest trying to cross the divide and be anything other than strictly formal in their dealings – let alone trying to befriend a member of staff: Trying to help yourself to food rather than wait for your personal butler to serve you was an unfortunate faux pas in everyone's eyes. For socially aware, left wing visitors it was an uncomfortable situation – and was a circle which could not be squared.

Their life was split into two very different phases. For long periods Jack would be away and if Janet wasn't with him she was fairly isolated, in the big house with just her two young children and the domestic staff. At other times, when he was home, they had a normal family life, except when Jack's drug habit meant that he needed nursing, or he admitted himself to a private clinic. One problem was that when he got on top of the drugs, he would often compensate by drinking too much. Life wasn't as easy as anyone looking at the glorious trappings of their rock lifestyle might have imagined.

Jack was a very good father to the boys, and did lots of things together with them, Janet says, but adds, 'When he was there, and when he was physically fit to do it.'

Janet consulted her doctor, and told him that she was feeling tired and a bit down. She says that she was expecting iron tablets or vitamins, but – as was very much the way in the Seventies – he immediately gave her amphetamines, and then both sleeping pills and Valium to counter the side-effects of the amphetamine. It wasn't a help, to say the least. The medication got her through it, she admits; 'I was a young mother and I was trying to support a musician who needed a lot of support.'

Eventually, when Jo and Malcolm were older, they were enrolled at a boarding school. Their parents looked for one which wasn't too far from home, and one which took both boys and girls. Malcolm says that he enjoyed boarding school, probably because there was a structure in place and a timetable to be obeyed, which he hadn't really had at home. Life at Le Mote was unpredictable and children tend to be happier with routine. He says, 'My parents were very loving but they weren't nine to fivers, and there wasn't a sense of stability and security.

Although British public schools are generally populated by the children of the

*A birthday celebration at Le Mote Hall; Jack and the boys were very happy at the
large East Anglian house, but Janet Bruce felt out of place
and missed her London friends. (JB)*

wealthy, most of the pupils at the school which Jo and Malcolm attended were from
military families, where the father was posted abroad. The Bruce boys were different
because their father was wealthier – or flashily wealthier – than the average. It seems
completely inappropriate to the man, but as a boy Malcolm was nicknamed Little Lord
Fauntleroy by his classmates.

Jack's thinking was that once the boys were away at school Janet would be able to
always travel with him. That wasn't what she was hoping for though; she had been
looking forward to furthering her ruptured education. She wanted to go to college.

It was to be some time before she got to further education. She sums up her perspective on their marriage, saying, 'I adored him. He could be a pain, and there were
some terrible things that went on, but I was with him regardless. I was married for life.
He always had affairs, but I colluding because I didn't say don't – but I didn't like it.
That was what men were like – that was what musicians were like. I didn't like it but I

just allowed these things to happen. I was tired and down with the life, and with trying to help Jack all the time.'

Towards the end of 1979 everything began to change. Jack was touring across Europe with John McLaughlin, Stu Goldberg and Billy Cobham, and was in pretty good shape. In the October of that year the band played in Stuttgart, and after the show a lady friend took Jack to a disco in the city. His attention was caught by a tall young woman who was dancing, and went out of his way to catch her eye. She was Margrit Seyffer, a graphic designer and a member of a well-to-do local family who ran a print business. It was, he said later, love at first sight, and Margrit described them as being 'like two magnets which could not be pulled apart'. Margrit dotted in and out of the rest of the tour, and at the end of the year she flew to London and they met up again – and indeed have been together ever since.

For a short while everyone was lodged at Le Mote, but it was obvious that Jack and Janet's marriage was over. The situation grew increasingly difficult, and in early 1980 Le Mote was put up for sale, the contents were dispersed and divorce proceedings were initiated.

Margrit had an established business in Germany and was understandably reluctant to abandon it, so it was agreed that when the dust had finally settled they would move over there to live. The boys were to live in London with Janet. Jack and Margrit married in Stuttgart on August 25 1982.

Janet says that it took her a long time to recover from the split and the divorce, but when she had, she at last felt that she had got her own life – almost for the first time. She went to Middlesex University and then started a career as a social worker. She spent just over five years specialising in child protection.

Both Jo and Malcolm became talented musicians, and had played instruments from a very early age. Together with their father the boys recorded a full-length album, which they cut in their home studio. Jack treated them like professional musicians and both boys rose to the challenge. Jo would have been sixteen and Malcolm fourteen. Malcolm remembers all three of them jostling to see whose songs would be recorded; politely but firmly insisting that their own material went on the album. Just like a real band. And a couple of the songs, written by Jack, not by either of the boys, re-surfaced on Jack's later album.

Jo's preference was for the electric guitar, the one musical instrument which Jack didn't have at home (though there were acoustic guitars around the place). By the age of three his hero was Jimi Hendrix, and Janet came into the kitchen once to find him on his knees on the floor, with his plastic Woolworth's toy guitar in front of him and a box of matches in his hand - trying to set it alight.

He was funny, quick and very good company. He was also quiet and somewhat introverted; when they were children it had always been the younger brother who was the spokesman. Malcolm says that though they vied for their parents' attention, as one would expect, they actually got on very well, and were each other's closest ally. He adds though that there was an area of competitiveness between them, and that was on the subject of music. Jo was supposed to be the keyboards player and Malcolm the guitarist, but Malcolm started to prefer piano, and they began to compete for who played what – as well as who wrote the best songs and played their instrument more adroitly.

Perhaps because he was older and perhaps because he was more attuned to what was going on in the house, Jo seems to have been more aware of the difficulties between his mother and father, and more affected by the break-up. He sailed through his schooling, and as an adult he was an enthusiastic cook, and he hugely enjoyed creating meals for his friends.

Janet says of her two sons, 'I have always talked a lot with Malcolm. He and I talk about everything. With Jo though it was different. He and I could communicate everything that needed to be said with just a look.'

By the mid-Nineties Jo was playing keyboards in the world music band Afro Celt Sound System. His work can be heard on their album 'Volume One – Sound Magic', which was released in July 1996. His is described as a quiet, thoughtful, self-contained – but one who came to life on stage. He was the youngster member of a band that included a broad range of ages, as his father had been in The GBO, and was regarded as 'the kid brother.' Simon Emmerson, who founded Afro Celt, says that he was very important to that first album, which of course set the tone for the band's development. Simon says that Jo rather 'stumbled' into the band – he was a musician, one of many, who was searching for his own musical language. He describes Afro Celt as 'very left-field, on the fringe of the fringe.' It was at the forefront of the World Music movement, and became the best-selling act on Peter Gabriel's Real World label, and was twice nominated for Grammy awards. Had he lived, Simon adds, 'He would soon have been in the position where he could have seen real success, and have turned round and said, 'Well, I did it, dad.''

Jo wrote News From Nowhere, which became the first track on the first side, long before the band was really under way, 'Jo was one of the first guys that I discussed what became Afro Celt with, and he came up with this amazing track.

'He was very proud of what Jack had done. I remember us discussing 'Songs For A Tailor' and me telling him that it was one of the greatest albums ever recorded. Jo used to play me stuff that he had recorded with Jack when he and his brother were kids.'

Jo had been asthmatic since childhood, and on the evening of October 8 1997 he suffered a very severe asthma attack in a friend's flat in London. He managed to get down the stairs to the front door, in search of help, but he wasn't able to open the door. Had he got through the door, had he received emergency treatment, he may well have survived.

He collapsed in the hallway, where he was eventually found by another resident. The oxygen had been cut off from his brain for too long though, and by the time he got to hospital he was clinically brain-dead. He was twenty-eight years old. News From Nowhere was played at Jo's funeral.

The death was a tremendous blow to the family. Jack cannot speak of it even now, and it cast a terrible shadow over Janet's life, which has eased somewhat with the passage of time but will certainly never lift completely. There was now nothing in common between her life and Jack's. She says that she 'has never stopped respecting and admiring Jack's music', and did go to one of the reunion concerts. She was nervous about going, but afterwards was very glad that she had been there. Malcolm Bruce spoke to Margrit, Margrit spoke to Jack, and a ticket was sent with his compliments. She enjoyed it enormously; 'It was good in the sense that I thought deep down that some bitter and twisted me might come to the surface, and I might be jealous, or I might think 'why am I not benefiting from this?' It was fine though. I went backstage to see them briefly, but it was okay to walk away, knowing that I had my own life.'

Thinking back on their eighteen years together, Janet says that their lifestyle was dictated by their circumstances; 'I know all the stuff that goes on behind the scenes, and it is a necessary thing that rock stars are partly removed from the average life.' She got used to going to public places such as restaurants and theatres, and Jack being recognised. People were awed. They would stand and point. And then they always had the limo waiting outside, ready to whisk them away. 'A lot of people who haven't had that experience can be a bit funny about the lifestyle, but a lot of it was necessary.

There are several musical instruments and a few odd bits of memorabilia in Janet's sitting room. Looking at the furnishings you wouldn't have to be an expert to guess that she is a child of the Sixties. In one corner stands a fretless Warwick bass. She is very close to Malcolm, who lives nearby. He has a daughter on the cusp of her teenage years, who Janet is teaching to play the piano, and she obviously adores her granddaughter. She has not re-married.

Jack isn't comfortable discussing his first marriage, but does say, 'Everybody falls in love when they're young and has children. That's what life is about. My experience was no different from anyone else's. It's not worth talking about.'

The area that he is happier to expand upon is the birth of his children. He and Margrit have had three children, two daughters and a son, and his sense of family is obviously crucially important to him. Like many – possibly all – first-time fathers he was 'walking on air' when his sons were born, and could hardly believe that anyone else had ever experienced that level of spiritual joy. He walked round Hampstead after the births of both Jo and Malcolm, happier than any man has ever been – and stopped complete strangers in their tracks to tell them his wonderful news.

Jack's family defines his sense of himself – at least that part which isn't related to his work and his music. It's also the area which, together with his marriage to Margrit, is the most private. Jack is a very private man, but his family life is the inner core. Speaking of Malcolm's birth he says, 'That was a very special moment but it's not something I want to go into.' The inquisitive are not welcome when it comes to his family, and questions are deflected. You're not likely to pick up a copy of 'Hello' and see a ten-page photo-spread in which Jack and Margrit 'welcome you to their fabulous family home.'

Both Jo and Malcolm took to Margrit readily. She certainly made an effort to become close to them, and to the boys this tall, slim and elegant woman seemed exotic and fascinating. They often holidayed in Germany, which they adored.

Malcolm remembers his father as a lot of fun, affectionate and 'very nurturing.' He and Jo saw a lot of Jack after the divorce, and it seems that he found being a parent easier under those circumstances – he could pour all his affection into those visits and then regain his freedom of movement when they weren't around.

He was always aware of his father's habit, even when young, and says, 'I didn't like it. It didn't sit right with me. I've always felt uncomfortable around heavy drug use, and still do. I don't like the way it makes me feel being around them. Some drugs make people act inappropriately. Maybe I'm a prude, but if something allows you to treat someone badly then you need to look at that.

'A drug is a pain killer, and if you don't feel pain then you don't feel empathy. You can hurt someone and not feel that you're hurting them. That can't be a good thing. It can be extremely dangerous to get used to being like that.

'There have been times when my father has behaved towards me, and towards other people, in a way that has been extremely inappropriate – and I don't think that he's really like that as a person. His drug use has allowed him to behave in those ways.

Malcolm has used transcendental meditation for many years, and he thinks that drugs can mimic the effect of practises such as meditation. He says, 'At a huge cost.' He feels that it's an easy option and that drug users can convince themselves that they have achieved enlightenment, 'But it's not a healthy option.'

It's obvious that Malcolm has been affected by his father's drug use – in ways which might actually be seen as positive – he's very cynical about those who proselytise drug use, and he keeps drug users themselves very much at arm's length. He has seen what the effect was on his father and doesn't want or need to experience that sort of damage again. He feels the same way about alcohol, and hardly ever drinks; 'Alcohol is just as bad as heavy drugs in terms of your health and its psychological effect –

but it happens to be legal.' He adds, 'I was aware of it from fairly early on and I don't like how drugs make people behave. To be honest it has been a big issue in my life.'

Malcolm is most certainly proud of his father, and is rarely embarrassed when someone makes the connection and he sees their eyes light up. It's not all a breeze being a rock star's son or daughter though. Some may seem to live gilded lives, but for many others there are cons as well as pros.

It is assumed that a musical career is easier for the scions of rock dynasties – like broadcasting dynasties – and that they just walk into positions and have an automatic advantage. There is something of a head start in that there are musical instruments lying around when they are young, and they are encouraged to try them. It's also true that the erratic life of a musician – and the even more erratic income – doesn't come as a terrible shock. In terms of their ability though they have to be as good as their parent, if not better. There is a standard which they have to come up to – or exceed. Then there's the question of how the industry sees them: Malcolm played in a band with Ginger Baker's son, and the marketing chaps wanted to dress them in paisley-print shirts, have them playing Sunshine Of Your Love, and call the band Sons Of Cream. Honestly.

Chapter 21

'**L**ifetime was in a class of its own', Pete Brown says; 'It is Jack's greatest musical achievement. It was an absolutely magic band live. It was like hearing Charlie Parker for the first time – it was scary. Nobody took it that far.'

Lifetime was formed in 1969 by jazz drummer Tony Williams. He was just 23, but had already built an almost unparalleled reputation. Born in Chicago and brought up in Boston, Tony had been playing professionally since he was eight years old. In 1962, at the age of sixteen, he moved (with his mother's reluctant permission) to New York City. His first job was drumming for Jackie Mclean's quintet but within a year he was playing alongside Herbie Hancock, Wayne Shorter and Ron Carter in Miles Davis's band. He stayed in Davis's band for five years. He was that good. He was that good that young; a fact which would have resonated with Jack.

Miles Davis was the first person to attempt to bridge the gulf between jazz and rock. It was something that, for the sake of jazz, needed doing. It was also, on the level of simple musical adventurism, well worth doing. His 1969 double album 'Bitches Brew' came as a shock what few jazz purists were left, and pushed the music further than almost any other recording. It seems to have a reaction to what John Coltrane was doing within jazz, but it's more than likely that Miles worried that he was going to be marginalised by elements of the rock world – most notably Jimi Hendrix and Sly Stone. Tony formed Lifetime at exactly the right time to build on, and move on from, what Miles had achieved so far.

Tony was also a composer, and was rapidly moving on to free-flowing avant garde jazz, and incorporating strands from a wide range of sources. He also had influences from outside the jazz world, and he acknowledged that these stretched from The Beatles to Hendrix. Having decided that it was to time to put together his own band, he was joined by John McLaughlin (who had first been recruited by Miles, having been introduced to him by Tony – though John refused a permanent place in the Miles Davis line-up, preferring to with Tony's new project). The third man in the trio was organist Larry Young. The band was described as the first fusion band, though many would despite that label, and Tony himself said, 'It was really a throwback to what was going on when I started out in Boston.' That's understating the case though; Lifetime became the first, true jazz/rock fusion band, and as such was a landmark.

After a year or so Tony decided that what the band needed was a bass player, and of course it had to be a great jazz bass player. John McLaughlin introduced Jack to Tony while Jack Bruce and Friends (the Friends being Larry Coryell, Mitch Mitchell and Mike Mandel) was touring in the States in support of 'Songs For A Tailor.' John brought Tony to see Jack and the band playing at The Fillmore East on January 30 1970.

It was the first gig of the American tour to promote 'Songs For A Tailor', but Tony invited Jack to join Lifetime there and then, and Jack immediately agreed; 'I had lost interest in my own band almost before the tour had happened. It was quite a good band, a great band in some way, but the idea of joining Tony's band was right up my street.'

As soon as the Jack Bruce And Friends tour was completed, Jack told Larry, Mitch and Mike that he was folding the band. He then threw himself into his new role in Lifetime. He came off the road with his own band in early March and was out on the road with Lifetime in April. They went straight into a huge tour, first of the USA – with more than fifty shows played - and then of the UK. There were two odd dates in Switzerland, and then the band went back to the States at the end of the year. They played the Newport Jazz Festival that year and had a short residency at Ungano's in NYC.

For a progressive jazz band trying hard to make an impact on the American club and college circuit Jack was quite a catch, and a draw in himself. His recent experience was more in rock than in jazz, or at least, he had a lot more pure rock experience than the other members, so adding Jack to the line-up pulled the band quite a way further towards rock.

As well as playing bass, Jack wasn't really required to sing – within the jazz/rock notion Lifetime was very much an instrumental-based jazz band rather than a lyric-based rock band - though what was required, rather than lyricism, was what Hal Horowitz described as 'creepy, other-worldly vocals.'

Talking about the band's music, Hal says, 'Songs, actually jams, were often built on riffs, only to be abandoned for wildly innovative (and loud) improvisation, and hooked back up at various points throughout their extended lengths.'

Pete Brown adds, 'It was a fusion of black Americans and white Brits. It wasn't rock. It was a form a jazz. It was the most terrifying band. Earth-shattering. Hardly anyone else could produce music like that. They were so fucking good that people couldn't

A publicity shot for Lifetime after Jack had been recruited;
from left, Larry Young, Tony Williams, John McLaughlin and Jack. (Public Domain)

believe what was happening. Unfortunately that band never really made a proper record.' Jack explains, 'It was a pioneering band, and was so far ahead of its time that they couldn't get us to sound good, either on record or in studio. There were so many notes at such high volume! It wasn't that easy to make good records in those days. They didn't have the technology. They couldn't get the power of the band onto vinyl.'

Lifetime's lack of commercial success meant that there was a real danger of the band breaking up earlier because of lack of income. For a long time it was only sustained by Jack reaching into his wallet and funding it. That couldn't go on forever though.

'The problem with Lifetime', Jack says, 'Is that it was elitist, and we all knew it. That's something that Cream, for example, never was. Because of the problems that exist in the jazz scene you have to have that sort of arrogance. We were given a hard time from both the rock and the jazz sides, and it was hard. It was a supreme band in its own way.' Jack adds that he still meets people whose musical experiences were completely shifted by Lifetime; 'They say that it was the greatest thing they'd ever seen, and it changed their life. The critics didn't understand it – they never understand anything

– but the people who saw us, they understood.'

He adds that Lifetime was very much ahead of its time. Lifetime didn't receive the recognition it truly deserved, but he believes that no one who ever saw the band live has ever forgotten it – or has heard such great music.

The band made four albums in all, but none of them was a commercial success. Tony was to see greater success in later years but died aged fifty-one in February 1997.

In the autumn of 1970, as Lifetime was breaking up, Jack and Tony started talking to Jimi Hendrix about forming a band. All three men were keen on the idea and, in the informal way of those times, they agreed that it ought to happen, but made no specific plans of discussed musical themes and directions; 'We met, and Jimi was all for it. In those days we didn't have very deep discussions,' Jack says. 'When Cream happened it was one question, 'Do you want to come and play', and the answer was 'Okay.' We didn't have a meeting about a meeting. Jimi was definitely up for it. He knew me and he was enamoured of Tony because Tony was just the guy at the time. It would have been a dream for him as well as for us. He was definitely going to do it.'

The next thing would have been to simply get together and play, and see what emerged. Music lovers can only imagine what glories might have sprung from that trio, and deeply regret that it never happened.

'We'd have played the sort of music that the three of us would have played, like Eric, Ginger and me had played the sort of music that happened because we were playing.' Jack believes that – with all respect to Mitch Mitchell and Noel Redding – Jimi's side men had never really tested him; indeed, Tony Williams wasn't backward in telling him that, and Jimi agreed. In a group made up of equals, exactly as Cream had been, Jimi would have reached even greater heights.

The week after their discussions, on September 18 1970, Jimi was found dead in his flat London. Jack denies that Jimi was ever a really heavy drug user, and says that his was a completely unnecessary death. The major element in his death, Jack believes, was alcohol; Jimi was 'experimenting with drinking', which he had hardly ever touched before, and the alcohol in his system - to which his body wasn't acclimatised – reacted with his sleeping pills and killed him. His death certificate bears this out; the cause of death was the inhalation of his own vomit, linked to the suppressive action of the prescription drug Quinalbarbitone, which is used in the treatment of severe insomnia. Jack absolutely insists that his wasn't a death waiting to happen.

Jack's only reservation might have been that such a group might have been technically ahead of its time, and that neither the PA systems used for live gigs not the analogue recording systems would have been able to cope with the complexity of sound they would have created. Cream experienced these problems and, playing live, were delighted when the state of the art PA system proved to be up to their requirements, as it was at the Fillmore. Jack, Jimi and Tony Williams would have made possibly impossible demands on the technology of the time.

Pete Brown knew about this planned band at the time and is very sorry that it didn't happen. It would certainly have been a very exciting new outlet for his material. He has no doubt whatsoever that the band would have come together if Jimi had lived.

Hendrix was a great admirer of Jack, Ginger and Eric as musicians, and also loved their music. He often played Cream songs. As well as playing Sunshine on the Lulu show, Jimi played it at Winterland in Los Angeles on each of three nights he played there in October 1968. The shows were recorded and can be heard on the unimaginatively named 'Live At Winterland' album. Of all the musicians he came across in Britain, it was Cream that he connected with most intimately.

Jack's next solo album, 'Harmony Row', was recorded early in 1971 and released the following July. It was named after a street in Govan in Glasgow, where the longest continuous tenement block could be found. It was close to the ship-building area south of the Clyde, and a short walk to the Ibrox football stadium. The name had been changed from Washington Road at some point – and re-named with a touching degree of optimism.

Jack recruited just two familiar and empathetic musicians to work on the album with him; John Marshall and Chris Spedding. All the lyrics were by Pete, and Jack is credited as producer. It was recorded at Command Studios on Piccadilly in London.

Jack wrote almost all the music at the piano in his home, and recorded his playing straight into a tape player. Interviewed at the time Jack said, 'I prefer Harmony Row' to 'Songs For A Tailor' as a piece of writing. Six songs were written one very stoned afternoon in about one hour. I sat down and one after another they came out as complete songs. The songs are so varied, with many different types of feelings, and Chris and John are both capable of that. They're not just a good rock guitarist and a good jazz drummer ... they have all those different things in their playing. Chris has come on a storm - I haven't heard anyone else with that kind of free rhythm he plays.'

Jack, with his feet up his music room, argues that he is a lazy man by nature – though that can hardly be very true – and he says that he liked that album because it was easy to write, because a lot was improvised (which cut the necessity for complex arrangements right down to a minimum), and because the recording simply flowed; the songs appeared on the record in the order in which they were cut.

The album was recorded very quickly. The three of them spent just two days at Command recording the basic tracks - with Chris and John nervous of what they were going to be asked to play, and slightly awed by demands and challenges of this new jazz/rock fusion. Chris says that it was much harder work than 'Songs For A Tailor', particularly when it came to mastering all the different time signatures Jack wanted.

It took Jack just another two days to complete most of the overdubs. In that time he added keyboards, acoustic bass and 'Dozens of voices and cellos and hundreds of harmonicas and piano and organs.' It was a week of energetic creativity, which he truly relished. The finest work follows on naturally and stylistically from 'Songs For A Tailor', but it's already possible to see that commercial considerations are way down the list of priorities. For good or ill, Jack is creating the music that he wants to play, regardless of whether anyone will feel a need to follow his lead.

Interestingly, Chris Spedding says that when he was working on 'Songs For A Tailor' he had wanted to go to Felix Pappalardi on several occasions, wanting to know if he had got the right sound and if what he was playing was being well received. He had no interaction with Felix at all though, and received no feedback of any sort. When it came to 'Harmony Row' and Jack handling production himself, Chris was much happier. He describes Jack's work as efficient, and 'He knew he what he wanted to do and he went and did it.' He disagrees with the theory that Felix – or, at least, a Felix figure – was a great advantage when Jack was in studio; 'I've not worked with many musicians who have known quite so distinctly what they want. He's unique in that respect.'

John Marshall had first met Jack when he was playing with the Mike Gibbs Orchestra, which Jack had guested with in October 1969, and of which Chris was also a member. Mike Gibbs aimed to steer an even-handed course between rock and jazz, and can be counted among one of Britain's greatest fusion pioneers. Jack had also played with Nucleus, which was fronted by Ian Carr. John played drums for the band and Jack played occasionally. Ian founded Nucleus in late 1969, and the following year they represented Britain at the Montreux jazz festival.

It was from those meetings that Jack invited John to play on, firstly, 'Songs For A Tailor' and then on 'Harmony Row.' 'Jack liked to record late at night', John recalls, 'And on into the early hours.

'When I first walked into one of Jack's recordings they were putting the horns onto Never Tell Your Mother She's Out Of Tune and I was completely over-awed. It sounded so good.'

Jack was a hero to John, dating back to when John had seem him play with Alexis Korner and then in The GBO. He was delighted to be asked back to play on the next album. He remembers the sessions as very straight forward; 'There was just us, and Jack was in charge. We just got on and did it.'

Like Chris, John was slightly taken aback by Jack's way of working. The drum parts were all written out, to establish a structure, as a jazz drummer would expect. On most tracks though he was asked to play drums to accompany Jack on the acoustic guitar, and he found it difficult to play without a bass guitar accompaniment. 'I just relied on Jack to know what would work and what wouldn't', he says, 'He was specific about what he wanted, but if anyone came up with anything then that was great.'

'Harmony Row' opens with a surprising – almost shocking - ninety second-long track, Can You Follow, with Jack singing characteristic Pete Brown lyrics and playing piano. There were no echoes of Cream on 'Harmony Row', in the way that there had been on 'Songs For A Tailor.' It was as if those influences and hangovers had finally been wrung out of his system, just as the stock of songs written by him and Pete during the Cream years had been exhausted. It was other, more innovative and personal strands from the first album which were now picked up and taken forward.

The Consul At Sunset was originally written as an instrumental for Dick Heckstall-Smith, but Pete added lyrics. Dick had discovered the novel 'Under The Volcano', written in 1938 by Malcolm Lowry and had recommended it to both Jack and Pete. Set in Quauhnahuac in Mexico, it uses a stream of consciousness technique to tell the story of an alcoholic British consul. It has been compared to the novels of Joseph Conrad and James Joyce, and Lowry re-wrote it many times, adding more mysticism each time, before it was finally published in 1950. All three men were influenced by it and the portentous, atmospheric song was their tribute to it.

You Burned The Tables On Me was one of the highlights on the album, with Jack's confident vocals, the chunky, rocky arrangement, and Pete's dark, wry wit ('My life was the table and you have dined off of it'). There's a lot of humour on the album, both in the lyrics and in some of the arrangements. In short, it sounds like a real joy.

You Burned The Tables On Me is followed by the very substantial, almost monumental There's A Forest, which connects directly with Weird Of Hermiston and To Isengard from the earlier album. There was a poignancy and a romanticism to this album – something which could never have been said of Cream – just as there was a delicacy and heightened sensitivity to Folk Song and which wasn't even found in Jack's most personal earlier songs, such as We're Going Wrong.

All in all it was a very successful album. It hung together as a single body of work with a strong tone of voice. John and Chris backed Jack up very solidly; they weren't flashy heroes and yet they were certainly much more than mere side-men. Many of Jack's fans hold 'Harmony Row' in very high esteem, and while it was never in the spotlight in the way that 'Songs For A Tailor' was, it's certainly a very satisfying and very accomplished album. Jack says of it, 'It wasn't very commercially successful. I think it was so miserable, and miserable wasn't commercial! I mean, it wasn't Chirpy Chirpy Cheep Cheep. The music scene is much more to my taste now because miserable is in!'

Chris thinks that the discipline of being in studio has always been a very good thing for Jack; 'If it's going to be a success on any level you have to leave all your troubles outside the studio door', he says.

With Graham Bond on organ and Art Themen on sax, alongside John and Chris,

Jack toured in support of the new album. Jack remembers that line-up as 'A great band. A really fine band.' They played some forty-five dates, with Graham actually leaving the band on two occasions. Most of the gigs were in the UK but they also travelled to Germany, Switzerland and Italy. As well as making an In Concert recording for BBC radio, the band made television appearances both in Britain and Germany.

Jack often seemed troubled on that tour, and on occasion certain demons seemed to be getting the better of him. John says that Jack was always great to be with, but describes the tour as 'quite eventful … it got quite hairy.'

Early on the band played a week at Ronnie Scott's in Soho, which culminated in Jack picking up his bass amp and throwing it at Larry Coryell, who was guesting with the band. It had been a great week, and Larry had thanked the audience for a great week and told them that Jack and John were one of the best UK rhythm sections. Not one of the best in the world, but one of the best in the UK. That went down very badly and things only got worse when Jack's amp fused in the middle of a bass solo. Jack lobbed his amp at Larry but it missed and hit John's drum kit. The shouting match continued in the dressing rooms. Jack announced that he was never going to work with Larry again.

At one of their first foreign gigs, in Italy, there was a full-scale riot organised by the local anarchists; the tear gas even crept into the dressing room where the band had retreated away from the mayhem.

It wasn't unusual for Jack to get upset on stage. He often shouted at the audience and would attack his speaker stack. He seemed very eager not to be there, wherever 'there' was; he would leave the stage and jump straight into a waiting car, and be gone even before the audience had left their seats. At one show he played three numbers and was then unable to go any further. He threw his bass into the audience and simply left the stage. There was never any explanation. Apart from the spat with Larry Coryell he got on well with the other musicians. His anger seemed to be directed more at himself than in any other direction.

The tour could be a touch weird; Graham was immersing himself ever deeper in magick. He insisted on calling his girlfriends Diana (after the mythological huntress), no matter their real name. And picking up any of his artefacts that might be left around was a very bad idea. When the band was playing Rome he was ejected from Saint Peter's basilica for laying out his tarot cards on the high altar. He also used to order two drinks – always the most expensive cocktail on the menu - from the hotel bar; one for him and the other to be poured straight onto the carpet as a sacrifice to the gods.

Despite the weirdness John remembers his days in The Jack Bruce Band with great fondness. It was a time of memorable musicianship; he describes Jack as a delight for a drummer to play alongside; 'He's got so much energy and he's so inventive. I've learned a lot from him about rhythm and timing. He told me once that some drum-

Hyde Park, 1971. From left, Jack, John Marshall on drums, Chris Spedding and Graham Bond on saxophone (Maurizio Comandini)

mers don't like playing with him because he's 'too busy', but that's what it's about. He's a joy to play with.'

Also in '71 Jack's work could be heard on a new album recorded by his EMI label-mate Duffy Power - 'Innovations.' Duffy has never seen the success he deserved, and can be said to have had one of Britain's best blues voices. This wasn't new material though; parts of it dated back to 1965.

In September of that year Jack Bruce And Friends headlined at the fourth and last free concert in Hyde Park. These events had been kicked off back in '68 with some of the very best bands in the country, and had helped to launch the notion of progressive rock. Pete Brown's band Battered Ornaments had played in '68, and again in '69 when they supported The Rolling Stones. That gig was recorded by a Granada TV film crew, just days after Brian Jones had died; Mick in white frock, hundreds of doves released, Shelley quoted on stage.

In '71 the bill was much smaller than in the previous three years: Jack's band was supported by King Crimson and Roy Harper (a late substitute for The Third Ear Band, who failed to show up). The concert was enthusiastically and extensively reviewed in the British rock press. Roy Carr, writing in New Musical Express, noted that the band played some Cream songs, but added, 'Jack Bruce to his credit has managed to shake off most of his past associations, to concentrate on his new career. Looking extremely happy and with Graham Bond, John Marshall and Chris Spedding for musical compa-ny, Bruce maintained the stature he has built up over nearly a decade on the interna-tional scene.' Roy enjoyed You Burned The Tables On Me, which he described as 'hard rockin' and noted that as well as being in fine voice, 'He thundered out a strong bass riff while Graham Bond played some rolling and very rocky interjections at the piano.' He wasn't so keen on some of the other material though; the damnation coming right at the end of the sentence; 'In complete contrast, a rather doomy interpretation of Carla Bley's Detective Writer's Daughter lasted for some time.'

Ray Telford, writing about the same concert for Sounds, was also moved to put a sting in the tail of his review; '[Jack] has around him now what I consider to one of the best bands on this side of the Atlantic and they proved it as they literally stormed through every number. Opening with You Burned The Tables On Me, the distin-guished voice and bass guitar playing and the equally unmistakeable guitar playing of Chris Spedding cut through magnificently. It looked as though nostalgia played a big part in this Bruce comeback. I say comeback because, to the rock fans present, this was the Jack Bruce of Cream and he had at last come home to them. "Politician" hadn't changed much since the days of Clapton, Baker and Bruce played it and although it was so obvious that this was no Cream, I guess that a lot of people were closing their eyes and imagining.'

John Marshall can't remember what they played that day, but describes the gig as, 'The most wonderful experience. The sort of gig you always remember.' Jack says, 'It was great. Quite phenomenal. There should be more of those!'

Early the following month Jack went back to the politics of his roots. He and his band played a benefit at Bumpers club in London for the ship-workers of the Upper Clyde Shipbuilders in Glasgow. UCS was a huge operation formed in 1968 as a result of The Geddes Enquiry into ship building on the Clyde, and brought together five of the historic yards. It was always a unhappy marriage though, and closures and lay-offs started to occur very soon afterwards. By 1971 the UCS experiment had collapsed.

Jack was approached to help out, and he agreed readily, as one would expect. A large number of the shipyard workers were travelling to London to demonstrate against closures at the yard, and as well as playing the benefit for them, Jack acted as hotelier; 'They were from my roots. If I'd said no they have turned up and slept at my house anyway. Every floor of the house had people sleeping on them, and my house had a lot of floors!'

Again he was lionised by the rock press. The reviewer from Sounds was exhausted by the ten hour-long gig, but was exhilarated by The Jack Bruce Band (as it was billed at that time) and described the band was being 'full of power and fire.' He went on to say, 'I don't think I can ever remember being disappointed by Bruce's bass playing and it was the same here. He was majestic and unpredictable at the same time, happy to play the blues, a ballad or edge towards the improvisations of jazz.'

Other reviewers noted that it was a shame that, as the headliners, The Jack Bruce band had come on so late – 10.30pm – and many fans had had to leave early for fear of missing the last bus home.

NME's writer made an incisive point in saying, 'The beautiful thing about the band is it doesn't blast you all the time; it gives you the chance to recover from the heavier numbers with searing solos by playing numbers in a quieter vein. The sound was solid yet allowing individual freedom. Throughout it all, Jack's bass was the fulcrum of the rhythm.' Melody Maker, on the other hand, said how good it was to see a band that actually took a stand on political issues on a practical level, and didn't just sit around preaching revolution – which will have pleased Jack. One hopes his dad read that.

Chapter 22

Jack sees his early solo records as a diary; the diary of a musician and song-writer, rather than any structured attempt to turn out more conventional rock albums – and certainly not rock singles. To say that he wasn't interested in being in the Top Ten and appearing on Top Of The Pops again is something of an understatement. It's hard to say what, if anything, he had in common with what was going on in the Seventies music scene. There again, he says that he was largely unaware of what was going on around him so far as new music was concerned. Like Eric he was impressed by the work of The Band during the Seventies, and what Stevie Wonder was doing, but that was about it. He was aware of landmarks if they were brought to his attention, and he knew what his friends were doing, however he says that, musically he has always inhabited something of a bubble, entertained more than adequately by the music in his head.

A lot of the music which influenced aspects of his composition had some roots in soul, or jazz or folk, but more was owed to the music he actually listened to for relax-ation; composers such as Bartok, Beethoven, Stravinsky, Schoenberg: 'My influences happened when I was a lot younger and I was still assimilating them. Your influences happen during childhood and adolescence, and you spend the rest of your life mulling it over. You then express yourself through those things rather than keeping up with the latest stuff. I'm still in love with Bach … and Louis Armstrong and Percy Heath. If I hear something now that's truly great I don't go off and try and emulate that or use it in my own stuff.'

Jack acknowledges that he had a lot of freedom of movement thanks to the success of Cream. The band's records were still selling in large numbers, but by the mid-Seven-ties sales had died off a lot, and then his management started to pay rather more atten-tion to what he was doing. 'They expected me to be making a lot more money than I was', he says.

There was a break of three years before Jack released another solo album; he moved on to another band and suspended work on what was exclusively his own music. That was to take the rock/jazz indicator needle right over to rock, but before then he let it slip well back into the jazz zone.

'Escalator Over The Hill' by The Carla Bley Band was a huge project initiated by the American-born jazz organist, originally described as a jazz/poetry opera, with the words written by poet Paul Haines – who was living in Pakistan at the time. It was inspired by her seeing Jack playing with Cream, and most specifically, by her seeing Jack perform on his 'Songs For A Tailor' tour.

Carla was seen as 'one of the greatest jazz composers of the post-bebop era', and 'Escalator Over The Hill' was a huge undertaking which went through a considerable number of musicians and wasn't finished until 1972. It was released as a whopping triple album, which restricted its potential market slightly. It was not accurate to call it an opera because it doesn't have any sort of narrative structure, and to be honest you have to be devoted and well-informed modern jazz enthusiast to sit through all three albums (or, now, two CDs).

Jack sang on several tracks, including Rawalpindi Blues, with its hints of Kurt Weill, and Detective Writer Daughter – which could have been a Bruce/Brown song and a Bruce production if it was wittier and less chaotic.

Jazz critic Trevor MacLaren said of it, '[The album] consists of equal parts rambling beat poetry and interesting yet nonsensical lyrics that work more in the context of Captain Beefheart's 'Trout Mask Replica' than inside a unified story structure.' He goes to say that the lyrics do at least reflect the 'Surrealism and Dadaism' that seemed to have a role in jazz of that period.' McLaren goes on to describe it as jazz's answer to 'Sergeant Pepper's Lonely Hearts Club Band.' Richard S Ginell of All Music Guide wrote, 'Escalator is a late-'60s attempt to let a thousand flowers bloom and indulge in every trendy influence that Bley could conceive. There is rock music, early synthesizer and ring modulator experiments, the obligatory Indian section, repeated outbreaks of Weimar Republic cabaret in 3/4 time that both mock and revere European tradition.' He went on to describe the libretto as incomprehensible, and the writing as lugubrious, and dismisses the work as 'avant-garde pretension.'

The work with Carla Bley was never anything more than a side-line, and soon afterwards Jack had a new band to get involved with – a move back into the rock world. It was time for a dramatic change, and that was brought about by Felix Pappalardi re-entering Jack's orbit.

Immediately after working with Cream, Felix was asked to produce a couple of singles for a band from Long Island, New York City called The Vagrants. They had an excellent local fan base but couldn't translate that into record sales and they folded after a short run of singles crashed. Felix got on well with their guitarist, Leslie West (who had abbreviated his surname from Weinsten to sound more rock ' n roll) though. Felix was then asked to production Leslie's album, called 'Leslie West – Mountain.' He wasn't a small man.

They decided to collaborate further, and put a three-piece band together, recruiting drummer Corky Laing. Curiously they decided to name themselves after West's solo album, so they became Mountain.

The music they started playing was heavily influenced by Felix's work with Cream, and they were soon being described as America's answer to Cream. In August 1969 they played at the Woodstock festival. The title track on their second album, 'Nantucket Sleighride', is instantly recognisable to any Briton, having been used as the theme music of the Granada TV current affairs programme World In Action for many years. They also covered a number of Bruce/Brown compositions, including Theme For An Imaginary Western. They became very big in the States, but made no impact in the UK.

The band never had the concentrated power that Cream managed to convey, and their versions of those Bruce/Brown songs sound scrappy and a stodgy. Corky and Leslie were more conventional rock musicians than the members of Cream; they didn't have the same blues and jazz backgrounds, and somehow the magical quality of true genius was missing from their work.

Jack says that he was drawn to the band because he admired the warmth of tone that Leslie brought to his guitar playing. He'd been described by promoter Bill Graham as 'a three hundred-pound psychedelic canary', which Jack says was a very accurate description. Leslie visited Jack at his home when Mountain where playing a gig in London, and the two became friends immediately. After 'the long grind' and lack of commercial success he'd seen with Lifetime, Jack was ready to get involved in a new project which wouldn't be such an uphill struggle. 'I was also ready for a return to simpler rock 'n roll', he adds.

Felix decided to return to working as a producer, and Leslie and Corky invited Jack to replace him. Jack wound up his own band, but not before Chris announced that he was leaving. In a statement his manager said, 'He hasn't been enjoying playing with Bruce. Chris likes simple happy music and Jack's music over the year has become increasingly more complex.' Chris says that he was at his happiest playing straightforward rock 'n roll, and what he had wanted to do most was be up on stage backing Jack playing Sunshine Of Your Love.

That press statement, with its implied criticism, didn't go down at all well with Jack. Chris says now that what he failed to appreciate back then was that he was merely a hired hand, and it wasn't for him to comment on his employer's music. In interviews for the music press he had criticised Jack for not playing the Cream hits, and had said that the new music made people nervous. Jack, Chris says, has never forgiven him

Jack with Seventies perm and Leslie West in West Bruce & Laing, 1972 (Redferns)

for the slight. In recent years, thirty years on, a mutual friend suggested that they ought to play together again; Jack jabbed a finger at Chris and told him that he hadn't forgotten what he'd said and would never play with him again.

At the end of January '72 Melody Maker reported that Jack was now a member of Mountain – but that wasn't quite right.

The new band wasn't Mountain, but was called West Bruce And Laing – though it played mostly Mountain material. The news came as a blow to the members of his existing band, and more than something of a surprise. Jack, never afraid of tackling problems head on, phoned the three musicians and told them the band was no more.

Over the next couple of years West Bruce And Laing made a couple of excellent studio albums – 'Why Dontcha?' in '72 and 'Whatever Turns You On' the following year - and a less successful live album, 'Live 'N 'Kickin'' released in 1974. Several of their songs had lyrics by Gail Collins, Felix's wife.

Although it was in theory a trio, in practice keyboards player Steve Knight often made up the numbers. To the fans they didn't look like Cream and they didn't sound like Cream, but although Jack disagrees that it was so, it does appear that their management and the record company seem to have believed that they had the second coming of Cream on their hands. Pete damns West Bruce And Laing very simply, 'The other two simply weren't good enough.'

The studio albums included two new songs by Jack and Pete, which were some of the best they had ever written. Both November Song and Out Into The Fields were sparse songs, with far fewer words than the Pete Brown lyrics on 'Songs For A Tailor.' Those lyrics, coupled as ever with Jack's singing, made them gloriously atmospheric and evocative songs. They are some of their best ever work, and though Jack has thankfully re-visited Out Into The Fields on his own albums, November Song seems to have been forgotten.

The band undertook two American tours though 1972, and played sixteen shows in Europe in late March and April. There were only five gigs in England, and one – at Green's Playhouse in Glasgow - in Scotland.

Jack was with West Bruce And Laing between '72 and '74, but then Felix and West got back together in 1974 to re-form Mountain. They surprised everyone by coming back with a live album. This was 'Twin Peaks' (nothing to do with the TV series of the same name) and mostly comprised old Mountain songs, on which Jack rather than Felix had established the bass lines. Pete damns West Bruce And Laing very simply, 'It was an abomination. On the records Jack ended up doing all the backing vocals and all the other stuff. The other two simply weren't good enough.'

After a second New Mountain album, 'Avalanche' (which included versions of Whole Lotta Shakin' Goin' On and Satisfaction) the band dissolved. Felix returned to producing and he and Gail lived in Japan for a few years. On April 17 1983 Gail used a .38 two-shot Derringer, which had been a present from Felix, to shoot him dead during a row at their home at the exclusive Waterside Plaza apartment block in New York. Gail was found guilty of the relatively minor charge of criminally negligent homicide and was sentenced to four years in jail.

In 1973 the Robert Stigwood Organisation had released the first of many compilations that were to appear over the years. Entitled 'Jack Bruce - At His Best', it was a companion album to an Eric Clapton anthology. They had almost identical sleeves, which will have saved a bob or two; the title strap was blue on Jack's and red on Eric's. Half of the album was made up of tracks from 'Songs For A Tailor.'

Jack's next solo album, 'Out Of The Storm' was, he says, supposed to be a more commercial record – though how anyone could tell is hard to say. 'Out Of The Storm' is emotionally his most powerful album', Pete Brown says. 'It's very tied up with his roots and his struggle to be himself. As a recording it's not as well produced as others, but it has incredible emotional under-currents. There are songs about addiction, and leaving home. It's very powerful.'

The record was originally to have been called 'Into The Storm', and Jack and photographer Roger Phillips set off for Scotland to find a storm to photograph for the album sleeve. Although they drove around the west coast and then through the Highlands and over to the north-east coast, they couldn't find bad weather, let alone a photogenic storm.

What they did find was a clearing in a wood, with an old abandoned bicycle lying in the grass. They propped the bike against a tree and Jack was despatched to stand in the middle distance while Roger created a pool of light in the foreground. As an image it worked very well, and Jack was particularly happy with as he was small in the frame, which he prefers; he dismissed the cover of 'Songs For A Tailor' as 'just a picture of my nose.' There was nothing 'out of the storm' about it, so the album was re-titled. The track Into The Storm had already been recorded, so that stayed as it was – confusingly.

Production credits were shared between Jack and Andy Johns (younger brother of the famous producer Glyn Johns), and it was Andy who suggested that it be recorded in Los Angeles. Andy had been the engineer on 'Songs For A Tailor' and had then gone on to work with The Rolling Stones on 'Exile On Main Street' – recorded in the south of France in 1972 while they were in self-imposed exile for tax reasons ('He was never the same again, like anyone who ever worked with The Stones.' Jack says, 'My advice to anyone, even now, is never work with The Stones!').

The plan was to spend ten days recording at The Record Plant studio in LA. As it happened The Bee Gees had recently recorded their curiously-named album 'A Kick In The Head Is Worth Eight In The Pants' at The Record Plant (the album was refused by

Atlantic and has never been released).

The studio wasn't going to be cheap, and ten days there would take them up to budget for their basic recording work. The plan was that the record would then be mixed back in England. That was the plan. The way it turned out Jack and Andy were there for ten months. Even then it wasn't really finished, and some recording was done back home. Jack remembers that period it as a complete nightmare.

LA session drummer Jim Keltner was based at The Record Plant, but he had problems giving Jack what he wanted in terms of percussion, and brought in another LA session drummer. This was Jim Gordon, who had played on (and co-wrote) Layla for Eric Clapton, and he finished the session. The only other musician who played on the album was Steve Hunter, who had previously been with Mitch Ryder, and was recruited to play electric and acoustic guitar.

The previous year Lou Reed had recorded his third solo, post-Velvet Underground album, 'Berlin', at Morgan Studios in London. He had a very impressive line-up of musicians on the session, some of which he brought in from the States, but also including Britons Steve Winwood and Aynsley Dunbar. Lou had asked Jack to guest on the recording – and he played bass on all but two tracks. Steve, who was Lou's guitarist at that point, was on his first trip to London, and was having the time of his life. He says that Cream was 'my favourite all-time band', and he was delighted to be playing alongside Jack. They spent the best part of a week together, and 'We just got along really well', Steve says, and a year later he was delighted to get a call asking him to play on 'Out Of The Storm.'

Steve turned up at the studio with no idea what he was going to be asked to play, though as a Cream fan he was hoping to play Sunshine Of Your Love and White Room. He was to be disappointed on that front; Jack still wasn't interested in playing Cream songs (though Steve says he was very patient with his endless questions about 'How Clapton played this or that, or what amp he used'). He was amazed and thrilled to learn that he was part of a trio. 'As soon as I heard Jack play the first track I thought it was really deep, and I was worried that my blues/rock style wasn't going to fit. After we ran through it a couple of times it just fell into the groove. I think that what I brought to it added a different flavour.

'It was very challenging. He threw some very difficult things at us. Jack wrote very complex harmonies, and I was just trying to find my way round what he gave me. I learned an enormous amount on that session about harmony structure.' Steve adds that Jack knew what sound he wanted, but within that he gave him a lot of freedom to try out new ideas – and anything that worked got used.

He does think that at times Jack wasn't comfortable in Los Angeles, which isn't surprising. Where he has had the choice he has always recorded in familiar surroundings, near to home. Given the choice he will always sleep in his own bed rather than stay in a hotel. He adds that although The Record Plant was a great studio, he thought that Jack would probably have preferred to record the album in London (Jack adds that New York is always his a preference, in fact!), and Steve himself would definitely been happier to work there.

Steve also recalls that by way of relaxation he played Scrabble with Pete and Jack, and adds that he never ever won against them.

Pete Brown recounts how, during the recording of one song in the 'Out Of The Storm' session, Jim had slowed down in the middle of the break on one of the tracks. This annoyed Jack considerably, so he had a 'not very good' drum kit brought into the studio, and he played just one phrase, which was then dropped into the mix; 'It was absolutely seamless; you couldn't hear the difference.' Especially as they were only using 24 tracks and two-inch tape, it was a remarkable ability. It was one of many times when Pete admits to being awed by Jack's music talents.

Pete (who Steve Hunter describes as 'the coolest, funniest guy I've ever met') adds that it was on this record that he acted, more than on any other, as Jack's translator. He says that he found all the imagery already there, in Jack's music, and what he had to do was put translate those musical images into lyrics; 'I could hear what the music was saying and my job was to articulate it. That record was a hurdle for both of us. We did easier stuff before and after, but that was very much a watershed.'

The endemic sins of LA soon caught up with Jack and sucked him in. Drugs were a way of life, more so than almost anywhere else, and anything you might want was readily available. Many musicians have found that every third person in Los Angeles is a pusher, or so it seems. It also didn't help that, with the Vietnam war coming to an end, the city was flooded with disillusioned and frequently unhinged veterans, who found that had no place back home, and who took their refuge wherever they could find it. Given the chance to indulge more than ever, Jack didn't hesitate. Neither Pete nor Steve was interested in drink or drugs – women, most certainly, for both of them, but not substances of any kind - but Andy and Jack made up for that.

Recording the album was undoubtedly a very worthwhile experience musically; at one point the next studio to one side was being used by Stevie Wonder, and in the other direction, John Lennon. 'There was a big party every Sunday. I can remember playing Stand By Me on one occasion, with John Lennon and Mick Jagger. It was complete madness. I tried to fly off the top floor of the Hyatt hotel one day – but I didn't succeed in taking off.'

Stevie Wonder was recording 'Songs In The Key Of Life', one of his most important albums, and James Jamerson was with him – though the bass player wasn't well and was fairly heavily dependent on drugs. The first time they met Jack was running through some bass over-dubs and James came in, took the instrument off him, and told him in no uncertain terms that he was playing the bass part all wrong ... before realising that he was in the wrong studio, and it wasn't his Stevie Wonder session at all.

The two men became friends and on a couple of occasions James asked Jack to cover for him on recording sessions that he couldn't make; which is how Jack came to play, unrecognised and uncredited, for Tamla Motown.

James Jamerson died of pneumonia in 1983, aged just 45. His flame is kept alive by the third of his four sons, James Jamerson Junior, who is a very highly regarded bass player.

Another local drummer was present at one of those jam session; Bruce Gary, who dropped in from time to time simply because he lived nearby and several of his friends worked at The Record Plant. He very surprised to find himself playing alongside Lennon, Jagger and Jack. He was understandably delighted to be playing with John and Mick, but was most impressed by the fact that he was playing with his greatest bass hero. He had first heard Jack playing on imported GBO albums, and had listened to every note that Cream had recorded; 'I was blown away to meet Jack as I was such a huge fan of his.'

The first thing they played together was a Willie Dixon blues called Too Many Cooks, with both Jim Keltner and Bruce Gary on drums (though Jim's part was cut out on the final mix), and a phenomenal line-up, which included, as well as Jack, Mick Jagger, Danny Kortchmar on guitar, Al Kooper on keyboards, Jesse Ed Davis playing saxophone, Bobby Keys and Trevor Lawrence on brass, plus a choir of female back-up singers conducted by Harry Nilsson. David Bowie and Lou Reed were also said to be in the studio at the time. It was never released but has appeared on bootleg albums, and in 2003 an acetate of the recording was sold for £1,400 – though it's uncertain what the new owner could legally do with it.

Bruce remembers, 'Even though John and Mick and all these people were in the room, my focus was on Jack. For a drummer he is the ultimate bass player. There is no finer bass player, so he was my focus. I was so honoured to play with him.'

Jack and Bruce were playing really well together, and after the session Bruce gave Jack and Pete Brown a lift back to their hotel in his old Dodge van. On the journey Jack praised his playing and asked for the drummer's phone number. He couldn't believe how kind the two Britons were to 'this young hippy kid.'

The spring after 'Out Of The Storm' was recorded, Jack went out on the road with a new version of The Jack Bruce Band, and did indeed call Bruce and ask him to join the band. By then Jack was playing with Tony jazz drummer Tony Williams, and Bruce wondered how on earth he was going to follow that. Jack brought the American to Le Mote, and as there was a delay in getting the rest of the band together, Jack and Bruce spent every day playing together in the music room at Le Mote. Bruce, still only twenty-four, was having the time of his life.

Jack's management also phoned Steve Hunter and asked him to join them on the road, but Steve was committed to working with Alice Cooper, and very regretfully had to decline. Instead this band included Mick Taylor on guitar, along with Carla Bley playing organ, synthesiser, clavinet, Mellotron and electric piano, Ronnie Leahy (from Springburn, just outside Glasgow, where Jack's mother's family had come from – so Jack would introduce him on stage as Ronnie O'Springburn) on keyboards - who had been with Leslie Harvey in Stone The Crows - and Bruce Gary on drums.

Jack had been aware of Carla Bley's work since the very end of the Fifties, when he started playing jazz in Glasgow. In the city at that time there was a scarcity of printed music which they could play from, but some of the few works available on paper were hers. Born in Oakland in California in 1938, she made her first public appearance aged four, playing piano in church. She then became a very highly regarded roller skater, but by 1957 she was in New York, writing and performing. Carla, who had a husband, children and a newly built house in New York State with its own recording studio, dropped everything and came to England to join the band. Musically speaking she was completely enamoured of Jack's work, and would have followed him anywhere to play.

Jack also liked the idea of having a woman in the band. It was a rare thing; there were female jazz singers around, and female rock singers too, but female instrumentalists were not a common sight.

Mick Taylor was a very interesting addition to the band. He had replaced Peter Green in John Mayall's Bluesbreakers after Peter had left to join Fleetwood Mac in 1967, and two years later had joined The Rolling Stones following the death of Brian Jones.

It was Andy Johns who suggested bringing in Mick once it was clear that Steve wasn't available. There was a connection between Andy's brother Glyn, who worked with The Stones and had just produced their album 'It's Only Rock 'n Roll.' Jack thought that was a great idea; Mick's profile was of course very high and was unhappy with life in The Rolling Stones. It's a moot point as to whether or not he had already left the Stone; if he hadn't then he was very much on the point of doing so. Of Mick's playing with his band, Jack says that when it was good it was great, but when it was bad it was dreadful; 'When it worked he was a very tasty guitar player, but he seemed to be switched off a lot of the time.'

Ronnie Leahy was very surprised to get a call from Jack asking him to come to an audition. They had never met before, but he went along and played piano for Jack and Mick in a flat on the King's Road. He recalls that Jack spent a long time, getting him to play ever more difficult pieces. He was, Ronnie says, 'Very intense. Every note had to be the right note.' Mick's patience finally ran out though and he firmly suggested that Jack simply give him the gig there and then.

The band was, for once – Bruce Gary says – 'well-organised and well put together, and the band was getting tighter night by night.' Jack was off heroin, relatively briefly as it turned out, but was in fairly good shape, and the tour went well. The audiences on the mainland of Europe, in particular, were particularly enthusiastic for the music. Bruce Gary remembers wonderful gigs as far apart as Scandinavia and Spain; at San Sebastian, 'Guys in the audience were hugging each other with delight. They were really into the music. Britain didn't love Jack as much as other countries in Europe did.'

This line-up of The Jack Bruce Band recorded a live album at The Free Trade Hall in Manchester on June 1 1975 (a venue which had a fine history as a rock venue and was the real venue for Bob Dylan's 'Judas!' concert), or at least, recordings were made, and eventually turned into an album. It wasn't released until 2003, and Bruce Gary describes it as 'not one of our best gigs.'

The opening track, Can You Follow is shaky, but the album – now a two-CD presentation – gets into its stride as the band go into Morning Story. The penultimate track on the first CD is a twenty four and a half minute version of Weird Of Hermiston, which then shifts slightly awkwardly into Post War from 'Harmony Row.' The track has rather too long a modern jazz piano intro, which would have left 1970s rock fans yawning or heading for the bar. The last track on the first CD was the brisk instrumental Spirit, which was an almost-epic at nearly eleven minutes.

By now Jack was happy to play the occasional song written for Cream, and the second CD closed with Sunshine Of Your Love – a jazzier, funkier cut which becomes slightly messy and frantic - and which was more than twelve minutes long. That followed a startling twenty four minute version of Smiles And Grins, also from 'Harmony Row', which really was far too long; as the intro goes on and on the listener does feel their will to live slipping away. You got real value for your money at gigs in the Seventies – especially, sadly, when it came to drum solos.

Ronnie remembers that tour as one of the best things he has ever been involved in, and says that the standard of musicianship was terrifically high and he greatly enjoyed the tour. He describes it as 'a fantastic band.' He adds, 'The music was so complex. It had classical music in it, jazz roots, blues roots and Jack's roots – all those things rolled into one, and that's what made it so distinctive. I'd not played music like that before.'

He makes the point that the band was particularly distinctive because not only were there two keyboards players, but they came out of very different musical disciplines. Carla's music was, primarily, modern jazz, of course, and was playing a more melodic groove on a Meletron. At the same time, Ronnie – who was much more a straight-ahead rock 'n roller – playing in a more rhythmic, more aggressive style on

In 1975 Jack played The Free Trade Hall in Manchester with the band that included Carla Bley and Mick Taylor. The show was recorded and was released as a live CD many years later. (Bruce Gary Archive)

electric piano and organ. He was following Jack, Ronnie says, while Carla played counterpoint.

The band wasn't to last long though. The band disintegrated following major disagreements between Jack and Mick over heroin use. Jack was again trying to get clean and didn't want the drug anywhere near him, and Mick reacted very strongly against being told what he could and could not do with and to himself. There was a gig at The Apollo in Glasgow in June 1975, to which Jack had invited his father, and Charlie had the misfortune to witness these two rock stars brawling in the dressing room before the gig.

Unfortunately the band never undertook a studio recording: An album was planned and after a fortnight's holiday for everyone to relax and re-group, almost everyone re-assembled in studio. They waited and waited but Mick didn't turn up. Eventually a message came through that he had decided to leave the band. Ronnie urged Jack to go ahead and start recording, and a few tracks were cut, but it was the end for the band. It was, Bruce Gary says, a great disappointment to him; 'That band was poised to be one of the best bands in the world. No one sounded like us.'

Back in the Sixties Jack had encountered Frank Zappa in Greenwich Village, where he played a residency in a tiny theatre with The Mothers Of Invention. They played through the afternoons, every day. Jack and Eric went to see him play on several occasions - 'doing these insane concerts', as Jack describes the gigs. One of his tricks was to haul in bums and winos from the alleyways and give them plastic trumpets and ukuleles and get them to play them on stage. The Britons adored the humour of the performances; 'There was no humour in Sixties rock. It took itself very seriously. He was an American version of The Bonzo Dog Doo-Dah Band, must musically much more advanced. He was obviously a schooled musician. 'It wasn't Frank Zappa for me. I was very much the Mothers Of Invention. Frank was the band leader but it was very much a band.'

They invited Zappa and The Mothers to support them at a huge auditorium in Chicago, and after the show Frank and Jack met by chance in the lift. Frank went out of his way to praise, in particular, Jack's singing, saying that his voice was unique in rock. That made quite an impression on him because, he says, it was the first time that anyone had actually been complimentary to his face.

Six years later Frank phoned Jack quite unexpectedly, and asked him to play cello on the album he was working on. This was to be 'Apostrophe' (or '), which was released in May '74. As Jack was in New York and his cello was in England he replied that he couldn't. Frank's solution was to rent one, which didn't go down well; 'The cello is such a personal instrument. It's not like a guitar or a piano, which you can rent. It's part of your body.'

Jack went along to the session and was presented with 'a machine-made cello which was falling apart', and he was on the point of walking out. Frank didn't want to lose him completely so he stopped him leaving by asking him to play bass, which he did. 'Apostrophe' turned out to be Frank's most successful album, far more so at the time than the better-remembered albums. It reached number ten in the American album charts.

The one record from this period which – in Pete Brown's opinion - should have been a big commercial success, was 'How's Tricks?' In his opinion it's the greatest of Jack's records after 'Songs For A Tailor.' Jack disagrees. The album has always brought back memories of what was a difficult time. He tried hard not to use drugs while the record was being made, 'And I was suffering because of that.' He adds, 'I found it difficult to make. It was a funny cross between a Jack Bruce album and a band album. Other people were contributing. We should have had a name for a band.'

It was recorded between October and December 1976 at Virgin Records' Manor Studios near Chipping Norton in Oxfordshire, and released in March '77. Jack was supported by a completely new line-up - Hughie Burns on guitars, Tony Hymas playing keyboards and vibraphone, and Simon Phillips on drums (and glockenspiel). Everyone is credited as vocalists.

Hughie recommended Tony and Simon to Jack, and they were all invited down to Le Mote hall ('Remote Hall, as we called it', Simon adds) and they began rehearsing. Tony Hymas recalls there first meeting as 'a very nice afternoon.' There was no sense of them being lesser mortals turning up at the rock star's mansion; exactly the opposite. Jack came across as 'just a bloke.' He is at his happiest with other musicians, relaxed and at ease. Tony, like the others, had previously been a jobbing musician for hire, working sessions, and was understandably delighted to be asked

Jack and Tony had a lot in common in that they were the same age and both had a very rich musical background which encompassed both jazz and classical music.

Simon was only nineteen in 1976, but his musical thinking had mirrored Jack's, albeit half a generation on. He had been brought up playing jazz and was an out-and-out purist, disdainful of rock music and only interested in playing big band jazz (he first went on the road professionally, playing with his father's band, in 1969 – aged twelve); 'I didn't listen to the Top Forty like the other kids, he says, 'That music didn't do it for me. I needed to hear far more complex harmonies.' He did, later on, recognise the jazz influences in both Cream's music and Jack's solo work. He had also read about Jack in the music press; indeed, he says, he knew of him from the papers but had hardly heard his music. He had then been very surprised to find that this 'rock star' had turned up playing with Tony Williams in Lifetime; 'That was intriguing. I thought 'How did that work?.'' He then heard 'Out Of The Storm' and was immediately converted; 'It was darker and more complex', and he made a point of catching Jack's band with the Carla Bley, Mick Taylor line-up.

Some critics saw Simon as a great asset to Jack, and a spur to his playing. Author Chris Welch observes, 'Jack has always worked well with a good drummer. When he was working with Simon Phillips, you can hear the difference immediately.'

Not all the songs on 'How's Tricks' were by Jack and Pete: Times and Lost Inside a Song were credited as being written by Hughie Burns as well as by Jack and Pete. Baby Jane was written by Hughie alone: It's a standard issue rock 'n roll song, and to be honest it doesn't have the charm of a Bruce/Brown composition. If you were played it blind, having not heard it before, you'd be hard pressed to identify it as being by a band led by Jack Bruce – which is not something you can ever usually say of tracks on his albums.

Pete says, 'It's exceptionally well produced – by Bill Halverson, who was the engineer on Cream's live recordings at The Fillmore West. The other albums had great performances on them, but 'How's Tricks?' is the record that stands out as having the kind of production that Jack needed.' There are some touches on the production which date the record somewhat; particularly the use of electronic effects on the drum parts.

Bill was a physically large man who knew what he wanted, and though he wasn't a dictator in any sense, he didn't invite contradiction. The recording took place over three weeks, and Tony found them to be, 'The most intense thing I'd done up to that point.'

'I've grown to like 'How's Tricks' an enormous amount over the years', Pete says; 'Partly because it was a working band and it has got this band feel to it, and partly because the production was first rate.'

Pete has said that the song Waiting For The Call is a prescient political song which anticipated the rise of Margaret Thatcher. It's a slow, tortured blues, complete with wailing harmonica; Pete called it 'a worthy successor to Politician and Ministry Of Bag', though in truth it's lyrically rather more obscure than Politician. The last track on the second side, Something To Live For was re-jigged for release as a single, edited down from more than five minutes to just under four. It didn't entirely work though; Jack's solo work was never about producing hit singles, and it wasn't released.

The album's front cover was an attractive piece of artwork by Don Murray, made up of several 1920s vaudeville and fairground image, from dancing girls to a human cannonball. The figure at the centre of the cover, hair slicked down and looking like Terence Rattigan, seemed to be rising up from the fires of Hades - and into a large orange question mark. Very enigmatic. The least said about the soft focus photo of the band on the back of the album – with all four in white tuxedos and bow ties, and topped with hair styles which seemed to eagerly anticipate the Eighties and the rise of Bucks Fizz – the better.

The Jack Bruce Band, with the line-up as on the record, toured the UK and Europe through March and April 1977. For a while they tried to come up with a different name for the band, one that showed it was a 'real band' rather than one big name and three side men. Nothing seemed right though, and The Jack Bruce Band was decided upon by default. It wasn't Jack's preference. It made obvious commercial sense though.

Simon Phillips, whose talent was really starting to be recognised, had been offered a couple of very high profile, well-paying jobs, which unfortunately clashed with the tour dates. They were very tempting but he didn't hesitate; he stayed on with Jack Bruce And Friends; 'I was offered gigs that would have taken me to the States, playing big arenas, but they didn't excite me at all. Playing with Jack was so cool. I loved the music and I felt it was a real learning experience. That was what I wanted to do.'

Most of the British gigs were at university student unions, which were then enjoy-ing their heyday, but weren't the biggest shows in town. There were dates in all the north European and Scandinavian countries, and after a break over the summer, the band went to the States and played eighteen shows through until the middle of December. In Los Angeles the band played six shows over three nights at The Roxy Theatre on Sunset. Tony Hymas remembers it as a great band, and recalls 'The intensity and the speed of a lot of the playing; it was extraordinary. There were gigs when we were on fire.'

The band also played a BBC radio 'In Concert' performance which was recorded in the middle of April and broadcast at the end of the month.

Jack's last album cut during the Seventies was 'Jet Set Jewel', in the early autumn of 1978. It was again recorded at The Manor Studios in Chipping Norton, and was co-produced by Jack and Dennis McKay (who was also billed as the engineer), and the personnel was unchanged from 'How's Tricks?'

His colleagues describe him as being in a very fragile state at this point – 'It was a very fraught time', Simon Phillips says - but the studio was almost an escape route. He had no option but to leave the outside world, with all its worries and harshness, outside the studio door. Inside he was with solid, sympathetic, empathetic souls, who were supportive and encouraging – and whose only desire was, just as his was, to produce and record the very best music they could. Throughout the recordings he again didn't act as band leader or paymaster; he was in charge, of course, but anyone wandering in would have got the impression of a band – a single unit, a team, a collection of equals – with one guy only slightly more equal than the others.

'Those sessions weren't as much fun', according to Tony Hymas, 'We didn't have a strong producer. The US tour had been a bit fracuous. Jack and I had our disagreements. There were egos involved. It wasn't easy.'

It's a very attractive album, and across many tracks it's softer than a lot of Jack's work earlier in the decade. His voice is stronger than ever before and seems to have an increasing maturity. The band had been together for some time and it showed; they had that ready-made band tightness that Jack thought had been missing previously. Simon Phillips says that because the songs were so well-written they were very easy to record, and they 'almost played themselves.'

The title track is Pete railing against the decadent super rich with their yachts and their self-centred selfishness; a thought process not unlike Bob Dylan's Like A Rolling Stone. Pete has always been proud of the song, and says it was partly inspired by the decadence of The Rolling Stones in the late Sixties, which he saw at first, being a regular visitor to Marianne Faithful's London home; 'I was so amazed by all that, it leaves a bad taste in my mouth to this day.' Jack sings the lyrics softly and thoughtfully, accompanying himself on the piano; there none the anger one might expect. The musicians cut in as the song progresses, and Jack's bass dances round Hughie Burns's guitar and Tony Hymas's keyboards.

The writing credits on the album were complicated. Apart from Jet Set Jewel, which is the only tracked credited just to Bruce and Brown, tracks credited to Jack and David Hart, some to Tony Hymas and Pete, one to Tony Hymas alone, and one to Jack, Pete and Tony. Dick Heckstall-Smith guested on The Boy and Neighbour Neighbour.

For once the songs which aren't blessed with Pete's lyrics aren't less impressive. The Boy is a surprising opening track, but in catching the listener off guard with its gentle lyricism its all the more effective. It's an impressive and completely original track, which is neither jazz nor rock – nor obvious anything else. Perhaps it's an electric folk song; it's possible to imagine Fairport Convention covering it. The same can be said of Maybe It's Dawn; a very beautiful, anthemic song with distinct celtic hints.

Pete Brown says that Jack had convinced himself that his days on this earth were numbered. He had one piece of music that he had written, and he implored Pete to write optimistic, upbeat lyrics to it. Pete has often used his lyrics to communicate important thoughts to Jack; trying to say things to Jack which couldn't be said man to man. On 'Out Of The Storm' the song Keep It Down was purely directed at him. It voices Pete's concern over Jack's drug taking – though it's not a reference which is easily spotted. On this occasion he wrote The Best Is Yet To Come, which became the last track on the album, to try and reassure him. Pete says that he found his own lyrics far from convincing though.

If anything doesn't fit on the album it's the raucous Neighbour Neighbour, which breaks up the flow of an otherwise very melodic string of songs. Jack has revisited Neighbour Neighbour on a number of occasions, and the album of the first Alexis Korner memorial concert, recorded live at Buxton Opera House in 1995, opens with him playing it. His band on that occasion comprised Dick H-S, Norman Beaker on guitar, Dave Bainbridge on keyboards and Tim Franks on drums. Neighbour Neighbour was followed by four Cream songs – which pleased the audience hugely – and Jack's old mucker Paul Jones then joined him to play Sonny Boy Williamson. The CD of the concert is a joy; Jack is relaxed, well and on great form. His bass playing on White Room in particular is best described as playful as, particularly on the run-off, he runs right up and down the scales and coaxes top end notes out of his bass which would have bothered bats in flight. And a lengthy cut of Sunshine Of Your Love, at nearly seven minutes in length, as good as any recording of that song he has made. To say that Norman Beaker was playing his sneakers off is an understatement too.

At the time that 'Jet Set Jewel' was being recorded and mixed, Robert Stigwood was selling RSO to PolyGram, and men in suits were despatched to Chipping Norton to listen to the master tapes. They declared there and then that they didn't like what they had heard and had no intention of releasing it. Simon says, 'The A&R man wandered in and listened to it, and he didn't hear any Top Forty hits.' Jack was stunned, and understandably very frustrated; 'It wasn't quite finished, and their decision was very unfair. It was a good record.'

Tony Hymas was less surprised that it didn't go down well; 'It seemed a very dark record.' This meant that all their work had been in vain. Three tracks did surface in 1989 on a PolyGram compilation album ('Willpower'), but it wasn't until Universal Music bought PolyGram's catalogue in 1999 that the full recording saw the light of day. It was finally released, twenty five years on, in 2003, just as it had been recorded, without any re-mixing.

Unfortunately it was given a cheap and cheesy cover; a photo of a jet aircraft taking off, laid over a shot of a full-lipped lady in a 'we're off to a smart wedding' hat. These are obviously standard-issue photo agency shots, and it looks like a travel brochure. It's a shame; the album deserves better and if you weren't familiar with Jack's music the sleeve probably wouldn't encourage you to buy the CD.

In May of that year Jack was a guest at the wedding of Glyn Johns. The other guests included Charlie Watts, Mick Jagger and Keith Richards of The Rolling Stones (Glyn had by then produced the majority of The Stones' albums), Paul McCartney and Ringo Starr and George Harrison, and Eric. Everyone played at some time or other, and Jack joined in of course, playing Jerry Lee Lewis and Little Richard songs. Sadly no recording exists of Eric and Jack (and their mildly famous side men) playing classic rock ' roll. The three Beatles played tracks from 'Sergeant Pepper's Lonely Hearts Club Band' – the only time the songs were ever performed live and in full by the band (albeit only three members of the band), and despite the fact that all four Beatles were deeply entrenched in legal action.

In July 1979 Jack played a handful of gigs alongside his old friend Charlie Watts in his boogie-woogie band Rocket 88. It was a terrific line-up, which also included Alexis Korner and The Rolling Stones' keyboards player and ass-kicker Ian Stewart (who had been a member of the band until Andrew Oldham decided that he didn't look cool enough). Jack also played on the live Rocket 88 album recorded at the Rotation Club in Hamburg in 1981, and called 'Rocket 88.' The album included the Bruce/Brown song Waiting For The Call from 'How's Tricks?', which was a nice touch.

Writing of that album, Ian Stewart said, 'Anyone reading the line-up of musicians on this album would be forgiven for thinking that this is yet another jazz-rock fusion. It is, in fact, a straight-forward, mainly instrumental blues album with boogie woogie as its foundation.' He added that Jack, 'played his ass off, and by the time Roll 'Em Pete ended the set, his fingers were bleeding profusely from playing double bass – something he has only rarely done in recent years.' Jack remembers all his gigs with Rocket 88 as nothing less than enormously good fun, and maybe even light relief in a way.

Ian Stewart died of a heart attack while in a doctor's waiting room in 1985, aged just 47. In February 1986 Jack performed along with Jeff Back, Pete Townshend and all The Stones at a memorial concert held in his memory.

In 1986 Jack played in Charlie Watts' Big Band – big in the sense that there was an average of thirty-two people in it, including three drummers. They recorded a live album at Fulham Town Hall in London in the March of that year. He asked Jack to join them for those shows because, as he put it, he was one of his favourite bass players. In an interview in America a year or two later he talked about seeing Jack with Alexis Korner back in the Sixties, and described it as 'the best band in London at the time.' In total Jack's playing can be heard on five Rocket 88 albums; the eponymous first album from 1981, 'Blues & Boogie Explosion' the same year, 'It's Boogie Time' in 1982, 'Live at the Fulham Town Hall' in '86, and 'Blues & Boogie Explosion' released 1998.

There was then a lengthy European tour for The Jack Bruce Band. This ran through October, November and early December 1979, which took Jack, John McLaughlin, Billy Cobham and Stu Goldberg right across the continent – ending up at The Rainbow in London.

Chapter 23

I t was time for Jack to stop using heroin. No one could have ever persuaded him to do that; he just had to reach the point where it became obvious to him. It had to be his decision. He had managed to ensure that his use hadn't affected the music in the main, though he does admit that if he couldn't get supplies then things could become very difficult. 'I was very careful not to work when I was sick', he says, 'The music was too important to me for me to allow it to be affected.'

There were times in the Seventies and Eighties when he felt under pressure to come up with new music simply he was desperate for the income it would generate. He fiercely denies though that such an imperative ever led to him turning out inferior or commercial albums. What he had to do was sell the idea of a new album to a recording company so that he could be paid an advance. With that banked he could then forget all about that side of things and simply engage his creative abilities.

Although coming off the drug is certainly possible and isn't life-threatening – John Coltrane, Miles Davis and Ray Charles all simply stopped, survived the withdrawal period and never used the drug again – but the craving for it can become highly insidious. The simplest cues, such as walking past a place where one used to score or shoot up, can set off the highest level of need and desire. That's why Jack was at least right to move out to Suffolk to alter both his lifestyle and his pattern of movement, to help him get out of heavier drugs. Around 40,000 American troops in Vietnam were regular heroin users, but a study has shown that by far the majority simply stopped using it completely once they returned home. They were out of the situation and the drug didn't present itself. For most people it's almost impossible to move out of a damaging environment. For a wealthy rock star such as Jack that was easy, but unfortunately he also had fast cars – which, while he was in Suffolk, allowed him to get him back to the pushers. He was a junkie commuter.

When Bruce Gary was staying at Le Mote in 1975 Jack was trying to kick the drug, and he vividly recalls walking through the house and seeing Jack slumped in a corner, retching violently. His first thought was that he had been taken ill but in fact he was in the worst stage of withdrawal. Jack was on the Meg Patterson cure, which worked for a while. Bruce says that Jack said to him, 'Take a good long look at me and let this be a lesson to you. I want you to promise me that you'll never do heroin. It's like a living thing – it takes a part of your soul.' Bruce adds, 'He was about as sick as you can be. I've never, to this day, touched heroin.'

When he became truly serious about kicking heroin he and Margrit went to live in her native Germany. He wasn't known as a junkie there, he didn't know any pushers and he didn't even know how to ask for a fix in German.

It was going to be very difficult for Jack because, as he says, 'I had such a huge habit.' He tried every route available; he was in and out of clinics and tried every treatment available. Eric Clapton had recommended the treatment by Meg Patterson that he had received. She was a Christian who required her patients to go and live in her house and be attached to a 'black box' machine, which Jack believes was actually no use at all (though it might have been of some psychological use, giving the impression of their being a formality and a science behind the treatment). Jack says that the biggest single impetus was that you got to know her children, and they knew all about your problems, and he hated the thought that he might be letting the Patterson children down if he failed. He actually ran away on one occasion and managed to get stoned. He then felt so guilty that he went back to the house and apologised. It worked for a while. Not for long. Soon he was using as much as ever before; more than ever before, on that eternal upwards curve.

He overdosed on several occasions and needed emergency hospital treatment, and has lost count of how often he went through cold turkey as he tried to stop and the drug began to drain from his body.

One thing that didn't work for him was Methadone; 'You've then got to kick the Methadone and that's harder than kicking heroin.'

The impetus for giving up the drug completely came from meeting Margrit. It was the very end of the Seventies and perhaps, as he had been injecting heroin almost for the whole of that decade, that this was a natural break point; that he should start the new decade clean. It wasn't that easy though, and certainly wasn't that clearly defined. It took a long time to finally get off heroin, but he says that when he was with her he knew that, one day, he would be able to get off the drug completely. It was simply a matter of the right moment.

He achieved it. The answer, simply, was willpower. He and Margrit wanted to have more children together but Jack knew that it would be a terrible mistake to father more children while he was a junkie. He wanted to be a father again and he wanted to have his life back.

There was one last cold turkey; it was as simple as that and as final. 'It wasn't easy', he says, and then after a moment's thought he changes the adjective; 'It was awful.'

When he did finally stop, he stopped completely. There's been the occasional pull on a joint at a party, but nothing heavier than that. That's the way it has to be. It's like murdering your granny; you either did or you didn't. There's no middle ground. You either kick drugs completely or not at all.

There's no doubt that ten years of hard drug use took a terrible toll on Jack's body, and did damage that cannot be repaired. He has no doubt that his illness in recent years is directly attributable to heroin. 'It wrecked my health. No one does what I did to myself and escapes unscathed.'

When asked what he would say to young people about drugs, Jack's answer is 'Don't try it because you'll like it.' There can be no doubt that fans related to him on the subject just as he had to Charlie Parker or whoever; if it worked for them then it's going to work for me. He agrees that it's a difficult argument. It sounds like the hoary 'Do as I say, not as I do' mantra.

Extending the thought, he adds, 'Saying 'don't' alone isn't good enough. You can't tell kids that they'll end up in the gutter because in some cases that's just not true. You can tell them not to try drugs because they'll make you ill, but the one reason not to try drugs is that will probably really like it. That's the danger.'

So far his children are concerned, he says that he has always tried to be completely open on the subject. They know that their father had a long and dreadful relationship with hard drugs; when they were young there was no escaping the fact – and on occasions were exposed to some of the more unpleasant details. His family have certainly seen references to their dad as an 'ex-junkie.'

He finds it very difficult though. There is an ambiguity within the thinking, and that gap between his own experience and what he would advise is considerable. He certainly hasn't felt that he was ever in any position to lecture any of his children, or actively warn them off drugs. It is surprising that he hasn't taken a harder line or wanted to know, and there is an argument that his experiences would have made any advice impossible to ignore. In effect though it may be the case that his children are more abstemious than they might otherwise have been.

'In this country the politicians just have no idea. They made this ex-cop Drugs Czar, but what the hell does he know about it? The cops are either out of touch with what's going on, or are actually selling drugs on – which is a very common thing both in this country and in America.

'The politicians don't know what they're talking about when they go on about drugs. They lump everything together. They think that someone smoking a joint socially is the same as somebody shooting up or smoking crack. It's not the same. These things have to be separated. Everything has to be taken for what it is. Because they've made the mistake of lumping all drugs together and there's the 'drug horror' jargon, they're unable to separate it out and say that they condone this or that. But then, governments take too much upon themselves; what right do they have to do that? If something is harmful to the public good then I'm all for the government stepping in – like the smoking in public thing; I agree with that. It's right that you should be able to go to a restaurant or a cinema and not have my old man with his thick black tobacco cloud blowing in your face.

'For someone to smoke a naturally growing plant, in the privacy of his or her own home – why should that be the government's business? Mind you, this government is more and more taking away the freedoms that we took for granted. The more they talk about not wanting to control the people, the more they actually want to. This present government is a very sinister one indeed; these people, like Blunkett and Straw, are very shifty characters in my opinion. They use the high-flown ideals that they might once have had to take away the few liberties we still have. We're not citizens, we're subjects.

'The 'horror' of drugs goes back a long way – hashish and assassins, and all that murky things. That's foreign. They don't understand that if you smoke dope, moderately, it's not nearly so bad as drinking alcohol in moderation. It does make you more peaceful. If you drink ten pints of lager you're more likely to get in a fight than if you've smoked a couple of joints.

'But then, how many people are taking prescribed drugs? Especially as you get older you take things for your arthritis or your blood pressure. Those are drugs too, and some of them are pretty dangerous, as we know. The fact that Multiple Sclerosis sufferers are persecuted [for using cannabis], the ones who grow a bit at home to help themselves out and get nicked for it, is terrible.

'Also, they have this thing about always getting the dealers, but most dealers are just users who are financing their own habit. I met one or two dealers who were dodgy individuals, of course, but mostly they were quite sad individuals who were financing their own habits by selling small amounts of drugs. They were also trying to live as normal a life as possible. The only answer to any drug problem – and 'the drug problem' is always exaggerated in order to create the scare stories which are so important to governments – is to legalise all drugs. I'm almost surprised it hasn't happened because just with marijuana, they would make so much money if it were legal and taxable. Look at the money that they make out of the legal drugs. Alcohol and tobacco are much more damaging, and kill many more people than so-called drugs ever will.

'You get 'shock horror' things on the front pages of the papers. The parents of the poor girl who died from an ecstasy overdose became almost celebrities. Again, I think those people are ignorant of the facts. They don't know about drugs. The only people who really know about drugs are the people who have used drugs. Football commentators have either been footballer players or know what the game's about, but you get these pundits talking about drugs, and they really don't know what they're on about. The few good medical people, there are a few, haven't got the power that they would need to do some good.

'The problem would disappear. I don't mean that you should be able to buy heroin and cocaine in a sweetie shop. It should go back to the way it was. They should allow doctors to prescribe drugs to users, so that they don't have to resort to the street, and then the black market would disappear. It would take a courageous government to do that, and it would take time now that it's become such a mess, but it would work.

'The politicians know that and they don't want to do it because it's not a vote winner.'

Politician came out of the feelings shared by Jack and Pete Brown. They weren't joking. Jack has absolutely no faith in politicians and is completely cynical about their motives and them as people. Pete Brown's declared policy was once to make all the dustbin men politicians and give the politicians the refuse-collecting jobs.

He says that he does vote in elections – has always voted - but points out that the rural constituency in which he lives is very much the Conservative heartland and any vote of his is rather a straw in the wind. In the spring of 2005 he was undecided about how we would vote in the then-forthcoming general election. There was hardly likely to be a party or a candidate, deep in the picturesque Constable country, which exactly reflected his political thinking.

In fact, because of the reunion concerts, Jack was in London on election day and did not vote. For him here's no escaping his personal, political upbringing. The right to vote was fought for and people died to gain it. It was a long hard struggle and it's a right of immeasurable value, which mustn't be neglected, let alone lost.

'Until Tony Blair got in, it was easy. It also seemed obvious; there was the evil of Conservatism and what they seemed to stand for. When Blair got in I thought that at last we can fix this country up. We can take it to where it should be – take it back to where it should be. Because of the tone of his speeches and what he said in his manifesto I thought we could go back to the idealistic state of 1945. It didn't quite work out that way.

'Thatcher ripped this country apart, and the people she targeted are still being affected. She said that there was no such thing as society, and proved it by destroying the working class – which doesn't exist any more. She was really hated by the people she dispossessed. But the good thing was that the lines were drawn – there were the goodies and the baddies. Now there's only spin and lies from this government. There's no freedom of information, only spin.

'Thatcher was more successful at screwing this country up than Hitler was. I found it ironic that it was the first woman prime minister who did that, but I wasn't surprised by it. She had to prove herself to be tougher than the men, and she surrounded herself with men – I don't remember her having women in her cabinet. And coming from her background, she had a lot to prove. You expect a Leftie to have ideals, but a Tory with ideals is a very dangerous thing.'

As one would expect, Jack is outraged by honours being heaped upon retired politicians, let alone rock stars. He says that he has tried to talk politics with his peers, and has always been stunned by how right wing most of them are. The idea that a musician could accept a knighthood appals him. He insists that he would refuse any honour – though laughs at the idea that one might be offered, suggesting that he would be offended by somewhat in the establishment even thinking that he would consider the notion.

'It's easy for me to say that because it's not going to be offered. If I accepted an honour though I'd be recognising that I'm a subject, and that the Queen is at the top of this pyramid and I go along with the status quo.' He argues for a 'clean sweep' to consign the Honours List, men in tights in the Houses of Parliament, and be-wigged judges to the pages of the history books.

He believes that music and politics do not make for comfortable bed fellows. He doesn't feel that there is a direct link between the two elements, and has no time for overtly political, polemical bands and their music. He shies away from making statements and waving placards. Above all, he has no time for Live Aid and its progeny; 'I'm quite cynical about a lot of those things. I think that the original one – the concert for Bangla Desh – was done for altruistic reasons, but the people who get involved in them tend to use them for their own ends. The money never seems to go anywhere. If I actually saw some huge difference, even going back to the first Live Aid, if you could take me somewhere and show me that that had transformed things .... these sums of money are drops in the ocean.

'It's never been about money anyway. It about awareness, yes, but it's about changing the whole of the world's attitude. You're not going to do that with a concert.

'I guess they [the organisers of Live Aid] are much better than me because they try, and I don't try. I suppose it's better there are people who try, rather than people like me.'

He remembers a charity gig in aid of environmental concerns that he played in Saint Andrews in Scotland, and though it did raise a small amount of money, the biggest single impact was on the park where it was held – which was comprehensively trashed by the staging of the event. The musicians and organisers stayed at the very expensive Old Course Hotel, and were very freely drinking as much as they could, and charging their drinks to the charity's account.

'Recently, the Make Poverty History thing in Edinburgh was hijacked by the Live 8 concert. It a smaller, more effective thing, but it became this other thing. There was a load of issues of course; a thing for Africa with no Africans, which is kind of typical for those rock people. They're very narrow-minded.'

On the other hand, he has no problem with rock stars appointing themselves to roles as quasi-political spokesmen, but he adds, 'I know how little those rock people are aware of what's going on, having been involved in a few things with rock stars.'

He dismisses any suggestion that one might have expected more overtly political themes in his work, and makes the point he has his political opinions but they have no place in his music. His history shows that what he says is certainly true; there are very few songs which have any level of political slant, and those that do tend to be cynical and anarchic rather than biting commentary. Which is more Pete Brown's influence than Jack's. It's a somewhat surprising stance, given his political awareness, his background and his ability to articulate his thinking.

Several of Cream's classic songs were part of the soundtrack of the Vietnam years, and Jack's opinion on that war and the broader international and quasi-imperialist situation which led to it, are unambiguous to say the least. Yet they took no part in the debate or the protest movement; which is to say, Jack took no part, being far more politically-minded than either Eric or Ginger; indeed, far more politically-minded than virtually any British musician of his generation.

Perhaps that is the key; his nationality. John Lennon seemed very naïve throughout his late-Sixties and early Seventies Give Peace A Chance phase, whereas The Rolling Stones' Streetfighting Man and The Who's Won't Get Fooled Again were far more typically British – healthily cynical and cautiously self-defensive. In California in '68 Jack joined in the anger against the American government's actions in South-East Asia, but he wasn't going to man the barricades, let alone put his head over them. If his family had not returned from Canada in 1947, and if he had been raised a North American then maybe he would have joined the likes of Country Joe McDonald in lobbing fiery lyrics into the laps of the National Guard.

At the same sort of time Jack was finally coming to the end of his time with Robert Stigwood, but for whatever reason he wouldn't release Jack from his contractual obligations. He had the frustration of receiving the offer of a 'tremendous' recording contract from CBS, but the legal situation didn't allow him to accept.

The result of this was that for several years at the end of the Seventies and stretching into the Eighties, he didn't have either management or a recording contract. The situation took away his ability to work, to make music, but it also was financially disastrous.

The royalties from Cream's heyday were long gone, and that band's records were only selling in small numbers. Jack's divorce had been a financial disaster for all concerned, and Le Mote had achieved a relatively modest price when it was sold. There was also the drug habit, which was of course costing large sums of money. Cash was becoming a real problem: 'I went from having a very comfortable life, to say the least, to sleeping on the couch at Ronnie Leahy's flat in Earls Court.' Indeed he was there for about six months in all.

He and Margrit relocated to south-western Germany in 1980, a year after they met. The rationale was that it would be an idea to get away from London, and Jack considers that it was a very good move and exactly the right thing to do. It took a while to really establish a new base there, but he was able to start a new band, and travel from Germany to the States as often as he needed; 'There'd been all this traumatic stuff happening but I was able to function quite soon.' They finally moved back to Britain in 1986 and bought the house they still own in East Anglia. By then Margrit was Jack's manager and was credited on albums as executive producer. She had undertaken a determined campaign to win control on un-paid royalties, and monies were apparently discovered in all sorts of corners of the world.

The Eighties was a long hard road for Jack; re-establishing his finances, protecting his family, and trying to finalise the long battle for royalties due to him since the mid-Sixties. Because of his drug use, the Seventies had been hard, but for different reasons the Eighties often seemed rather worse.

He was also determined to get the recognition which he was certain was his by right. There was a perception that his star had burned brightly but was now dimmed, and Jack was absolutely certain that there was a lot more for him still to do, and he wanted it to be known that he was a lot more than 'just' the singer and bass player with Cream. He wasn't going to be written off as a has-been for anyone.

On the one hand he could use his personal history to his benefit – the reputation still opened doors, but on the other he had a lot to live up to. Because Jack wasn't a sideman in a band, or dependent on other band members in a set line-up, he could now make the decisions and act on them. Supported and now managed by Margrit, he started writing, recording and performing – as if starting from scratch almost. It was simply going to be a long hard slog, and he knew it. There wasn't another Cream waiting around the corner. He might describe himself as lazy, but he's never been afraid of hard work.

He was well into the Nineties before he felt that he and his family were secure. He toured incessantly and, he adds, 'I did everything I could to make a bob or two' – and then he adds hurriedly, 'Without compromising!'

Chapter 24

The band Jack fronted from 1980 was, he considers, one of the best. New Jersey-based manager and impresario John Scher represented the band and got them a deal with CBS, and they were definitely on their way. The other musicians were Billy Cobham on drums, his old friend David Sancious playing keyboards and guitar, and Clem Clempson on guitar. That year they recorded 'I've Always Wanted To Do This' and then immediately started on a lengthy tour which in fact stretched into 1981 and included dates in the UK as well as dozens in America.

The album is, interestingly, credited as being 'Produced by Jack Bruce in association with Clem Clempson, Billy Cobham and David Sancious', which is very fair minded, and reflects the fact that it was a band effort rather than Jack insisting that everything be played as he laid down.

Clem Clempson first became aware of Jack's playing when he was a teenager living in Tamworth in Staffordshire, and the B-side of Pretty Flamingo, You're Standing By Me, was played on the juke box in the local café. He was impressed by the bass line and wanted to know who was playing it. They first met when Clem was playing with Colosseum, and he was required to play bass on the 'Daughters Of Time' album. He didn't own a bass, but Dick Heckstall-Smith knew where they could borrow one, and took Clem round to Jack's home, where they relieved him of his Gibson for as long as the session was going to take.

After that point, although they had lived within a few miles of each other in East Anglia for three or four years during the Seventies, they had never really got together – until they were both guests on Cozy Powell's 1979 album 'Over The Top' and played together on The Old Grey Whistle Test.

The following year Jack asked Clem to play on 'I've Always Wanted to Do This' – he turned up at his house in Shepherd's Bush, and announced that he wanted Clem to work with him. As it happened, Clem was out, but he got the message soon enough.

He was delighted to be asked; he had been doing a lot of studio work but was, as he says, 'Desperate to play some real music, and music didn't come any more real than playing with Jack.' He was to be with Jack on several tours through the Eighties.

There were gigs booked, and it was in New York, in the rehearsal room, that all four met up for the first time; 'It was daunting to be working with Jack, but to be working with Billy Cobham and David Sancious as well was a bit intimidating.' As soon as they were underway the band gelled immediately. It was very much a meeting of equals; it wasn't Jack and three sidemen, it was a solid gigging band with four excellent, equally talented musicians, all giving 100% every night.

They played a few gigs through March and then went straight into studio to record the album. The four musicians went to north Devon and rehearsed there for a week, and then flew back to the States to record. Clem says that there are some great moments on the album, and it includes some of his favourite songs. He also says that touring with that band was 'possibly the most satisfying thing I've ever done.' He explains, 'Jack's material was so much fun to play every night. He had such a vast repertoire of songs, and a lot of his music is very challenging from the musician's point of view. His music was always very rewarding to play; it's got great depth, very emotional. It was also musically quite challenging; I always enjoyed that aspect as well.

'He is also one of the most fantastic singers I've ever heard - I used to just get goosebumps listening to his voice every night, and it was so inspiring to play with him when he was singing like that.'

The album was cut at The House Of Music in New Jersey, and there were some fraught times; 'Jack isn't always the easiest person to work with. There were tense moments, particularly when it came to Jack doing vocals on other people's songs', Clem says. He adds though that whatever issues there were, they were only ever about the music. Whatever else was going on in Jack's life was left outside the studio door. On the other hand, Clem has happy memories of relaxing in the studio's swimming pool, and indeed teaching his girlfriend to swim there.

The opening track, Hit And Run, even has hints of the dreaded disco craze about it – as do several other arrangement on the album. The second track, Running Back, is a band composition and sounds almost like a shot at a hit single. It's not hard to imagine a female vocalist of the period recording it as a power ballad – and it then becoming a karaoke classic.

One of the strongest tracks on the album is the attractive and lyrical ballad Wind And The Sea, composed by Billy Cobham, and with an excellent jazzy intro. It needs a bigger, heftier arrangement though – and someone should have brought in Pete Brown to edit Billy's lyrics. Wind In The Sea is followed by the bluesy Out To Lunch, which is fun, and an accomplished dip into a contrasting genre.

The album finishes with its best track; the Bruce/Brown composition Bird Alone, which is a very original and exciting work – typical of their work but very fresh and exhilarating. As Clem says, 'Bird Alone is possibly my favourite song out of all the things we ever played. I could play that forever without getting tired of it. There was always something really special and magical about that song. Every time Jack sang the middle section I just got goosebumps. Sometimes it would bring tears to my eyes.

His other favourite on the album is Mickey The Fiddler; 'It's a very haunting tune. After I play it I can't get it out of my head for days. It's just magical.'

The illustration on the album cover is curiously irrelevant to the music; it shows a girl in what looks like a floral-print dressing gown hovering, as if levitating, over an Edwardian sofa. That wasn't what Jack had wanted. Given the album's title he had wanted a photograph of himself leaping through a plate glass window. The record company decided against it. The band did manage to veto the art department's suggestion of a photograph showing the band's backsides. The idea was that as two of the guys were white and two were black, there'd be an out of focus shot which, the art director said, would look like the surface of the moon. There was a stunned, appalled silence as the notion was digested, before Billy Cobham said quietly, 'My momma told me never to do that.'

The band played forty dates in the USA alone, from March through until the end of 1980. They returned to the UK for four nights at The Venue in London in July, and early in 1981 they played live on the prestigious American television show Saturday Night Live. There was then a short European tour through May. They also played on The Old Grey Whistle Test for the BBC, and that performance was released as a DVD in 1998. A performance for Rockpalast in Germany is also available on DVD, and they come across as a very genuine rock band. Apart from the four musicians there are two backing singers; a guy and a girl who looks an Eighties period piece in herself, wearing a jump suit and an early-Kylie hair do. It's fascinating to watch Clem playing bass – Jack's Warwick in fact – while Jack plays piano on Theme From An Imaginary Western. The concert ends with David Sancious playing a double-necked guitar – playing it quite wonderfully indeed - on an almost-instrumental version of NSU. Obviously a real crowd pleaser.

1981 saw Jack involved in a new collaboration though – with guitarist Robin Trower. Robin was born in 1945 is south-east London, and saw some success in the early to mid-Sixties with the r 'n b band The Paramounts. They mostly played covers, but did release a small number of singles between 1963 and 1965. In 1967 though Robin joined Procol Harum just after the group had seen a huge, worldwide hit with A Whiter Shade of Pale. They had had a hit single but didn't have a good enough band to stand up to the exposure. That's where Robin came in. He eventually left in '71 and formed a power trio before breaking up that band and releasing a short series of solo albums through the rest of the Seventies. When he and Jack met neither man's star was in the ascendant, and a collaboration seemed a good way to shuffle back into the spotlight.

Robin had been recording some new music, and he simply got in touch with Jack and asked him to play on the over-dubs. Everything else had been virtually finished. Jack went into the Konk studio in north London and laid down his parts, which he remembers as very straight forward and easy. They recorded two albums – 'BLT' with drummer Bill Lordan – and 'Truce' (the 'tr' of Trower and the 'uce' of Bruce …) with Reg Isidore replacing Lordan.

Jack remembers the first as a very successful effort; simple and effective, straight ahead rock 'n roll. The record sold well – at a time when both men were grateful for both the exposure and the income. Robin changed the modus operandi for the second record at the end of the year though; 'Instead of sticking with that formula, unfortunately he changed things. That sort of music thrived on that sort of approach. It was basic but good music. Very loud; almost like American-style rock as opposed to British stuff.' Jack saw the change of drummer as a mistake; Bill's straight forward style suited the music, he felt. The new drummer had to play to a click track, which wasn't a good idea. The second album didn't sell nearly as well.

'BLT' is an attractive album but can't be described as inspired. The song writing – by Keith Reid, who had been in Procol Harum with Robin, and who had co-written most of their songs, including A Whiter Shade Of Pale – isn't his best work. It's best described as rather ordinary soft rock; jolly, good time music, but essentially inconsequential. There's no sense of passion in the work, and certainly Jack seems to be just walking through his parts. Robin has been criticised for being overly influenced by Jimi Hendrix, which is not the worst thing in the world, and tracks such as No Islands Lost certainly confirm that. It would have been a better idea to simply acknowledge that influence and cover Hendrix songs, which would have stretched Jack more and been a better use of both men's talents. The most effective track on the album is the last – End Game – a slow striding blues with Jack singing.

'Truce' was more of the same; great playing on weak songs, but no real sense of passionate commitment. The lyrics on half of the songs were by Pete Brown, and the other half by Keith. The album isn't obviously weaker than 'BLT' – Gone Too Far and Little Boy Lost are both an outstanding tracks, and Take Good Care Of Yourself is a near miss. A lost opportunity. Both 'BLT' and 'Truce' were released in 1981.

Jack was keen to tour following the success of 'BLT', but Robin wouldn't do it. Robin's thinking was they didn't have enough material, but Jack couldn't see why they couldn't play a mix of tracks off the album and from their respective back catalogues. There was enough material on the two albums for two-thirds of a solid live set. What could have been a very promising rock 'n roll collaboration went no further. 'It's a great pity', Jack says, 'I've got a lot of admiration for Robin. I saw him about five years ago in San Francisco and he was tremendous. A great, very under-rated player.'

In 1980 a four-album box set had been released in Germany, but apart from that Jack was to release nothing until 1983 when his 'Automatic' album came out.

He had always been interested in the avant garde, and was always fascinated by the music of the French composer Olivier Messiaen. Having been involved in other people's more left-field music, now was the time to try some of these experimental themes himself. In the Sixties he had bought two professional tape recorders, and had been criss-crossing sound between the two – proving that if nothing else he was a very good sound engineer! Jack created an entire suite of electronic music which has never been heard other than by his friends.

There are some great moments on 'Automatic', but the heavy use of synthesizers dates it; indeed dates it to one of music's stiffest and most awkward periods. When songs from the album were played live a sequencer was used, which meant that the musicians had to play to clicks in their monitors. Thus three guys could be heard to play two tracks each.

"Automatic' was all synthesised saxophone solo and sounds of machinery and things. Jack was in such a weird state when that was recorded. It was horrible', was Pete Brown's verdict on the project. It's the only one of Jack's albums which isn't easily found today.

1983 was another busy year so far as live gigs were concerned. Jack started the year playing a short tour of Germany with the Jan Hammer band (as composer and arranger, Jan has worked with many great names over the years – Jeff Beck, Mick Jagger, Carlos Santana, Sarah Vaughn and the Mahavishnu Orchestra and despite a distinguished history in jazz fusion, is best known for writing film scores - and the music for ninety episodes of Miami Vice).

Then, through the summer, The Jack Bruce Band was reunited (with Clem Clempson, Bruce Gary and Ronnie Leahy) for fifteen dates in the UK – all but one of which was in Scotland, which Jack enjoyed enormously. They played theatres, dance halls, clubs and even pubs. And even left the mainland to play a club called Cabarfeidh in Stornoway - on the Isle of Lewis in the Outer Hebrides. Bruce Gary, who in the interim had been working with the likes of Dr John and Robbie Krieger (late of The Doors), recalls that Jack was welcoming home like a conquering hero; 'He was a huge celebrity. They absolutely adored him.' Ronnie recalls that the venues were always absolutely packed to capacity, and there was rarely a sober man or woman in the place. On the way to Stornoway the band drank and sampled 'Trawler' rum – made and blended in the West Indies and aged in oak casks like a fine malt whisky - and Ronnie says that he has never seen audience quite so paralytic and so delighted to see them; 'I think they'd all been drinking all day. I never saw anything like it', he says, 'They were gobsmacked that Jack was playing for them. It was a great gig.'

There wasn't a lot of money around, so they all travelled on the tour bus and stayed in cheaper than usual bed and breakfast accommodation. Bruce Gary had enjoyed a big hit with his band The Knack, having seen the pop ditty My Sharona go to number one in the States (and number six in the UK), so unusually (other than for Charlie Watts' Rocket 88 or Ringo's All-Starrs) the band's drummer was feeling remarkably well off.

He and Jack spent a few days at the house in Wester Ross, which Bruce found utterly enchanting; he fell in love with the landscape and wanted to stay on there forever – which wasn't really that practical an idea.

The band christened it 'The Midgey and Mackerel Tour' because of the attentions of the blood-thirsty gnats that are the curse of many parts of Scotland in the summer. They wore their 'Jack Bruce Band – The Midgey and Mackerel Tour' T-shirts with pride.

Jack flew up to Scotland so that he could visit his mother before he started the tour, but Clem, Ronnie and Bruce went by train. As they were approaching the border between England and Scotland the two Britons double-checked with the American that he had his visa to enter Scotland. Bruce was horrified. Not only did he not have one but he didn't even know that he needed one. It was pointed out to him that if he was caught at the border without the correct documentation he would be refused entry into the country, and he'd be off the tour. The poor man was terribly worried, and after a short conference it was decided that the best thing he could do was hide under the seat until they were safely north of the border. Bruce, well over six feet tall, crawled under where the other two were sitting, and lay there quietly, curled up in the dust, until they were well into the Lowlands.

There were then eighteen shows to play Germany, Austria and Switzerland, which Jack played as a trio with David Sancious and Bruce Gary as the other two were unavailable. Then, in November, Jack played played some of his songs with a full-size classical orchestra conducted by Eberhardt Schoener. The show was recorded for television in Munich and broadcast as a Rock Klassic Nacht special. At the end of the show Jack sat in with Ian Anderson of Jethro Tull and the Fela Kuti Band.

Jack brought back Clem, Ronnie and Bruce Gary to play a dozen dates on the American east coast in the summer of 1984, and those was followed by a repeat visit to Scotland (though they didn't get off the mainland this time, and had the Western Isles had to go without), and – in the November – a short tour of Germany.

At the end of 1984 Jack was one of a highly impressive roster of musicians who played a charity concert at The Usher Hall in Edinburgh to raise funds for famine relief

Clem Clempson, Bruce Gary and Jack play The Capital Theater in New Jersey. December 1981. David Sancious out of shot.
(Mitchell Kane)

in Ethiopia. Jack played alongside Charlie Watts, Rory Gallagher, Ian Stewart, Rick Wakeman, John Martyn and Bert Jansch.

In 1982 producer and composer Kip Hanrahan had sent Jack a tape of an almost-complete album, and asked him if he would add the vocals to finish the project. Jack describes it as 'Phenomenal, beautiful, amazing Latin fusion music, like I hadn't really heard before. I'd been a long-time fan of Latin rhythms, and grew up listening to things like the Dizzy Gillespie Big Band – all those things that were part of the language to me. But when I heard this, it was phenomenal – and he wanted to pay me to sing on top of it. I said 'sure.'

Kip was brought up in the Puerto Rican district of the Bronx in New York City, of Irish-Jewish descent. His childhood and teenage friends were almost all Latin, and he was constantly exposed to their music and rhythms. Having received a bursary to study art was originally set on a career as a sculptor. He moved over to film studies though, was greatly influenced by the films of Jean Luc Godard, and then spent a year in India with Carla Bley's collaborator Paul Haines, studying architecture. Having travelled widely, he started his musical career as a percussionist and also worked as a promoter. By the late Seventies he was composing, and he founded the American Clave label in 1979, when he was only twenty seven years old, specialising in extreme left-field and experimental music. He forged an alliance with Sting's Pangea label, and first came to broad acclaim when he produced an album by Argentinian musician Astor Piazzolla, 'Tenderness', on which Sting played and sang.

Malcolm Bruce knows him well, and says that though he lives in Virginia nowadays he is New York City embodied; 'He's an interesting character. He's bright, tortured and creative. Very self-deprecating in a way that gets tiresome after a while!' He makes the point that Kip and Jack are alike in some ways; in the complexity, romanticism and 'unresolvedness.'

The album (actually a double album) which Kip wanted Jack to work on was 'Darkness Develops An Edge', which was released in June 1983. It was ecstatically reviewed by the music press, and Downbeat magazine trumpeted it as their album of the year. Jack came in for particular praise; writing in Musician magazine, Rafi Zabor said, 'Bruce is sensational, unforgettable. He is impassioned, without losing his grip on the particulars of any song, and commands a surprising emotional range: this is the work of a mature artist, the speech of an honest voice. There is expertise in every atom of this music and detail upon detail of invention in each of its aspects and admixtures.' New York Beat also singled out Jack's singing for particular praise, and the American magazine Spectator added, 'Bruce sings like his heart and soul are at stake. Incessant, occasionally urgent, counter and polyrhythms permeate all four sides.'

Jack describes the sessions for that album as life-changing, and everyone around

*Kip Hanrahan, centre, founded the American Clave organisation is the late Seventies.
Its Afro-Caribbean musicians and their rhythms have been a source of great inspiration
for Jack and a powerful influence on his music. (MK)*

him agrees. He had entered a new and hugely stimulating world; within his American Clave organisation Kip had a stable of stunningly talented Latin-American musicians, and Jack was very warmly welcomed into their midst. Not as a famous rock star, importantly, but as a fellow musician and musical adventurer. It was as if he had found a new spiritual home; he had certainly discovered fresh inspiration, and it seemed that the sessions had unlocked new musical themes from somewhere within his imagination. His music was about to change considerably, but before he brought all the Latin strands to his own music, he worked on several American Clave projects.

In '84 he worked on Kip's album 'Vertical's Currency', released the following year, of which Robert Elms, writing in The Face, said, That most rare of things, a genuinely new music. Wonderful.' Jack's singing was again warmly praised when the five-song EP 'A Few Short Notes For The End Run' was released a year later. The line-up included three percussionists and the New Orleans pianist Allen Toussaint.

Over the years Jack has played and sung on most of Kip Hanrahan's albums, and several other American Clave records, including a music and poetry album with a cast of dozens of musicians (including British musician Robert Wyatt and Carla Bley's ex-husband Paul Bley), which set the poems of Paul Haines to music. A reviewer wrote of Kip's 1993 album 'Exotica', 'Jack Bruce is tackling material as challenging and new for the 1990s as psychedelic bluesy rock was to the 1960s.' Which is an interesting thought.

Kip was to become a considerable force in Jack's music, and, as importantly, a very close friend. He has produced two of Jack's albums – albums which have been very important to the development of his music - and has guided him as he has explored Latin musical forms.

The American Clave musicians who came together under the Latin tag were African, Caribbean – Cuban in particular – and several of the finest became members of Jack's band later on. He describes them as 'Just beautiful people'; he greatly enjoyed both their company and the atmosphere in New York in around where they worked. The whole experience had a huge effect on him; it was exhilarating and revitalising: 'Darkness Develops An Edge' was a great record, and we just went from there and did lots of recording together over the years. Kip has been a big inspiration to me and to some degree I think I have been to him. He became very much part of my life and he's definitely my closest friend.'

In January 1986, in what was then a very unusual move, Jack played three nights in Israel. Backed by Clem Clempson, Ronnie Leahy and Anton Fier on drums, they played two nights at The Liquid Club in Tel Aviv (the second night of which was recorded for radio broadcast), and one night at The Bin Yanei Ha-ooma National House Theatre in Jerusalem.

In 1987, by way of a complete contrast, Jack made his debut as an actor. The production was 'The Tooth of Crime' written by Sam Shepherd, which has been described as 'a play which brought leather and foul language to mainstream audiences.' Sam, who was brought up in California, is almost exactly the same age as Jack, and wrote the screenplays for the movies Zabriskie Point and Paris Texas. He wrote 'The Tooth of Crime' in 1972 and it has been widely performed.

Jack was asked, right out of the blue, to appear in a new production of the play at a small theatre in Battersea, and play the leading role – of Hoss - for a five week run. It was very demanding part to prepare for, with long soliloquies to learn and a lot of complicated business to work to. He was on stage virtually the whole time – indeed, he off stage for just two minutes of the performance. He had to master a number of different American accents, and, at one point, play his own father.

'I wanted to see if I could do it, and I did it. It was difficult; I was the only non-actor involved, and it was a bit of a nightmare because real actors are protective of their craft, and they think that anyone coming in, anyone who's not a real actor, is going to be terrible. But I don't think I was. I think I acted a lot of them off the stage. I was proud of myself; I remembered all the lines – I was amazed. I can't remember the words of my own songs, but I was able to do it.'

Jack describes the play as 'A sort of Western duel of words and physical fighting. It's like the old gunslinger being challenged by the young gunslinger – except that the old gunslinger is the king of rock 'n roll. The young guy is an upstart musician. So you have duels in music, in dialogue and actual physical fighting.' The contact was only too real most nights, and he ended the run bruised and battered – though happy that he had given as good as he had got.

There were no more new releases under Jack's name until 1989, when PolyGram issued 'Willpower', which was a retrospective compilation. The album wasn't completely new; it included four tracks from the unreleased 'Jet Set Jewel.'

Later the same year Jack embarked on a new album; 'A Question Of Time' was recorded in San Francisco and New York in 1987 and was released in January 1990. Overall it sounded much more commercial, much more mainstream, and was a gift for American FM radio. It was an album of many different styles and moods, from fast rock – Vernon Reid playing riotous electric guitar and Jack tumbling up the bass scale on the opening track, Life On Earth – or more typically lyrical Bruce/Brown songs such as Make Love and the beautiful, dreamy Flying, which almost harked back to 'Songs For A Tailor.' Having sat around for more than twenty years, Hey Now Princess surfaced – as a fast and funky song with Ginger guesting on drums and Jimmy Ripp playing superbly effective guitar. Ginger also played on a second track, Obsession, which opened side two

The Willie Dixon song, Blues You Can't Lose, was taken slowly, with Jack playing harmonica, Albert Collins on guitar and Nicky Hopkins on piano. Having included a blues, Jack added a folk song – the charming, haunting Only Playing Games, with both Jack and Jimmy Ripp playing acoustic guitars … and backing vocals from The Golden Gate Boys' Choir.

Both Malcolm and Jonas Bruce played on the album; Jonas played piano on one track and Malcolm played guitar on two. Jack describes having his sons playing on the album as, 'Beautiful. It was always beautiful to play with them. Always. Working with them was a joy.' Malcolm says that he wasn't there as long as would have liked – he had to get back to college in the UK - but it was a delight. The album was co-produced by Joe Blaney, who had previously produced Prince's 'Lovesexy', of which Malcolm was a big fan, and he was delighted to be working with him.

Of Jack's style of working in studio, he says, 'It was pretty loose. I got the feel in studio, got the vibe. He let me find my own level in studio. He can be direct at times but he's not overly controlling.'

There were two other musicians of great note on the album – the Indian tabla player Zakir Hussein and the Lebanese-American drummer Mark Nauseef. The song Kwela was different though. It was Jack writing very authentic world music, and it not only added another colour to the album, but it was the precursor of how his music was going to turn over the next decade.

From the end of '89 The Jack Bruce Band was out on the road again – the line-up now being Bernie Worrell, Blues Saraceno, Gary 'Mudbone' Cooper, Tom Goss and Ginger. They played a forty-date American tour, including a live performance on David Letterman's late night show.

Jack and Pete had a major disagreement during the recording of 'A Question Of Time.' It was recorded in San Francisco, where, Pete says, he wasn't made to feel welcome by Jack, for whatever reason - regardless of the fact that he had done a lot of work on the lyrics for the album, and had abandoned all his other projects to be able to do so. Feeling unloved, Pete flew home, and Jack reacted very angrily. He felt that

Jack, Gary Husband and Blues Saraceno on tour in 1992 (Gary Husband)

Pete had deserted him, and when Jack asked for re-writes Pete did them – for once – by fax. As a result the two men sulked for a long while and went through one of their many phases when they didn't speak to each other and wouldn't hear the other's name uttered in their presence.

Pete says that Flying is one of his favourite songs, and was recorded despite all this. They had been working on some film music, for a movie that was never made, and the raw material became the basis for several songs. Jack played Pete a piece of new music, which Pete was enthusiastic about, and started to work on lyrics for it. Jack told him it was about flying – or rather having a fear of flying. He started work on that basis, but Jack then got back in touch and said, 'It's not actually about flying. It's about Roy Orbison.' Pete sighed and started again. When that lyric was finished, Jack announced that it wasn't about Roy Orbison at all, but was to be in his style, needs to have the feel of one of his songs. Pete wrote another set of lyrics.

Pete admits that his reaction has usually been just to throw up his hands and walk away shaking his head. His next move is then to write letters, which he describes as 'very, very unpleasant', and given his command of the English language it's not hard to imagine that a furious missive from Pete is a fearful weapon. He feels guilt about doing it, because, 'Although he is always very hard on people, in some ways Jack is quite fragile', and such a broadside is going to have a huge effect. Pete never feels he can approach a problem face to face; his anger, he says, makes him physically ill.

He had sent a vitriolic epistles to Jack on several occasions (and once to Ginger), the words scorching through the paper. Each time, Jack, who is not slow to take offence, would become even more furious, and swear that he'll never work with Pete again. Pete then swears he'll never work with Jack ever again, and they go their separate ways for however long it takes for things to calm down. The 1989 spat lasted for four years. Eventually Jack phoned Pete, ahead of his fiftieth birthday gig in 1993, and they started worked together again – albeit somewhat warily.

The result of their work was the album 'Somethin Els.' Seven of the nine songs were Bruce/Brown compositions, with one co-credited to Tony Hymas, and the last song on the album, FM, being written by Jack alone. The album had been a long time in the gestation, with the recordings stretching from 1986 through until '92.

It was as if, suddenly, all the malaise of the Eighties had fallen away. The album was very different; fresh and sophisticated. The opening track, Waiting On A Word, is absolutely classic Jack - with beautiful lyrics ('I left my heart down at the pawnshop, can't afford it anymore'), and sparse but stunning guitar playing by Eric Clapton. All in all, it was a very impressive production.

Eric played guitar on three tracks, and his playing on the second of those, the hefty, rocky Willpower, is magnificent and couldn't have been played by anyone else. It's a big production, with two saxophones, trumpet and trombone. He was never in the same studio as the rest of the line-up though. The tapes were flown to London and went into a studio and over-dubbed his guitar part.

Ships In The Night is one of Jack's favourite tracks on the album. He plays cello, piano and keyboards, and is backed on the vocals by Maggie Reilly. Eric again plays guitar. It's a delicate and thoughtful song, but though Bruce and Brown can do softness very effectively, this isn't the strongest song on the album. The jazzy, funky, piano-based GB Dawn Blues, with Dick adding sax and Jack striding through the bass line, is a great track – exuberant and full of life; typical of the best Bruce/Brown jazz-based compositions. The album ends with the elegant simplicity of Jack playing piano unaccompanied on FM.

There are a few electronic effects and sound quotes which sound slightly awkward and a touch old-fashioned now, but in some ways 'Somethin Els' was possibly Jack's most impressive album since 'Songs For A Tailor.' 'Parts of 'Somethin Els' are absolutely terrific', Pete Brown says.

Jack agrees that the album was somehow different from what he had done before. It was his first digital album, which made a big difference to the quality of the recordings, and he also gives a lot of credit to the engineer, Walter Quintus. Another important figure was Kurt Renker, the owner of both the Zerkal studio (near Duren, west of Cologne) and the CMP record company, who used his wealth (derived originally from the family paper-making business) to finance the sort of music that he loved. Kurt's first recording was made in 1977, and was of Ian Carr's Nucleus – so there were links there with Jack – and the following year he founded Creative Music Productions. Kurt says that he has only ever worked with people he likes, and whose music he loves; the company's catalogue spans jazz, rock and very many aspects of world music. Jazz critic Bill Milkowski describes CMP thus; 'With its rich catalogue of artistically challenging music, CMP has established itself as a vital force in the jazz, rock and world music arenas. A renegade player in the industry, CMP has boldly followed its own inner-directed course without paying heed to musical trends, record charts or radio play lists.'

The atmosphere at Zerkal had Jack feel very much at home, very comfortable; he's always at his happiest when he is surrounded by like-minded, high skilled musicians with the broadest musical horizons. Kurt Renker was a genuine fan of Jack's music – of, indeed, all the music that he recorded at Zerkal, and of all the musicians he signed to his company – and he gave Jack the support and encouragement he needed, and on which he thrived. This was crucial to the near-renaissance in his music.

The album's name came from the local drink, which was called Els, which is described as 'not strong but disgusting.' The session was equipped with a large bottle of the substance, and – unlike what would have been the case with any other known alcoholic beverage – there was hardly any gone by the end of the session. The band was invited on to a tour of the factory where it was made, but with little enthusiasm for the free samples it never happened.

The same year Jack recorded 'Somethin Els' he worked with the Hungarian-born jazz composer Leslie Mandoki on the album 'Soulmates.' It was a curious work, and in every case the heavy jazz-funk intros to the songs promised a lot more than they delivered. The lyrics were all naff and cloying, and the overall effect was of easy listening for hotel lounges that had been pumped up out of all recognition.

The albums always had the most impressive line-ups, and Mandoki seemed to achieve that by juggling the personnel; asking X to play on the basis that he'd be working alongside Y, and then assuring Y that it was his great chance to play with X ... and then telling Z that X and Y were definitely in the mix. His organisation operates from large studios in Munich, but he would think nothing of flying over to Britain, recording Jack's part in a British studio and flying out again. Jack agrees when it is suggested that it is 'funny music', but adds 'The money's good.'

Mandoki is also involved in the large-scale, big-budget television shows that used to be made in Germany, and on which Jack has appeared several times. These are smaller than they used to be, but in their heyday in the Seventies and Eighties they were transmitted right across Europe and had phenomenal viewing figure. He performed on one which also featured David Bowie, Madonna and Michael Jackson – all on the same show.

Also in 1992 Jack was asked to perform at the Guitar Legends Festival in Seville, which he greatly enjoyed. It was split into different nights for blues, jazz, rock and so on, and Jack played alongside Bob Dylan, Keith Richards and Steve Cropper; Brian May played a set with Joe Satriani, Joe Walsh and Steve Vai – which must have been something to have seen and heard. B B King played with Bo Diddley and Albert King – again, a line-up to die for.

Simon Phillips backed Jack and friends, and remembers the rehearsals in London, held at a huge space on the Fulham Road called The Furniture Cave – 'It was like going back to the Seventies – everyone was stoned. We were supposed to be rehearsing with Bob Dylan, and Jack is a big, big fan, but Bob didn't want to rehearse, and he was playing old blues songs – but with the wrong chords.' At the gig they played All Along The Watchtower. Asked what it was like to play with Dylan, Jack says, 'It was great. He's Bob Dylan.'

The other thing that Simon remembers about the gig was a huge jam session at the end, but with too many guitarists on stage. In those pre-radio mike days they all had cables connecting them to the amps, and as they moved around the cables got more and more knotted; 'They started all spread out, but by the end all the guitarists were clustered in the middle because the cables were pulling them all closer, and they had to move as a single unit.

Back in 1969 Jack had considered putting together a band with guitarist Allan Holdsworth and Jon Hiseman; songs had been written and a few demos had been cut. At the same time Gary Husband was playing with Barbara Thompson, Jon's wife, in her band, Paraphernalia – or at least, had been; Gary was fired for playing too loudly, which is a reason for dismissal which has a great pedigree. Not wanting to see his wife's band dip, Jon stepped into the breach and began drumming with Paraphernalia, so it looked as if Gary was going to join Jack and Allan. For whatever reason that band didn't happen, but in early '92 Gary got a call, asking him if he was free to play a modest gig at The Bull's Head in Barnes in London. Jack was to be supported by Clem and Ronnie, but needed a drummer. The show, Gary says, went very well; 'It was wild, and was a very nice feeling.' Like so many drummers he had been an admirer of Jack's playing for many years, and had pored over every one of his solo albums.

That led to an invitation to join Jack and a new guitarist, Connecticut-born Blues Saraceno, who had first come to broad notice playing lead with the band Poison. The trio played an American tour, which though not long, took them all over the country, and then a handful of gigs in England and Europe – including three nights at the recently-opened Birmingham branch of Ronnie Scott's. That saw them through to July, and the following month Blues left, to be replaced by ex-Thin Lizzie guitarist Gary Moore.

Gary Husband remembers that band with great affection, but says that there were always great tensions between the three of them; 'It was volatile. He's not the easiest man in the world. And then there's Gary … there were definitely temperaments flying around.'

Asked how he found him, at this point in the mid-Nineties, with the worst of his problems behind him (for now), Gary Husband says, 'Complex! He could be difficult, warm, angry, incredibly generous – the whole gamut. Every day was a new journey.'

The music was a mix of Cream numbers and new material, but Gary Husband was disappointed that they didn't play much from Jack's – by then – quarter of a century-long history of solo work. He didn't want to be playing Cream songs, and wasn't too comfortable playing drum parts made all too famous by Ginger; 'I had to try and make the drumming really live, in a new way, and not just be a copy. I had to find a point where I remained faithful to Ginger's definitive approach, but hopefully there was an area where I could bring something to it, and be me.' This was a different thing though; Jack has always seen a distinction between his own music and collaborative work. With Gary Moore there it wasn't really his band, so his more personal music didn't fit.

Gary Husband had been approached by Billy Cobham to work on a recording he was making, and there was a clash of dates; Gary had committed to Billy and told Jack and Gary Moore that he wasn't available for a recording session of theirs. Someone phoned Ginger, he sat in, and then he was in the band, and a new entity – BBM – was born.

The catalyst for the trio being formed in the first place was the two-night show held in Cologne to celebrate Jack's fiftieth birthday, and filmed for television. Although the birthday was actually in May, the shows were played the following November. It was Margrit's idea, and she spent a huge amount of time getting all the musicians in the right place and arranging the filming and the recording. The show had an astonishing line-up, and included many musicians who Jack had played with down the years, including both Jonas and Malcolm Bruce, and – in full - Gary Moore, Simon Phillips, Gary Husband, Clem Clempson, Pete Brown, Dick Heckstall-Smith, Art Themen, Henry Lowther, John Mumford, Gary 'Mudbone' Cooper, Maggie Reilly, Bernie Worrell, Francois Garny, Kip Hanrahan and Ginger Baker. Malcolm did a lot of work for Jack beforehand, transcribing music and arranging.

Simon Phillips remembers an awful lot of waiting around, because the support musicians were only playing for a small part of the overall performance. He spent the first half of the show in the audience, watching Jack, Ginger and Dick re-creating the GBO days. It was, he says, fascinating to watch Jack and Ginger's interaction on stage, but when he came to play his set alongside Ginger, and they were drumming together, the only way to handle the situation was for Simon to drop back slightly and let Ginger lead; 'When it came to playing Sunshine Of Your Love I was always going to defer to him.' Both played drum solos, but on the morning of the second show Jack made a point of finding Simon and told him that Ginger was insistent that Simon shouldn't play a solo that day. It seems that he didn't like competition, but Simon wasn't going to step aside so easily. He asked Jack how he felt about it; Jack wasn't going to take sides – so Simon ignored the instruction and played his solo.

Gary Husband remembers it as a delightful occasion; 'It was one big party, and a great celebration of Jack and his work. Everybody who was taking part was completely into it.

'Jack opened playing Bach on the cello, and from there he went on to play with Dick Heckstall-Smith and Ginger – taking a look back at his life. It culminated with an awful lot of people on stage at the end of the second night!' Clem Clempson adds, 'Being in the 'house band' and playing with all the guests meant I was in a very privileged position. It was a lot of fun.

'I got to live out one of my teenage fantasies; I played with Jack and Ginger, so I was Eric for the night! That's one of my fondest memories.' And if there's one song that Clem always enjoyed playing above all the others, it was White Room; 'It's got that extra something, with the five/four section and the beginning, and the lyrics are a large part of it as well. The lyrics are absolutely fantastic.' The song was a regular part of the set – often saved for the encore – as was Sitting On Top Of The World. Clem did, he admits, get just a touch tired of playing Sunshine Of Your Love, which they could never get away without playing.

The three-disc album of the fiftieth birthday was called 'Cities Of The Heart', and some of the matter has also appeared on a later compilation – though this rather breaks up the flow of the gig.

Chapter 25

W hat had been said about West, Bruce And Laing being a re-creation of Cream was repeated, unsurprisingly, about BBM. Gary Moore had been to see Cream when they played at his native Belfast on March 1 1967. It was the day that 'Fresh Cream' was released in the States, and Gary was still a month off his fifteenth birthday. For many years he harboured an ambition to play with Jack and Ginger so that he could create his take on Cream. It was understandable and laudable; he thought they were just about the greatest rhythm section of all time, so why not aspire to work with them? The problem was that he tried to step into Eric's role. It wasn't a question of being better or worse, but of that job already having been done. It was always going to be second hand news in a way. If there had been a new Sunshine Of Your Love, as it were, it would have been very different. But there wasn't.

Jack has said that he and Gary were consciously trying to write the kind of songs which they believed Cream would have been playing if the band was still around, which was a tortuous and artificial thought process, and led to some of the songs sounding very artificial. In an interview he made the point that Led Zeppelin had done extremely well having 'ripped off' Cream, but that BBM was castigated by the reviewers for trying to emulate what two-thirds of the band had done with Cream. It's not an argument that's very easy to defend under fire.

Jack has played with Gary many times and says that it's different from playing with, say, Eric, but can't define how exactly; 'You play to whatever is going on around you. It's like a conversation. Gary is a very different sort of guitar player from Eric; you have different conversations with different people, and you say different things. If I was in a country and western band I wouldn't play that four-strings-at-time bass – it might not work!'

The band toured, and recorded 'Around The Next Dream', which was released in June 1994 on the Virgin label. It was a considerable commercial success, reaching number nine in the UK album charts but was to be their only recording. 'It was great fun to do', Jack says.

In itself the album was quite magnificent, though it was very much at – or indeed almost off – the heavy blues/rock end of the scale. Fans of Jack (or Ginger) as jazz musicians would have been demanding their money back. Again though, if anyone was expecting 'The New Cream' they were to be disappointed, though playing 'Spot The Cream Influence' throughout the record was a rewarding` game. No one could fail to spot the similarities between Why Does Love (Have To Go Wrong)? and We're Going Wrong. The BBM song is very strong – one of the best tracks on the album - but the earlier, leaner song is the more effective. Again though, the sheer musicianship of the three men is awe-inspiring. After each surviving a couple of very difficult decades there was no doubting the fact that both Jack and Ginger could still pull out all the plugs, and keep up with this young whippersnapper.

The musicianship is truly inspirational, and Jack had never been in better voice. This was huge scale stadium music; big music, best played very loud at huge venues.

Just about every track was a showcase for Gary's guitar work – with the effects slightly overdone at times (especially the wah-wah) – but never sounding like Eric, which was good. Throughout Gary's guitar is well to the front of the mix, with Jack and Ginger a little too far back. That gives a very, very slight impression of it being a Gary Moore band, accompanied by two side man – though less of a problem if you know that the bass player is the main vocalist.

The problem was the lyrics. They were terrible. Someone had been trying to copy Pete Brown's style and it definitely hadn't worked. At worst they were simply naff. Such glorious music deserved better.

One real surprise was a pair of power ballads. One came complete with orchestral backing; Where In The World was an uncharacteristically big production but it worked very well. The second was Glory Days (not the Bruce Springsteen song, of course). It's easy to imagine Celine Dion covering either of these, doing her big inspirational bit – and taking them to platinum sales levels worldwide.

Where In The World is followed by Can't Fool The Blues, which is refreshing, straight-down-the-road slow blues, and it sounds as if it was born fully formed as a classic blues standard. Again, the lyrics aren't subtle enough to be as effective as they might be – not bad but in need of editing – but that's not such a problem when it comes to the blues.

The tracks that stop the listener dead in their tracks though are the slower ones. Naked Flame was a very slow and thoughtful song that sends shivers down the spine. The song was a masterpiece, and Wrong Side Of Town – which you could easily imagine Billie Holliday singing, wearing a black dress and standing in a single spotlight –

isn't far behind it. Both were written by Gary. 'Around The Next Dream' is an absolute delight for any blues-rock aficionado. It should be far more highly regarded today.

There were no earlier songs on the album, though the CD includes four bonus tracks, including a live cut of Sitting On Top Of The World. It's not greatly unlike how Cream played it, though, as ever, Gary's guitar solos sound subtlely different from Eric's.

The album cover was a curious work; the front showed Ginger, dressed in black, dragging on a cigarette and with his eyes closed. Behind him was a pair of white angel's wings, inappropriately, but in fact they looked rather more like giant ears. It could have been a billboard that was standing against. It didn't work – though one's natural disinclination to see Ginger Baker as a seraph didn't help. The back cover had a bleached-out Polaroid of each member of the band, and all of them looked unspeakably villainous. One wouldn't have needed much urging to cross the street to avoid them.

It has to be said though that, ever the professionals, and as ever glorying in each other's music, Jack and Ginger worked exceptionally well together. For all their differences, the hostility and the mutual antipathy, they have always been a world-class rhythm section. They have always understood each other and been able to predict what the other is going to play, and when and how. If one was looking for comparisons, in terms of how other musicians, soloists in particular, who can really meld with their drummers, one would find them first in jazz. Philly Jo Jones and Miles Davis always produced magic together, as did John Coltrane and Elvin Jones, or Benny Goodman and Gene Kruger. The equivalent rock duos would all be rhythm sections rather than a drummer and a soloist; John Paul Jones and John Bonham, John Entwhistle and Keith Moon (and, subsequently, John Entwhistle and Zak Starkey), and even Paul McCartney and Ringo Starr.

BBM was a very interesting excursion for Jack. He could still be a team player. He could front his own band or he could subsume himself into a meeting of equals. That was nothing but a good thing. It was also a boost to the morale; the interest in the band was considerable right from the start, and they played good venues, and to large crowds right through the summer of 1994; 'We played the top flight venues, and for top-flight money.' It's simply unfortunate, though perhaps inevitable, that the band eventually 'imploded', and the rest of the European tour that was slated had to be cancelled. ''Around The Next Dream' was a great record, and live we were even better. Ginger was playing tremendous – up to the standard of how he was playing with Cream at the reunion. But it imploded ...

'You could say that it was about personalities, though that would be over-simplifying things. Although it seems like a long time ago it's too close, and I'm too close too the other two guys in the band.' Beyond that Jack refuses to be drawn. 'Maybe it was my fault. I don't think it was my fault ... but then I never do.'

In May 1995 Jack returned to Kurt Renker's Zerkal studio in Germany to record 'Monkjack.' This was to be another shift, and a move away from the hefty blues/rock of BBM. The only other musician on the album was the keyboards player Bernie Worrell, who played Hammond B3 organ. Jack sang and played piano. Born in New Jersey in 1944, Bernie was a child prodigy, who could play piano at the age of three and wrote a full concerto at eight. He's best known for his work with George Clinton, who he first met when he was a member of a doo-wop combo, and the band George's funk outfit Parliament. He also worked with Talking Heads throughout the Eighties.

The idea behind the album, Jack says, was that he would strip everything down and simply play piano and sing. It was a notion he had harboured for a long time. He decided to add a second keyboard instrument and recruited Bernie, and the album was recorded in just two days, with almost all new material. The two men have a lot of common ground, musically and intellectually, and when they are working together simply slip into a relationship of complete empathy.

The album begins with a depressing, almost maudlin song, The Food, being the lament of a cuckolded husband; a noticeably downbeat opening which could well depress and distract listeners, and was uncharacteristic of the album as a whole. Tightrope was a song Jack had performed with the Clempson, Cobham and Sancious band, and which he decided was worth re-visiting, and there were two tracks from 'Songs For A Tailor'; Weird Of Hermiston and Folk Song – which is just about the best thing on the album simply because it is such a well-written song, and suits the minimal treatment of piano, organ and voice perfectly. On the other hand, stripping down Hermiston doesn't work quite so well – though Bernie's elegant organ-playing is a joy.

The very slowly-paced, eight minute-long Laughing On Music Street by Jack and Pete is a late night, last-glass-of-wine-and-now-the-bottle's-empty song. The last track on the album, the instrumental Immortal Ninth, is a song which Jack wrote when he was just eleven years old. Overall, it's a quiet, understated and reflective album, but not Jack's best.

In September Jack and Bernie played music from 'Monkjack' at the Queen's Hall in Edinburgh, and then at The Queen Elizabeth Hall in London; just the two of them on stage, with a piano and a Hammond. It was, essentially, two classically-trained musicians performing modern classical music.

In 1996 Jack had again been involved in a more esoteric project, when Viennese-born, American-based composer Michael Mantler (who was Carla Bley's husband at that time) asked him to sing on a new opera. In '91 Jack had sung a specially commissioned work written by Mantler and Mike Gibbs in Vienna in front of a full orchestra. The '96 work, entitled 'School Of Languages', was described by Mantler as 'a sort-of-but-not-really-an-opera.' Jack and seven other voices were backed by horns and strings.

The first performance was at The Arken Museum of Modern Art in Copenhagen, and there was a second outing, where it was re-titled 'School Of Understanding' at The Hebbel Theater in Berlin in November 1997. Jack describes the music as 'Very challenging but fun. Not commercial music though.'

In the spring of 1997 Jack joined Ringo Starr's All-Starr band and embarked on a hefty tour of the USA. As well as Ringo – playing drums of course, and singing – the Starrs included keyboards player Gary Brooker from Procul Harem, guitarists Marc Rivera and Peter Frampton, Timmy Cappello on keyboards and sax, and drummer Simon Kirke – who was originally with Free and then Bad Company. Ringo had been touring with the band, on and off, since the beginning of the decade, and at various times the line-up had included Dr John, Levon Helm and Rick Danko of The Band, organist Billy Preston, Dave Edmunds, Clarence Clemons from The E Street Band, Ringo's son, Zac Starkey, and many others. Jack was in great company; he described is as like being in one big, never-ending, travelling party.

Ringo ran the show like a review, sometimes drumming or singing, and at others times acting as the master of ceremonies. The other musicians all got to play some of their best-loved music, and Ringo was a famously generous band leader – giving everyone lots of space and time. Jack usually performed I Feel Free, Sunshine of Your Love or White Room, and often contributed a bass solo.

Ringo comes down front while Simon Kirke drums –
Timmy Cappello on far left, Jack in the centre and Todd Rundgren on guitar (MK)

Reminded of his time with Ringo's All-Starrs, Peter Frampton says immediately, 'Oh, it doesn't get much better than that!' Peter is seven years younger than Jack, and when he was a teenager he used to sneak out of his parents' home so that he could go to The Flamingo Club in Wardour Street, and listen to The Graham Bond Organisation. He remembers fighting his way to the front to get a closer view of the playing, so it's no surprise when he says that playing with Jack in The All-Starrs was a milestone for him.

Peter adds, 'When I first looked at the set list, when we were going to rehearse, I laughed – it was all of my favourite numbers. It was a dream – but the icing on the cake for me was playing with Jack on the Cream numbers. I had to be about five guitar players with that band, but every night we'd play the Cream numbers and I had to be my version of Eric.

'There's nothing like going head to head with Jack Bruce – I mean literally; we'd be almost touching, head to head, when we got into a solo.'

Eight gigs into the American tour the band was due to play a huge outdoor gig at the Fiddler's Green Amphitheatre in Denver, Colorado. During the sound check a lanky and familiar figure wandered in, and he walked up to Peter Frampton. In a very distinctive south London accent, Ginger Baker demanded to know where Jack Bruce was. Peter's first thought was that this could only mean trouble, and it occurred to him that they might be playing that night's gig with their bass player lying in hospital – or worse, the mortuary.

What Ginger wanted to do though was sit in with the band. The ever-genial Ringo was characteristically relaxed about the idea, so Ginger joined them on stage to play one of the Cream numbers. Peter remembers, 'Ginger took Simon's kit, Ringo stayed on, and we played White Room. I was locked onto my wah-wah pedal and my neck almost came off as I kept turning round to watch the interaction between Jack and Ginger. What an experience to play with the two of them – and Ringo! The crowd went absolutely bananas.'

Not long after the European tour had ended, towards the end of 1998, Jack, Peter and Gary Brooker talked very seriously about forming a band. The two others went out to Gary's farm, and spent a week jamming, writing new material and recording demo tapes. They were all relaxed, fresh back from a very successful couple of tours, and it worked well. In fact it looked very promising. The tapes – which Peter still has – sounded great. They worked with a drum machine, and although a few names for the other personnel were mentioned, no one was seriously put into the frame, let alone approached.

It wasn't to be though. Other commitments loomed and the idea fizzled out. Again, it was a great shame. Music lovers can only guess at what the band would have

Jack with Gary Brooker (Timmy Cappello in background) in 1999 on the Ringo's All-Starrs tour (MK)

played and how they would have sounded, and with the large numbers of fans that each of the three already had, it's hard to imagine that band not being a huge success.

Jack again toured Europe and the UK with The All-Starrs in the autumn of '98, and the following year the band undertook a huge tour of the States, but with Peter, who had other commitments. The guitarist on the first half of the tour was Todd Rundgren, and then Dave Edmunds on the second leg. There are several All-Starrs albums but only one Jack track on one album (I Feel Free on the three-CD box set).

There was a flurry of retrospective album releases in the second half of the Nineties, starting with a live recording made for the BBC at the Paris Theatre in Regent Street, London in 1971, with Graham Bond, Art Themen, Chris Spedding and John Marshall. That came out in 1995 and was followed the next year by 'The Jack Bruce Collector's Edition' which was a compilation of CMP recordings. The 1997 'Sitting On Top Of The World' album was the edited highlights of the fiftieth birthday concerts, and that was followed in 1998 by another BBC live album. This dated from 1975 and 1981, and featured two Old Grey Whistle Test performances. The line-up for the first, earlier, set was

Mick Taylor, Carla Bley, Ronnie Leahy, and Bruce Gary. The second was Clem Clempson, David Sancious, and Billy Cobham. Material by the same band, dating from 1981, was released in 1999 under the generic 'Concert Classics' label. In 2003 another retrospective would be released, 'Rope Ladder To The Moon', from Polygram's archives.

The new millennium seemed to bring a new direction and a new spirit: Many of the thoughts which gelled to create 'Shadows In The Air' had been in Jack's mind since the mid-Eighties. He went into the studio wanting to come back to both White Room and Sunshine Of Your Love, and also had two ballads finished – Dark Heart and Heart Quake. He also decided, during the session, to record new cuts of Boston Ball Game 1967 and He The Richmond, both from 'Songs For A Tailor.' The band persuaded him to also re-cut Out Into The Fields, which starts the album.

Jack hasn't always chosen the best tracks to open his albums, but 'Shadows In The Air' opens with a glorious new cut of Into The Fields. The song was well worth revisiting, and this version is much heftier than the West Bruce and Laing version, and features very adroit guitar playing by Vernon Reid over delightfully complex percussions lines.

The new songs were as successful as the classic songs; the lyrics on 52nd Street are

The core of The Cuicoland Express is its stunning percussion section;
from left, Robbie Ameen, Ritchie Flores and El Negro Horacio Hernandez. (MK)

typical of Pete Brown's wit, and the treatment, with Jack playing sparse bass above playful Afro-Caribbean percussion, works exceptionally well. As does the moody and slightly bleak Dark Heart.

The album very successfully mixed new and old music, and what made all the difference was the joyous exuberance of the band, which was something that they also managed to communicate effortlessly at live gigs. The album also managed to be obviously more commercial with compromising any of its musical credibility.

Seven tracks were written by Jack alone, while three – 52nd Street, Directions Home, and Surge were written by Jack and Kip Hanrahan. Kip is in the credits as co-producer. As he was recording the slightly Celtic-sounding Directions Home, which was improvised in the studio, Jack started to think of lost friends – Tony Williams and Larry Young – and dedicated the track to them. He now regards it as one of the best pieces of music he ever recorded.

The majority of the musicians on the album were his 'Latin' band, drawn from the American Clave stable - Vernon Reid, Bernie Worrell, El Negro Horacio Hernandez, Robby Ameen, and Richie Flores. 'Basically, I stole Kip's band', he jokes. 'No, it's not like that, we're a pool of musicians who all work together. They're mates.'

Talking about the way the percussion works, Jack says, 'There's a place where everybody operates within the rhythm. You would never get in the way – it wouldn't be possible. It's not like two rock drummers playing, where they either play the same or they have to work out things to do.

'Robby Ameen is the main trap drummer, and he plays the basic 'down' rhythm, and you've got El Negro Horacio Henendez – probably the greatest in the world – playing around him. Then, on top of that, you've got Richie Flores playing congas or whatever, decorating on top of that. And there I am – doing whatever it is that I do ...'

There was also a very impressive roster of guest musicians on the record. Eric Clapton played on both the Cream songs, which was a great treat, and Gary Moore played guitar on two of the new songs, Heart Quake and Mr Flesh. The great New Orleans piano player Dr John played on This Anger's A Liar and Windowless Rooms (originally he was to have sung as well, but Jack changed his mind – an unfortunate decision in the minds of many – and he only played). Jack had always loved his music, so he simply phoned him up and asked him to play on a couple of tracks. Dr John – Mac to just about everyone – turned up for the sessions in New York, and decided not to go home once his tracks were finished and just hung on, enjoying the atmosphere and the music; 'We couldn't get him to go', Jack says. He hung around bullying Malcolm Bruce while the woman with him kept reprimanding him for 'being horrible to the kid.'

'Making that album was a dream', Jack says, 'You can tell that it's not been wrestled with. It was just plucked out of the air. More than any record I've ever done – like some of the Cream records, but the music was more complex on this. I love this record.' The album was recorded in New York and Gary and Eric's parts were over-dubbed back in London. Malcolm noticed that his father was very at home in New York, and was relaxed and invigorated in the presence of the American Clave musicians; 'They love him and respect him, and he feels close to them in spirit.' He describes them as 'very down to earth.' He makes the point that Jack is to, but the difference is that Latin musicians have no interest at all in then rock star baggage he carries around with him, and are only interested in him as musician. 'You don't want to mess around with them; they're the evilest people to be on the wrong side of, but with Jack they're respectful and kind. Very giving. They come out of a very warm culture.'

'Shadows in The Air' was the first of his solo albums on which Jack re-visited songs which he had written and recorded with Cream. He offered new but undisguised treatments of both Sunshine and White Room. Eric Clapton played on both, and they sang

Bernie Worrell and Jack have a lot in common. They were both classically educated and showed their musical abilities from an early age. They have worked together for more than ten years. (MK)

together on Sunshine. He had realised by then that he had played a large part in breathing life into a creature which then had its own organic life force - one which simply wasn't going to go away. His fans wanted him to hear his Cream songs – not Tales Of Brave Ulysses or Blue Condition; songs on which he only played, and which he had had no hand in creating – but his own compositions, which were arguable more his than Cream's. That desire on the part of his audience wasn't going to go away, and Jack was at last comfortable enough with his own history to satisfy it. Those tracks were also included, pragmatically, to get some radio air time, and in that Jack was fairly successful.

Eric Clapton came back to Cream songs in May 1985, playing live on Late Night With Letterman on American television. He had played Badge and Crossroads very occasionally, but now he ran through Sunshine Of Your Love, and from then on he seemed happy to dig into that particular corner of his back catalogue. Two months later, when he played the Philadelphia side of the Live Aid concert he opened a three song set including White Room (despite getting an electric shock off the microphone as he started the song). Eric performing that song was a huge delight and a source of deep satisfaction to many millions of fans around the world.

When it came to touring in support of 'Shadows In The Air' – as they did from the autumn of 2001 – the band was called The Cuicoland Express (pronounced kwee-ko). The name came from an Australia fan who picked up the word 'cuicoland' – which is a Chilean name for a private gated community. Jack had heard the word and used it, but the Australian turned it into Cuicoland Express and made it the name of his on-line newsletter. Jack saw the site, liked the name and borrowed it as the name of his band. They toured as The Cuicoland Express but didn't record under that name. It started off as a nine-piece band, but economics dictated a reduction in the line-up, and in the end there was just the three drummers rather than four.

That year the band played The Canterbury Fayre, and the show was released on DVD. The quality isn't what one would hope for, but it's a very interesting set and shows Jack in very good humour – as he could hardly fail to be in that company. The cut of Sunshine Of Your Love is very slightly slow and sounds ponderous, but is set alight by Vernon Reid's stunning guitar playing, for which Jack provided some witty new bass lines. The Afro-Caribbean themes are best displayed on 52nd Street and Windowless Rooms – the former hustled along with magnificently funky keyboards playing by Bernie Worrell. He plays organ up against Jack's piano on Theme For An Imaginary Western, which – even now – is one of the most inspirational, most moving songs in the Bruce/Brown catalogue.

There was to be another slightly weird project after the 'Shadows In The Air' tour and before work began on the next album: Through June and July 2002 Jack joined

Alan Parsons, Todd Rundgren and a host of others on a show billed as 'A Walk Down Abbey Road: A Tribute to the Beatles', and they criss-crossed the States as an eight-piece band.

There was also an intriguing collaboration mooted, which unfortunately came to nothing. After Jack's last tour with Ringo he went into studio in Venice, California with Andy Summers (previously with The Police) and drummer Dennis Chambers. They had written twenty eight songs and recorded many of them. They did attempt to put together a band, putatively called Hot Flash, but couldn't get the support of management and the project was shelved.

Released in the autumn of 2003, 'More Jack Than God' was even more heavily influenced by Afro-Caribbean music than 'Shadows In The Air.' The musicians were again the percussionists Robby Ameen, El Negro Horacio Hernandez, and Richie Flores, with Malcolm Bruce playing guitar and piano, Bernie Worrell on organ and Vernon Reid on guitar. Godfrey Townsend joined the line-up to play guitar on one track. The album was a mix of Bruce/Brown and Bruce/Hanrahan compositions, and the sessions felt, Malcolm says, 'More spontaneous. Jack let a lot of things happen in the studio.'

This album took the influences of World rhythms much further and the delight and exuberance is carried over from the previous album. The label Afro-Caribbean isn't really accurate, though it's better than the old-fashioned catch-all 'Latin.' In an interview for Vintage Guitar magazine Jack explained, 'What I was trying to do was show the development of rhythm from Africa, through the Caribbean, though New Orleans – then to Glasgow, if you like. The rhythm came through West Africa, then went into places like Cuba and Haiti.'

The Bruce/Brown song Kelly's Blues (the true story of a schoolgirl who was bullied so badly that she took her own life) was one of the most powerful and memorable tracks on the album, while Progress – with Jack, alone but for a small contribution from Bernie, singing and playing the piano, was pensive and essentially pessimistic, mourning unfulfilled promise. Jack dedicated the track to his father, saying that Charlie's favourite song was Buddy Can You Spare A Dime?

On The Night That Once Was Mine Jack duetted with himself, which was both novel and effective. The slow ballad Cold Island was dedicated to the drummer Cozy Powell, with whom Jack had worked with a few times down the years, who died in a car crash in 1998.

There were three memorable new versions of old songs; We're Going Wrong, stretched out to over five minutes, an honest re-recording of I Feel Free, and the evergreen Politician – now a couple of seconds under six minutes long. We're Going Wrong and Politician were absolute triumphs; the former slightly slower than the original, and with the percussions forming an elaborate mesh beneath Vernon Reid's inspirational

The Cuicoland Express plays BB King's club in New York, December 2001.
Vernon Reid on the right (MK)

guitar playing. Politican was more portentous and claustrophobic than ever, but the percussion gave it a surprising lightness. The cut of I Feel Free seemed to add nothing to the original though, and sounded slightly stodgy by comparison – bass riffs excepted.

The title was much misunderstood in some areas; reviewers saw it either as a gesture of self-aggrandisement or a sly dig at Eric (via the old 'Eric Clapton Is God' graffiti angle). It was neither. The album didn't have a title, and when they were recording Kelly's Blues Kip Hanrahan suggested that in the mix they needed 'more Jack than God', meaning slightly more of Jack and slightly less of Godfrey Townsend. Jack was amused by the phrase and decided that it was as good a name for the album as anything they'd come up with so far. It's not likely that any secondary meaning occurred to him.

At the time of writing, Jack is planning a new album with The Cuicoland Express line-up. He has some material in mind but also expects to generate a lot more in studio. The plan is to record in Cuba in the early months of 2006. Asked if he would then go on tour, Jack replies, 'I'd love to, but a lot depends on my physical strength. I haven't got all of my strength back. Time will tell.'

What he is alluding to is the fact that, having been diagnosed with liver cancer earlier in the year, he underwent a liver transplant in the autumn of 2003. The operation took place at Addenbrooke's Hospital in Cambridge, an internationally-renowned centre of excellence for organ transplants.

Nowadays it is almost a routine procedure and the success rate is very high. Despite everything having gone well in surgical terms though, it is said that Jack did not recover as expected and his condition deteriorated rapidly. It is thought that at the eleventh hour, at the point where the doctors were giving up any hope of saving his life, it was realised that he was the one person in tens of thousands who was allergic to the anti-rejection drug, and the pharmaceuticals which should have been easing back to health were in fact killing him. He may then have suffered from secondary infections.

Asked to talk about all this for his biography Jack refused point blank. Despite having talked about it off the record at great length, on the record he simply dismissed the whole episode, saying 'It's not an important part of my life.' Obviously that's not true. Going through an experience like that and coming very close to death is a hugely important part of anyone's life story, and can't fail to be life-changing. For a creative artist the impact is all the greater, and it can't fail to have a massive impact on both his work and the way he views the world.

Beyond his complete refusal to talk openly about his illness, all that can be added is that Margrit Seyffer posted a statement on the internet, giving news of the success of the operation – and plugging the new album:

'After Jack was diagnosed with liver cancer earlier this summer, we went through a very difficult period of uncertainty, not knowing whether it would be life threatening. Jack spent three weeks on and off in hospital for examinations. When we were told Jack could have a liver transplant, then we knew that there was real hope and we were overjoyed! Jack had his successful transplant on 19th September 2003 and after being critically ill for a period in which we almost lost him, Jack is now making a successful recovery. The whole family is very relieved, that Jack will be with us for many years and obviously we are looking forward to more new songs, concerts and records to come! I am sure that our friends and fans all over the world will feel the same as the Bruce Family.

'We hope you will enjoy and celebrate the new album 'More Jack Than God' which was released by Sanctuary Records worldwide almost on the day of Jack's transplant. The pictures in the album booklet could well have been the last pictures of Jack. He has proved us wrong, after all, he is a strong Scotsman!

'We would like to take this opportunity to thank the staff at Addenbrooke's Hospital in Cambridge for the dedication and expertise they have shown.

The Bruce Family'

Chapter 26

When the band walked on stage of The Royal Albert Hall on May 2 2005, it was the first time they had been together since January 12 1993. Another heavy power trio, ZZ Top – had inducted them into The Rock 'N Roll Hall Of Fame - and they played Sunshine Of Your Love, Born Under A Bad Sign and Crossroads. It was ad fairly ad hoc performance – they had run through a brief rehearsal just the day before - and might not have been their best ever (Jack says that the rehearsal was better than the show). The fact that the three of them had shared a stage and thundered through three Cream classics was the headline though. Each had worked with the other; Jack with Ginger separately, and with Eric – indeed, Eric had played on three of his albums, and Ginger had been in one of Jack's bands. It had been slightly more than a quarter of a century since all three of them had last been together on stage. Despite that gap, Jack says, 'It was great. It just felt as if we'd had a week off. We tore the place apart.'

The Rock and Roll Hall of Fame Foundation had been established in 1983 in an act of music industry self-aggrandisement. The Foundation's function is to 'recognise the contributions of those who have had a significant impact on the evolution, development and perpetuation of rock and roll by inducting them into the Hall of Fame.' Artists become eligible for induction twenty-five years after the release of their first record. Criteria include 'the influence and significance of the artist's contributions to the development and perpetuation of rock and roll.' The Foundation inducts half a dozen people or bands each year – including the likes of producers and arrangers as well as performers, and they are chosen by one thousand 'rock experts.'

They had all been uncertain about the wisdom of accepting the invitation so, Jack says – certainly he and Eric were. The problem wasn't the fact of playing together so much as the occasion; 'I'm not comfortable with anything like that, awards ceremonies for rock – they just don't go together. It's like Mick Jagger getting a knighthood – which he really sought – it doesn't fit.

'There's also the evil side of the business – the ripping-off and the thievery which someone gets conveniently forgotten at these events. It's about an industry that has exploited musicians, and especially black musicians, for years. One of the guys who were honoured at that time was Frankie Lymon; he was a very good performer, but the record company and his management deliberately got him hooked on smack when he was fourteen so they could control him. He was being inducted, despite being dead for many years. So I had mixed feelings, but you do get sucked into it.'

Jack's enduring memories of the event are, firstly, that they had to wait far too long before they got to play, secondly that Bob Dylan was very kind to them and was 'entirely encased in a leather suit and looked like a lizard', and thirdly that he sat alongside Naomi Campbell all evening.

He has been invited to The Rock And Roll Hall Of Fame museum in Cleveland but says that he has never wanted to go, 'I'm a member of all that though, and the good thing is that I get to vote for all my friends. I do so shamelessly! If I'd gone to the museum I'd have been presented with a jacket, so I got them to send it. It's one of those with 'leather' arms, but they're plastic really … and it's got my name on it.'

Ginger said that he would have been far more impressed if he had been inducted into a jazz hall of fame. Eric would think the same thing about a blues hall of fame.

Jack tried to add a hint of rebellion by refused to go along with the black tie dress code – hardly very rock 'n roll in itself – which upset Eric. He wore a purple Versace suit with a green shirt. The award sits on a shelf in Jack's music room, but is a bit battered as a result of it being used as a goalpost for a hotel room game of football against Eddie Van Halen.

What did delight Jack about the induction was the fact that he was the first Scotsman to become a member of The Rock And Roll Hall Of Fame. In his brief speech he said that it seemed like a long way from Glasgow to Hollywood. Eric spoke for longer, and then Ginger leaned forward and, ever to the point, said, 'I agree with what they said.'

The three talked seriously about recording an album of new material; 'We talked about trying to do something comparable. It wouldn't have been as great, but you never know …'

That was Jack's suggestion, and he says that Eric was very interested in the idea, but it wasn't to happen; 'Eric had commitments, then BBM started, which I really liked. It just didn't work out …'

Asked who, among the galaxy of musicians he has worked with, has most impressed and delighted him, Jack immediately mentions Eric and Ginger. He describes them as 'the greatest musicians I've ever played with.'

Equating rock guitarists with jazz musicians, Jack says that what Eric was to Charlie Parker, Jimi was to John Coltrane.

The one man who he would describe as a genius though is Larry Young, who converted to Islam and became Khalid Yasin. Jack says of him, 'It's hard to describe his genius. I once saw him bring a Glasgow audience to tears by playing the Hammond organ. It was so moving. I still get shivers thinking about it.'

Talking of Larry, Jack again makes a comparison with John Coltrane; .' 'Coltrane has this very deep thing going on that transcended music. So deep. Emotional. The only other person who could get that depth from his music was Larry Young. Coltrane was like a prophet, and people who worked with him were given this gift of achieving depth and truth. I saw Larry play things on the organ which you wouldn't think were possible. He played a little L100 and he played with one hand and operated the draw bars with the other, but he made sounds you just couldn't believe.'

Larry died of pneumonia in 1978 during treatment for a stomach infection, aged just thirty-eight. Talking about Larry Young moves Jack on to John McLaughlin, who he says was also greatly changed by his interest in religion; 'He went from being a fairly straight Wes Montgomery type of player, to being a wonderful, inspirational, transcendental player. A lot of that was to do with the recognition that he got from Miles Davis and Tony Williams.'

Jack's fan base in Europe has been rather different from that in the USA. Since the Seventies he has always been very well received in Germany (German fans being very heavily into rock and blues-rock anyway), and in the UK the people who buy his records have fallen into two groups. There are old Cream fans who have always followed what the three members have gone on to do individually, and those who came out of a sophisticated musical tradition and know his work from the jazz/funk fusion channels. Both these sorts of fans have had to work fairly hard to keep up with his work, in a world dominated by Kylie, Robbie and Britney. Very little music of real quality is well promoted in Britain, and there are few media outlets where it can be heard. Paul Jones's blues show on Radio 2 is an excellent and important forum for that genre, but there's no equivalent for many other forms of modern music. The situation has improved somewhat in recent times, with the launch of BBC Radio 6, the widening of the remit for Radio 3, and more mature music magazines such as Mojo. It's far from good though; for every hour of Jools Holland's Later, there's several thousand hours of MTV and its clones. Similarly, on-line stores make buying more esoteric music a lot easier.

In the USA music lovers seem to be better informed and supplied. There is also a far broader range of music on offer, and because the market is so much larger promotional activity can be justified in pure accountancy terms for acts which aren't going to sell a million records. It is also a monied market; people aged between thirty and sixty can spend money on CDs and concert tickets a lot more easily than can the pubescent audiences at whom boy bands are aimed.

There is also, of course, a vast live music scene in the States, which there isn't in this country; so many venues have gone, and in their place are soulless stadia which are okay for really big name bands, but are too large for middle-ranking attractions. There is a small number of new and beautifully-designed, comfortable, architecturally exciting and acoustically brilliant smaller concert halls, such as The Bridgewater Hall in Manchester and SAGE in Gateshead – which perfectly fit performers like Jack.

It hasn't been easy being a Jack Bruce fan. He has expected his audience to run and keep up with him; no easy task. And if one's tastes lay more at one end or the other of the jazz-to-rock line, then him suddenly accelerating off into the distance was almost inevitable confusing and alienating.

Jack acknowledges that at times he made life very difficult for his audiences. He remembers his early British 'Town Hall' tours ('all those big, echoing places') which was sold out on the strength of his earlier reputation, 'and I came on and played this weird music.' Some of those fans will have fallen by the wayside at that point – and transferred their affections to other rock bands and artists – while others stuck with it and developed their tastes within the emerging pattern of his music. For those who were younger, and didn't have the grounding in jazz, it was much more difficult than for those of his own generation.

He quickly denies that he ever had a responsibility towards his fans in the sense that he might have led them more sympathetically and gently towards different forms of music. 'My job is just to stand up there and play', he says.

It would be a brave man who suggested to him that compromise might have been appropriate – that dreaded 'C' word! He says that, right across the band, he is more uncompromising now than when he was younger. Age has most certainly not mellowed him.

He harks back to his time with Manfred Mann more often than he thinks, justifying the fact that on that one occasion at least he did compromise, and did join a commercially successful band simply because it paid well. It's as if he never quite forgiven himself for that one small lapse.

In truth, post-Cream, there was no way that he was ever going to move towards his audience. If they'd loved White Room but didn't understand Lifetime then that was unfortunate. It was for them to keep up, not for Jack to stop moving.

Like most musicians Jack has surprisingly, even frighteningly, little control over the use of his recorded music. The ability to sell the music rests with the publisher, and Jack often won't know of a compilation until he sees it advertised or in the shops, and won't know that a few bars of one of his songs is being used in a television programme unless he sees it or someone tells him. Odd snatches of Bruce/Brown compositions from the Cream years crop up frequently, but as Jack says, 'If it's big enough they've got to ask me, but in practice if I say no they'll do it anyway. I don't own the performance. I have more rights over the music itself but I can't stop them.

'A few years back there was a tremendous amount of money offered to use White Room for the launch of the Apple computer. A lot of money was paid but I don't remember ever being asked. Actually, the publishers do ask me nowadays, but for years they wouldn't ask so that you couldn't say no.'

The only area of compromise he will ever admit to though is in the use of his music for commercials and film and television soundtracks. For a long time he always refused permission; 'I considered that to be a cheapening of my art.'

He has been very flattered by the producers of The Sopranos wanting to use his music – at the time of writing Jack had just been asked for his permission for the of We're Going Wrong - as he was by Martin Scorsese using Sunshine Of Your Love in the film Goodfellas (it was also used in the Arnold Schwarzenegger/Jamie Lee Curtis movie True Lies and in the more recent film School of Rock). His music has twice been used in Matt Groening shows, to the delight of both Jack and his youngest son. A few bars of Sunshine was played in Futurama, and White Room was used in The Simpsons; 'That's real fame! Though when that episode came on, when they used White Room as some sort of drug reference, I was sitting down to watch it and my wife made me go and do something. I came back in and I'd missed it!' If Matt Groening ever wants the use of Jack's voice as one of the guest celebs, he only has to ask; 'Ringo's done that, and Peter Frampton – he was in a very good episode about his floating pig flying away. That's real fame!'

In the Eighties I Feel Free was used in a television advertising campaign for a car company … no, not Ferrari, but Renault. Pete mentioned at the time that the money came in very useful, and Jack felt the same way. There again, even while Cream were still working, they recorded a one minute-long radio advertisement in the USA for the Falstaff brand of beer. It's not certain who wrote the lyrics:

'Falstaff the thirst slaker, Falstaff the thirst slaker.
The beer that can slake any thirst, any thirst.
The beer you reach for first when you want to quench your thirst'

The question is best not asked, though it's unlikely to have been Pete Brown.

Jack adds that if the music is going to be used to promote tobacco or alcohol he won't agree to it, which actually has a certain irony as he has availed himself of both with some generosity in his time.

Apart from that, Jack doesn't have any particular concerns about the use of his music in other media in general and in advertising in particular. He's certainly not dead set against it as some musicians are. He only regrets that I Feel Free hasn't been used to promote free-range chickens, which he thinks would be an excellent idea …

Chapter 27

E ven at the time of the May 2005 reunion concerts there was speculation that Cream would play dates in America, and on September 12 tickets went on sale for their gigs at Madison Square Gardens in New York on October 24, 25 and 26 2005. Two days later pairs of tickets were for sale on eBay for $3,300.

It's highly unlikely to become a regular gig at The Royal Albert Hall. The band is surely not going to re-form year after year; no, it's impossible to imagine, and they are too astute to do it. They've done what they wanted to do. Jack says, 'It should remain a very special occasion for the band and the audience.' He appreciates that to join the international rock circus – with corporate sponsorship from a bank or Pepsi – wouldn't be right; 'The music wouldn't survive it. There's an unspoken agreement between the guys that the music is so precious that we mustn't do it to death. I'm looking forward to the next time very, very much.'

Malcolm Bruce says that he was hugely impressed by the sheer musicianship at the Royal Albert Hall reunion concerts. He went to three of the four of the gigs, and says, 'I was really blown away.

'If they play dates in America I would love to get over there and see those shows as well. When Jack is at his best the music is timeless, and that can mean two things – that you can't date it and also that time stands still when you experience it. On the first night of the reunion concerts time did stand still for me when they played We're Going Wrong. It made me feel a space and an energy, and that's something that rarely happens – it's like chanting, that resonates with the nervous system in a certain way. It's what truly great art does for people. When he propels himself into the moment it's incredible. There's nothing like it.'

There can be no doubt but that the reunion concerts have been enormously good for Jack. Although the concerts were physically taxing, they did reassure him that he can still do what he has always done, so long as he paces himself for now at least. He can still get up on a stage in front of thousands of people, and can not only entertain them – but can thrill and really move them too. This won't have entered his conscious-ness in such black and white terms, but semi-consciously it'll be there. He can share a stage with the best, in a stripped down trio, even when expectations are astronomically high, and shine.

Malcolm says of him, 'He has never been given the respect he deserves; it's a very cynical, fickle industry – especially in this country. But I have felt a real healing energy through this experience. The balance has been redressed. It has given him a sense of validation.'

In theory, it was always going to be wonderful, or else they wouldn't have done it. They have always been highly critical of their own and each other's abilities, and they would have known if it was going to be anything less than monumentally successful; why would they dare risk the reputation of the band? Eric, especially, who most cer-tainly didn't need to undertake the reunion, and perhaps had the most to lose – would-n't have put a foot on the Royal Albert Hall's stage if it wasn't going to work. But could he have pulled it up? Could they? Once the concerts had been announced they had their own momentum. They were unstoppable. It would have been dreadful for them if they had had to cancel. No matter what had been said, the painful rumours would have started within minutes. Despite not having played together for many years, were they all simply so certain that it was going to be better than terrific, better than won-derful – simply perfect?

It wasn't, of course, about now. This was for the history books. It was to put the band back very definitely into the narrative of rock music that stretches over the past fifty years. It was to switch on a spotlight and illuminate Cream so fiercely that it could never be ignored or forgotten. No other band of their stature has ever left it so long, and then returned in such style and with such impact. There are no comparisons that can be made.

On a personal level, the motivation of the three men differed. Many younger music lovers have never heard Ginger Baker play, and far too many may know the name but actually know very little about him. Since he last stepped off a Cream drum riser there has been an untold number of rock drummers thumping out the rhythm and holding their bands together. The money will have been more than useful, of course, but The Albert Hall gigs were to put him back in the reference books, and at the top of the pile. He is one of the most talented, innovative and creative drummers that late Twentieth century music has ever known, and his age only served to reinforce his dom-inance. If Ginger dies tomorrow then he can die knowing that he fuckin' told them so. If you ever want to know Ginger's epitaph then fuckin' listen to this.

Eric's reasons were even more personal. He was very wounded by the demise of Cream, and spent a long time searching for a new musical identity. Although great music came out of the years '66 to '68, for decades Cream represented a nadir in his musical development. After the frustrations and limitations of The Yardbirds and The Bluesbreakers, Cream was supposed to be a short cut to creative fulfilment. For the fans it was, but for Eric it certainly wasn't. For a long time he had wanted to avoid being reminded of the difficulties of the period. To return to them could be seen as a process of publicly thanking everyone who had helped him reach such heights. To be able to re-address these moments now, and turn some painful memories into a triumph, is a sign of maturity. Perhaps too he thought it was simply 'the right thing to do.'

The concerts were also good for Eric as a musician. It's not hard to imagine sessions or concerts where Eric has been very much the boss, very much the most famous and important person in the place, and he has been able to coast. Some of his best work in recent years has been his duets with BB King, where drifting through the session was never going to be an option. So it was with the re-formed Cream; the old competitiveness was there in full, and he knew it was good for him.

Malcolm says that he hasn't been hugely impressed by what Eric has done since Cream; 'He does some really nice songs but I don't listen to his stuff and think it's amazing. When I heard him with Jack and Ginger though, I thought 'Wow! This guy is phenomenal.' He was blowing me away. I couldn't believe what I was hearing.'

If you had only ever heard Eric Clapton play one of those concerts and nothing else, you would recognise him as an unparalleled blues/rock guitarist. For many fans it made up for the Armani years. It became possible to forgive him for Wonderful Tonight. Like all great musicians, Eric is at his best fully stretched, and whether that was a conscious part of his thinking when he initiated the reunion or not, he must be admired for it.

Jack was genuinely delighted by how well he and Eric played. It was, he says, as if the improvisations had been going on even in the years they didn't play together, and they simply tapped into a continuous strand; 'The improvising that Eric was doing was just out of this world, and for me it felt like the bass was an extension of myself. It was like breathing; part of my unconsciousness.

He goes on to say that the three of them hadn't given Cream 'the love and respect' that it deserved, within their individual musical histories, but, 'Once we had done the concerts I think we all realised that Cream was the high spot of our musical careers.'

What Jack achieved with the reunion concerts was to re-focus history in a more personal direction. Because of the very wide success which Eric achieved through the Seventies and Eighties, Jack's role in Cream was diminished. Just as Ginger so resented being known as Eric's drummer, so Eric hated the portrayal of Cream as Eric's band. The musical merits of the three men, disparate though they were, were equal in importance, but whereas Eric played guitar and sang some of the time, Jack had a three-fold role in the band; he played bass, he co-wrote some of their greatest music and he was undeniably the front man. His was the voice that defined the band. That was the position that he had to re-establish. Some of the fans remembered it like that, but the focus had undeniably been distorted. The critics, the rock writers and the reference books tended to see Cream as Eric Clapton and a couple of other blokes. That was what he had to correct, and that's what he did. If he had never played or sung another note after the last night of the reunion gigs, that would have been okay. The reference books had been re-written.

Jack has both resented and been envious of the global success which Eric went on to see, but Malcolm says that to a large degree the difference between their two careers has been shaped by the decisions Jack made after Cream; 'He has felt he got a raw deal, but there was his self-abuse over the years, and he can be a very driven, very abrasive character. That's what makes him what he is but that can rub a lot of people up the wrong way and can alienate a lot of people.'

He was never going to be a musician whose personality made him easy to promote and market, and his work has only reinforced that. Eric's recordings with Phil Collins was the most marketable music this side of The Spice Girls; Jack's work has often been too left-field, too adventurous, too jazz-based (if you want to sell rock records and CDs by the million, blues is good, jazz is bad). He can hardly have been surprised that he had a far smaller audience than Eric enjoyed. Jack and Pete wrote many truly excellent songs together after Cream, but none reached the audience achieved by Sunshine Of Your Love or White Room. None had that huge success or stood up on their own as great anthems.

Jon Hiseman has a very interesting theory about what has limited Jack's career, and, in a nutshell, it is the collaboration with Pete Brown – the fundamental which has produced what the vast majority of his fans think of as his very best work: 'Jack hasn't been a megastar of the Sting variety because he chose the wrong words. The words were far too clever; they were poetry, and poetry doesn't make good lyrics for ordinary people.

'Jack has taken incredibly difficult words and set them to music in inventive ways, and he has never lost his way of doing that. He hasn't thrashed around trying to find different ways. That's what he does brilliantly. He's a true original and he didn't nick anything from anybody.

'But at the highest level the lyrics are high art-pop, and on a commercial level that doesn't reach out and touch ordinary people. I've got the greatest respect for Pete Brown, you can tell that by the number of his songs that are in the Colosseum repertoire, but Jack created his own world by relying on esoteric lyrics.

'I think Jack wanted, and in my view deserved, a bigger listenership, but the lyrics blocked that. He's a preacher, and he wanted people to hear and enjoy, but he aimed higher than the public could accept. The deeper you go the more limited the market becomes.'

*Just a few weeks after the Royal Albert Hall gigs Jack played a memorial concert
for Dick Heckstall-Smith at The Astoria in London (MK)*

Talking about the reunion concerts at his home, two months later, Jack mused, 'I don't think anybody expected it to be as amazing musically as it was. I can stand aside from it now and it was amazing. We just reached the heights. It was a good thing to do, maybe a great thing to do, and we did it.'

He appreciates that the experience has changed him; the increased financial security is very welcome of course, but as important is that he is far more positive about himself and his ability to realise his musical ambitions. That is a very strange thing to say about a musician who has seen such success over so long a career, but the truth is that Jack only ever travels – he never arrives.

Now he can afford to relax and be fairly sanguine about being pigeon-holed as 'the bass player with the Sixties super-group Cream.' He makes an analogy with an actor, who is well known for one starring role, and that's the work that's always quoted, but who has in reality been working non-stop for decades and has performed in hundreds of roles. He points out that being 'type-cast' as being the bass player with Cream is actually pretty bloody good. Rather better, at least, than if he was only known now for having been the bass player with Manfred Mann.

What matters is exactly who is mentally filing him away. If it's a dedicated Cream fan who, for whatever reason, hasn't kept up with his career since 1968, then that's okay. If it's a critic looking for some facile shorthand, then that's simply annoying. What does matter is that the full story of his career is known to both the cognoscenti and his fellow musicians. It's that old thing of having the respect of the people whose respect is worth having. That's pretty good.

It is possible that the success of Cream was unhelpful for Jack in the sense that it allowed him to do exactly what he wanted to do. That ought to have been nothing but a good thing, but there's an argument that it allowed him far too much freedom. It can be said that he wasn't going to be swayed by potentially wiser counsel from any quarter, just as he felt he could dispense with the services of a strong producer. To say that is to accept a conventional career trajectory, but there are certainly things that Jack could have done which would have brought him a broader audience and greater commercial success. However, in the way that you wouldn't say that of Harrison Birtwhistle, there's no reason to say it of Jack Bruce.

Like Eric, Jack has never been at all comfortable with the fame that comes with being a rock star – probably for the fundamental reason that neither man has ever seen themselves as a rock star. Jack can't decide if he is happiest playing big stadium gigs, at the rock end of his rock-to-jazz scale, or the more musically creditable, more intimate gigs at the other extreme, where he feels his musicianship is being better appreciated. It almost seems that when he's doing one, he wishes he was doing the other. Is a smaller but possibly more musically literate audience better than a huge, more broadly-based one? Jack chose the latter but never stopped regretting that he didn't have the former. In theory he could have had both; in practice that was never going to happen simply because of his terror of 'compromising' – as he saw it. There's no point of contentment in the middle.

This leads to his essential professional paradox; is Jack a successful and famous rock star or is he a highly-regarded serious musician? On the one hand there are rock stars, who are very broadly but shallowly appreciated, and on the other, more serious artists who are regarded in a narrower field, but far more deeply. It is possible to be both, but that number is very small. The two roles are contradictory, and there has always been a conflict in terms of how he regards himself on that front.

The sense of some unspecific inadequacy has never left him. He does live behind walls of his own construction. There is still the same lack of self-esteem. It might reduce but it never goes away completely. He saw exactly the same quality in Jimi Hendrix, who he says had no sense at all of his own worth. On stage, like Jack, he might have looked like the master of the universe, but in private his opinion of himself and his abilities could hardly have been lower.

Deep down Jack's probably still not certain that he has lived up to his mother's high expectations of him. Jack knows that he has achieved as much as anyone could have wanted – far more than he or his parents could ever have imagined – and he can list his achievements with pride. Then he asks himself if it all really matters, if he's actually that good, if he has honestly had the impact that he might have done and made music that is truly valuable.

Being detached from his mother for the first few months of his life – and the way that she over-compensated for that - has had its effect. He has always felt, he says, 'an emptiness', which he dates from that crucial point in his life. What is missing is a sense of worth and context; knowing and understanding one's true place in the universe.

Malcolm Bruce is a very shrewd and well informed critic of his father's work. He says of him, 'He's not a totally resolved person. He's not content – and never will be. He's always had a good time, but without being content with what he has got. He has always wanted more.'

Malcolm is right; Jack does not know contentment and will never know true placidity. However, in the wake of the reunion concerts, he is closer to that state of perfect grace than he has ever been. He certainly isn't creatively content though; there's always more to do and so much more that ought to have been done. Ability often comes hand in hand with a feeling of responsibility that one must live up to the talent. That's what pushes an artist ever further, but it's a hard and unyielding master. Unforgiving too. The job is never finished – and when one piece of work is at least complete, any sense of satisfaction is very brief. There's no sitting back and enjoying the pleasure of it all. That's done; what's next?

He describes himself as lazy, which is probably not exactly accurate; it's the motivation, the impetus, which is hard to summon up on demand. Any form of creativity is, in the long run, very hard work. Lyrics might be scribbled on an envelope in moments, but the whole process invariably takes a long time and a lot of intense, very concentrated, very demanding work. Inspiration might be instantaneous, but putting it into practice, translating it, takes much longer.

It might be appropriate to ask why, as he reaches his mid-Sixties he doesn't think about retirement. His health might suggest that that's a good idea, and though he had become financially comfortable before the reunion concerts, they will add enough to the family coffers to ensure that he and Margrit can live very well for the rest of their lives. As a rule though, musicians – like writers and artists – simply don't retire. You can't just turn off the creative tap overnight. New art always wants to force its way through.

In Jack's case there's also something else. He has known difficult times, and no matter how secure the financial situation might look, there will always be the tiny nagging doubt that things might go wrong again. It's a lower middle class and working class instinct, and is one that, no matter how successful one becomes, cannot be contradicted. The worry will always be there at some level or other.

The notions of self-confidence and self-assuredness have surfaced often in Jack's story, but what people are seeing is no more than body armour. Many have thought Jack overly self-confident, and it's a short step from there to arrogance. Those people would be amazed to learn that he was physically sick before the Cream reunion concerts, as he often is before going on stage. The problem for Jack has always been that he knows what he is capable of; he knows that he can take his music further, and that audiences expect that of him.

It's not the audience which drives him though. He propelled by these demonic doubts about his abilities. His fear is that he won't be able to reach up quite high enough to touch his own greatest moments – because, for him, that has to happen every single time he steps onto a stage. Going through the motions is not an option; giving a performance which is one percent below what it might be is simply unacceptable. Every show is a great responsibility. Every one has to be brilliant, and anything less than brilliance is failure. That's why he regards his bass guitar as the tool of his trade – a work instrument. He doesn't play bass for recreation. The bass is like a Gurkha's kukri – once drawn, the instrument cannot be put away until it has drawn blood.

There are many paradoxes apparent within Jack's make up, not least of which is the fact that he is a very traditional man, a child of the Fifties rather than the Sixties. He has a very strong work ethic. He's not one to sit around and wait for things to drop into his lap, and if he's going to do a job then he's going to do it to the very best of his abil-

Reunited with Gary Moore and Gary Husband at the Astoria,
Jack was on good form and looked relaxed (MK)

ities. In that sense he is his father's son, as he is in so many ways (one difference though is that the attitudes and lifestyle of the son seem to entirely run contrary to his political beliefs – and he knows it. It's the dichotomy of all wealthy, privileged people who embrace left wing politics opinions).

At the same time he is utterly modern and completely forward looking. He's more interested in the future than the present, and is only concerned with the past so far as it helps him to achieve his goals.

Jack is, superficially at least, a very sociable man, who is more than happy to simply sit and chat, talking about politics or cars, but that contrasts with a sense best summed up by the question 'Don't you know who I am?' When the portcullis comes down and the drawbridge goes up the crash is deafening.

He can often seem to need to be the centre of attention wherever he goes, but that may well be a defensive mechanism rather than a true reflection of his character. He is a very intelligent and sensitive man, and it is true to say that he has to have a barrier between him and the wider world. In that mode he can be a very scary guy indeed;

something that he denies and perhaps doesn't understand, but he can be very forbidding. He is still someone who you don't mess around. You don't make jokes at his expense.

It's also true to say that Jack is, at whatever level – consciously or not - very concerned by how history will regard him. He's quite unlike the majority of his contemporaries in this; indeed it simply wouldn't occur to them. In the main Jack's true heroes are long dead – be they Johann Sebastian Bach or Robbie Burns – but their work is still very much a part of our culture. No one will remember Freddie And The Dreamers, The Bay City Rollers, or the very transitory success of the winners of Pop Idol come the twenty-second century. Their moment of fame will be long gone. At the other extreme, Chuck Berry, Keith Jarrett, John Taverner and (dare one say …) Eric Clapton will all be part of the musical curriculum. Time is the most trustworthy filter.

It would give Jack great satisfaction indeed, and set a large part of his troubled psyche at rest, if he could know for sure that his own star will still be twinkling brightly in a hundred or two hundred years time. If his music is still being played and appreciated. If his work is seen to represent the very best music of the second half if the twentieth century, and the subdivisions of jazz, rock, or whatever have long become irrelevant. If critics are saying then that so-and-so is 'the Jack Bruce of our time.' If there was a blue plaque on the house in Chalk farm, and the brightest musical scholar at Ballahouston is awarded The Jack Bruce Prize every year. That would be perfect. Ars longa vita brevis, as they say.

Afterthoughts

Bruce Gary: 'You'd expect a drummer to talk about other drummers so far as his influences are concerned, but my biggest influence in my life musically, bar none, has been Jack Bruce. He taught me so many great things about music. All the things I'd heard – Jack just tapped a nerve that made everything become obvious. If you've got the ability to begin with you can't help but rise when you play with great musicians. It was that way with Jack. When I first started playing with him I suddenly felt I was ten years better. If you're close to someone who is that gifted you can't help but soak it in. He influences me to this day.'

Simon Phillips; 'I've never told him this but Jack was my musical guru. Most bass players are very rhythmical, and harmonically are a little limited. Jack thinks very harmonically; that's what I love about him, that's what is exciting. It's just more musical. There are a few bass players in the world I love to play with, and with Jack it's always great.'

Ronnie Leahy: 'Jack never lets up and never lets you down. He's supportive and listens to everything you're playing. He hears everything! Every gig with him is very special. He's a fantastically generous person, particularly with him time; generous with his friendship and his music. Very well-read, very cultured. He's temperamental, yes, he has his moments, but he'd do anything for you.'

Peter Frampton; 'As a bass guitarist Jack is one of a kind. Every true musician hopes that they can create a style, and Jack is very much a stylist. He has phenomenal technique, and has such a great musical mind. Before Jack a bass playing was very simplistic; after Jack Bruce you got other bass players. He took bass to a completely different level. Everyone else's bass was pure, but Jack's bass had an edge to it – he could make it sound like a tuba sometimes. It's in the fingers; it doesn't matter what amp he plays through. It always sounds like him.'

Gary Husband; 'For me, Jack's singing has some of the qualities you find in Sinatra. As soon as he opens his mouth I know that he believes it. It's just the truth. But there's a demon in there; one which isn't out of control, but born of passion and lust for music. People play how they are, and Jack plays exactly as he is, with this visceral, powerful urge.

Clem Clempson; 'Jack is intense and passionate, and he's a genius. There's no bass player that I'd prefer to play with. He's got such a fantastic feel.'

Pete Brown; 'Jack really is a musical heavyweight. He could go into virtually any musical area and simply wipe the floor with the competition.'

Bernie Worrell: 'Jack Bruce is my baby!'

Index